PRAISE FOR

For the Thrill of It

"[Leopold and Loeb] had the world on a string in 1924: rich, smart, good-looking, well connected, and with the brightest of futures ahead of them. So why did they murder a fourteen-year-old schoolboy, stuff his naked body in a drainage pipe, and send his parents a ransom note demanding $10,000? The answer is in the title of Simon Baatz's altogether **absorbing** history of the case, *For the Thrill of It*. It was that, and they wanted to prove to themselves they were smart enough quite literally to get away with murder. **Mr. Baatz . . . has done meticulous research, and he writes extremely well.** As a result he brings to vivid life the major characters. Not just the two murderers, but also the judges and lawyers. . . . **A page-turner of a book.** . . . Simon Baatz's book on the Leopold and Loeb case is the best we'll have for a long, long time." —*New York Times*

"Simon Baatz's *For the Thrill of It* is likely to be **the definitive work** on this infamous crime. . . . It is impressive in its research, evenhanded in its tone, and **immensely readable**. . . . Without falsely heightening the drama, Mr. Baatz keeps the reader entranced by a story whose central event—the murder itself—is well-known, though its aftermath less so. . . . The crime may now be forgiven, but it is not forgotten, as Simon Baatz's **excellent book** demonstrates. Although the names Leopold and Loeb can no longer be used to frighten young children, the calculated viciousness of their crime, so **compellingly** captured by Mr. Baatz, remains a major event in the annals of human depravity." —*Wall Street Journal*

"**Meticulously researched.** . . . More than eighty years later, [the crime] still has the power to daze us, one of those benchmark crimes that is burned into our consciousness, even as an increasingly violent world desensitizes us to the most horrific atrocities."

D0190599

"*For the Thrill of It* is **a page-turner that you'll have trouble putting down**. . . . A carefully detailed work that is likely to be definitive. It's **immensely readable**, filled with drama and suspense."

—*Chicago Jewish Star*

"Baatz lucidly lays out the complicated courtroom maneuvers and also provides **a fascinating, skillful analysis** of two different legal philosophies. . . . A solid true-crime thriller that's also a masterly analysis of postwar shifts in society's ideas about crime and personality."

—*Kirkus Reviews*

"Simon Baatz has worked for six years unearthing every detail of the proceedings—court reports, newspaper accounts, witness recollections, and a host of other sources—but this has not produced the tunnel vision that might be expected. His obvious intention is to step back from the dramatic events and personalities he's writing about and let them do all the talking. His book is full of direct quotations taken from a variety of official transcripts, and as a result **the pages read like the very best crime fiction.** This kind of editorial restraint is rare in cases like that of Leopold and Loeb, and for good reason: they don't deserve it. And even when on occasion Baatz slips in an opinion, the reader is grateful for it—he's the expert, after all, so any of his thoughts on the case are of interest. . . . Reading **Baatz's compelling, definitive book** brings it all back to life."

—*Open Letters Monthly*

"Baatz breaks his **fascinating narrative** into two distinct *Law & Order*–type sections. He starts with the kidnapping and murder of fourteen-year-old Bobby Franks, abducted while walking home from an after-school baseball game. While it might be easy to dismiss the murderers—Nathan 'Babe' Leopold Jr. and Richard 'Dickie' Loeb— as bored rich kids, Baatz shows that there was much more to this story." — *Library Journal*

"Baatz . . . has written a narrative history that aims, he says, 'to recapture the drama of the events that it describes' but also to deal with the 'complex issues that give the subject its significance.' By and large he has succeeded. . . . *For the Thrill of It* is **meticulous and thorough**, and it puts the case in historical perspective as a clash between two conflicting views of criminals and crime, one espoused by Robert Crowe, the state's attorney, and the other by Clarence Darrow, who represented Nathan Leopold and was the most famous American lawyer of his day, perhaps indeed of any day." —*Washington Post*

"Simon Baatz's *For the Thrill of It* is the kind of book that can ruin late-summer vacation plans. It's **a riveting nonfiction thriller** that will turn you into an activity-hostile recluse who shouts, 'Go away and let me read!' . . . What makes *Thrill of It* so **exceptional** is the way Baatz balances all the elements: the killers, the crime, the police, the media, and the trial's impact." —*USA Today*

"An acute portrait of the two murderers bound together in a web of fantasy." —*Publishers Weekly*

"Baatz's thorough research, and particularly his analysis of the flaws and strengths of the medical and psychological testimony offered by the defense, are **singularly impressive.** He tellingly dissects Darrow's crude (to us—they seemed quite modern and progressive in the 1920s) attempts to explain the crime as a freakish result of glandular imbalances or psychological scarring." —*U.S. News & World Report*

"Exhaustively researched and rivetingly presented. . . . **One of the best true-crime books of this or any other season.**" —*Booklist* (starred review)

"**A masterful book.** . . . Both Crowe and Darrow were capable of surprises, and the judge himself, John Caverly, pulled off the biggest surprise of all. . . . In addition to his **meticulous** research, the author **knows how to tell a story.**" —*Chicago Lawyer*

"*For the Thrill of It* is a thrill in its own right, not only for its spine-tingling subject matter but also for its meticulous research and **relentlessly powerful prose**. In telling the story of Nathan Leopold and Richard Loeb, Simon Baatz has given us **a gripping murder mystery and a compelling courtroom drama** that just happen to be true."

—John Matteson, winner of the 2008 Pulitzer Prize for
Eden's Outcasts: The Story of Louisa May Alcott and Her Father

"Richly illustrated and **highly readable**, *For the Thrill of It* offers a startling new interpretation of the infamous Leopold-Loeb case. Simon Baatz has written a definitive account that corrects long-standing errors and myths. The result is a tale of privilege and arrogance, forbidden sexuality, and human tragedy that is **consistently enthralling**."

—Nancy C. Unger, Associate Professor of History,
Santa Clara University, and author of
Fighting Bob La Follette: The Righteous Reformer

"The story of the Jazz Age thrill-killers Leopold and Loeb has never been told in so gripping a style. **A significant work of historical scholarship that reads like a page-turning thriller**, Simon Baatz's masterly book now stands as the definitive account of this legendary case."

—Harold Schechter, Professor of English,
Queens College, City University of New York,
and author of *The Devil's Gentleman:
Privilege, Poison, and the Trial That Ushered in
the Twentieth Century*

"In 1924 Clarence Darrow set out to save Nathan Leopold and Richard Loeb from the gallows after they had confessed to the murder of a young child. Simon Baatz's **superbly crafted book** tells the story in an eminently readable and accessible style. The Leopold-Loeb case has finally found its historian. *For the Thrill of It* will be the standard work on this infamous crime for decades to come."

—Ronald L. Numbers, Hilldale Professor of
the History of Science and Medicine,
University of Wisconsin, and author of
The Creationists: From Scientific Creation to Intelligent Design

Photographer's Gallery

About the Author

SIMON BAATZ holds a joint appointment as associate professor of history at John Jay College of Criminal Justice and at the Graduate Center, City University of New York.

ALSO BY SIMON BAATZ

*Venerate the Plough: A History of the Philadelphia
Society for Promoting Agriculture, 1785–1985*

*Knowledge, Culture, and Science in the Metropolis:
The New York Academy of Sciences, 1817–1970*

FOR THE
THRILL OF IT

LEOPOLD, LOEB, AND THE MURDER
THAT SHOCKED JAZZ AGE CHICAGO

SIMON BAATZ

HARPER ● PERENNIAL

NEW YORK ● LONDON ● TORONTO ● SYDNEY ● NEW DELHI ● AUCKLAND

HARPER ● PERENNIAL

A hardcover edition of this book was published in 2008 by Harper,
an imprint of HarperCollins Publishers.

FOR THE THRILL OF IT. Copyright © 2008 by Simon Baatz. All rights
reserved. Printed in the United States of America. No part of this book may
be used or reproduced in any manner whatsoever without written
permission except in the case of brief quotations embodied in critical
articles and reviews. For information address HarperCollins Publishers,
10 East 53rd Street, New York, NY 10022.

HarperCollins books may be purchased for educational, business, or sales
promotional use. For information please write: Special Markets
Department, HarperCollins Publishers, 10 East 53rd Street,
New York, NY 10022.

FIRST HARPER PERENNIAL EDITION PUBLISHED 2009.

Designed by Ellen Cipriano

The Library of Congress has catalogued the hardcover edition as follows:

Baatz, Simon.

For the thrill of it: Leopold, Loeb, and the murder that shocked Chicago /
Simon Baatz—1st ed.
    p. cm.
ISBN 978-0-06-078100-2
    1. Leopold, Nathan Freudenthal, 1904–1971. 2. Loeb, Richard A., 1905–1936.
3. Murderers—Illinois—Chicago—Biography. 4. Murderers—Illinois—
Chicago—Case studies.

HV6245.B27 2008
364.152'3092—dc22   2007050877

ISBN 978-0-06-078102-6 (pbk.)

09 10 11 12 13 WBC/RRD 10 9 8 7 6 5 4 3 2 1

1. THE DEFENDANTS WITH THEIR LAWYER. From left: Nathan Leopold, Richard Loeb, and Clarence Darrow.

The problem I thus pose is . . . what type of man shall be bred, shall be willed, for being higher in value. . . . This higher type has appeared often—but as a fortunate accident, as an exception, never as something willed. . . . Success in individual cases is constantly encountered in the most widely different places and cultures: here we really do find a higher type that is, in relation to mankind as a whole, a kind of superman. Such fortunate accidents of great success have always been possible and will perhaps always be possible.

Friedrich Nietzsche, *The Antichrist*, Sections 3, 4

"I'm reminded of a little article you wrote, 'On Crime,' or something like that, I forget the exact title. I had the pleasure of reading it a couple of months ago in the *Periodical*."

"My article? In the *Periodical Review*?" Raskolnikov asked in surprise. . . . Raskolnikov really hadn't known anything about it. . . .

"That's right. And you maintain that the act of carrying out a crime is always accompanied by illness. Very, very original, but personally that wasn't the part of your article that really interested me. There was a certain idea slipped in at the end, unfortunately you only hint at it, and unclearly. . . . In short, it contains, if you recall, a certain reference to the notion that there may be certain kinds of people in the world who can . . . I mean not that they are able, but that they are endowed with the right to commit all sorts of crimes and excesses, and the law, as it were, was not written for them.

"The heart of the matter is that . . . all people are divisible into 'ordinary' and 'extraordinary.' The ordinary must live obediently and have no right to transgress the law—because, you see, they're ordinary. The extraordinary, on the other hand, have the right to commit all kinds of crimes and to transgress the law in all kinds of ways, for the simple reason that they are extraordinary. That would seem to have been your argument, if I am not mistaken."

Raskolnikov smiled again. He understood at once what was going on and the direction in which they were trying to push him. He remembered the article, and decided to accept their challenge.

"That's not quite the way I put it," he began simply and modestly. "Still, I must admit, you've got the gist of it. Even completely right, if you wish."

Fyodor Dostoyevsky, *Crime and Punishment*, Part 3, Section 5

CONTENTS

PART ONE   THE CRIME

PART TWO   THE ATTORNEYS

PART THREE   THE COURTROOM

ILLUSTRATIONS

PREFACE

This is a true story. The events described here occurred in Chicago in the summer of 1924. The conversation and dialogue in this book, indicated by quotation marks, are taken verbatim from the transcript of the courtroom proceedings, from the records of the office of the state's attorney of Cook County, or from contemporary newspaper accounts. The University of Chicago and the University of Michigan generously provided me with the academic transcripts of Nathan Leopold and Richard Loeb, respectively. I wish also to thank the archivists at Northwestern University; the Wisconsin Historical Society; Columbia University; the University of California, Berkeley; Stanford University; and the National Archives in Washington, D.C., for permitting me to quote from materials in their possession.

PART ONE

THE CRIME

1 | THE KIDNAPPING

This cruel and vicious murder ... this gruesome crime ... this atrocious murder ... the most cruel, cowardly, dastardly murder ever committed in the annals of American jurisprudence.[1]

Robert Crowe, state's attorney of
Cook County, 23 July 1924

Everybody knows that this was a most unfortunate homicide. That it is the cruelest, the worst, the most atrocious ever committed in the United States is pure imagination without a vestige of truth. ... A death in any situation is horrible, but when it comes to the question of murder it is doubly horrible. But there are degrees ... of atrocity, and as I say, instead of this being one of the worst ... it is perhaps one of the least painful.[2]

Clarence Darrow,
defense attorney, 23 July 1924

FLORA FRANKS GLANCED AT THE CLOCK. Already past six o'clock and still no sign of Bobby! The cook had prepared dinner and the maids were waiting patiently for the family to move to the dining room. Normally she could rely on her eldest son, Jack, sixteen years old, to keep an eye on his younger brother, but Jack lay upstairs in bed, ill with chicken pox; he had not been to school all week. Her daughter, Josephine, seventeen years old, tried to calm Flora's fears—Bobby always played baseball after school; perhaps he had gone to a friend's home for supper after the game.[3]

Jacob Franks agreed with his daughter. Admittedly it was not like Bobby to be late for dinner; but nothing serious had happened to the boy. It was only three blocks from the Harvard School to their house and Bobby was now fourteen years old, old enough to know not to talk to strangers. The boy had probably fallen in with a classmate after the game and had forgotten the time. Still, he was annoyed that his son should be so thoughtless and forgetful, annoyed with Bobby for causing his mother to worry.

Jacob Franks was proud of his four children: Josephine had been accepted at Wellesley College for the fall, and Jack, a junior at the Harvard School, was planning to attend Dartmouth College. Jacob Jr. was the youngest child, still a student in grade school, but already showing signs of academic prom-

2. ROBERT (BOBBY) FRANKS. Bobby Franks was a pupil at the Harvard School for Boys. This photograph appeared as the frontispiece to a collection of poems published in his memory by his brother Jack.

ise. Bobby, the darling of the family, was a bit of a scamp who got into his share of scrapes at school, but he was, nevertheless, his mother's favorite. She loved his assertiveness, his independent spirit, his ambition; he had already announced to the family that he too would go to Dartmouth and then would study for the law. No doubt he would keep his promise: the principal of the Harvard School, Charles Pence, had reported that Bobby was a precocious child. Only a freshman at the school, he was a member of the class debating team. He was a popular boy at school, a keen tennis player and an avid golfer; he had joined with some other boys in establishing a reading group, and only a few days earlier, he had won a debate on capital punishment, arguing for a link between criminality and mental illness—"most criminals have diseased minds"—and protesting against the right of the state "to take a man, weak and mentally depraved, and coldly deprive him of his life."[4]

FOR FLORA AND JACOB FRANKS, their four children were the capstone of their lives. As a young boy, Jacob Franks had lost his own father. His mother had run a clothing store and then a pawnshop in Chicago, and in 1884 Jacob had set up in business for himself, opening a pawnshop on Clark Street south of Madison Street. It was a good location and an auspicious time—gambling was then unregulated in the city and there were at least a dozen gaming houses within a block of Jacob Franks's pawnshop.

Jacob soon built up a loyal clientele—the gamblers could rely on Jacob to lend them as much as ninety percent of the value of the diamonds, watches, and rings that they pawned—and once their luck turned, they could easily redeem their property. Michael (Hinky Dink) Kenna, Democratic alderman of the First Ward and one of the most powerful politicians in Chicago, remembered Jacob Franks as an honest businessman who earned the loyalty of his customers: "He ran the business strictly on the square and he had the respect of every man who ever made a loan. . . . He knew who he was dealing with, and for that reason would take a chance."[5]

Jacob Franks never ran for political office, yet he was well connected—"Franks," according to one politician, "has for years been a big factor in the Democratic party"—and he used his connections to make his fortune. An opportunity to buy stock in the Ogden Gas Company was a lucky break for Franks and his business partner, Patrick Ryan; the two entrepreneurs sold the stock to the People's Gas Light and Coke Company at an enormous profit estimated by one friend to be as much as $1 million. Franks bought land in the downtown district and watched its value soar when the city moved the grog shops, gambling dens, and brothels farther south, to the Levee between 18th and 22nd streets. By 1924, Jacob Franks was wealthy beyond his wildest dreams; he was worth, at a conservative estimate, more than $4 million.[6]

IT WAS NOW AFTER seven o'clock. The youngest son, Jacob Jr., had finished eating and was fidgeting, anxious to leave the table. His father let him go. Flora, Josephine, and Jacob remained at the table talking; they could no longer pretend that Bobby was delayed at a friend's house.

Jacob went to the phone to call his lawyer, Samuel Ettelson. Jacob Franks had known Ettelson for many years—the two men were close friends. Ettelson, undoubtedly one of the most influential lawyers in Chicago, had served as corporation counsel during the mayoralty of William Hale Thompson from 1915 to 1923 and was now state senator for Cook County in the Illinois legislature. A prominent Republican, Ettelson still had considerable influence with the police department and with the state's attorney, Robert Crowe. If anything had happened to Bobby, Jacob Franks could rely on Ettelson to help launch a massive police investigation.[7]

Ettelson arrived at the house on Ellis Avenue around nine o'clock that evening. The three adults talked briefly in the living room; both parents were now consumed with anxiety. Ettelson started calling the teachers at the Harvard School. Had they seen Bobby Franks that afternoon? Could they remember when he had left to go home? Only Richard Williams, the athletics instructor, could provide much information.

Bobby had been the umpire at an impromptu baseball game between some schoolboys on a vacant lot at 57th Street and Ellis Avenue. Williams had seen Bobby leave the game to walk home around 5:15 p.m.[8]

Had Bobby returned to the Harvard School on his way home? Perhaps, Ettelson reasoned, he had popped into the school to retrieve something and had been locked inside by the janitor. The two men grabbed their coats and hats and made for the door—it was a five-minute walk to the school. When they reached the main entrance, the building was dark; there was no sign of the janitor. A window was open on the first floor. Ettelson helped Jacob Franks climb into the building and both men began hunting through the classrooms. They also searched the school grounds, but there was nothing—no clue, no trace of the boy's whereabouts.[9]

At home, Flora Franks waited anxiously for her husband. It was now almost half past ten; Jacob had been gone for more than an hour. The children were asleep and the servants, except for one maid, had all retired to their quarters—the house suddenly seemed very quiet.

In the hallway, the phone rang. Flora could hear the maid pick up the receiver and answer the caller—she was bringing the telephone into the living room—had Bobby been found? It was a man's voice—Flora Franks remembered later that it was "more of a cultured voice than a gruff voice."[10]

The caller spoke rapidly yet clearly—Flora did not miss a word. "This is Mr. Johnson . . . your boy has been kidnaped. We have him and you need not worry: he is safe. But don't try to trace this call. . . . We must have money. We will let you know tomorrow what we want. We are kidnapers and we mean business. If you refuse us what we want or try to report us to the police, we will kill the boy."[11]

The receiver clicked—the caller had hung up. Flora stood motionless for a moment, still holding the phone in her hands; then she fainted and fell to the floor.

Six minutes later, Samuel Ettelson and Jacob Franks returned. The maid was still holding Flora in her arms—she had revived her mistress with spirits of ammonia, and at that moment Flora had regained consciousness.

At least they now knew what had happened to the boy—and, thank God, he was still alive. Perhaps Mr. Johnson would telephone again that night—Samuel Ettelson called the phone company to put a trace on incoming calls.[12] Admittedly this was a risky maneuver—the kidnapper had explicitly warned against it. Ettelson was in a difficult situation: as a friend of the Franks family, he wanted Bobby returned home, alive and safe; yet as a public official, he was loath to truckle to blackmailers. From his years as corporation counsel, Ettelson had vast experience in managing the city's affairs, and in negotiating contracts with labor unions, utility companies, building contractors, and streetcar companies, yet nothing had prepared him for this. He was uncertain how best to proceed. Should they inform the police? Or should they wait for another phone call? If they merely obeyed the kidnapper's commands, were they nevertheless putting the boy's life at risk? Perhaps it would be better to have the Chicago police out searching for the kidnapper. Perhaps the police had a list of likely suspects who could be rounded up.

At two o'clock in the morning, Ettelson decided they should go to the police. Jacob Franks could stand their inaction no longer; anything was better than waiting for the phone to ring. Ettelson was well connected with the Chicago police—he was a personal friend of the chief of detectives, Michael Hughes, and of the deputy captain of police, William (Shoes) Shoemacher. Why should he not use that influence to rescue Bobby?

The central police station was almost deserted. Ettelson had never previously met the young lieutenant, Robert Welling, in charge; could he trust Welling not to leak news of Bobby's disappearance? And suppose Bobby was not in danger? Suppose that this was a juvenile hoax by some of his classmates? Unlikely, of course, but Ettelson was reluctant to mobilize the Chicago police department and find, the next morning, that Bobby was safe and sound, having spent the night with a friend. His reputation would be tarnished, and Ettelson, who always hoped for a revival of his political fortunes, could not afford to be made a laughingstock.

Robert Welling listened thoughtfully to Franks and Ettelson. He would, if they liked, send out detectives to search for the boy. Ettelson demurred; perhaps, he advised the lieutenant, it was all unnecessary; the boy might turn up in the morning. "We are not sure. Perhaps it is only some prank, some foolish joke. Perhaps—" Ettelson's voice trailed off. What should they do? He spoke again: he did not himself believe it was a hoax. "If the boy really has been kidnapped, then we must be very, very careful. He may be in the hands of desperate men who would kill him." Ettelson could not bear the risk that the kidnappers might kill Bobby. "Perhaps," he decided finally, "we would better wait until morning before doing anything about it."[13]

THE NEXT MORNING, AT EIGHT o'clock, a special delivery letter arrived. The envelope bore six two-cent stamps, was addressed to Jacob Franks at 5052 Ellis Avenue, and had a Chicago postmark; it had been mailed either the previous evening or earlier that morning.

In one sense the arrival of a ransom letter provided a measure of relief, however minor, for Bobby's parents. It confirmed that he was still alive and provided instructions for his recovery. The writer of the letter, George Johnson, promised that Bobby was "at present well and safe. You need not fear any physical harm for him providing you live up carefully to the following instructions. . . . Make absolutely no attempt to communicate with either the police authorities nor any private agency. Should you already have communicated with the police, allow them to continue their investigations, but do not mention this letter.

"Secure before noon today $10,000. This money must be composed entirely of old bills of the following denominations: $2,000 in $20 bills, $8,000 in $50 bills. The money must be old. Any attempt to include new or marked bills will render the entire venture futile. The money should be placed in a large cigar box . . . and wrapped in white paper. The wrapping paper should be sealed . . . with sealing wax.

"Have the money thus prepared as directed above and remain home after one o'clock P.M. See that the telephone is not in use. You will receive a future communication instructing you as to your future course.

"As a final word of warning, this is a strictly commercial proposition, and we are prepared to put our threats into execution should we have reasonable ground to believe that you have committed an infraction of the above instructions. However, should you carefully follow out our instructions to the letter, we can assure you that your son will be safely returned to you within six hours of our receipt of the money."[14]

The family felt a tremendous sense of relief. Here was assurance that Bobby was still alive. Merely for the payment of a trivial sum, a bagatelle, they would soon have Bobby back, safely home. Samuel Ettelson was sanguine—this was a professional kidnapping gang, no doubt about it; the boy was not, as he had feared, the victim of a child molester. There was now no apprehension that Bobby would end up dead.

SEVERAL MILES AWAY, TONY MINKE, a recent immigrant from Poland who worked as a pump man for the American Maize Company, walked along a path that ran parallel to the Pennsylvania Railroad tracks near Wolf Lake. Few people ever ventured out to this remote part of Cook County. Farsighted action by the state legislature a decade earlier had led to the creation of the Forest Preserve district southeast of Chicago as an area of natural beauty, and by 1924 more than 20,000 acres of wetlands and marshes had been permanently set aside. It was an ornithologist's paradise—the thick brush and low trees provided a safe haven for migratory wading birds, and during the spring and fall it was possible to spot such exotica as the yellow-crowned night heron and the snowy egret. Pawpaw trees, shingle oaks, spicebush, sycamores, and hawthorn trees were everywhere; wild prairie roses ran alongside the few paths through the wilderness; and occasionally one might discover dewberry and raspberry patches in the meadowland openings. The Forest Preserve was a magical spot, yet its distance from the city and a lack of public transportation rendered it inaccessible to most Chicagoans. Occasionally one might see a hunter, and on the weekends schoolboys would come out with field glasses to observe the migrating birds passing overhead, but otherwise the Forest Preserve remained inviolate.

Tony Minke lived nearby, on the edge of the Forest Preserve, but he did not usually take this route home. That morning, Thursday, 22 May, he was coming from the factory where he had worked the night shift. Now he was on his way to Hegewisch to pick up his watch from a repair shop before returning home to sleep. The sun was at his back, and as he passed a large ditch on his left, he looked down momentarily. The sun's rays shone into the ditch, and Minke looked more closely: was that a foot poking out of the drainage pipe? Minke stopped and looked closer—he peered into the pipe. Inside, he could see a child's body, naked and lying face downward in a foot of muddy water.[15]

In the distance, Minke could see four men, railroad workers, on a handcar traveling slowly along the tracks in his direction. He climbed the embankment and, as the handcar approached, he signaled to it to halt. The handcar came to a gradual stop. As the workmen climbed down, Minke walked a few steps toward them, pointing back at the ditch. "Look," he exclaimed, "there is something in the pipe, there is a pair of feet sticking out."[16]

As the men pulled the body out of the pipe and turned it on its back, Minke could see immediately that the boy had been killed: there were two large wounds on the forehead—deep gashes, each about an inch long—and toward the back of the head he could see large bruises and swelling. And those marks on the boy's back? What had caused those scratches running down the back all the way from the shoulders to the buttocks? But the most peculiar aspect was the appearance of the face—there were distinctive copper-colored stains around the mouth and chin; and the genitals also—they were stained with the same color.[17]

As his fellow workers were carrying the body to a second handcar on the tracks, Paul Korff, a signal repairman for the railroad, glanced over the scene. He wondered if any of the boy's clothes were lying around; if so, they should gather them up and take them along. Korff could see nothing—no shirt or trousers, or even shoes and socks—but he did find a pair of eyeglasses with tortoiseshell frames, lying on the embankment, just a few feet from the culvert. Perhaps they belonged to the boy; Korff put them in his pocket and joined his comrades waiting by the handcars.[18]

At around ten o'clock that morning, Anton Shapino, the sergeant on duty at the Hegewisch police station, took charge of the body. Paul Korff had handed him the tortoiseshell eyeglasses, and Shapino, assuming that they belonged to the boy, placed them on the child's forehead. Later that morning, at the morgue at 13300 South Houston Avenue, the undertaker, Stanley Olejniczak, laid the body out; as he did so, he noticed the unusual discoloration of the boy's face and genitals and the bruises and cuts on the head—someone had obviously beaten the child violently.[19]

JACOB FRANKS WAS LOOKING FORWARD to seeing his son again. He had spent that morning in the Loop, the city's business district, obtaining $10,000 ransom from his bank. The teller was surprised at the request for "all old, worn bills" but said nothing; it was not his place to question such a customer as Franks.[20]

Back at Ellis Avenue the family waited. They expected the kidnappers to call sometime after one o'clock, but time dragged on—two o'clock passed and still there was no call. Jacob Franks continued sitting in his armchair staring out of the window onto Ellis Avenue; his wife sat by his side, quietly crying.[21]

Samuel Ettelson stayed in the library answering calls and talking with visitors. Ettelson was annoyed that the press had learned of the kidnapping—but it was perhaps his own fault. After Ettelson had asked the phone company to put a trace on incoming calls the previous evening, the family had discovered that the company's telephone operators had been gossiping about the tracing of calls. No doubt someone had alerted the press to Bobby's disappearance.

Even now, there was a reporter from the *Chicago Daily News*, James Mulroy, badgering him about the body of a boy found earlier that morning, out near the Indiana state line near the Forest Preserve. Of course, this was not Bobby—Mulroy had said that the boy was found wearing

3. THE DRAINAGE CULVERT. Tony Minke, a workman for the American Maize Company, discovered the body of a naked boy in this drainage culvert on Thursday, 22 May 1924.

eyeglasses and Bobby had never worn eyeglasses in his life—but perhaps someone from the family should go down to the morgue and ensure that it was not Bobby lying on the undertaker's slab. Ettelson turned to Edwin Greshan, the brother of Flora Franks and Bobby's uncle: would he mind driving to South Houston Avenue with the reporter?[22]

And if, by some chance, Ettelson continued, it was Bobby at the undertaker's, he should say only one word—"Yes"—over the phone, and nothing more. There was a telephone extension in the living room; Ettelson did not want Flora Franks to overhear the news of her son's death.

Thirty minutes later, the phone rang. Ettelson picked up the receiver. He recognized Greshan's voice. Only one word now mattered—"Yes." The phone clicked off at the other end and Ettelson walked deliberately to the living room.

Flora had left the room but Jacob was still sitting in his armchair, gazing out of the window. He looked exhausted, pale and tired and crumpled; his right hand twitched and fidgeted aimlessly with a loose thread in the arm of the chair.

Ettelson leaned over to speak softly into Jacob's ear: "It looks pretty bad, Jake. It looks to me as if the worst has happened."

Jacob Franks glanced up into his friend's eyes: "What do you mean?"

"That your boy is dead."[23]

At that moment the phone rang. Ettelson picked up the extension: "Hello?"

"Hello. . . . Is Mr. Franks in?"

"Who wants him?"

"Mr. Johnson wants him."

"Who is that?"

"George Johnson."

"Just a minute."

As he passed the receiver to Jacob Franks, Ettelson whispered that it was the kidnapper, but Jacob was still in a daze. He was stunned at the unexpected news of his son's death. How could he tell Flora that Bobby was dead? She was already in shock at her son's disappearance; his death would break her heart.

"Mr. Franks?"

"Yes?"

"This is George Johnson speaking. . . . There will be a yellow cab at your door in ten minutes. . . . Get into it and proceed immediately to the drug store at 1465 East 63rd Street."

"Couldn't I have a little more time?"

"No, sir, you can't have any more time; you must go immediately."[24]

What was this? Bobby was dead—but the kidnapper still expected to get the ransom money? Perhaps, Ettelson thought, Edwin Greshan had misidentified the body in the morgue and Bobby was still alive.

And, look, there at the front gate, there was a yellow cab pulling up at the curb. What should they do? If Jacob Franks got into the cab, could they still save Bobby's life? Or would that also put Jacob in danger?

The cab was waiting in the street, its engine running. Ettelson was struggling with the possibilities. Jacob Franks was exhausted—he had gone more than thirty-six hours with very little sleep. And he was flustered and confused, shocked and sad; so perhaps it is not surprising that, by the time Ettelson turned back to speak to him, Franks had forgotten the address of the drugstore—he remembered only that it was on 63rd Street.

Samuel Ettelson pleaded with Jacob to recall the location of the drugstore. Had the kidnapper identified it by name? Was there any other detail that Jacob could remember?

No. Jacob struggled to remember, but it had gone. Ettelson paid off the cabdriver and stood silently on the sidewalk, watching the cab drive down Ellis Avenue; eventually it disappeared and Ettelson sensed that their last chance to rescue Bobby had disappeared with it.[25]

THE HUNT WAS NOW ON for the killers. Morgan Collins, chief of the Chicago police department, promised that he would commit all his resources to tracking down the murderers. Collins undoubtedly exaggerated when he described the killing as "one of the most brutal murders with which we have had to deal. Never before have we come in contact with such cold-blooded and willful taking of life." His exaggeration was for effect; Collins was a political appointee, selected the previous year by Chicago's Democratic mayor, William Dever, with a mandate to enforce prohibition. Collins could not possibly, in a city such as Chicago, end the liquor trade—better to divert attention to a crime more tractable. "The children of our schools must be protected against the possibility of any such crime as this. . . . We intend to hunt down the slayers if it takes every man in the police department to do it. I have assigned some of our best men to the job and told them that I would supply every aid necessary. They can have as many men as they want."[26]

Fortunately, Collins already had his eye on a group of likely suspects: the instructors at the Harvard School. In the early hours of the morning, around three o'clock on Friday, 23 May, the police began rounding up the Harvard teachers. Walter Wilson, the instructor of mathematics; Mott Kirk Mitchell, the English teacher; and Richard Williams, the athletics coach, were dragged out of bed and taken to the Wabash Avenue station. Within the next two days, the police brought in Fred Alwood, the chemistry teacher; George Vaubel, the physical education instructor; Charles Pence, the school principal; and Edna Plata, the French teacher.[27]

The teachers were suspects because they had access to the boy; because they knew that Jacob Franks was wealthy and able to afford a $10,000 ransom; and, tellingly, because the ransom note was flawless. The letter contained few grammatical errors and no typographical mistakes; only an educated person could have composed it. Hugh Sutton, an expert with the Royal Typewriter Company, thought that the kidnappers had used an Underwood portable typewriter, probably less than three years old; the typist had used two fingers to compose the letter. "The person who wrote this letter," Sutton concluded, "never had learned the touch system. . . . The touch system strikes the keys pretty evenly, with an even pressure on the keys. The man who wrote this was . . . a novice at typing. . . . Some of the letters were punched so hard they were almost driven through the paper, while others were struck lightly or uncertainly." The kidnapper had written Jacob Franks's address on the envelope in block letters; handwriting experts determined that the letters displayed a uniform slant, and a regular spacing and character; it was obviously the penmanship of a capable writer.[28]

Since the kidnappers were educated and literate, the murder was clearly not the work of the Black Hand kidnapping gangs linked to organized crime in Chicago. And the motive? The instructors at the Harvard School may have taught at one of the city's most prestigious private schools, but they were paid startlingly low salaries: the typical teacher received less than $2,000 a year—the $10,000 ransom was thus equivalent to five years' salary.[29]

As the police questioned the Harvard School staff throughout

Friday, clues began to emerge to indicate the leading suspects. Walter Wilson, the mathematics teacher, had shown an unusual interest in the Franks children. Several months earlier, he had taken Bobby Franks and his younger brother, Jacob Jr., on an excursion to Riverside and had not returned with the boys until one o'clock in the morning. Was Wilson, the police wondered, a pedophile? He was single and had no girlfriend; he admitted to the police that he did not "know any young ladies around Chicago." Wilson had visited the Franks home that Wednesday evening after Jacob Franks had phoned him with the news of Bobby's disappearance; then, not long after Wilson had left the house, Flora Franks had received the first phone call from one of the kidnappers—had Wilson made that phone call?[30]

Both Richard Williams, the athletics coach, and Mott Kirk Mitchell, the English teacher, were held in police cells for five hours that Friday; the police beat both men with a rubber hose to force them to confess. The detectives had searched Williams's apartment and had found four bottles of brown liquid. There had been copper-colored stains on Bobby's face; could the liquid in Williams's possession be the poison with which the murderer had killed the boy? Williams protested his innocence. The liquid, he explained, was merely a liniment which he used to rub on the boys' muscles after strenuous exercises. But his explanation did him no good; the athletics instructor remained a leading suspect.[31]

The revelation that Mott Kirk Mitchell, the English teacher, had a semiannual mortgage payment due the day of the kidnapping hardened the suspicions of the police. When the detectives learned that the mortgage on Mitchell's house was exactly $10,000—the kidnappers had demanded precisely that amount—they felt sure they had the murderer. Mitchell had taught at the Harvard School for fourteen years and was popular with the boys—perhaps, Charles Pence hinted, too popular. "He always impressed me as being a very fine man," the principal informed the police. "He was interested in his work and his pupils. Why, whenever one of the boys was ill at home he always sent flowers." The police dug up the sewers around Mitchell's house in a search for Bobby's clothes but found nothing; they questioned Mitchell again and again about the killing, but he was obdurate. He insisted on his inno-cence.[32]

Fortunately for the teachers, they all had alibis for the evening of Bobby's disappearance. Mitchell's neighbors could testify that he had been working in his garden at the time of the kidnapping; Richard Williams had had dinner at the Delphi Restaurant on 47th Street near Lake Park; and Walter Wilson's landlady stated that her boarder had been home the entire evening. For friends, neighbors, and acquaintances it was impossible that any of the three should have killed the boy: the three teachers were conscientious, irreproachable, and considerate—perfect gentlemen.[33]

Robert Crowe, the state's attorney for Cook County, was still suspicious. True, he had no evidence linking any of the teachers to the crime. The police held the suspects for four days and beat them regularly yet were unable to force a confession. The men's lawyers, Charles Wharton and Otis Glenn, filed a petition for a writ of habeas corpus on Monday, 26 May, alleging police brutality; Glenn pointed out that there was little justification for their clients' continued detention. "The police have nothing on them and I don't see why they should be held." But Crowe insisted to the judge, Frederic Robert DeYoung, that he needed to keep them in the police cells: "We feel they can help us materially in solving the mystery surrounding this murder. It is true we have no warrants for these men, but we are very desirous of questioning them further and getting what aid we can from them." Perhaps, Crowe slyly suggested to DeYoung, the judge would continue the case to enable the police to hold them for a few days more; but that, the judge replied, would run counter to the law. If Crowe did not have the evidence to charge the teachers with murder and kidnapping, then there was no basis for their continued detention. "Under the law," DeYoung stated, "these men are entitled to their liberty. There is no escape from it."[34]

Samuel Ettelson was furious that the killers might escape justice. The teachers were guilty—no doubt about it. In a rare display of anger, Ettelson was quoted by the Chicago newspapers as condemning their release—he asserted that at least two of the instructors had plotted to kidnap Bobby. "One instructor at the Harvard School," Ettelson declared, "killed Robert Franks. Another wrote the polished letter demanding $10,000 from the family. The instructor who wrote the letter was a cultured man—a man with perverted tendencies—the man who committed the actual crime is a man who needed money and who had mercenary motives."[35]

Ettelson's outburst reflected the authorities' frustration; one week after the murder, they had several clues, plenty of theories, dozens of leads, but no arrests. To their amazement, the police discovered that they even had a witness to the kidnapping: just after five o'clock on Wednesday afternoon, Irving Hartman, a ten-year-old pupil at the Harvard School, had been trailing thirty yards behind Bobby as the two boys walked south on Ellis Avenue. Irving's attention had been momentarily distracted by some flowers in a yard; he stopped to look at them, and when he glanced up, Bobby had disappeared. At that moment, Irving reported, a gray Winton automobile moved away from the curb at the exact spot where he had last seen Bobby.[36]

Philip Van Devoorde, a chauffeur for the Fay family, had noticed a gray Winton, spattered with mud, outside the Harvard School on Tuesday, 20 May, the day before the kidnapping. Van Devoorde provided a detailed description of the car to the police: it was a 1919 model with a gray-black top; the driver had been between twenty-five and thirty years old; and in the front passenger seat there had been a second man, red-faced, with a pointed nose and wearing a tan cap. Equally significant, the same car was standing near the front entrance of the school on Wednesday at around five o'clock, almost exactly at the time of the kidnapping.[37]

Soon sightings of gray Wintons were pouring into police headquarters. One witness had seen a gray Winton at 113th Street and Michigan Avenue, not far from Wolf Lake, around eight o'clock on Wednesday evening. A man had been behind the steering wheel and a woman had sat in the front passenger seat, and in the back there had been a large bundle that might have been a huddled human form. William Lucht, a tax assessor, had seen a Winton, with two bundles in the rear seat, near Cottage Grove Avenue and 67th Street on Wednesday evening. Stanley Miner had reported a gray Winton on Lake Park Avenue and

48th Street. Frederick Eckstein, a watchman, had noticed a gray touring car—"old and decrepit looking"—on Railroad Avenue in the vicinity of Wolf Lake.[38]

Robert Crowe, the state's attorney, attached especial significance to such accounts. Irving Hartman had no reason to deceive the police with his initial account of Bobby's disappearance—Crowe could trust his veracity. And the Winton automobile was not a popular model; it would not be difficult to track down owners of Wintons in Chicago. Moreover, it was a distinctive car: its boxy appearance, elongated hood, and capacious tonneau made the Winton instantly recognizable.[39]

Anyone with such a car was liable to be arrested on sight. Two days after the murder, the police took Adolph Papritz, a draftsman at Armour and Company who owned a gray Winton, to headquarters for questioning. Papritz was eventually cleared, but not before the newspapers had concluded that he was most probably the murderer. Nevertheless, he harbored no malice: "I expected it. Everybody with a gray car is being taken in."[40]

Joe Klon had the misfortune to drive a gray Winton *and* to wear tortoiseshell glasses. Klon eventually decided to leave his car in his garage and walk to work—too many busybodies were turning him in to the police in hopes of winning the $5,000 reward offered by the family. "This has got to stop somewhere," Klon protested. "I'm going to have that car painted black. . . . I've got to wear glasses to see, but I'm going to do away with those tortoise shell rims. This is the third time I've been arrested for murder in as many days."[41]

The state's attorney, Robert Crowe, and the chief of police, Morgan Collins, had enlisted the aid of the press in advertising the clues as widely as possible. As a strategy, it was a double-edged sword: on the one hand it encouraged the public to report possible suspects to the police, but on the other hand it often involved the detectives in a fruitless pursuit of leads based on an entirely false premise. So it was with the gray Winton automobile. Collins's men searched out gray Wintons in every corner of the city, hauled in their owners for questioning, and interviewed countless mechanics at car repair shops—but all for naught. Not a single gray Winton could be conclusively linked to the murder. Irving Hartman's eyewitness account, Crowe wearily concluded, had been mistaken.

AND THE KIDNAPPERS' MOTIVE? The authorities had as little certainty about motive as they had regarding the clues. Could the killing of Bobby Franks be an act of revenge against the father for a business deal gone sour? Jacob Franks had a good reputation as an honest businessman, but it was difficult to believe that in his long life as a pawnbroker and realtor, often dealing with gamblers and pimps, he had never crossed someone. Indeed, Bobby's death had sparked an avalanche of hateful, vengeful letters to the Franks household. One anonymous writer promised "to strangle you to death. . . . You shall suffer minute by minute, you lowdown skunk"; and this writer concluded by threatening to kill Franks's daughter, Josephine. The threats against the Franks family might be the work of cranks, but they could not be taken lightly. Might the other children be at risk? No one was prepared to ignore the possibility that someone was planning a second act of violence against the family; and so, on Saturday, 24 May, a police guard, consisting of eight sergeants, was set up around the Franks home.[42]

Had Bobby been the victim of a child molester? Publicly, at least, the coroner's physician, Joseph Springer, claimed that "young Franks had not been the victim of a pervert"; yet in his final report, Springer hinted that someone may have raped the boy: "the rectum was dilated and would admit easily one middle finger."[43] Chicago had no shortage of pedophiles; and everyone could recall the rape and murder of six-year-old Janet Wilkinson in 1919. Perhaps the abductor had molested Bobby and, fearing identification by the boy, had decided also to kill him.

Morgan Collins detailed a police squad to arrest N. C. Starren, a notorious pedophile who had taught at Lindblom High School; and on the Monday following the murder, Collins issued a general order to arrest all "persons known to be perverts, those who have ever before been charged with or convicted of any unnatural act." It was a comprehensive roundup of pedophiles and homosexuals that included anyone either fined or sentenced in the criminal and municipal courts and anyone who had served a term for sexual deviancy in the state penitentiary. John Caverly, the chief justice of the Cook County Criminal Court, endorsed Collins's draconian measures. The kidnapper, Caverly believed, was most probably a mental defective who had taken Bobby Franks in order to sexually abuse him. There were other possible motives, of course; perhaps it was a straightforward kidnapping case with the ransom as the principal object, or perhaps the kidnapper bore a grudge against Jacob Franks. But Caverly had little doubt that the abduction was the work of a child molester. "All evidence so far," he pronounced in support of Collins, "points to the moron theory as the most plausible."[44]

But would a pedophile attempt to extort a ransom from the boy's father? Would a kidnapper interested in sexually abusing the boy also phone the boy's parents, arrange for a cab to arrive at the Franks home, and mail a letter asking for a ransom? That was possible, of course—anything was possible—but in the opinion of the state's attorney, Robert Crowe, it was highly unlikely: "It is not to be considered tenable that the boy's attackers were perverts. They would not have bothered about sending letters and chauffeurs to complicate the matter."[45]

Crowe believed the murder was the consequence of a ransom demand gone awry. The kidnappers had lured Bobby into an automobile (but how? did the boy know his abductors?); perhaps one kidnapper had sequestered the boy in a remote location (near Wolf Lake?) while the second kidnapper had stayed in Chicago to phone the parents and mail the letter. Bobby had probably recognized the captor who had killed him not long after the kidnapping; the second man, unaware that their victim was dead, had proceeded with the plan.

Crowe hinted that cocaine addicts, in the pay of a criminal mastermind, had abducted Bobby Franks. Never mind that there was no evidence to support this assertion—Crowe knew that, by linking the use of illegal drugs to the murder, he could legitimately call on outside assistance without losing face. If the resources of the Chicago police department were inadequate, perhaps federal agents from the Bureau of Investigation could find the culprits: "We shall, by a process of elimination, try to find some one user of drugs who was sufficiently well acquainted with the habits and movements of the Franks family to have contrived a kidnapping plot. . . . Dope will be found at the bottom of it all."[46]

Whether or not cocaine addicts were behind the kidnapping, it certainly appeared that the desire to obtain a ransom was the least improbable motive for Bobby's disappearance. Some detectives wondered why the kidnappers would choose a fourteen-year-old; if ransom was the motive, why not abduct a younger child, who would be less likely to recognize the kidnappers at a later date? But this reasoning failed to disturb the emerging consensus: the ransom provided the motive.[47]

On Monday, 26 May, five days after the murder of Bobby Franks, the police learned that another child, a sixteen-year-old schoolgirl, had also disappeared the previous Wednesday. Gertrude Barker had left St. Xavier's Academy on Cottage Grove Avenue to walk north toward her home on Blackstone Avenue. She would have arrived at 49th Street and Ellis Avenue—the scene of Bobby's abduction—at almost exactly the moment when Bobby had disappeared. Had she witnessed the kidnapping?

Had the kidnappers bundled Gertrude into the car to prevent her from informing the police? The girl's aunt could not imagine that Gertrude had done anything foolish—she was not one to fall in with a bad crowd. "She preferred her home and her books to the school friends she had made. She loved to fish and ride, and expected to take up horseback riding as soon as the weather got warmer." Her family was frantic with worry; Gertrude had been missing for almost a week. Perhaps, her aunt speculated, she also was lying dead in a ditch. "I feel sure something untoward has happened to her. She . . . would have been on 49th Street just about the time that poor little Franks boy was kidnaped. . . . I am afraid she saw those terrible kidnapers, and they abducted her also, fearing she might tell the police the license number of their automobile."[48]

Gertrude was not so innocent as her aunt had imagined. Later that week, the police discovered her living with a twenty-seven-year-old stable boy, Bert Jeffery. Gertrude explained that she had met Bert in a local diner. "I flirted with a nice-looking boy in a drug store where I stopped to get a soda." Bert declared his love for Gertrude and his intention to marry her, but the police had other ideas: they bundled Bert into a cell in the South Clark Street police station and returned Gertrude to her family.[49]

THEIR QUICK SUCCESS IN FINDING Gertrude Barker was the only bright spot for the police in an otherwise grim week.

On Monday, 26 May, the Franks family held a funeral service for their son at their home on Ellis Avenue. It would have been impossible for the family to have held a funeral service in a public place; the crowds would be too large and the ceremony might turn into a circus. Every day since the kidnapping, hundreds of sightseers had milled outside the house, gawking at the drawn curtains, hoping to catch a glimpse of Bobby's father and mother.

Thus a select group—members of the family, twenty of Bobby's classmates, and a few close friends—gathered around the white casket in the library for the service. Banks of flowers crowded the room; lilies of the valley, bouquets of peonies and mignonette, wreathes of roses, and baskets of orchids surrounded the small coffin.[50]

The Franks family had converted from Judaism to Christian Science. Elwood Emory, the first reader of the Fifth Church of Christ, Scientist read the Lord's Prayer, the Twenty-Third Psalm, and other passages from the scriptures. Glenn Drake, a choral singer from the church, sang two hymns, and then the mourners moved silently and slowly toward the front door, where black limousines waited to drive to Rosehill Cemetery. Eight boys carried the coffin to the hearse; the other boys from the Harvard School clustered in the hallway at the bottom of the large staircase. As Flora Franks passed them, she looked wistfully over their faces: her son had belonged to that group, and now he was gone—never again would Bobby talk to her excitedly about hitting a ball out of the baseball lot; never again would he tell his mother of his plans, his disappointments, and his victories.

There was now a crowd of 300 waiting in the street. The family slipped out of a side door with a police escort to escape the photographers. There were no disturbances: Morgan Collins had sent out a large detail of police to keep order. At Rosehill Cemetery, Elwood Emory offered prayers, and Bobby Franks was laid to rest in the family mausoleum.[51]

The police investigation seemed to be at a standstill. The detectives had been unable to connect anyone to the gray Winton car seen by Irving Hartman; they had no evidence linking the teachers at the Harvard School to the killing; they could not identify the author of the ransom note.

Only one promising clue remained: the tortoiseshell eyeglasses found by Paul Korff near the corpse. Gradually, during the first week after the murder, the police had come to realize that the eyeglasses constituted an extraordinarily valuable clue—perhaps their only way to track down the killer. Crucially, the lenses could have been obtained only with a prescription; they had not been purchased over the counter. Somewhere there must be an optician who had ground the glasses; that optician had doubtless kept a copy of the prescription in his files.[52]

But the prescription was a common one, given to "persons suffering from simple astigmatism or astigmatic farsightedness," explained one Chicago optician. "The lenses are of a convex cylindrical type, also a common pattern." Thus the prescription alone would not materially advance the search—there could be thousands of Chicagoans with such glasses—but what about the frames? Were they distinctive?[53]

Yes, they were unusual. Composed of Newport zylonite, an artificial composite, the frames had distinctive rivet hinges and square corners. No firm in Chicago, or even in the Midwest, manufactured Newport zylonite frames. They originated in Brooklyn, and only one optician in Chicago sold such frames: Almer Coe and Company. The owner of the firm recognized the glasses immediately. "We . . . identified them as of a type sold by us and not by any other Chicago dealer. The lenses had markings used by us, and as far as we know, not used by any other optician in Chicago. The lenses are not unusual; such prescriptions are filled often by us, possibly once a week. They are lenses for eye-strain or headache, and would not materially improve vision. . . . They might be used only for reading or for what is known as mild astigmatism. Their measurements are average in every way."[54]

Average in every way. Perhaps the killer would slip away again. But for the first time in eight days, state's attorney Robert Crowe sensed that the net was gradually closing. That Thursday, 29 May, the clerks at Almer Coe began the laborious task of checking the thousands of prescriptions in the company files: they were looking for a distinctive frame and a common lens prescription. How many would they find and to whom would these belong?[55]

THAT AFTERNOON, THE POLICE KNOCKED at the door of Nathan Leopold Jr., a nineteen-year-old law student at the University of Chicago. The journalists following the Franks murder were mildly curious that the police had taken Leopold into custody—but this was certainly only a routine matter. Everyone knew Leopold's father as one of the wealthiest Jewish businessmen in Chicago; the family was socially prominent, with influential connections. And Nathan Leopold? He was a brilliant student—Phi Beta Kappa at Chicago—who had recently applied to transfer to the law school at Harvard University that fall. The journalists shrugged their shoulders at the news. There was no copy to be filed with their editors about this—obviously Nathan Leopold had nothing to do with the murder of Bobby Franks.

2 | THE RELATIONSHIP

Their criminal activities were the outgrowth of an unique coming-together of two peculiarly maladjusted adolescents, each of whom brought into relationship a long-standing background of abnormal life.[1]

Psychiatrists' Report for the Defense
(Joint Summary) [July 1924]

[Nathan] was very egocentric. Practically all the time I was with him, in ordinary social conversation, he attempted by any sort of ruse possible to monopolize the conversation. It didn't make any difference what was being said or what was being talked about, he always attempted to get the conversation revolving around him so he could do most of the talking. . . . He thought his mentality was a great deal superior to the ordinary person.[2]

Arnold Maremont, student at the University
of Chicago, 7 August 1924

[Richard] smoked very much, constantly. . . . We were in the habit of seeing him drunk a good deal. . . . We would be sitting in the house playing a game of bridge and Dick would walk in and one or two of us would say he is drunk again and one or two of us would say no he is not. Half of the time it would work out he was drunk.[3]

Theodore Schimberg, student at the University
of Chicago, 8 August 1924

NATHAN LEOPOLD WAS JUST FIFTEEN YEARS old; but already he felt that he was passing into adulthood, gratefully slipping out of his adolescence, gladly discarding his high school years. That month—October 1920—he was to begin his freshman year at the University of Chicago.[4]

The university had been in existence less than three decades, but to Nathan it seemed to have been around forever. He had grown up in its shadow—the Leopold house was just ten blocks from the campus. He had often walked past the imposing, monumental Gothic buildings, constructed of gray Bedford limestone, that stretched south from 57th Street to the Midway. There was much to admire about the campus: Mitchell Tower—reminiscent of the tower of Magdalen College, Oxford—with its august presence on 57th Street signaling the approach to the university; Cobb Gate, linking the anatomy and zoology buildings, the fantastic gargoyles on its inclines representing the upward progress of the classes; the student dormitories with their red-tiled roofs, ornamented doorways, and heavyset bay windows; and Harper Library, a massive, brooding building looking out over the green fields that stretched south of the Midway.

The architects had constructed the campus in the late Gothic style. It might have seemed anachronistic to build in Chicago—the most modern of American cities—a university that resembled the medieval colleges of Oxford and Cambridge, but there was a pleasing regularity about the campus. Everything was in proportion; nothing was too large or too small; and the Gothic style allowed for an astonishing diversity of embellishment and ornamentation. Innumerable gargoyles studded every building, peering down on the students making their way to class; crockets and finials—elaborate decorations shaped in the form of foliage—ran hither and thither over the buildings, stretching across the tops of doorways and around the arches of bay windows; and the generous use of stained and leaded glass in the windows provided an essential ingredient to the riot of medievalism that constituted the University of Chicago.[5]

Already—even before his matriculation—the university dazzled Nathan Leopold with its promises of future achievement: academic triumphs in the classroom, acclaim from the professors, scholastic awards and honors. His mother—his gentle, loving, affectionate mother, Florence—had extracted a promise from him, willingly given, that he would make Phi Beta Kappa before graduation. Nathan intended to keep his promise—and perhaps, also, he hoped, he would attain what had almost always eluded him in high school: companionship and friends.

For Nathan Leopold—fifteen years old, five feet three inches tall, weighing 110 pounds, with a sallow complexion, gray eyes, thick black hair, and a curiously asymmetrical face that gave him an evasive appearance—had always been a lonely and unhappy child.

His grandfather Samuel F. Leopold had emigrated from Germany to the United States in 1846, eventually settling in northern Michigan. Samuel had opened several small retail stores, each one close to the copper mines, first in Eagle River, a second in Eagle Harbor, a third in the town of Cliff Mines, and a fourth in Hancock. Business was good, and within a few years he had been able to open several more stores, so that his reach extended along the Upper Peninsula. But obtaining supplies to sell on to the miners and laborers had become a constant struggle: there was no railroad connecting Chicago to the copper mines, and shipping facilities were rudimentary.[6]

In 1867, Samuel Leopold bought his first steamship to carry grain and other provisions to the mining towns; then came his second, the SS *Ontonagon*; and in 1872, he added the SS *Peerless* to his fleet. He moved to Chicago with his wife, Babette, and their six children; invested wisely; and gradually built up his shipping business so that, at his death from septicemia in 1898, the Lake Michigan and Lake Superior Transportation Company was the largest shipping line plying the Great Lakes.[7]

His first son, Nathan F. Leopold, born in Eagle River in 1860, proved as astute a businessman as his father. Nathan inherited the family business; married his childhood sweetheart, Florence Foreman; purchased a large house at 3223 Michigan Avenue; and made a second fortune manufacturing aluminum cans and paper boxes. Through his marriage to Florence, a daughter of the financier Gerhart Foreman, Nathan F. Leopold Sr. was now connected to some of Chicago's most prosperous and prominent bankers. Within a single generation, the Leopolds had won a place among the wealthiest families in Chicago.[8]

In 1915, Nathan and Florence moved their family—three sons: Michael, Samuel, and Nathan Jr.—from Michigan Avenue to the residential neighborhood of Kenwood, eight miles south of the Loop. Their new home, 4754 Greenwood Avenue, a three-story mansion set back from the street, was one of the more unusual homes in a neighborhood distinguished by architectural diversity: the Leopold house included, on the first floor, an enormous rectangular living room built in the modernist style, facing the garden on three sides, around which the architect had attached the remainder of the mansion built in traditional nineteenth-century style complete with gabled roofs.

The youngest son, Nathan Jr., had reason to welcome the family's move to Kenwood. For two years Nathan had attended the local public school, the Douglas School, just a few blocks from their home on Michigan Avenue. It had been an unhappy experience. Nathan was one of those unfortunate children who attract the relentless, unforgiving attention of schoolboy bullies, and during his time at the Douglas School his classmates taunted and teased him remorselessly. He was different from the other boys, Nathan realized: he was naturally shy and more studious than his peers; he had little interest in baseball and no athletic ability; his parents were affluent; and, each afternoon, at the end of the school day, his governess would embarrass him by appearing at the school gate to escort him home. And when his classmates discovered that Nathan had, as a six-year-old, briefly attended a girls' school—the Spaides School on Buena Avenue—his humiliation was complete. Nathan's acknowledgment that he was different—"I realized I was not like other children, that I had wealthy parents, that I lived on Michigan Avenue and had a nurse who accompanied me to and from school"—did nothing to ease the pain and distress that accompanied the daily torture inflicted by his classmates.[9]

To whom could he turn for help? His father was aloof and remote, preoccupied with his business ventures; his two brothers, Michael and Samuel, older than he by several years, had never taken him seriously; and his mother, Florence, was an invalid, bedridden after contracting some mysterious illness during her pregnancy with Nathan.

There was only one person in whom he could confide. His governess, Mathilda (Sweetie) Wantz, had joined the Leopold household in 1911. She was an attractive, strong-willed woman, around thirty years old, with a heavy German accent and a flirtatious manner. Mathilda quickly established herself as a presence in the Leopold household, less as a governess to the two younger boys, Samuel and Nathan, than as a substitute for their invalid mother. Florence Leopold loved her three sons, and had a special regard for Nathan, a weak, frail boy; but because of her illness, she had gradually given up control of the household to the governess.[10]

It was not long before the maids were exchanging gossip about Mathilda's increasingly eccentric, even outrageous behavior. Everyone remarked on her obvious familiarity with the two younger boys, and soon it had become common knowledge among the household staff that Mathilda was having sex with seventeen-year-old Samuel; even more scandalously, she had become sexually intimate with twelve-year-old Nathan.[11]

The youngest boy, especially, was smitten with his governess. Nathan recognized that Mathilda had taken the place of his mother— "She had a very great influence over my brother and myself. She displaced my mother"—but any regret that his mother's illness had reduced her importance was overwhelmed by the affection

4. THE HARVARD SCHOOL. The Harvard School for Boys, founded in 1865, moved in 1917 to a new location at 4731 Ellis Avenue. This illustration first appeared as the frontispiece to the school catalog.

and love that he now felt for his governess: "I was thoroughly devoted to her."[12]

His home life was in turmoil; Nathan, nevertheless, excelled at his studies at his new school. After the family had moved to Greenwood Avenue, his father had enrolled him at the Harvard School for Boys. The school building, located at 47th Street and Ellis Avenue, was unremarkable—a single three-story redbrick building facing onto Ellis Avenue with chemistry laboratories at the rear and an asphalt playground at the side—but the teachers were, without exception, conscientious and hardworking, devoted to their pupils, and determined that each boy should, if he desired, have the opportunity to attend college.

Fewer than 200 boys attended the Harvard School. The primary school included eight grades, with approximately fifteen boys in each grade; the high school consisted of four classes, ranging from the freshman class to the seniors. The Harvard School emphasized academic excellence; the size of each class, along with an extensive counseling program, enabled the teachers to give each boy individual attention. Very occasionally, a boy might forgo university to enter directly into his father's business, but more typically, every member of each graduating class went on to college: in the majority of cases, either to the University of Chicago or to an elite private institution in the East such as Yale, Cornell, or Dartmouth.

The classes at the Harvard School were too small to support sports teams, and success in sports was always elusive. In 1919, the school abandoned football because of a lack of interest among the seniors; and, although the school fielded baseball ar d basketball teams, other, larger schools, most notably the Francis Parker School, Chicago Latin, and Wendell Phillips, invariably trounced the Harvard boys.[13]

Nathan Leopold had no interest in sports—he was indifferent to the lack of success of the Harvard teams—but he excelled in the classroom. At the Harvard School, he took, in addition to the assigned courses, electives in German and classical Greek, and he succeeded, year after year, in standing at the top of his class. He was still an outsider—his classmates regarded him as an eccentric loner—but by his junior year, he had won a few friends through a shared interest in ornithology. Nathan had a passion for collecting birds, a passion that had begun six years earlier through the encouragement of a teacher at the Douglas School. His bird collection, kept in a study adjoining his bedroom, encompassed over 2,000 specimens; on weekends, he would drive to the lakes southeast of the city near the Indiana state line to hunt up new species for his collection.[14]

By spring 1920, Nathan, fifteen years old, now a junior at the Harvard School, felt that he had nothing more to learn from his teachers. He had accumulated sufficient credits to forgo his senior year and was eligible to matriculate at the University of Chicago. He was eager for the challenge. And so, in 1920, Nathan prepared to enter the university's freshman class.[15]

But that summer, in June 1920, Nathan met a new acquaintance, a boy six months younger than himself, an impossibly good-looking boy, slender but well built, tall, with brown-blond hair, humorous blue eyes, and a sudden, attractive smile.

RICHARD LOEB CAME FROM a wealthy, well-connected family. His father, Albert Loeb, was vice president of Sears, Roebuck and a close friend of the millionaire philanthropist Julius Rosenwald. Richard's mother, Anna, was a prominent member of the Chicago Woman's Club and an associate of Jane Addams, the founder of the settlement house movement in Chicago. His uncle Jacob then, in 1920, a lawyer in private practice, had been president of the Chicago Board of Education until 1919, responsible, most notoriously, for the Loeb Rule enjoining teachers in the city's public schools from going on strike.[16]

Albert Loeb had begun his career as a lawyer—he had been admitted to the Illinois bar in 1889 and had worked for the firm of Loeb and Adler for twelve years. In 1901, he accepted Julius Rosenwald's invitation to work for Sears, Roebuck, and within the decade he had become vice president of the company. As the business expanded during the early years of the century, Albert accumulated a personal fortune that by 1920 exceeded $10 million. Albert and Anna Loeb had four sons: Allan lived in Seattle, where he was the manager of Sears, Roebuck on the West Coast; Ernest was a student at Vanderbilt University; Richard, fifteen years old, had recently completed his freshman year at the University of Chicago; and the youngest, Thomas, was in the eighth grade at the Harvard School for Boys.[17]

Richard had always been the intellectual of the family. At an early age, with the benediction of his governess, Emily Struthers, he read widely in history and literature. Emily introduced Richard to the novels of Charles Dickens and William Makepeace Thackeray and encouraged him to read the adventure stories of Ernest Thompson Seton. Historical novels, loosely based on actual events, were all the rage in the United States in the early years of the century, and Richard, too, was caught up in the craze: as a young boy, he read Henryk Sienkiewicz's *Quo Vadis* and Lew Wallace's *Ben-Hur*. Emily Struthers was ambitious for Richard—

she imagined he might choose a career as an ambassador or a diplomat—and she encouraged him to read not only the literary classics but also such serious historical works as John Lothrop Motley's *The Rise of the Dutch Republic* and Herman Grimm's *Life of Michael Angelo.*[18]

Richard was a dutiful pupil who conscientiously read those books that Emily picked out for him. But he never divulged to his governess his real passion, which was for crime stories and detective mysteries, a genre that he knew would never win Emily's approval. He had discovered a copy of Frank Packard's *The Beloved Traitor* among his brother's books. Out of sight of his governess, alone in his bedroom, Richard would spend hours reading Packard's stories about a famous criminal who could extricate himself from the most complex and dangerous situations. Richard was enthralled by such adventures; the more intricate the story, the greater his fascination. He could not stop reading the Packard stories. No sooner had he finished *The Beloved Traitor* than he purchased Packard's *The Adventures of Jimmie Dale*, a collection of tales in which the eponymous hero, an expert crook with noble motives, carried out a series of dazzlingly clever robberies. Richard had a passion for detective stories. He quickly read the Arthur Conan Doyle oeuvre, taking particular pleasure in *The Sign of Four*; he followed Sherlock Holmes with Jules Verne's *Michael Strogoff: The Courier of the Czar*, Maurice Leblanc's *813*, and Wyndham Martin's *Anthony Trent, Master Criminal.*[19]

5. RICHARD (DICKIE) LOEB. Born 22 June 1905. This photograph shows Loeb as a seven-year-old pupil at the University Elementary School.

.   .   .

IN OCTOBER 1917, RICHARD, THREE months past his twelfth birthday, entered the freshman class at University High School. The school, adjacent to the University of Chicago, was the creation of John Dewey, professor of philosophy at the university. In 1896 Dewey had established an elementary school, for pupils younger than eleven, as part of his initiative to overturn traditional pedagogical methods. In 1902 Dewey added a high school on the same site in new buildings on the north side of the Midway, immediately east of the university campus. The teachers at University High School would forgo the traditional pedagogy then current in American high schools—rote learning and memorization—and replace it with a pedagogy that encouraged innovation, initiative, and experimentation. Students, Dewey believed, should be educated in a way that best prepared them for the demands of daily life; the pupils at University High were expected, therefore, to solve practical problems creatively and in cooperation with their classmates.[20]

As a consequence, University High, in the first two decades of its existence, was a riot of creative activity both inside and outside the classroom. The University of Chicago took especial pride in the high school and its innovative pedagogy and provided the resources, including financial support, to enable the faculty to introduce a many-sided curriculum. By 1917, 500 boys and girls were enrolled at University High; many of them were sons and daughters of the university professors.

Extracurricular activities flourished at the school. The students organized a jazz band, a symphony orchestra, a Glee Club (for theatrical performances), Sketch Club, Discussion Club, and Engineering Club. Each class organized a Literary Society (exclusively for members of the class) to meet for readings, debates, and musical recitals. There were three academic honor societies: Kanyaratna (for girls), Tripleee (for boys), and Phi Beta Sigma (for pupils with an outstanding academic record). Boys from all four classes could join together as the Boys' Club for informal discussions and meetings; the girls quickly established the Girls' Club as a counterpart. Students at University High organized three publications: *The Midway*, a literary magazine that appeared each fortnight; *The Correlator*, the high school yearbook; and that most extraordinary of accomplishments, the *University High School Daily*, a four-page newspaper that appeared on Tuesdays, Wednesdays, Thursdays, and Fridays during the school term. Finally there were the sports teams: football, soccer, and baseball for the boys; basketball for boys and girls.

Richard Loeb entered the freshman class in 1917 with a sense of anticipation. His elder brother Ernest, a senior and captain of the soccer team, could provide guidance to Richard if he needed it; but Richard had been a pupil in the elementary school and was now entering University High with his classmates. It was not difficult, therefore, for Richard to adjust to his new situation. He was an extroverted, outgoing, enthusiastic twelve-year-old, with no hint of shyness or diffidence. He had no particular talents that set him apart from his classmates—no outstanding athletic ability and no aptitude for playing a musical instrument—but he was likable, engaging, and popular, someone who readily joined in school activities.[21]

In his first term at University High, Richard joined the Discussion Club and the Engineering Club, two groups that recruited their members from all four classes. Predictably, the upperclassmen—seniors and juniors—dominated the affairs of both groups; Richard attended sporadically during his freshman year but said little during the discussions. His enthusiasm was reserved for meetings of the Freshman Literary Society. No seniors and juniors could dominate the proceedings of this group, and the freshmen—nicknamed "the molecules" by the upperclassmen—could organize their own activities without interference from their elders.[22]

Each fortnight members of the Freshman Literary Society would meet to debate some pressing issue, to hear a musical recital by one or more members, and to listen to extemporaneous talks. Richard was irrepressible and indefatigable, and scarcely a meeting went by without one of his many contributions. He was an enthusiastic presence, always volunteering his thoughts and remarks, and perhaps, therefore, it was a cruel disappointment that, in May 1918, when he ran for president of the Freshman Literary Society, he lost narrowly to Henry Abt.[23]

Richard's failure to win the election was the sole blemish on an otherwise successful freshman year. Everyone liked Richard—he was one of the most popular boys in the class. He rarely missed a homework assignment, and his teachers regarded him with affection and admiration as someone who always did well in his studies. In January 1918, at the start of the winter term, his classmates elected him treasurer of the freshman class, and in February Richard helped organize the freshman-sophomore dance. At the end of the school year, in May, Richard was manager of the freshman class party. It was a tremendous success; there had been plenty of ice cream and cakes and, of course, lots of bottles of Bevo, more than enough for all the boys and girls present.[24]

Richard's freshman year had been a triumph—but his governess, Emily Struthers, was ambitious for him to aim higher. Emily, an attractive woman in her early thirties, had a strong sense of duty. She had moved to Chicago in 1910 from her native Canada; she felt fortunate to have found such a generous and considerate employer as Albert Loeb, and she was determined to raise Richard in the best way that she knew. She was neither harsh nor cruel—she never applied the rod—but she expected to be obeyed.[25]

6. RICHARD LOEB. Loeb became a pupil at the University High School in 1917, at the age of twelve. When this photograph was taken, in 1918, Loeb was a freshman at University High. He matriculated at the University of Chicago at age fourteen.

Until he was eleven years old, Richard remembered, he never questioned Emily's commands ("I always obeyed her to the minute—second. Her word was law"), but as he grew older, he resented her diktats as onerous and excessive. Other boys could spend their evenings playing baseball and their weekends fishing in the Jackson Park lagoon. Why, Richard complained to himself, did Emily compel him to spend so much of his free time studying, studying, always studying? It was not fair; it was not reasonable; and gradually a spirit of rebellion and resentment crept over him. Emily's demands were unceasing; every evening, after dinner, she would sit down by his side and compel him to stay at the desk until his homework was completed to her satisfaction. "As a boy," Richard recalled, "I was kept under and did not do the things other boys did."[26]

Nor was there any recourse to a higher authority. His father, Albert, was a busy man and had neither the time nor the inclination to worry about his sons' education. Julius Rosenwald, the president of Sears, Roebuck, had absented himself from the day-to-day management of the firm and, in his place, Albert Loeb effectively ran the company. It was an all-consuming task, and in any case, and as far as Albert could tell, the governess, Emily, seemed to be doing a good job with Richard's upbringing. Albert was content to leave matters in her hands. Anna Loeb, also, was not unduly concerned about Emily's management of her son's education. Anna, too, was busy, busy with the affairs of the Chicago Woman's Club; she knew only that Richard was doing well at school and that Emily was clearly a capable woman who could be trusted with the children.[27]

It was, for Richard, an unbearable situation and, increasingly, he chafed at his governess's supervision. His resentment grew and, more and more, he slipped into the habit of lying to Emily in order to avoid her watchfulness. "To myself," Richard remembered, "I would think certain things were not as they should be. I would brood some. To 'get by' her I formed the habit of lying."[28]

Richard entered the sophomore class at University High in September 1918. He was just thirteen years old, but Emily had already decided that he should graduate from high school the following summer, two years ahead of his class.

It seemed, to Richard's teachers at University High, a nonsensical decision. It served no purpose. It might even be harmful to force him to carry such an accelerated course load; Richard was a bright boy but not as exceptional as his governess seemed to believe.

But Emily was not to be dissuaded. She had always felt her own lack of education as a disadvantage; she resented her inferior status as a governess and blamed it on her failure to progress beyond high school. Richard would be different, of course. He would be a great lawyer or perhaps a professor, she believed. But that would come only through constant effort; and, so, during his sophomore year, Richard took those courses that would enable him to graduate in 1919.[29]

During the autumn term, Richard gamely attended gatherings of the Sophomore Literary Society, occasionally speaking in the debates. But he was taking too many courses—he had too much schoolwork—and Emily's demands were too insistent; it was a struggle merely to complete his homework each week. He could no longer afford the time to participate in extracurricular activities.[30]

Throughout his sophomore year, Emily coached Richard in his studies, sitting with him each evening over his schoolwork, discussing his progress with his teachers each week, and ensuring that he completed his assignments. Her persistence paid off. Richard graduated from University High in June 1919, just a few days past his fourteenth birthday.[31]

Emily was exuberant. It had been a singular accomplishment. Richard had earned all the necessary credits and would be able to enter the freshman class at the University of Chicago that fall.

But Richard's success had come at a heavy price. He resented Emily's insistence that he take so many courses; he was embittered that his parents paid no heed to his complaints that he was overworked; and he envied his classmates their freedom. And it quickly became apparent that Richard, despite his high school diploma, was ill prepared for college. He was fourteen years old when he first attended classes at the

University of Chicago in October 1919. Many of his new classmates were three, four, even five years older than himself, and Richard struggled to keep pace with the demands of the college curriculum. He worked hard during that first year at Chicago, and Emily continued to supervise his course work, but Richard was a mediocre student and his grades were disappointing. Even in history, his favorite subject, Richard performed dismally, earning B-minus in the winter quarter and B in the spring quarter for courses in European history. Other courses were equally disappointing: C in English literature; C in geography; B-minus in mathematics; C in French literature; and B in rhetoric and composition.[32]

It was an inauspicious start to his college career. And Emily, who had played such an important role in Richard's life, from his early childhood to his adolescence, left the Loeb household in summer 1920 after his parents had decided that Richard, now fifteen, no longer needed a governess. Emily had made some ill-advised decisions—it was her ambition for Richard that had caused him to enroll at the university at fourteen—but she had been a constant source of emotional support, and without her steadying presence, Richard, by his own admission, went off the rails: "When she left, I sort of broke loose."[33]

THAT SUMMER HE HAD BECOME friends with a student at the Harvard School, an awkward, self-conscious, diffident boy, six months older than himself. Nathan Leopold would begin at the university that fall. Richard had the advantage over the other boy—he had already spent one year at Chicago—and he took the trouble to explain the demands that Nathan would confront at the university.

Could there have been a greater contrast among the students at Chicago than that presented by Richard Loeb and Nathan Leopold? Richard was gregarious and sociable; Nathan misanthropic and aloof. Richard impressed everyone with his easy open charm, his pleasant affability, and his humorous mannerisms; Nathan, who projected a disdainful, supercilious, arrogant attitude, appeared exactly opposite in character and temperament.

They seemed, to all appearances, to have little in common. Richard, absent Emily's steadying influence in his life, now had no reason to devote much time to his studies. He had hoped to join a fraternity, perhaps Phi Sigma Delta or Kappa Nu, but none of the Jewish fraternities on the campus had taken his pledge, perhaps because he was still so young. Early in his sophomore year, Richard had joined the Campus Club, a social organization for those students who had yet to pledge a fraternity. Members of the Campus Club gamely copied the rituals and rites of a fraternity organization, sponsoring frequent dances and smokers in Hutchinson Commons, but the club was a poor imitation of the real thing. And, in any case, the Campus Club was far too sedate, too stolid. Richard preferred to spend his evenings drinking and gossiping with friends at one of the many speakeasies south of the Midway—the Granada Cafe on 65th Street was a popular spot among the college students—or looking to pick up a girl at the Trianon Ballroom, a dance hall on the corner of 62nd Street and Cottage Grove Avenue.[34]

Richard's friendship with Nathan was a puzzle. What did each see in the other that made them such close companions? They had no shared interests, nothing that could provide a basis for their friendship. Nathan had no desire to accompany Richard on his drinking sprees or to join him in his quest to pick up girls. He, too, had joined the Campus Club and occasionally appeared at one of the smokers in Hutchinson Commons. But Nathan had set himself the task of graduating from the university as quickly as possible, and to that end he spent much of his free time studying. He earned good grades: he did so well in his freshman year, earning A or A-minus in Latin, introductory psychology, political economy, European history, and experimental psychology, that the university awarded him advanced standing. Nathan was neither the best nor the most brilliant student in his class—he earned B or B-minus in several other courses—but he was tenacious, hardworking, and determined to make his mark.[35]

. . .

IT HAD NEVER BEEN EASY for Nathan to make friends, and he was delighted to have won Richard's companionship. Richard was six months younger than himself but, nevertheless, there was so much to admire about him! His good looks, his gregarious attitude, his apparent sophistication, his worldly knowledge—Richard seemed to lead a charmed life. And as Nathan grew to know Richard better during the winter quarter, he began slowly to realize that Richard led a secret life. Perhaps, had Nathan not been so enamored with his companion and so anxious to retain his friendship, he might have dismissed Richard's purposeless, destructive behavior for what it was, but by spring 1921, Nathan had fallen in love with Richard. There was nothing he would not now do for Richard, and so, when Richard devised a plan to cheat at cards, he fell in with the scheme readily. It was not for the sake of the money—the boys received generous allowances from their fathers—but more for the thrill of the experience. There was pleasure in the anticipation of their success in fooling their friends, in pulling it off successfully, in evading detection.[36]

And when Richard suggested other adventures, Nathan acquiesced, even if he could not fully share Richard's pleasure in them. Some evenings Richard would have had too much to drink and he would insist that they find some deserted street close to campus—Kimbark, Greenwood, or Dorchester, perhaps. Then, as Nathan waited in the car, the engine running, ready to make good their escape, Richard would smash the windshields of parked cars with a half brick.[37]

Each such adventure seemed only to whet Richard's appetite for something more daring. Richard had discovered that the ignition key to his mother's car, a Milburn electric automobile, would fit any Milburn electric. It was inevitable that Richard would get his hands on a spare key and equally inevitable that he would use this key to steal Milburn electrics parked on the street. They had some narrow escapes. On one occasion an owner spotted Nathan and Richard sitting in his car and gave chase; on another occasion, the police questioned them about a stolen car—but they were never caught in the act.[38]

Richard loved to play a dangerous game—the more dangerous the better—and he always sought to raise the stakes. It was difficult to explain, even to himself, the pleasure that his vandalism provided; he knew only that he experienced a thrill—a more rapid heartbeat, a pulse of exhilaration and well-being—whenever he planned such adventures. Perhaps the knowledge that he was breaching a prohibition gave him the thrill; or perhaps it was his seeming ability to evade detection, the assuredness that came from the careful planning of his misdeeds, which provided him with a sense of his own potency.[39]

Richard's fascination with crime stories and pulp mysteries fueled his imagination. He was, at least in his own mind, a master criminal who, no matter how complex the crime, could always escape detection. There was no deed so difficult that he could not accomplish it, and in his fantasy, his ingenuity and cleverness commanded respect and admiration from other members of the criminal underworld. There was no detective—not even Sherlock Holmes—capable of catching him, nor was there any police force that could solve the crimes he had committed.[40]

Richard's narcissism could be completely fulfilled only in front of an audience that expressed its admiration for his ingenuity and guile; his fantasy that he was a master criminal was complete only if he could commit his crimes in front of one, two, or several associates. And such was his notoriety that if he were to be caught and placed in prison, he would attract a crowd of spectators who would simultaneously admire and pity him. The prison guards had whipped and beaten him, he imagined, and as he stood in his cell, bruised and bloody, dressed in old, ragged clothes, a group of onlookers, mostly young girls, regarded him through the prison bars with a mixture of fascination, awe, pity, and admiration. "I was abused, but it was a very pleasant thought," Richard said; "the punishment inflicted on me in jail was pleasant; I enjoyed being looked at through the bars, because I was a famous criminal."[41]

It was a powerful fantasy that provided Richard with endless pleasure. The drama began with a scheme—expertly planned—to commit an ingenious crime, carried out to perfection in front of respectful and admiring associates. It was never clear why Richard, if he was a master criminal, able to evade capture, should ever end up inside a prison cell;

nevertheless his imagined imprisonment provided Richard with masochistic and narcissistic sensations that heightened his fantasy.

Just as each detail provided Richard with pleasure that, as he experienced it, resembled sexual ecstasy, so in real life the planning of his actual misdeeds thrilled and excited him. In his sophomore year at the University of Chicago, Richard, always accompanied by Nathan, would carefully plan his acts of vandalism in advance. On several occasions he set fires, none of which, however, resulted in any loss of life. Less seriously, Richard would leave his house in the dead of night to smash storefront windows in Hyde Park and Kenwood. The preparation of such episodes was as pleasurable as their execution. It was almost as though the anticipation of the act, foreshadowing the violation of legal and moral imperatives, stood as the justification for the actual event.[42]

Nathan was a willing participant in Richard's adventures. He experienced neither enthusiasm nor regret over their vandalism; in truth, he was largely indifferent to the mayhem they inflicted. But his affection for Richard and his desire to be in Richard's company were now so strong that there was nothing he would not do to hold on to the friendship. It meant everything to him to have Richard as a companion. Richard needed him as an accomplice; if that was the requirement for gaining Richard's friendship, then of course he would willingly agree.[43]

Nathan also had a vivid fantasy life. He imagined himself as a slave, handsome, intelligent, and strong, the strongest man in the world, who had earned the gratitude of the king by saving his life. The king had offered Nathan his freedom, but Nathan preferred to remain in servitude, protecting the king and saving him from his enemies. When the king chose a slave to fight on his behalf, Nathan was always his choice, and in his battles Nathan was the victor, effortlessly vanquishing hundreds of fighters determined to kill him.[44]

It was a powerful fantasy; Nathan would be absorbed in his reverie for hours, imagining the admiration bestowed on him by the king, listing the opponents that he had defeated in battle, counting the times he had saved his king's life. This fantasy had first possessed him when he was eight years old, and it had persisted through puberty and into adolescence; it remained as potent and as pleasurable as ever.[45]

The fantasy had an enduring central narrative—a powerful slave serving a grateful king—but varied in its details. In one version, the king had first discovered Nathan as a young boy, beaten and abused by slave drivers; he had rescued the boy from neglect and poverty and had made him a member of the royal household. In time Nathan himself had come to possess slaves, despite his own condition of servitude—he marked his slaves by branding a crown on the inner calf of each slave's leg.[46]

The stronger his feelings for Richard Loeb, the more Richard appropriated the role of the king in Nathan's fantasy. Richard, as the king, might issue any command, for any reason, at any time, and Nathan would have no choice but to obey. But Nathan had reserved for himself the role of a strong, good-looking, powerful slave whose servitude was more apparent than real, dependent on his own acquiescence, and liable to be dissolved at any moment. It was a curiously contradictory fantasy, one that allowed Nathan to be both submissive and dominant; it gave over authority and power to the king while providing Nathan himself with potency and virility.[47]

Each imagined life—Richard's ideal of the master criminal and Nathan's self-portrait as the powerful slave—fulfilled the other. Richard, in his imagination, was capable of committing the most intricate and complex crimes, but he needed an audience to applaud his ingenuity: what better, more appreciative, onlooker could he choose than his subservient companion, Nathan Leopold? And Nathan secured gratification in imagining himself the slave to an appreciative king: could anyone other than Richard Loeb fill such a role?[48]

BUT THEIR FRIENDSHIP WOULD not endure. Richard was restless at the University of Chicago; during his freshman and sophomore years, he had continued to live at home while studying at the university; but now that he was about to become a junior, he was anxious to slip off the family bonds. He had friends at the University of Michigan at Ann Arbor, about 300 miles east of Chicago; he had visited the Michigan campus for football games, and by comparison the University of Chicago seemed too quiet, too sedate. In 1921 he suddenly announced to his parents that he intended to transfer to Michigan to finish his degree.[49]

Nathan was devastated—his closest companion, his most intimate friend, was to leave Chicago for Ann Arbor! He would lose Richard—perhaps forever! In his desperation, Nathan announced that he too would transfer to Michigan; and so, in September 1921, both boys prepared for the journey eastward.

Nothing went right for Nathan that fall. He contracted scarlet fever shortly before the start of the semester and arrived on campus only after the beginning of classes. In October his mother, Florence, finally died, succumbing to an illness that had persisted for many years. Nathan had grown close to his mother during his adolescence, and her death was a bitter blow that hardened his cynicism and mistrust; how could there be a God, he reasoned, who would allow the death of such a loving, sweet mother? Nathan remained in Chicago until Yom Kippur so as to attend the memorial service for his mother, and when he returned to the university, he discovered that Richard no longer cared to continue their friendship. On 17 October Richard had passed for pledgeship at Zeta Beta Tau fraternity. Members of the fraternity had cautioned him, however, that he had been seen too frequently in the company of Nathan Leopold, a suspected homosexual. Such an association would surely torpedo his chances of election—better, they advised him, that if he hoped to join Zeta Beta Tau, he should entirely cut Leopold.[50]

Nothing could have given Nathan more pain that to realize that Richard had abandoned him for new friends at Zeta Beta Tau. Nathan led a solitary existence at Ann Arbor, eating his meals alone or with one or two other Jewish boys, who, like himself, had neither enthusiasm nor aptitude for fraternity life. He spent most of his time immersed in his studies; he earned good grades, but there was now little reason for him to remain at the university and so, in fall 1922, Nathan transferred back to the University of Chicago.[51]

It was an auspicious move. Nathan's final year at Chicago was a time of self-realization, when he was able to break free of Richard's influence. He began to seek out friends and to develop extracurricular

7. IL CIRCOLO ITALIANO. Members of Il Circolo Italiano, an undergraduate group at the University of Chicago for the study of Italian culture, pose for their 1923 yearbook photograph. Nathan Leopold, holding his hat, is standing in the front row.

interests. Il Circolo Italiano, an undergraduate society devoted to the study of Italian culture, had been established on the campus the previous year; Nathan quickly became one of the group's most enthusiastic members, serving on committees, speaking in the discussions, and helping to organize joint meetings with the French and Spanish clubs.[52]

The Undergraduate Classical Club, another literary society, had been a fixture on the Chicago campus for at least a decade but by 1922 there were only twenty-five members, most of them women studying Latin or classical Greek at the university. Despite its small size, the Classical Club was one of the liveliest literary groups at Chicago, sponsoring talks by faculty members in a room lent by the classics department, organizing dinners, and staging a production of *Iphigeneia in Tauris*. It seemed appropriate that Nathan, who could both speak and write Latin and Greek, should join the Classical Club on his return to the university in September 1922. Such literary societies were intellectual oases at a campus where few undergraduates cared a great deal for academic achievement; and Nathan enjoyed the sense of exclusiveness that the fortnightly meetings conferred on the members.[53]

No other student at the University of Chicago performed so brilliantly in his studies during that academic year as Nathan Leopold. In autumn 1922, he earned an A-minus in Latin, A in classical Greek, A in Romance languages, A-minus in Russian, and A-minus in Sanskrit. The following quarter, in winter 1923, he took four courses for credit—earning an A in philosophy, A-minus in sociology, A in modern Greek, and A in classical Sanskrit—and he audited a reading course on Cervantes's *Don Quixote of La Mancha* in the Romance languages department. It might have seemed foolhardy to take so many courses—the normal course load at Chicago was three courses each quarter—but Nathan had surpassed all expectations.[54]

Nathan had distinguished himself as a philologist and linguist, proving worthy of election to Phi Beta Kappa, one of only fifteen students from the university to receive that honor in 1923. But his aptitude for languages was not his only talent. Ornithology was still an avocation for Nathan, something he pursued in his spare time. On weekends, if he had nothing better to do, he would drive to the Forest Preserve, south of Chicago, to the marshland around Wolf Lake, near the Indiana state line, in pursuit of new bird species to add to his collection. Ornithology was a hobby, nothing more, yet so proficient had he become in his studies that during his final year at the University of Chicago, Nathan was able to prepare two scientific papers for publication in *The Auk*, the leading journal for professional ornithologists in the United States.[55]

During his year at the University of Michigan, Nathan had made field trips to the northern part of the state to observe the Kirtland's Warbler, a rare, finchlike bird that laid its eggs in ground nests among the jack pines common to northern Michigan. The Kirtland's Warbler had been seen only infrequently within the United States, and in the 1920s it seemed destined for extinction. Nathan's account of its nesting habits, which appeared in *The Auk* early in 1924, was a model of detailed observation; and together with an earlier article by Nathan on bird migration and instinct, it earned its author instant recognition among professional ornithologists.[56]

Nathan had redeemed himself. His stellar academic record during his final year at Chicago, his election to Phi Beta Kappa, and his successful graduation, one year ahead of his class, amounted to a fulfillment of the promise made to his mother, before her death eighteen months earlier, that he would distinguish himself at the university. That spring, shortly before his graduation, Nathan decided on the law as his profession; he planned to enroll at the University of Chicago law school in the fall.

RICHARD LOEB ALSO GRADUATED—from the University of Michigan—in 1923. By his own admission he had coasted along, always taking the easy option and doing the minimal amount of work. Yet he had achieved satisfactory grades in his senior year—A in Euro-

pean history, A in American history, B in political economy, B in philosophy, B in zoology—and when he received his degree, still a few weeks shy of his eighteenth birthday, he was the youngest graduate in the history of the University of Michigan.[57]

8. NATHAN (BABE) LEOPOLD. Born 19 November 1904, Leopold attended the Douglas School (1912–1915) and the Harvard School for Boys (1915–1920) before graduating from the University of Chicago in March 1923 at age eighteen.

It was an accomplishment that spoke more for the ambition of his governess, Emily Struthers, than for Richard's intellectual ability. Richard had never fulfilled the promise with which, four years earlier, Emily had endowed him; and his seeming triumph in graduating at such a young age obscured a darker reality. His university career had been lackluster; he had never joined any of the many student societies or participated in any extracurricular activities. Richard had never tried out for any of the sports teams or volunteered his services for a student publication or joined a debating society or discussion club. He had attended lectures desultorily, preferring to spend his time hanging around the fraternity house on Washtenaw Road, playing cards, reading dime novels, gossiping idly with friends—he seemed, even to his fraternity brothers, to have lost any will to do very much with his life. And Richard had taken to drink; he was so often drunk, even in the early afternoon, that it was sometimes difficult to tell when he was ever sober. There was something childlike in Richard's mannerisms and behavior: in conversation he could often seem quite normal, even serious, but without any warning, he might suddenly break off a topic and talk in an irritatingly frivolous, infantile manner. Upperclassmen were supposed to set an example for the freshmen and sophomores, but Richard's eccentricities had become too embarrassing even for his fraternity brothers, and in his senior year the executive committee of the fraternity formally censured him for his drunkenness and suspended his privileges as an upperclassman.[58]

It was a pitiable conclusion to an inglorious year. He had received his degree but he had neither chosen a career nor made plans for the future. But Richard had always enjoyed studying history—it was the one subject that had caught his interest at Michigan—and so, in September 1923, he returned to the University of Chicago for graduate work, taking a course in American constitutional history during the autumn quarter.

Nathan Leopold was also at Chicago that fall. He also had received his degree earlier that year, and with his customary energy, he was taking four law courses that quarter. Nathan and Richard renewed their acquaintance in September 1923, and very quickly Nathan succumbed, once again, to Richard's charm. How, indeed, could he have resisted? Richard was too handsome for Nathan not to fall in love a second time, and Richard was sexually complaisant, willing to indulge Nathan's desires. To his friends, Richard would boast of his sexual conquests; he claimed to have many girlfriends among the coeds on the Chicago campus but, in truth, sex was only moderately pleasurable. "I could," he confessed, "get along easily without it. The actual sex act is rather unimportant to me." His indifference toward sex usually (but not always) translated into acquiescence whenever Nathan importuned him so passionately—why refuse when it mattered so little one way or the other?[59]

Nathan's devotion flattered and pleased him. True, Nathan was annoyingly egotistical—he had an irritating habit of bragging about his supposed accomplishments; and it quickly became tiresome to listen to Nathan's empty, untrue boast that he could speak fifteen languages. Nathan also, in Richard's opinion, had a tedious obsession with the philosophy of Friedrich Nietzsche; he would talk endlessly about the mythical superman who, because he was a superman, stood outside the law, beyond any moral code that might constrain the actions of ordinary men. Even murder, Nathan claimed, was an acceptable act for a superman to commit if the deed gave him pleasure. Morality did not apply in such a case, Nathan asserted. The only consideration that mattered was whether it afforded the superman pleasure—everything else faded into insignificance.[60]

It was not that Richard had any moral objection to murder; he too had only contempt for conventional morality. But Nathan was full of pretense, forever prating on about his intellectual superiority, forever sneering at the rest of humanity as dolts who obeyed the laws that he, Nathan, affected to disregard. Nathan's braggadocio, with its exaggerated self-regard and its casual dismissal of others, seemed spoken as though for effect, as though designed to shock whoever heard it into granting Nathan the respect that had always been denied him. There was an angry edge to Nathan's words; it betrayed the bitterness—hidden beneath his calm, equable manner of speaking—with which he remembered the taunts he had endured as a child and the loneliness he had experienced as an adolescent.

But Richard, nevertheless, was glad to have Nathan as a companion. There was no pleasure in committing crimes alone. He had to have a confederate who would appreciate his careful planning and preparation; Nathan's admiration made it all worthwhile. And Richard had been thinking, ever since he had returned to Chicago in fall 1923, how to commit the perfect crime. He had vaguely thought of it as a kidnapping, of a young child perhaps, and there should, of course, be a ransom demand as an essential part of the plot. Richard knew that to obtain the ransom and yet still avoid capture would present a challenge that would surely tax even his ingenuity and guile—but even now, as he thought of it with anticipation, it excited and aroused him.[61]

3 | PLANNING THE MURDER

SATURDAY, 10 NOVEMBER 1923–TUESDAY, 20 MAY 1924

A superman . . . is, on account of certain superior qualities inherent in him, exempted from the ordinary laws which govern men. He is not liable for anything he may do.[1]

Nathan Leopold Jr., 10 October 1923

THE FOOTBALL PLAYERS REPRESENTING THE UNITED States Marine Corps had arrived the previous day—Friday, 9 November—to an official reception from the city of Ann Arbor, and that Saturday morning, five special trains had arrived from Quantico with 2,000 marines and a military band in support of their team against the University of Michigan. The streets of Ann Arbor were packed with jostling crowds, eager to see the game. Blue and maize—the colors of the university—were everywhere: Michigan's supporters waved their pennants and flags enthusiastically in anticipation of an easy victory over the Devil Dogs.[2]

Forty-five thousand spectators crammed into Ferry Field. The University of Michigan stadium had opened in 1906, only seventeen years earlier, yet already it was too small to accommodate the crowds that flocked to the football games on Saturday afternoons. At the east end, on either side of the new field house, the university had recently installed temporary wooden bleachers, but still spectators overflowed the benches and spilled into the aisles.

Marion Burton, the president of the university, and Fielding Yost, the director of athletics, were both present to welcome their guests. Henry Ford had driven from Detroit to watch the game. Both Alex Groesbeck, the governor of the state, and James Couzens, the Republican senator for Michigan, were in attendance. Edwin C. Denby, secretary of the navy, and his assistant, Theodore Roosevelt Jr., sat on the opposite side of the field among the supporters of the Marine Corps. John Archer Lejeune, the marine commandant, had made the journey from Quantico to support his troops. It would be a difficult game for the Marine Corps, they realized; Michigan was undefeated, having already, that fall, vanquished Ohio State, Michigan Agricultural College, Vanderbilt University, the Case School of Applied Science, and the University of Iowa. True, the university would be missing some of its key players: Ed Vandervoort, the right tackle, had been injured in the Iowa game the previous week, and both Stan Muirhead, the left tackle, and Louis Curran, the right end, were unwell. But Michigan was a powerful team, nevertheless, and most experts predicted that the Wolverines would win the Big Ten conference that year.[3]

Against all expectations, the first quarter belonged to the marines. Their quarterback, Frank Goettge, played brilliantly. The Michigan defense did all it could against the run, but to no avail, allowing the Devil Dogs to march uncontested seventy-five yards downfield for a touchdown.

The crowd was shocked into silence. No one that season, not even Ohio State, had scored against the Wolverines at Ferry Field. Who would have expected the unheralded Marine Corps to have scored a touchdown before Michigan had even put points on the board?

But Irwin Uteritz, the Michigan quarterback, soon asserted control over the game and in the second quarter, the tide began to turn in Michigan's favor. Michigan repeatedly found holes in the marines' defense; Herb Steger, the Michigan right halfback, had an outstanding game and, on those few occasions when the Wolverines did give up the ball, Harry Kipke's punting pinned the Devil Dogs back to their goal line again and again. Michigan scored four touchdowns and made two conversions while the Marine Corps failed to score a second time; the final tally was 26–6. Michigan remained undefeated.[4]

THAT NIGHT THE MICHIGAN STUDENTS packed the fraternity houses to celebrate their victory. Only two more games remained—an easy game the following Saturday against the University of Wisconsin and the final contest of the season against the University of Illinois—and already there was talk on the campus that this would be a championship year. The celebrations continued through the evening, past midnight, but by two o'clock the campus was deserted. The football crowds had long ago left Ann Arbor; the students were now sleeping off their intoxication in the dormitories; nothing broke the silence of the night.

At three o'clock that Sunday morning, a red Willys-Knight sports car, with distinctive nickel bumpers and disk wheels, drew up by the side of Zeta Beta Tau fraternity. Nathan Leopold and Richard Loeb stepped wearily from the car and stretched their legs—it had been a long drive, almost six hours, from Chicago to Ann Arbor.

Richard and Nathan each held a flashlight in one hand, and each boy carried a loaded revolver in the pocket of his jacket. They cautiously approached the Zeta Beta Tau building, a large, three-story mansion set back from the street, and walked up the path to the front door. It had been Richard's fraternity during his junior and senior years at the university; it would be a challenge, he had suggested to Nathan, to burglarize his old fraternity house. Admittedly, someone might recognize him—he had graduated from the university that year—but he could explain their presence at Zeta Beta Tau by claiming that they had come up to Ann Arbor for the football game.[5]

The front door of the fraternity swung open at their touch. Inside, beer bottles and beer mugs stood empty on the tables; ashtrays overflowed with cigarette butts. On a side table, empty bottles of gin and whiskey stood stacked like soldiers. Nathan could see that someone had left a football program on the table; it was now soaked with beer.

9. ZETA BETA TAU fraternity house. Jewish students at the University of Michigan established the Phi chapter of Zeta Beta Tau in 1912. The building on Washtenaw Road, shown here, was constructed for the fraternity and first occupied in 1922.

Nathan and Richard paused in the center of the room and listened for sounds from the floor above. It was quiet; nothing moved. Carefully they went up the stairs. There was a coatroom, Richard remembered, on the second floor. Sure enough, several students had left their jackets and overcoats hanging in the large closet.[6]

They searched through the coats. One forgetful student had left his wallet in his jacket. Richard took out the money—almost fifty dollars. Nathan also discovered some loose bills—about twenty dollars. There were penknives, some watches, and several fountain pens but not much else.[7]

As they made their way downstairs and walked across the living room toward the front door, Nathan noticed a typewriter on a writing desk to one side of the room. It was one of the latest models, a portable Underwood. Nathan picked it up and admired it—he could scarcely believe that a typewriter could be so compact and light. He already possessed a Hammond typewriter at home, but it was heavy and rather awkward; this portable Underwood would be useful for typing up his notes from the law lectures.[8]

ON THE LONG RIDE HOME, back to Chicago, both boys began drinking from a half-empty bottle of gin taken from the fraternity house. Richard was exultant. To plan the robbery and to escape detection had been a challenge; to know that they had carried it off successfully was its own reward. The stolen items would certainly be missed in the morning, and news of the robbery would make its way back to his friends in the fraternity's chapter at the University of Chicago. Richard was almost gleeful in anticipating the buzz that the robbery would generate among his friends; it heightened the experience to know that he had inside knowledge of the burglary.[9]

But Nathan was tired and irritable, and Richard's excitement soon became wearisome. They had left Ann Arbor at five o'clock in the morning; they would probably not reach Chicago until around midday. When Richard had first suggested the robbery, it had seemed appealing, daring, almost courageous: Richard had convinced him that the planning and calculation involved would be a test of their mettle.

Now, in the early hours of the morning, their adventure no longer seemed appealing; instead it now appeared almost pointless, even futile. What was the purpose, Nathan wondered, of driving six hours to Ann Arbor, along bumpy country roads, to steal a few trinkets? The money taken from the wallets—seventy-four dollars—was inconsequential, and they had no use for the watches and fountain pens. The Underwood typewriter, a recent model, would be useful, but otherwise, Nathan reflected, it had been a great deal of effort for singularly little reward.

In Richard's company, Nathan was usually submissive and acquiescent. Now he was in a querulous, angry, argumentative mood. Their friendship was one-sided, he complained. Whenever Richard proposed some escapade, he always demanded that Nathan tag along. Nathan had willingly complied—but there was too little reward from their friendship. What, he demanded, did he gain from Richard's companionship?[10]

Nathan was especially aggrieved that they too rarely had sex together. In the early days of their friendship, Richard had willingly slept with him, but in the six months since Richard had graduated from Michigan to move back to Chicago, they had only infrequently had sex. Why, Nathan demanded, should he continue to participate in Richard's schemes if Richard continued to hold him at arm's length?

Richard knew he could not afford to lose Nathan's friendship. The other boy now had too much on him. He could never entirely trust Nathan to keep his confidences. If their friendship dissolved, Nathan might tell the world of Richard's crimes and misdemeanors. And if word ever got back to his father about, say, that time when he had burned down that hut or, even worse, that other occasion, when he had burglarized that house in Hubbard Woods—then who knew what might happen? Richard was afraid of his father, afraid of the punishment that Albert Loeb would visit on his head if he found out that Richard had been misbehaving.[11]

Richard would have liked to divest himself of Nathan's friendship—Nathan's cloying devotion had become irritating and even embarrassing—but who else would willingly participate in his adventures? There were no substitutes; Nathan's companionship could be irksome, but it served its purpose: Richard felt validated when Nathan took a part in his escapades.

Richard broke the silence. Would Nathan be happier if they reached some sort of formal agreement? How would Nathan feel, for example, if they agreed to have sex a certain number of times, proportional perhaps to the frequency of their criminal adventures? Or why not just continue as before, Richard suggested, with the promise that they have sex together three times every two months?[12]

It was not a particularly generous offer but, to Richard's surprise, Nathan accepted readily. It gave a guarantee that their friendship would continue. Nathan had always dreaded the thought that, one day, without warning, Richard would again suddenly end the friendship. That was an event too terrible to contemplate. This compact between them gave Nathan what he desired most of all: an assurance that Richard would continue as his friend.

As Nathan drove away from Ann Arbor in the darkness, Richard continued to talk. They had carried off the robbery without a hitch, but already he felt slightly dissatisfied: the burglary had been too easy. It had involved only minimal planning, and in any case it had not been a particularly complex crime. They should be more ambitious, he declared; they should commit a perfect crime, a crime so intricate and complicated that planning and calculating its flawless execution would be a challenge. They would leave behind no clues for the police; they would leave no trace of their involvement; it would stand forever as an audacious act that admitted no solution.

Dawn had broken now; there was no longer any need to use the car's headlights. They had finished off the gin but neither Nathan nor Richard felt especially intoxicated. The roads were deserted—occasionally they spied a Model T taking a farmer and his family to church; but otherwise they had the highway to themselves.

Soon they had passed Gary, and in less than an hour, they approached the outskirts of Chicago. On their right, they could see Lake Michigan shimmering in the morning sunlight, and on the horizon, far out on the surface of the lake, a large freighter was chugging its way slowly west in the direction of Chicago.

As he outlined his idea for the perfect crime, Richard steadily grew more excited. They should kidnap a child, he proposed, and to increase the intricacy of the crime, they should demand a ransom from the child's parents. The money was important, not for its own sake, but to magnify the complexity of the crime. They would have to leave directions in order to obtain the ransom, but they must make sure that they left no clues for the police. They would have to kill the child, of course; it would be foolish to leave open the possibility that their victim might recognize them at a later date.[13]

Had Richard a particular child in mind? Nathan asked. There were many wealthy families living in Kenwood and Hyde Park whose sons attended the Harvard School; and some of the children at University High School also had wealthy parents who would pay any ransom they asked.

Their victim should be a girl, Nathan suggested. One of his most vivid fantasies, he explained, had always been the image of a gang of German soldiers stripping the clothes off an attractive French girl and raping her while she was tied with ropes to a kitchen table. Sometimes in his fantasy, Nathan was the commanding officer who stood to one side and watched as his men raped the girl; on other occasions he would participate in the rape. If they were to kidnap and kill a child, therefore, they should abduct a young girl; it would give him enormous pleasure, he told Richard, if he could rape her before they killed her.[14]

But Richard had intended the kidnapping to be the perfect crime that he had always imagined himself planning. The rape of a girl had never been a part of his intention; he was not about to allow Nathan to hijack the fantasy for his own ends.

They bickered about it as they drove into Chicago. A boy or a girl? Would raping the child be part of their plan? In any argument with Nathan, Richard usually got his way, and this occasion was no exception. They would kidnap a boy, Richard declared with finality, most probably one of the pupils at the Harvard School, someone whose parents could afford to pay a ransom.

They had now entered the city limits. As Nathan wended his way through the streets of the South Side, Richard continued to talk about the kidnapping scheme. It was to be a brilliant crime, he mused, one that would shock Chicago with its daring. They would obtain the ransom, dispose of the body, and leave no clues behind; the police would never catch them. Already Richard could feel the thrill of anticipation; already he could sense the enjoyment he would derive from planning the murder.

No one, he believed, would ever know who had committed his perfect crime.

•   •   •

CHRISTMAS AND NEW YEAR CAME and went. After the holidays, both boys picked up their studies again: Nathan resumed his law courses while Richard attended the graduate seminars in the history department.

During the winter quarter, details of the kidnapping plan gradually developed. They proposed to lure a boy into their car; somehow render him unconscious, perhaps with chloroform; and drive him to a deserted spot near the Indiana state line, southeast of Chicago. There was a drainage culvert, almost three feet in diameter, running underneath the Pennsylvania Railroad tracks, close to 118th Street; this, Nathan volunteered, would be the perfect hiding place for the body. He knew the spot well; he had often passed by the culvert while bird-watching near Wolf Lake. They could stuff the corpse inside the pipe—it would accommodate a boy's body. No one would ever find it. Drainage water trickling through the pipe, along with the summer heat, would quickly decompose the body.

But how to kill their victim so that they would share equal responsibility for the murder? It would be easy to put a bullet through the boy's head, but in that case, Richard claimed, whoever pulled the trigger would alone be guilty of murder. Richard was adamant on this point: they must both participate in the killing. If both were directly guilty of murder, both would be liable for the death penalty and neither would have any advantage in confessing to the police. They should, Richard suggested, strangle their victim; if each pulled on one end of a rope around the boy's neck, they would then be jointly culpable.[15]

BY THE END OF MARCH, snow and ice no longer blanketed the campus; winter had turned to spring and leaves had appeared on the elms in the main quadrangle. It remained bitterly cold—harsh winds still swept in from Lake Michigan—but the sun shone more bravely on the students crisscrossing the campus, making their way to class.

The kidnapping plan slowly matured; the details became clearer.

There was, Nathan and Richard realized, one formidable difficulty that, no matter how they approached it, seemed insuperable. How were they to obtain the ransom money while avoiding capture? They had decided to demand $10,000 from the boy's parents for his release, but to obtain the money at no risk to themselves seemed impossible.

They talked it up and down, picking holes in each other's ideas, rejecting any suggestion that would not guarantee their safety. Their discussions eventually bore fruit; at last, it seemed they had a foolproof method of securing the money.

The Michigan Central train from Chicago to Boston departed from Central Station at 12th Street and Michigan Avenue and made its way south, parallel to the shoreline of Lake Michigan, stopping at branch stations on the South Side. Each day the train left Central Station at three o'clock standard time; eighteen minutes later it stopped at the 63rd Street station before heading east to Michigan City and on across Indiana and Ohio.

They would telephone the victim's father and instruct him to go to a drugstore on 63rd Street and Blackstone Avenue, adjacent to the local train station, to wait for a second phone call. This subsequent phone call would arrive shortly before the train reached 63rd Street. He was to board the train, walk to the rear carriage, and look in the telegraph box for a letter that would instruct him to throw the ransom, securely wrapped in a cigar box, from the train five seconds after he passed the distinctive redbrick water tower of the Champion Manufacturing Company. They calculated that the package would fall close to 74th Street; Nathan and Richard would be waiting at that spot, ready to grab the money and make a quick getaway.[16]

Would this plan work? There was only one way to find out; and so, on Wednesday, 24 April, Richard Loeb boarded the three o'clock train to Boston. It left Central Station punctually and made its way south; Richard, standing at the rear of the train, could see Lake Michigan on his left, and, to his right, the close-packed, narrow houses of the stockyard workers. The train reached the 63rd Street station on time, exactly eighteen minutes after leaving Central Station. It paused to take on passengers; the conductor shouted his customary warning; and gradually the carriages moved forward as the engine picked up speed. Richard looked to his left, out across a jumble of ugly factory buildings

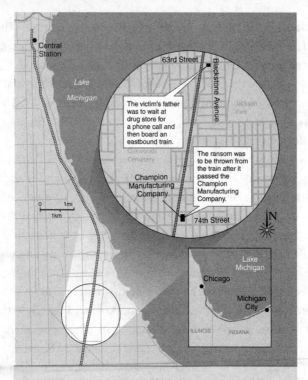

10. THE RANSOM DEMAND. The kidnappers intended that the victim's father wait for a phone call at a drugstore at 63rd Street and Blackstone Avenue. He would then board a train at the 63rd Street station and, after passing the Champion Manufacturing Company, would throw the ransom money from the train.

packed closely together. The water tower with its distinctive white lettering spelling out "Champion Manufacturing Company" suddenly came into view. Richard paused for a count of five and threw a package from his right hand as far as possible.

The rehearsal worked perfectly. Nathan, waiting in his car at 74th Street, watched the train travel above him on the elevated tracks. The package landed as they had expected; it was a moment's work for Nathan to retrieve it and drive away.[17]

Nathan and Richard congratulated themselves on devising such an elaborately clever plan. It could not go wrong. Even if the police accompanied the victim's father to the drugstore and even if they boarded the train at 63rd Street along with him, they would not be able to capture the kidnappers waiting in the car on 74th Street. And if the train suddenly began to slow down after leaving 63rd Street, Nathan and Richard would know that their plan had been discovered; they would abandon the ransom and make good their escape.

It was foolproof! What could possibly go wrong?

BUT THERE WAS ANOTHER DIFFICULTY, a second obstacle. Nathan's red sports car, a Willys-Knight, with its nickel bumpers and disk wheels, was too distinctive to use in the kidnapping. Nathan drove to the university every day and usually parked in a prominent place, close to the center of campus, on 57th Street; any witness to the kidnapping would certainly remember a red Willys-Knight sports model, and the police would have little difficulty in linking Nathan with the abduction. So it was necessary to use a rental car for the kidnapping.

However, to hire a rental car it was necessary to assume false identities. If even one witness connected the kidnapping with the rental car—perhaps while the car was parked near the Harvard School on the day of the kidnapping—the police would track their way to the kidnappers through the rental agency.

On Wednesday, 7 May, Nathan walked into the Hyde Park State Bank. The bank was almost empty; it had been a slow afternoon and Charles Ward, the cashier, was looking forward to closing up for the day. Ward noticed the young man even before he approached the desk—well dressed, with thick black hair and gray eyes, about five feet six inches tall but with a noticeable slouch. The customer walked up and began talking about opening a checking account.

Ward considered the applicant standing before him. Did he live locally? Could he provide a reference from someone in the neighborhood?

"Do you know anybody in Hyde Park?"

"No, I don't know anybody in Hyde Park."

The cashier reached down into his desk and pulled out a card; he handed it to the young man to write down his details.

"Well, have you any other address?"

"Yes, Peoria, Illinois."[18]

As the customer began writing on the card, Ward leaned over the desk to read the details. He found the application unusual. Why would a traveling salesman from Peoria want to open a checking account in Hyde Park if he knew no one in the area? Surely he would do better to open an account in one of the larger banks downtown, in the Loop? But, the cashier reflected, this was none of his business. Who was he to quarrel with a new customer? The customer, who had signed himself Morton D. Ballard, held out $100 as a deposit; Ward took the money and again reached down into his desk drawer: first for a checkbook, and then for a passbook showing the $100 deposit.[19]

That was sufficient. Nathan now had a new identity as Morton Ballard.

The same day, Richard Loeb walked into the lobby of the Morrison Hotel at Clark and Madison streets. He carried a rattan suitcase in his right hand, but it contained only books: four books that Loeb had previously borrowed from the university library. Loeb also claimed to be a traveling salesman; he, too, had come from Peoria and he also had assumed the pseudonym Morton D. Ballard.

J. B. Cravens, the clerk on duty that afternoon at the reception desk, gave the guest a key to room 1031 and waved an arrival slip at the bellboy waiting on the hop bench. The transaction took only a few minutes—the bellboy, distinctive in his cherry red uniform with green piping, jumped up from his place on the bench to show the salesman to his room before returning to the lobby.[20]

One hour later, Morton Ballard came down from his room to the reception desk. He was staying in Chicago only one night, he explained to Cravens, but he expected to be back in the city in a few weeks. There might be mail addressed to him at the hotel; would Cravens keep it for him for his return? Cravens nodded his assent: the guest seemed rather young to be in business—Cravens guessed that he was not much older than seventeen or eighteen—but he had an open, honest face and he seemed a trustworthy sort.

Two days later, on Friday, 9 May, at eleven o'clock in the morning,

Nathan Leopold walked into the offices of the Rent-A-Car Company at 1426 Michigan Avenue. Nathan had $400 in cash in the left pocket of his jacket, and in the right pocket he carried the passbook from the Hyde Park State Bank made out in the name of Morton Ballard.[21]

William Herndon, assistant manager of the Rent-A-Car Company, rose to his feet to shake hands with the young man who introduced himself as Morton Ballard, a salesman from Peoria. Ballard explained that he was in Chicago on business and needed a car to visit some clients that afternoon. He was new to the area; it was the first time he had covered the Chicago district for his company. As Ballard spoke, he produced the passbook from the Hyde Park State Bank and reached into his pocket for his wallet. Since he was a new customer, he told Herndon, he would be willing to put down a deposit of $400 for a rental car. And if there was any question about his honesty, he continued, he could provide references: he had the telephone number of an acquaintance, Louis Mason, who could vouch for him.[22]

Two blocks away, Richard Loeb entered a lunchroom at 1352 Wabash Avenue. He bought a telephone slug from the counter clerk, David Barish. Richard was hungry: he paid for a box of raisins, and as he slid his finger across the top of the box to open it, he asked Barish for the nearest phone. Barish indicated the booth against the wall at the rear of the store.

"Can I wait here for a phone call?" Richard asked. "I expect to be called."

"Yes, sir."[23]

Richard sat and waited. He listened absentmindedly to a conversation between the clerk and some customers at the front of the store. A large man with a mustache was telling the others, in a loud, boisterous voice, about a stag party the previous evening with some fellow Masons at the Auditorium Hotel.[24]

Richard wondered how long he would have to wait. Nathan was at the Rent-A-Car Company now; perhaps, he speculated, the rental agency would let Nathan have a car without asking for references.

The phone rang. Richard jumped up from his stool, almost, in his haste, knocking it over.

"Is this," a man's voice demanded, "Mr. Louis Mason talking?"

"Yes," Richard replied.

The anonymous voice explained that a salesman, Morton Ballard, was in his office wanting to take out a car; would he provide a reference?

"Do you know Morton D. Ballard of Peoria?"

"Yes."

"Is he dependable?"

"Absolutely dependable."[25]

Their conversation was brief, almost perfunctory. The rental agency provided Morton Ballard with a car for the day. Ballard mentioned that he would return to Chicago in a few weeks and would need a car then. In that case, the clerk replied, the company would mail an identification card to his address—the Morrison Hotel? Yes, of course . . . that would be no trouble at all.[26]

They had now worked out a plan to obtain the ransom without risking capture and had created false identities in order to obtain a rental car. Richard had thrown a package from the Boston train; it had landed near the anticipated spot at 74th Street. And Nathan had taken out a car from the Rent-A-Car Company on Michigan Avenue, establishing himself as a reliable customer.

They did not yet know the identity of their victim—he might be any one of a dozen boys. But the date of the kidnapping was set: Wednesday, 21 May, in the afternoon, when the pupils at the Harvard School were walking home after the end of classes.

Nathan spent the weekend before the kidnapping at Wolf Lake, close to the marshlands in the Forest Preserve. On Saturday, 17 May, he spent the afternoon at the lake with a school friend, George Lewis. They noticed some birds resembling sandpipers. Nathan, determined to obtain one for his collection, fired three shots at the birds as they flew across the Pennsylvania Railroad tracks that separated Hyde Lake from its neighbor, Wolf Lake, to the west. He missed and ran across the tracks in pursuit, stumbling in rubber boots that were slightly too large.[27]

The birds had disappeared in the reeds lining the edges of Hyde

Lake. The two boys searched for them along the shoreline, spotted them a second time, and fired at them but missed: Nathan's gun jammed and the birds made good their escape.[28]

He returned the following day, accompanied again by Lewis and a second friend, Sidney Stein. They parked Nathan's car by the railroad tracks, not far from a drainpipe culvert, and climbed up the incline to look out over Wolf Lake. There was no sign of the birds they had seen the previous day. The sun had already begun to dip low over the lake, casting an intense crimson glow across the horizon; soon it would be dark and time for them to start on the journey back to Chicago.[29]

ON TUESDAY, 20 MAY—the day before the kidnapping—Nathan and Richard purchased the equipment for the murder. Nathan bought writing paper and envelopes for the ransom note at a stationery store at 1054 East 47th Street. Nathan had a sweet tooth; as he waited for the clerk, H. C. Stranberg, to fetch the writing pad, he bought a box of chocolate creams from Stranberg's assistant.[30]

Later that day, Nathan entered a drugstore at 4558 Cottage Grove Avenue. The owner, Aaron Adler, was curious that the customer—a young man with a dark, sallow complexion, wearing an expensive gray topcoat and a slouch hat—was making such an unusual purchase.

"Give me a pint of hydrochloric acid," Nathan requested, "and let me have a half pint of ether, also."

Why did he need the acid? Adler asked.

For experimental work, Nathan replied, in a science laboratory at the university.

"Yes." Adler seemed satisfied with the answer. "All right."

"I have been to several other stores, and I couldn't get it."

Nathan paused—Adler was checking his inventory list.

"Do you sell much of it?" Nathan asked.

"Not a great deal," Adler replied.

Three minutes later, the pharmacist returned from the rear of the store with two glass bottles, each not much larger than a Listerine bottle. Nathan was surprised that the acid was so inexpensive—only

11. THE RANSOM LETTER. Nathan Leopold typed the ransom letter on a portable Underwood typewriter on the evening of Tuesday, 20 May.

seventy-five cents for a pint bottle. Adler indicated the glass stopper sealed with a dark-brown wax lining to prevent spillage.

"Be sure," he cautioned Nathan, "and keep it upright, because it might leak out and burn your clothes."[31]

That afternoon, Richard Loeb completed their purchases, stopping at a hardware store on Cottage Grove Avenue north of 43rd Street to buy a length of rope and a sharp-edged chisel with a beveled blade and a wooden handle.[32]

THERE WAS ONE LAST DETAIL remaining: the ransom letter. They had not yet, of course, chosen their victim, and the letter could not, therefore, be addressed to any specific person. Better, nevertheless, to compose the letter beforehand—they could then send it as soon as they had kidnapped their victim. That evening, after dinner, in Nathan's study, they composed the letter asking for $10,000. Earlier that day, Richard had shown Nathan a recent copy of *Detective Story Magazine*. It contained a tale about the kidnapping of a banker's wife by two ex-convicts. Perhaps, Richard suggested, they could use the ransom letters in the story as the model for their letter. Nathan agreed, and glancing occasionally at the magazine, open at page twenty-six, he began to draft the ransom letter, writing it out in longhand, pausing occasionally to read it back to Richard. Finally Nathan was done. He turned to the typewriter standing on the spinet desk by his side. It was the portable Underwood typewriter that he had stolen six months before from the Zeta Beta Tau fraternity at the University of Michigan. He fed the sheets of paper into the machine and, with Richard looking over his shoulder, typed out the demand for the ransom money. Nathan had never learned how to type, and he ponderously tapped out the letters one by one, searching out each key and striking it with his forefinger. But eventually he was done. He looked at the letter with a sense of pride—it was flawless; he could not see a single grammatical error.[33]

Everything was now in place for tomorrow. Nothing could go wrong. They were about to commit the perfect crime, a murder that would never be solved.

4 | THE MURDER

There was quite a bit of blood; the blanket . . . was quite saturated with blood.[1]

Richard Loeb, 31 May 1924

PRESTON DARGAN HAD TAUGHT ROMANCE LITERATURE at the University of Chicago since 1911. He was a neat and tidy man, somewhat short and small-framed; his ash-blond hair, brushed carefully toward the left, was graying slightly at the temples, but his mustache, cut in a military style, still retained its original auburn tinge.[2]

Dargan was forty-four years old. He had found a comfortable niche at the university: his teaching duties were not unduly onerous and he had ample time for research. He had written his first book, a study of Montesquieu, as a graduate student at Johns Hopkins University, and after receiving his doctorate in 1907, Dargan had taught successively at the University of Virginia and the University of California before landing at Chicago. He had established himself as a productive scholar, publishing a series of reviews and articles on nineteenth-century French writers, and in 1922 Dargan had been the coauthor of a magisterial survey of French literature, *A History of French Literature from the Earliest Times to the Great War*, with the chair of the department, William Nitze.[3]

Dargan was looking forward to the end of the school year. His course that quarter, on nineteenth-century French literature, had been successful—he was a popular lecturer—but teaching always consumed too much of his time, and he was keen to get back to his research. Dargan had already published several works on Honoré de Balzac, and he was planning a series of monographs, to be cowritten with his graduate students, on the novelist.[4]

On Wednesday, 21 May, Dargan's morning lecture was on the Parnassians, that group of late-nineteenth-century French poets that included René Sully-Prudhomme and Paul Verlaine. It was a literary movement, Dargan explained to the students sitting before him, that shared many characteristics with contemporary French culture and society; it had arisen in reaction to romanticism and emphasized exactitude, precision, and emotional detachment. The Parnassians had, the professor continued, initially grouped themselves around their journal, *Parnasse contemporain*, a literary magazine published in Paris from 1866 to 1876. José Maria de Heredia, whose reputation rested on his poem of 1893, *Les Trophées*, exemplified those qualities that distinguished the Parnassians: *Les Trophées* had attempted to reproduce the sensory effects of painting, music, and sculpture in poetic terms.[5]

The students seemed absorbed in his talk; most were taking notes on the lecture. Perhaps, Dargan reflected, it was the thought of the final exams that had concentrated their minds.

But one student, seated to his left, toward the corner of the lecture theater, on a bench several rows above him, seemed to pay no attention to his words. Dargan recognized Nathan Leopold, a sallow, dark-haired boy with a pale, unhealthy complexion. Leopold had taken a course with him the previous year. Dargan remembered him as an exceptional student, diligent and hardworking, one of the best students he had taught in his thirteen years at the university.

But Leopold now seemed distracted. Dargan noticed the boy fidgeting absentmindedly with his pencil, doodling on a notebook in front of him. From time to time, Nathan would look around the room, glancing, somewhat furtively, Dargan thought, at the other students. At other times, Nathan would stare directly ahead for several minutes, with an intense, fixed look, utterly absorbed in his own thoughts. What was the matter with the boy? Why was he so preoccupied?

THE PROFESSOR'S WORDS DRIFTED IN and out of Nathan's mind; he caught occasional phrases, but he had difficulty concentrating. He looked around the room: he could see Helen Robbins and Adelia Als-chuler sitting two rows directly in front of him and, over on the other side of the room, Susan Lurie was scribbling Dargan's words into a sketchbook.

Nathan had attended Dargan's class on an impulse. Ernst Puttkam-mer had lectured on commercial law at eight o'clock, finishing at five minutes to nine. Nathan had had an hour to kill before the ten o'clock lecture on agency and torts—and instead of stepping outside for a ciga-rette, he had attended Dargan's lecture on the Parnassians.[6]

But Nathan found it impossible to concentrate. He thought again of Richard Loeb; he turned their scheme over in his mind, asking him-self if they had missed anything. They had arranged the murder for that afternoon; could anything go wrong?

He knew the plan; they had rehearsed it together many times. They were to pick up the car from the rental agency on Michigan Avenue, return Nathan's automobile to his house, drive to Kramer's Restaurant in the rental car for lunch, and then continue on to Jackson Park. At two-thirty that afternoon the pupils would begin leaving the Harvard School; any one of the children walking by himself would be a suitable target—any boy would do, so long as his parents were able to pay the ransom.

Nathan and Richard had planned to kill their victim jointly. Each would pull on one end of a rope around the boy's neck. Nathan flinched involuntarily as he pictured himself pulling on the rope—it was an unpleasant image—but Richard had insisted that they both assume responsibility for the murder.

The clanging of the bell broke Nathan's reverie. It was ten o'clock, the end of class already! The other students were picking up their books and papers. Nathan had one more lecture to attend that morning. But first he would remind Susan Lurie about their date that weekend—she was going to a dance with him.

RICHARD LOEB STOOD IN THE sunlight, at the entrance to the law school. He watched absentmindedly a small group of students on the other side of Harper Court, directly opposite, talking animatedly among themselves outside the entrance to Haskell Hall.

Richard looked at his watch. Ten minutes before eleven. He had arranged to meet Nathan here, at eleven o'clock, at the conclusion of the law lecture.[7]

Richard lit another cigarette and stepped forward a few paces to look up at the law school. It was an impressive building, in the Gothic style, with large bay windows on the third floor indicating the law library. The heavy buttresses on the exterior gave the building a solemn grandeur and dignity. Richard noticed the four gargoyles above the entrance—a whimsical touch by the architect. There were two kings in the center, flanked on either side by a medieval scribe clutching a book.

At eleven o'clock, Nathan appeared. As they walked together across the campus through the main quadrangle, Richard reminded his companion that they must first drive to Nathan's home to pick up everything they needed: the chisel, adhesive tape, the bottle of ether, some pieces of cloth to gag the victim, a searchlight, the bottle of hydrochloric acid, hip boots, a length of rope, and the automobile blanket.[8]

They passed the botany pond on their right. Richard could see Nathan's car ahead of them, the red four-cylinder Willys-Knight sports model, parked on 57th Street, directly across from the football stadium. It was a beautiful car, resplendent in the sunlight, its nickel bumpers catching the light, but, Richard thought again, far too distinctive for their purpose. To kidnap a child using Nathan's car would surely invite detection and capture.

12. THE LAW SCHOOL, UNIVERSITY OF CHICAGO. Theodore Roosevelt laid the cornerstone for the University of Chicago law school in 1903. Built of Bedford stone with funds donated by John D. Rockefeller, the law school building was modeled on King's College Chapel at the University of Cambridge.

They arrived at the Leopold house at eleven-thirty. Nathan had prepared the equipment earlier that morning before leaving for the university; it was the work of a moment to load everything, wrapped securely in the automobile blanket, onto the backseat of Nathan's car. And if anyone interfered with the kidnapping, they would be prepared: each boy carried a loaded revolver.[9]

Thirty minutes later, at the Rent-A-Car agency on Michigan Avenue, Nathan presented his identification as Morton Ballard. The clerk gave it a cursory glance; would Mr. Ballard like to take out a Ford or a Willys-Knight? There was, he said, a green Willys-Knight, a five-passenger touring car, in the garage; it was, the clerk continued, a very solid, reliable car, easy to drive and furnished with the standard accoutrements. The Willys-Knight was slightly more expensive than a Ford but well worth the extra cost.[10]

. . .

Sven Englund, the Leopold family chauffeur, had spent most of that morning in the garage working on the engine of the Packard Twin Six; it was a luxury automobile, one of the most sophisticated on the market. Englund wanted to get the work finished as soon as possible. His employer, Nathan Leopold Sr., had asked him to get the car ready by the weekend, but Englund was finding the task more difficult than he had imagined.

He looked up to see the youngest Leopold boy coming up the driveway in his red Willys-Knight; directly behind, there was a second boy driving a dark green touring car.[11]

Nathan stopped his car and stepped out to greet Englund. He had been having problems with his brakes and he would like to leave his car in the garage that afternoon to allow Englund to fix the problem.

"The brakes squeak so much here." Nathan spoke with an air of exasperation. He was annoyed that so trivial a problem had disrupted his routine. "I want you to fix them."

Englund looked thoughtfully at the sports car; he had hoped to have the afternoon free to continue working on the Packard.

"I can put some oil on them and you can use the emergency," he replied hopefully. "If you are careful you will not run into anybody."

WILLYS-KNIGHT

MILEAGE

Big mileage! Smooth mileage! Economical mileage! The beautiful Willys-Knight gives you more satisfying mileage than you ever dreamed you could get from a car.

This fine car keeps youth in your veins and age out of mileage. Its beauty keeps you proud. Its action keeps you happy. Mileage makes your heart grow fonder.

The wonderful Willys-Knight sleeve-valve engine is utterly free from the woes of ordinary poppet-valve engines. It *actually improves with use!* No valve-grinding or carbon-cleaning. Owners report 50,000 miles and more without a single engine adjustment. As to total mileage—no *Willys-Knight engine has ever been known to wear out!*

WILLYS-OVERLAND, Inc., TOLEDO, OHIO
Willys-Overland Sales Co. Ltd., Toronto, Can.

The Day of the   Knight is Here!

5 Passenger Touring
$1175 *fob Toledo*

13. THE WILLYS-KNIGHT AUTOMOBILE. In the 1920s advertisements for the Willys-Knight touring car emphasized its reliability and economy. On Wednesday, 21 May 1924, Richard Loeb and Nathan Leopold searched for their victim while driving a dark green Willys-Knight automobile.

Nathan shook his head impatiently; the noise of the brakes had irritated him for several days already. He wanted Englund to dismantle the brakes and check that it was not a serious problem.

Englund watched silently as Nathan carried a large bundle, wrapped in an automobile blanket, from his Willys-Knight to the second car. Both boys drove off in the touring car, leaving Englund standing in the driveway.[12]

IT WAS STILL NOT YET one o'clock. Since afternoon classes did not finish at the Harvard School on Wednesdays until two-thirty, there was little point in driving across to Ellis Avenue to wait by the school. Richard turned the car south, toward the Midway, and out east to Jackson Park.[13]

It was a perfect day—there was not a cloud in the sky. In the far distance, by the edge of the lagoon, they could see a small group of schoolchildren sitting on the grass, listening to their teacher read from a book. On the other side, moorhens were darting in and out of the rushes, ruffling the water with their sudden movements, and in the center of the lagoon, a mute swan glided majestically over the surface, breaking the reflected patterns of the sun's rays on the water.

It was a peaceful, almost idyllic, scene. Nathan broke the silence first, turning to speak to Richard as they sat, side by side, in the front of the car. There were several boys on their list, he began, any one of whom would be a suitable victim. Armand Deutsch was their best prospect: Deutsch, an eleven-year-old pupil at the Harvard School, was the grandson of Julius Rosenwald, the president of Sears, Roebuck. The Rosenwald family was one of the wealthiest in the city and, because of the patriarch's philanthropy, also one of the best known.

Richard shifted uncomfortably in his seat. His father was vice president of Sears, Roebuck. Albert Loeb had known the Rosenwalds for two decades. Richard was uneasy that Armand Deutsch was a possible victim. Suppose they were found out? Imagine the embarrassment for his father if it emerged that Richard had killed Julius Rosenwald's grandson!

Well, Nathan continued, there was also Johnny Levinson, a nine-year-old boy in the same class at the school as Richard's younger brother, Tommy. Johnny's father, Sol Levinson, was one of the wealthiest attorneys in Chicago. He would certainly pay the ransom. Samuel Harris, a fourteen-year-old pupil at the Harvard School, was also on the list; his father was a building contractor who had made his fortune during the city's real estate boom at the turn of the century.[14]

Richard looked at his watch. They had been talking for almost an hour. It was quarter past two. He turned the key in the ignition and slowly moved the car out of Jackson Park toward the Midway.[15]

AS THEY TRAVELED NORTH, TOWARD Kenwood, Nathan reminded Richard that directly across the street from the Harvard School, facing its redbrick facade, there was an alley connecting Ellis Avenue to a parallel road, Ingleside Avenue. They could park the car on Ingleside Avenue, walk along the alley to Ellis Avenue, and from the alley observe the main entrance of the school.[16]

Nathan waited by the car on Ingleside Avenue while Richard walked through the alley to the Harvard School. Richard could see a few boys already by the main entrance; some classes must have ended already. He continued walking, past the entrance and along the north side of the school, toward the playground in the rear.

James Seass, an instructor, was in the playground, standing guard over the boys playing baseball. Richard recognized Seass as a senior at the university, a member of Delta Chi. He guessed that Seass was teaching at the Harvard School part-time to pay his way through college.[17]

Suddenly Richard noticed one of the boys on their list. Johnny Levinson, a thin wire of a boy with straight brown hair falling over his forehead, was scarcely ten feet from where Richard stood.

Could Richard lure Johnny away from his friends? What would persuade Johnny to leave the playground and walk with Richard to the car?

Richard found an excuse to talk to the boy. Johnny had a baseball in his hand; he was waiting for some friends, he explained to Richard, so that they could walk across to the lot at 49th Street and Drexel Boulevard for a pickup baseball game.[18]

Richard left the playground and made his way to the main entrance. His ten-year-old brother, Tommy, had finished his classes and was standing by the door, talking to another boy.[19]

At that moment, Nathan appeared on the other side of Ellis Avenue, directly opposite the school entrance. He whistled for Richard. He waved, urgently, signaling to Richard to join him. There were some children playing on Ingleside Avenue, he announced. Why not capture one of them? The street was otherwise deserted; there were no adults in sight.

No, Richard replied; he had a better plan. Johnny Levinson was going to 49th Street to play baseball; they should watch the game and then, when Johnny left to go home, they could grab the boy and kill him.[20]

But it was difficult to watch the game without being observed. They had to be careful: someone might see them watching the boys playing baseball, and if Johnny Levinson vanished, they would surely be linked to his disappearance.

While Nathan went back to his house on Greenwood Avenue to pick up his field glasses, Richard stopped at the drugstore on 47th Street and Ellis Avenue. He would find the Levinsons' address in the telephone book. Once they knew the street where Johnny lived, they could tell the direction he would take to go home.[21]

But by the time they arrived at 49th Street, Johnny Levinson had left the game. Perhaps he would return. They watched and waited for Johnny to appear. But there was no sign of the boy—he must have gone home.

Throughout the afternoon, they continued to drive around Kenwood, looking for a victim. Some children were playing near the corner of 48th Street and Greenwood Avenue, so close to the Leopold house that they could watch them from an upstairs bedroom window, but that opportunity also disappointed them—the children never departed alone but always left in small groups or with at least one other child.[22]

It was almost four-thirty. They had now spent almost two hours in

Kenwood, waiting and watching, hoping for the opportunity to kidnap a victim. Nathan was ready to abandon the attempt, at least for today; perhaps they should try again tomorrow.

Richard hesitated; it was worth one last try. They would drive around Kenwood a final time, and if they did not see anyone, they would postpone the kidnapping until another day.

Nathan drove the car west along 49th Street, turning left onto Drexel Boulevard. Richard sat in the back, behind the front passenger seat. At Hyde Park Boulevard, they turned left again, continuing east for one block. On Ellis Avenue, they drove north, passing the Loeb family home on the right-hand side.[23]

Richard Loeb had slumped back in his seat. It was already a few minutes past five o'clock and Ellis Avenue was deserted. It seemed futile to continue looking; no doubt all the children had made it safely home.

RICHARD SAW HIM FIRST. There—on the other side of the street—was a young boy, about fourteen years old, with chestnut-brown hair, walking south, alone, on Ellis Avenue. He was wearing a tan jacket with matching knee trousers, a colored shirt, and a necktie; he had on brown shoes and black-and-white checkered socks.[24]

Richard leaned forward and tapped Nathan urgently on the shoulder. "Here is an ideal victim."

Richard looked more closely; the boy seemed familiar. Richard suddenly recognized him. It was his cousin, Bobby Franks! Richard murmured into Nathan's ear, "I know him."[25]

The Franks family lived on Ellis Avenue, almost directly opposite the Loeb home. Richard knew the Franks children well—just yesterday, he had played tennis with Bobby on the court at the rear of the Franks mansion.

The car slowed down, but Bobby had already walked past. He had now crossed 48th Street.

Nathan turned the car in a circle so as to drive up behind the boy. He drove slowly down Ellis Avenue, gradually catching up with Bobby, pulling alongside the boy.

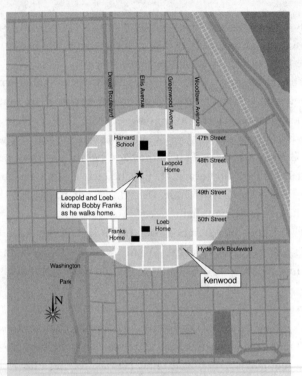

14. THE KIDNAPPING. As Leopold and Loeb drove north along Ellis Avenue, they spotted Bobby Franks walking south, about to cross 48th Street. They turned the car around to drive up behind Franks just before he reached 49th Street.

"Hey, Bob," Richard shouted from the rear window.

Bobby turned slightly to see the Willys-Knight stop by the curb. Richard leaned forward, into the front passenger seat, to open the front door.

"Hello, Bob. I'll give you a ride."

The boy shook his head—he was almost home.

"No, I can walk."

"Come on in the car; I want to talk to you about the tennis racket you had yesterday. I want to get one for my brother."[26]

Bobby had moved closer now. He was standing by the side of the car. Richard looked at him through the open window. Bobby was so close that Richard could have grabbed him and pulled him inside, but he continued talking, hoping to persuade the boy to step into the front seat.

Bobby had stepped onto the running board. The front passenger door was open, inviting the boy inside, and then suddenly Bobby slid himself into the front seat, next to Nathan.

Richard gestured toward Nathan, "You know Leopold, don't you?"

Bobby glanced sideways at Nathan and shook his head, not recognizing him.

"No."

"You don't mind [us] taking you around the block?"

"Certainly not." Bobby turned around in the seat to face Richard; he smiled at his cousin with an open, innocent grin, pleased to see Richard, ready to banter about his success in yesterday's tennis game.[27]

The car slowly accelerated down Ellis Avenue. As it passed 49th Street, Richard felt on the car seat beside him for the chisel. Where had it gone? There it was! They had taped up the blade so that the blunt end—the handle—could be used as a club. Richard felt it in his hand. He grasped it more firmly.

At 50th Street, Nathan turned the car left. As it made the turn, Bobby looked away from Richard and glanced toward the front of the car.

Richard reached over the seat. He grabbed the boy from behind with his left hand, covering Bobby's mouth to stop him from crying out. He brought the chisel down hard—it smashed into the back of the boy's skull. Once again—he pounded the chisel into the skull with as much force as possible . . . but the boy was still conscious. Bobby had now twisted halfway around in the seat, facing back to Richard, desperately raising his arms as though to protect himself from the blows. Richard smashed the chisel down two more times into Bobby's forehead, but still Bobby struggled for his life.

The fourth blow had gashed a large hole in the boy's forehead. Bobby now began to collapse onto the front seat. Blood from the head wound was everywhere, spreading across the seat, splashed onto Nathan's trousers, spilling onto the floor. Bobby was holding his hands to his head, curled up in pain on the front seat, whimpering and crying, his legs crumpled awkwardly underneath his body, as the blood continued to seep onto the front seat.

It was inexplicable, Richard thought, that Bobby was still conscious. Surely those four blows would have knocked him out?

Richard reached down and pulled Bobby suddenly upward, up over the front seat into the back of the car. He jammed a rag down the boy's throat, stuffing it down as hard as possible, forcing it in with his fingers past the boy's teeth, pushing against the resistance of the tongue. He tore off a large strip of adhesive tape from the roll and taped the mouth shut. Finally! The boy's moaning and crying had stopped. Richard relaxed his grip—Bobby slid off his lap and lay crumpled at his feet.[28]

NATHAN CONTINUED DRIVING. THE CAR left the city in the direction of Gary. Twenty minutes later, they were in open country, driving along a deserted road. They arrived at a spur road, not much more than a small two-lane track, leading from Calumet Boulevard to the Gary road.

Nathan parked the car off the road on a small bank of grass near a copse. The sun had already begun its evening descent and the summer heat had started to slacken its grip on the day. Fields of brown and blond stubble stretched out before them to the horizon. On the left, in the distance, they could see a small cemetery, and scattered across the flat, empty plains, dilapidated farm buildings broke the monotony of the landscape.[29]

Only occasional sounds disturbed the evening silence—the crows in the adjacent wood were cackling and cawing, and coming from the copse, there was the idiosyncratic whistle of a whip-poor-will—but across the vacant horizon, nothing moved. They were alone.

It was still only a few minutes past six o'clock. If they were to dispose of the body safely, they had to wait until nightfall. There was nothing to do but remain in the car.

Both boys were hungry—they had not eaten for six hours. Eventually Nathan started the engine and began driving along the Indiana country roads looking for a place to eat. He stopped at the Dew Drop Inn, a roadside convenience store with large billboards on its outside walls tempt-

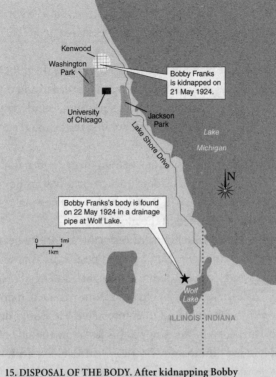

15. DISPOSAL OF THE BODY. After kidnapping Bobby
Franks, Leopold and Loeb drove south to Wolf Lake, near the
Forest Preserve, to dispose of the corpse.

ing passersby with promises of Cracker Jack and Coca-Cola. The owner,
Jim Tamis, was about to close for the night. Nathan returned to the car
with a couple of hot dogs and two bottles of root beer.[30]

They could see, across the fields, the evening sun begin to dip below
the horizon. Eventually Nathan started the car and headed back on the
road. Wolf Lake lay several miles southeast of the city. By the time they
arrived at the lake, it would be dark enough to get rid of the corpse.

THEY PARKED THE WILLYS-KNIGHT TWENTY yards from the culvert. As he pulled the body from the car and placed it on the blanket,

Richard wondered if Bobby might still be alive. But the corpse lay stiff and rigid on the ground; Bobby's glassy eyes stared up at them, unblinking.

Nathan held the blanket at the bottom, close to the boy's feet, while Richard took up the other end. The ground was damp and muddy from the recent rains; they could hear a faint squishing sound as they walked through the mud toward the culvert, holding the blanket between them as though it were a stretcher.[31]

The drainage ditch appeared before them in the darkness, the planks of wood framing its sides jutting out a few inches above the ground. The Pennsylvania Railroad tracks, elevated on a slight rise behind the culvert, gleamed in the moonlight.

Richard held the searchlight in his right hand; the beam of light flickered over the culvert as Nathan knelt beside the corpse to remove Bobby's jacket and shirt. It was a warm night and already Nathan was perspiring. His own jacket—an old jacket, one that he had not worn for several months—felt tight and uncomfortable. He would do better to work in his shirtsleeves—he dropped his jacket by the side of the ditch as Richard handed him the pint bottle of hydrochloric acid.

Bobby Franks, his arms by his sides, his legs slightly apart, lay naked on the ground. Nathan pulled on the glass stopper and held the hydrochloric acid high above the corpse, allowing the liquid to fall on Bobby's face. The acid would burn away the skin; now, even if someone discovered the body, the police would never be able to identify it. Nathan had learned somewhere—perhaps his brother had told him—that it was possible to identify an individual from the shape of his genitals; accordingly, he poured the remainder of the acid over Bobby's penis and testicles.[32]

There was a slight splash as Nathan lowered himself into the culvert—the water at the bottom of the ditch reached as high as his shins. Richard lowered the corpse into the ditch, Nathan seized hold of the legs, and the upper part of the body hit the water with a second splash.

Nathan shoved the corpse into the drainage pipe. It would not go in—the pipe was too narrow. He pushed the corpse insistently with his hands, trying to avoid getting the water in his mouth as it splashed backward toward him. He pushed again, trying to force the shoulders into the pipe—there! He had done it. Nathan kicked impatiently at the boy's legs, trying to force the rest of the body into the pipe. It was not easy—the water kept defeating him—but eventually he was satisfied.

He scrambled back out of the ditch and up onto the railroad tracks to remove his hip boots. But his shoes and jacket were still by the ditch—could Richard bring them up the embankment?

As Richard walked up the slope, he thought he heard a slight noise, a clink on the gravel, as though something metallic had fallen from the jacket. Richard paused; he held the flashlight in one hand and the hem of the jacket in the other, and, looking to see if anything had fallen, he slowly passed the beam of light over the ground. He could see tufts of grass and patches of dandelion poking above the gravel, but otherwise nothing. He must have been mistaken.

ON THE RIDE BACK TO the city, Nathan pulled the ransom letter from his pocket. He held the envelope by one of its edges; it flapped back and forth in his hand as he talked. They were back in Hyde Park already, close to the university.

Richard pulled up at a drugstore on 57th Street. It was almost ten o'clock; some students were passing them, talking and laughing in loud voices, walking back toward Hutchinson Commons. Inside the store, the clerk directed them to the phone booth at the rear; they would find a phone book there. Richard's finger ran down the page as he searched for the Franks address, and as he read it off, Nathan wrote it, in careful, almost precise, handwriting, on the front of the envelope. The clerk sold them the postage for their letter—six two-cent stamps—and, to ensure that it would reach its destination the next morning, they also purchased a special delivery stamp, which Nathan attached to the upper right-hand corner of the envelope.[33]

The nearest mailbox was two blocks away, across the street from the Hyde Park post office on 55th Street. Nathan lifted the latch of the box and slipped the letter inside the narrow gap; it would arrive at the Franks house at eight o'clock the next morning.[34]

Although it was still not yet ten o'clock, the Loeb house seemed almost deserted when they parked the car on 50th Street. A single light shone from a front window facing Ellis Avenue, but on the side looking south, by the side entrance facing the garden, all the windows were dark. Richard gathered together Bobby's clothes—trousers, shirt, underpants, jacket—and wrapped them in the blanket. He led the way, through the vegetable garden, into the side entrance of the house, along a corridor to the right, and down a short flight of stairs to the basement. The furnace was still alight: Richard could see the flames flickering behind the grate.[35]

As they unwrapped the blanket and fed Bobby's clothes to the fire, Nathan stopped in alarm. There was one of Bobby's socks, with its distinctive black-and-white checkered pattern, but where was its companion? They must have dropped one of the socks somewhere along the way—perhaps by the culvert![36]

But a single sock, Richard laughed, was not going to send them to the gallows! Even if someone found it, there was little likelihood that it would be identified as Bobby's. And, in any case, there was nothing about that sock that could lead the police to the murderers.

Richard picked up the blanket, but it was saturated with blood, too much blood to safely burn in the furnace—it would give off a pungent odor. For the moment, they would hide it in the garden, behind the greenhouse.[37]

ONLY ONE TASK NOW REMAINED. That evening they would call the Franks household to tell the boy's father that they had abducted Bobby and that he should expect a letter in the morning with details of the ransom.

The Walgreen's drugstore at the corner of 47th Street and Woodlawn Avenue was still open, even at ten-thirty in the evening. They could see the clerk through the window as they approached, alone in the store, leaning across the front of the counter, reading a newspaper spread out before him.

Nathan purchased a telephone slug at the counter and walked, with Richard by his side, toward the rear of the store. Nathan picked up the receiver and read the number to the operator from a piece of paper in Richard's hand. It was a tight squeeze for the two of them inside the booth; Nathan, waiting for the operator to establish the connection, could feel himself suddenly nervous.[38]

A woman's voice came on the line and, in response to his query, explained that Jacob Franks had left the house about an hour previously; there was no telling when he would return. He waited for the maid to put Flora Franks on the line. Nathan's apprehension increased at the delay—suppose the police had tapped the phone already? He should make the call as brief as possible. At last! A second woman had come to the phone.

"This is Mr. Johnson . . . your boy has been kidnaped." Nathan spoke rapidly yet clearly, intent on wasting as little time as possible. "We have him and you need not worry: he is safe. But don't try to trace this call. . . . We must have money. We will let you know tomorrow what we want. We are kidnapers and we mean business. If you refuse us what we want or try to report us to the police, we will kill the boy."[39]

He returned the receiver to its cradle with a sigh of relief and turned to Richard. They should go home, he suggested, and have a drink, play some cards, and relax.

Nathan's father was still awake when they arrived at Greenwood Avenue. He greeted them and shook Richard's hand warmly. Richard Loeb was an excellent influence on his son, he believed; Nathan could have done a lot worse in his choice of friends. They sat and talked in the living room, and after the old man had gone to bed, Nathan and Richard remained downstairs, playing casino.[40]

Soon it was time for Richard to return home; Nathan offered him a ride in his Willys-Knight.

As the car drove south on Greenwood Avenue, Richard felt the chisel in his jacket pocket—in the excitement, he had forgotten it. He threw it from the car; it landed on the sidewalk with a clatter, and as the car continued south, a night watchman, Bernard Hunt, stepped from the shadows. Hunt picked up the chisel and examined it curiously: someone had taped up the blade, and on the handle Hunt could make out traces of dried blood. As he put the chisel in his pocket, Hunt looked up, just in time to see the car, a red car with distinctive disk wheels and nickel bumpers, turn right, toward Ellis Avenue.[41]

5 | THE RANSOM

The thing that prompted Dick to want to do this thing and prompted me to want to do this thing was a sort of pure love of excitement, or the imaginary love of thrills, doing something different. . . . The money consideration only came in afterwards, and never was important. . . . The money was a part of our objective, as was also the commission of the crime; but that was not the exact motive, but that came afterwards.[1]

Nathan Leopold, 1 June 1924

THE CHAUFFEUR, SVEN ENGLUND, STOOD AT the window of his apartment above the garage, wondering what was amiss. Nathan and his friend Richard Loeb were in the driveway below him, cleaning a dark green car: the same car, Englund remembered, that Richard had been driving the previous day. It was unusual to see Nathan performing physical labor—in fact, Englund could not recall that he had ever before seen Nathan work.

Englund approached the car. Richard stood on the left, with a pail of water by his side. In one hand he held a brush, and in the other a cake of Bon Ami soap; he was lathering the brush with the soap and rubbing vigorously at stains on the rear door panel.

Richard momentarily stopped rubbing at the car and straightened his back to greet the chauffeur. He explained that they had spilled some wine over the car and now he and Nathan were trying to remove the wine stains before he drove the car home.

Could he assist them? Englund asked. No, Richard replied politely, they were almost finished. There had been a lot of stains both inside and outside the car but it had been easy enough to remove them. Perhaps, Richard asked, they might need some more soap—did Englund have any in the garage?

He had only some Gold Dust cleaning powder, Englund replied, but he wouldn't recommend using it on the outside of the car: it would probably take the varnish off the paint.

As they talked, Nathan cleaned the rugs in the rear seat; now he came around to their side of the car. He had obviously been working hard; Englund could see beads of sweat on the boy's forehead, and as Nathan stood before him in the bright afternoon sunshine, holding a can of gasoline in his right hand, a rivulet of perspiration trickled down the boy's left cheek.

Nathan wiped his face with the sleeve of his shirt. He held out the gasoline to the chauffeur. "Here is your can," he said. They were trying to remove the wine stains before their parents caught them, Nathan explained. "We've been out doing a little bootlegging," he added, with a wink to Englund. "We don't want the folks to find out. Don't say anything about it." Nathan turned to Richard and remarked that he had cleaned as much as he could—there was still some slight discoloration of one of the rugs but no one would ever notice.[2]

How UNLUCKY, RICHARD EXCLAIMED, as they drove away from the house, that Englund had seen them cleaning the car! But Englund could never have known that the stains were blood. And why should there not be wine stains on the car? It was a plausible explanation, surely?

Nathan was irritated. Couldn't Richard stop worrying? It was done; there was nothing they could do about Englund. Why, he asked, did Richard have to nag him so?

And there was still a lot to do that afternoon; they would have to hurry if they were to make the schedule.

That afternoon—Thursday, 22 May—they were to set up the ransom payment.

They still had to contact Jacob Franks with instructions; they had to lay a series of clues for Franks to follow, clues that would get him onto the three o'clock Michigan Central train. And then, once Franks was on the train, they had to drive to the drop-off position, not far from the Champion Manufacturing Company, to pick up the packet of money that Jacob Franks was to throw as the train made its way southward, out toward Indiana.

NATHAN WENT OVER THE PLAN one more time as they drove north along Greenwood Avenue. They would telephone Jacob Franks at his home, directing him to a litter bin at the intersection of Pershing Road and Vincennes Avenue, where he would find a letter, instructing him to drive to the Ross drugstore at 63rd Street and Blackstone Avenue. Franks was to wait at the rear of the store, by the telephone booth, for a phone call, for further instructions.

Nathan had always thought it a very clever plan and, as he rehearsed it again on the ride, it still seemed foolproof.

While Jacob Franks waited at the drugstore, he and Richard would telephone Franks from a second drugstore, instructing him to walk to the railroad station one block west on 63rd Street to catch the train that came down from Chicago, the train that left at three o'clock from Central Station. Once Franks was on the train, he was to go to the rear platform, where he would find a second letter in the box for telegraph blanks. This letter provided further instructions: Franks was to stand on the east side of the train, to wait until he had passed the large redbrick factory with a water tower on its roof—there could be no mistake;

a white Champion sign was painted on the water tower—to count to five, and throw the packet of money as far as possible.

It was brilliant!—what could go wrong?

THEY DROVE EAST ALONG PERSHING Road and parked the car near the corner of Oakwood Boulevard.

In his right hand, Nathan held the letter that would tell Jacob Franks to drive to the 63rd Street drugstore and wait for the telephone call.

But already there was a problem. No matter how they tried, they could not attach the letter to the inside of the box at Vincennes Avenue; the tape would not adhere to the black metal surface.

They could not run the risk that the letter would blow away in the wind—Jacob Franks might never know to drive on to the drugstore.

Better to omit this stage. They would call Franks: he should drive directly to the drugstore to wait for the phone call.[3]

There was not much time; it was already a few minutes past two o'clock; the train would leave Central Station in less than an hour.

THE MICHIGAN CENTRAL TRAIN TO Boston would leave at three o'clock and make its way south along the Illinois Central Railroad tracks, stopping at branch stations to pick up passengers before skirting south of Lake Michigan. Its final destination was Boston, but Jacob Franks, after entering the train at 63rd Street, would get off at Michigan City, the first stop after Chicago.

The train was waiting to depart from Central Station when Nathan and Richard parked the car close by. Richard looked at his watch—twenty-five minutes past two! It had taken them exactly twenty minutes to drive from Pershing Road.

Inside the station, steam rose from the train's engine; passengers preparing for the journey to Boston were climbing the steps, settling into their carriages, saying good-bye to friends and relatives, and stowing their luggage in the overhead racks.

In the bustle of departure, no one noticed Richard Loeb pay seventy-five cents for a ticket to Michigan City. And even if some casual observer had picked him out in the crowd, Richard's disguise—black-rimmed glasses, a black hat, and a heavy overcoat—successfully obscured his identity. He entered the train at the rear door, a letter in his hand, looking for the telegraph box in the last carriage of the Pullman car.[4]

The telegraph box was empty. Richard placed the letter in the slats, so that it would be visible; the edge of the envelope peeked out half an inch above the metal slat. Jacob Franks would retrieve the letter, read its instructions, and follow the directions to throw the money.

Richard jumped off the train onto the platform. It had taken less than five minutes to place the letter on the train; now he was walking back through the station, looking right and left, looking to see if any-one had noticed him, pushing his way through the crowd of passengers preparing to board the train—no, no one had noticed him.

WHILE RICHARD HAD BEEN PLACING the letter on the train, Nathan had called the Yellow Cab company to order a taxi to the Franks's home on Ellis Avenue. Now he must make a second call, to Jacob Franks, to tell him to take the cab to the 63rd Street drugstore. Nathan took a deep breath and tried to relax. He placed the number and waited for the op-erator to make the connection. Almost immediately, someone picked up the phone on the other end, as if he had been waiting for the call.

"Hello?"

"Hello." Nathan could feel his voice flutter with fright as he spoke into the mouthpiece. "Is Mr. Franks in?"

"Who wants him?"

"Mr. Johnson wants him."

"Who is that?"

"George Johnson."

"Just a minute."

There was a moment's silence. Nathan twisted the telephone cord around his fingers as he waited for Jacob Franks to come on the line.

"Mr. Franks?"

"Yes?"

"This is George Johnson speaking. . . . There will be a Yellow cab at your door in ten minutes. . . . Get into it and proceed immediately to the drugstore at 1465 East 63rd Street."

"Couldn't I have a little more time?"

"No, sir, you can't have any more time; you must go immediately."[5]

Nathan replaced the mouthpiece and pushed open the door of the phone booth. As he stepped outside, he glanced at his watch. It was now two-thirty. Jacob Franks would be leaving his house almost immediately; within ten minutes Franks would be at the Ross drugstore waiting for their second phone call.

There was no time to lose. They planned to call Franks from the Walgreen's drugstore on the southeast corner of 67th Street and Stony Island Avenue. From there, they could drive the short distance to the pickup stop underneath the elevated railroad tracks where Franks would throw the money.

But their intricate planning, their careful calculations, had come to nothing. The afternoon newspapers had already appeared on the newsstands. As Nathan and Richard drove up to the intersection, the headline on the early edition of the *Chicago Daily Journal* caught their eye. Nathan bought a copy of the paper and quickly scanned the article. The police had discovered the nude body of a young boy in a culvert near 118th Street! The body had not yet been identified, but surely it was only a matter of time before the police realized that the victim was Bobby Franks.[6]

Richard Loeb could scarcely believe that the body had already been found—less than twenty-four hours after he had killed Bobby! How could their plan unravel so quickly?

It shocked him that the crime had been uncovered. They had assumed that the body would remain undisturbed—they had never anticipated its discovery so soon after the murder.

THERE WAS, RICHARD ARGUED, no point in continuing with the ransom plan. Jacob Franks would soon learn that his son had been killed. If they attempted, nevertheless, to get the ransom, they ran the risk of being captured. Why take the chance? The police had no clues; why should they risk the possibility of capture?

But Nathan would not give up. He had worked too long to abandon his plan now. Perhaps Jacob Franks had not heard the news. They might still get the money!

They must hurry. The three o'clock train would leave from Central Station in twelve minutes. Jacob Franks might already be waiting with the ransom money at the Ross drugstore, adjacent to the train station, expecting instructions.

They ran to the drugstore at 6734 Stony Island Avenue. Nathan fished for a telephone slug among his loose change and inserted it into the slot. He placed the call and waited impatiently.[7]

At the Ross drugstore, James Kemp, the porter, answered the phone. It had been a slow day; only a few customers had been in the store, and Kemp heard the phone ring with a sense of relief that something, if only a phone call, was breaking up the monotony of the afternoon.

It was a man's voice, asking the question, "Is Mr. Franks there?"

Kemp looked around the store—at the front, he could see two women making a purchase from the pharmacist, Percy Van De Bogert, but otherwise the store was empty.

"No," he replied, "there is no Mr. Franks here."

There was a slight pause at the other end, and then the voice spoke again, in a low mutter, before hanging up: "Probably I have the wrong number."[8]

Kemp shrugged his shoulders in disappointment; somehow he had expected more. Reluctantly, he picked up his broom to sweep away at the dust in the back of the store.

Even Nathan now had to admit that there was no point any longer in pursuing the ransom. Jacob Franks was not at the drugstore—perhaps he had never left his house; perhaps he knew already that his son was dead.

And, in any case, the Michigan Central train had now left Central Station and would soon be at the 63rd Street station. Obviously Jacob Franks would not be on the train.

Their grand adventure was over—there was nothing more to be done except return the rental car.

It suddenly seemed so anticlimactic; disappointment hung in the air as they drove silently downtown, to the rental office on Michigan Avenue.[9]

THEY ARRIVED BACK AT KENWOOD shortly after four o'clock.

At the Loeb house on Ellis Avenue, Leonard Tucker, the family chauffeur, greeted Richard as he reached the front door. Tucker was leaning against a car in the driveway, absorbed in reading a newspaper, and as Richard approached, he showed him the news about the discovery of a boy's body in swampland south of the city. It was a terrible crime, Tucker exclaimed; the newspapers were reporting that the kidnappers had mutilated the body before stuffing it into a drainage culvert.[10]

At the Leopold house, everyone was talking about the murder when Nathan arrived home. His father was still downtown, working at the office, but Nathan's brothers were home, reading the newspapers in the living room, devouring the details of the murder, calling out comments to their aunt in the dining room, and speculating on the identity of the killers.

Nathan felt tense and uncomfortable listening to his brothers gossiping about the murder; he felt a slight nausea in his stomach—perhaps it was the tension that had accumulated throughout the day, or perhaps it was the failure of their plan—and he excused himself; he was going out to the corner store for a soda. He would be back in a few minutes.

As he walked along Ellis Avenue, Nathan spotted a familiar figure walking toward him: a young-looking, rather plump man, with a worried expression on his face, so absorbed in his thoughts that he seemed about to walk past, without acknowledging one of his former pupils at the Harvard School. Nathan had recognized his English teacher immediately. He remembered Mott Kirk Mitchell as a rather fussy teacher, too conscientious and well meaning to deal adequately with a classroom of rowdy fifteen-year-olds.[11]

"How do you do, Mr. Mitchell?" Nathan inquired sincerely. "I haven't seen you for a long time; how are you?"[12]

Mitchell peered at the young man in front of him—who was he? Yes, he recognized him now. Nathan Leopold had been a student at the Harvard School a few years back. Mitchell remembered him as an obnoxious pupil: clever, certainly, one of the best students in the class, but too arrogant and cynical to be likable.

"Have you heard," Mitchell asked, "about the Franks boy?"

"No," Nathan replied.

Everyone at the Harvard School, Mitchell explained, was worried at the disappearance of Bobby Franks. There was a rumor going around that someone had kidnapped Bobby, and now there was news that a boy's body had been found out by the Pennsylvania Railroad tracks near the Indiana state line.

"Do you know him?" Mitchell asked.

Nathan shook his head, "No."

"Robert Franks?"

"No."[13]

Mitchell stayed a few minutes more on the sidewalk, talking about the murder, as Nathan listened. It was inexplicable, Mitchell proclaimed, that someone would murder Bobby Franks—and what effect would it have on the Harvard School? Bobby had disappeared the previous day on his way home after school, not far from where they stood—was any child safe while the murderer was still at large?

Mitchell soon stopped talking; he was in a hurry, he explained. There was to be a meeting of the school staff that evening with the principal; in all likelihood, the Harvard School would be closed tomorrow.

They shook hands. As he made his way across the road, Nathan realized that his nausea had disappeared. In its place, he felt a sudden sense of exhilaration—they had succeeded in a crime that would be the talk of the town!

SHORTLY AFTER NOON ON THE following day, Friday, 23 May—just two days after Bobby's death—Richard stood in the entrance hall at the

Zeta Beta Tau fraternity on Ellis Avenue, smoking a cigarette and chatting with friends; he had already had lunch in the dining hall, and now he was killing time, wondering how to spend the afternoon.

He saw Howard Mayer enter and nodded a greeting. Howard was a senior at the university, and, although he had never rushed for the fraternity, he knew many of its members. Richard had heard that the *Chicago American* had hired Howard as a stringer; he detached himself from his group of friends and stepped across the hallway to ask what Howard knew of the murder.

Everyone knew about the killing; everyone knew all the details; but, Mayer realized, Richard seemed almost to have an insider's knowledge of the case. Mayer listened attentively as Richard talked about the ransom demand. The newspapers had reported that the kidnappers had telephoned Jacob Franks at his home, directing him to go with the ransom to a drugstore on 63rd Street. Was there some reason for Franks to go to a particular drugstore? And what was Franks expected to do once he arrived at 63rd Street?

Could it be, Richard speculated, that the kidnappers had intended to give Franks a second message, perhaps instructing him to hide the ransom somewhere? After all, Richard said, the kidnappers would hardly wish to meet Jacob Franks face-to-face.

"You know these kidnappers would not meet a man on a busy street," Richard exclaimed, exhaling cigarette smoke as he spoke, "that is common sense."

Howard Mayer nodded in agreement; clearly there had been some reason for the kidnappers to direct Franks to the drugstore.

"Why don't you," Richard continued, without waiting for an answer, "make the rounds of some of these drugstores on East 63rd Street, and see if you can't find the one at which some word was left for Mr. Franks?"

Despite Richard's enthusiasm, Mayer hesitated; it seemed a quixotic mission to hazard an afternoon searching out such a faint target; and, anyway, he was already behind on his schoolwork and he had hoped to spend that afternoon studying.

While Mayer hesitated, two others approached them. James Mulroy and Alvin Goldstein were alumni, contemporaries of Richard Loeb during his time at the university; now both were reporters for the *Chicago Daily News*.

As they approached, Richard addressed Mayer a final time, nodding in the direction of Mulroy and Goldstein,

"If you won't take my proposition, why I will put it up to them."[14]

What proposition, Mulroy asked? What scheme was Richard cooking up now?

He had the idea, Richard replied, to find the drugstore to which the kidnappers had directed Jacob Franks. There had to have been some reason, he guessed, for Franks to go to 63rd Street.

Would Mulroy and Goldstein care to go down to 63rd Street? It wouldn't take long to search out the drugstores, Richard pleaded, perhaps only an hour if they went by car.

It was raining outside; they could see a steady drizzle coming down and no sign that the weather would change for the better. But Mulroy and Goldstein were eager, and Mayer, anxious that he might be scooped, abandoned his schoolwork for another day.[15]

By the time they had reached Blackstone Avenue, the rain was pouring down. They had already scouted out several drugstores along 63rd Street, having worked their way west from Stony Island Avenue, but there was nothing, no clue, to indicate that they had found the kidnappers' drugstore. Mulroy was discouraged and at Blackstone Avenue he announced that he would wait in the car; if the others wished to continue looking, that was their business, but he was ready to return to the university.[16]

While Alvin Goldstein checked out the cigar store on the other side of the street, Richard and Howard Mayer went together to the Ross drugstore on the corner.

Richard interrogated the porter, James Kemp. Had he received any phone calls yesterday afternoon from someone asking for Mr. Franks?[17]

Yes, Kemp replied; it had been around two-thirty. He had answered the phone himself, while he had been at the back of the store, cleaning up. A man's voice had been on the other end of the line. "The man asked for Mr. Franks," Kemp explained to Richard. "I told him I didn't know Mr. Franks and then he asked me to look around the store. He gave me a very detailed description of Mr. Franks, even to saying that probably he would be smoking a cigarette." But no one answering the description had been in the store, and the caller had hung up.[18]

Richard turned to Mayer in triumph; his guess had worked out. "You see, I told you we could find it. Now you have got a scoop."

He stood at the door of the pharmacy; the rain had eased off. Alvin Goldstein stood by the car talking to James Mulroy through the open window. Richard waved at the two reporters excitedly; he shouted for them to come over, "This is the place!"[19]

As they drove back to the university, Mulroy and Richard talked together in the rear of the car. Mulroy had not realized before that Richard Loeb and Bobby Franks had been second cousins. Mulroy was surprised also at Richard's knowledge of the murder; he seemed to know more about the killing than anyone else Mulroy had met. Mulroy was curious to learn more about Bobby Franks. The principal of the Harvard School had said that Bobby was one of the best students in the school and an excellent athlete—had Bobby been as good as everyone claimed?

Richard replied caustically that he had never had much regard for his fourteen-year-old cousin; he remembered Bobby as an arrogant boy, accustomed to having his own way, spoiled and selfish. "If I was going to murder anybody," Richard remarked, "he was just the kind of cocky little son-of-a-bitch that I would pick."[20]

Richard's adventure in leading the journalists to the drugstore had seemed innocuous, inconsequential, at the time. Richard knew, nevertheless, how dangerously he had flirted with the possibility of discovery—one slip, one revelation that he knew too much about Bobby's death, and he might become a suspect. But, like the killing itself, his flirtation with the reporters excited and aroused him. He could not openly boast, of course, that he was the architect of one of the most sensational crimes in Chicago's history. But his secret knowledge of the murder was congruent with his self-image as a master criminal. While Mayer and the rest blundered about in confusion and ignorance, he, Richard Loeb, had been able to unveil an important detail. Richard knew how close to the flame he hovered, but it was irresistible; it thrilled him to lead his friends along a dangerous path.

LATER THAT NIGHT NATHAN WAITED in his car at the corner of 51st Street and Cottage Grove Avenue. It was almost two o'clock in the morning. The rain had stopped, but the night was cold and chill and a strong wind blew in from Lake Michigan.[21]

Nathan sat in the dark, waiting for Richard—they planned to dispose of the remaining evidence that night.

He was worried that the police had discovered the corpse so soon. Nathan had expected the hydrochloric acid to have burned away Bobby's face, but apparently it had not worked—the newspaper reports said only that the face was discolored—and the police had identified Bobby as the victim almost immediately.

And the detectives had also found a pair of eyeglasses near the body! No doubt they had fallen out of his jacket. How could he have been so careless? He should have checked the jacket pockets before going out on Wednesday. If the police were to question him about the eyeglasses, he had an explanation for their discovery near the corpse—he would claim he had dropped them the previous weekend while bird-watching near Hyde Lake—but it was unsettling, nevertheless, to realize that the police now had a clue that could link him to the murder.

Richard finally arrived. He was in a good mood. That afternoon, he recounted to Nathan, he had gone with three journalists—Howard Mayer of the *Chicago American* and Alvin Goldstein and James Mulroy of the *Chicago Daily News*—along 63rd Street, pretending to look for the drugstore and finding it at the last moment, just when they were about to abandon the search!

It was exasperating, Nathan replied, that Richard would behave so foolishly; did he not understand the risk? Their perfect crime, Nathan warned, was already beginning to unravel. Why would Richard behave in such a provocative way? Nathan hit the steering wheel with his open palm for emphasis as he admonished Richard; Nathan reminded him that the police had discovered the eyeglasses near the corpse—had Richard thought how he could explain their presence by the culvert?

Perhaps, Nathan wondered, they should prepare for the worst; perhaps they should create an alibi in case the police did question them in connection with the murder.

Richard agreed—better to be on the safe side. They would say that they had gone out to Lincoln Park on Wednesday in Nathan's car; that they had been drinking that afternoon; and that, in the evening, they had had dinner before meeting a couple of girls.

This alibi would stick if each vouched for the other. So long as they both held fast to this alibi, they would be safe—but if either one buckled under police pressure, then the other also was doomed. In any case, they would need to use the alibi only if the police apprehended them within a week of the crime. No one could reasonably be expected to remember what he had done on a given day if one week had since gone by.[22]

They had talked for almost an hour; it was already three o'clock in the morning. Nathan lifted the Underwood typewriter—the typewriter used to print the ransom letter—from the backseat of the car and, with a pair of pliers, began twisting and pulling apart the keys. Now, even if the detectives found the typewriter, they could never match it with the ransom letter they had sent to Jacob Franks.

They drove south, down Cottage Grove Avenue, and east along the Midway, out to Jackson Park. On their left, across the North Pond, the Palace of Fine Arts—the sole structure remaining from the Columbian Exposition of 1893—gleamed white in the moonlight; its silent presence was the only witness as Nathan, clutching the typewriter keys in his hand, stepped from the car onto the bridge, and allowed the keys to fall into the water of the lagoon.

At the outer harbor, on the stone bridge, Nathan stopped a second time to dispose of the typewriter; it fell into the harbor with a splash that echoed into the silence of the night.[23]

The automobile blanket—stained brownish red with Bobby's congealed blood—lay crumpled on the floor of the car. It had been too risky to burn the blanket along with Bobby's clothes in the basement furnace in Richard's house; they had to burn it in open air so that the acrid odor of the blood would not attract attention. Nathan knew a spot on South Shore Drive, close by a small copse, far from any buildings, where they could safely burn it. It took only a few minutes to burn and once it had been consumed by the flames, the last piece of evidence had disappeared.[24]

THE POLICE FIRST KNOCKED AT the door of the Leopold house on Sunday, 25 May. Thomas Wolf, a captain from the Eighth Police District, explained that he wished to talk to Nathan about the ornithology classes he conducted by the lakes near the Pennsylvania Railroad tracks. It was routine, the captain explained; in the hope of turning up clues to the murder, the police were questioning anyone who frequented the area.

Nathan spent two hours that Sunday at the Ewing Avenue station answering questions. Yes, he had often been out at Wolf Lake; only the previous weekend, he had spent the day with a friend, Sidney Stein, hunting birds. And he also took groups of schoolchildren out to the area to look for birds; he had frequently taken boys from the Harvard School to the lake, and occasionally he had classes of boys and girls from the University High School.[25]

It was reassuring, he realized, that the detectives had no inkling that he had any connection with the murder; it quickly became apparent that their questions were indeed routine. Nathan was not a suspect and, he calculated, if the police had not yet, four days after the discovery of the eyeglasses, connected him, through the eyeglasses, to the murder, then it seemed that he was safe. Nathan reported back to Richard—neither of them was under suspicion!

Nathan had no need for any more distractions; he had decided to apply to Harvard University law school, and that week he was taking the entrance examinations. He needed to concentrate—it would be inconvenient if there were any more questions from the police.

One week after the murder, on Wednesday, 28 May, Nathan took his law exams. On his way from the examination hall, he passed the office of Ernst Puttkammer, the popular thirty-four-year-old law professor. Puttkammer, despite his thinning blond hair and his steel-rimmed glasses, had a youthful appearance; students found him approachable and helpful, always willing to discuss the complexities of the law and to lend a sympathetic ear to any student struggling with his class work.

The door was ajar, and inside, Puttkammer was sitting at his desk, poring over a law journal. He glanced up as Nathan knocked and entered the room. Nathan was one of the brightest students in his class—a little eccentric, certainly, with his Nietzschean philosophy and his avowals that a superman need not regard the law; but, Puttkammer reflected as Nathan sat down, it was better to have an engaged student who talked too much than a student who talked not at all.

Nathan explained that he had wanted to discuss the legal ramifications of the murder of Bobby Franks; would the sentencing guidelines in Illinois necessarily mandate the death penalty for the kidnappers?

Suppose that the kidnappers had abducted Franks solely for the purpose of the ransom and suppose also that the murder had occurred accidentally, say, as the boy was being kidnapped. If there had been no intent to kill, would the kidnappers nevertheless receive the death penalty?

Puttkammer twirled his pencil in his hand, looking at Nathan from across the desk.

"Isn't kidnapping," Puttkammer replied, "a felony here in Illinois?"

"Yes," answered Nathan.

Puttkammer laid the pencil on his desk and leaned back in his chair. "Supposing a man causes somebody's death while he is intending to commit a felony? Is that murder or manslaughter?"

Nathan hesitated. Perhaps the kidnappers had intended only to rape Bobby. What then? "Suppose that the intent were simply to take improper liberties with this boy?" he replied. "I understand that that is a misdemeanor here in Illinois."

"Well . . . you still are talking about someone who had an intent to kidnap at the time, so that it is none the less a case where the intent is to commit a felony, even though other crimes might enter into it which are simply misdemeanors."

Puttkammer was pleased that Nathan was taking such an interest in the case. The majority of students seemed interested in the law only as a way to make a living; Nathan was one of those rare students with genuine intellectual curiosity.

Puttkammer confessed his ignorance of the case; he had been too preoccupied with keeping up with the decisions of the Illinois supreme court to spend much time reading the newspapers. But he had attended the Harvard School himself as a young boy, so, to that degree at least, the case was very interesting.

"I went to the school myself," Nathan interrupted.

"Well, then, your interest perhaps is even greater than mine, because you went there so much more recently and must know many more of the people."

Puttkammer had read in yesterday's papers that the police had arrested Mott Kirk Mitchell, the English teacher, as the leading suspect. That was unexpected—he had always thought of Mitchell as an outstanding teacher and a considerate and thoughtful person.

"Well, I don't know—" Nathan interrupted again. "I am not so sure about that."

All the boys knew, Nathan continued, that Mitchell was a homosexual; he was notorious for soliciting sex with the older boys at the Harvard School.

"Are you sure of that?"

"Yes; he made that sort of a proposition to my brother; that is straight enough, isn't it?"

The professor had picked up his pencil again and was drumming it lightly on the top of his desk, glancing at the clock, and starting to pick up a book. Nathan rose from his chair, saying, as he turned to leave the room, "I wouldn't put it past that man, Mitchell; I would like to see them get that fellow. . . ."

He stopped and turned back to Puttkammer as he reached the

door; there was a slight smile on Nathan's face. "But . . . I don't say he did it."[26]

THE NEXT DAY—THURSDAY, 29 MAY—NATHAN stayed home. The law exams were finished and that afternoon he was taking a group of schoolchildren from University High School on a bird-watching expedition to Wolf Lake.

He heard the bell at the front door but paid no attention; he was not expecting anyone to call. Two minutes later the maid was at his study door: three men, police officers, wished to speak with him.

How irritating! No doubt they wished to ask him more questions about his birding expeditions. But perhaps he could put them off; perhaps he could persuade them to come back at a more convenient time.

6 | THE INTERROGATION

Since you have been in my custody have you been beaten by anybody? . . . Have any of the police or my assistants been rough, or anything of the kind? . . . You haven't any bruises on your body, have you?[1]

Robert Crowe, state's attorney for
Cook County, 1 June 1924

THE LARGE BLACK CAR MADE its way slowly down Greenwood Avenue, halting occasionally and then again moving forward. Greenwood Avenue lay in the heart of Kenwood, one of Chicago's most exclusive residential neighborhoods, and at that time of the day—two-thirty on a Thursday afternoon—the street was deserted; nobody observed the car as it slowly passed between the large mansions on either side.

The car finally stopped in front of 4754 Greenwood Avenue. Three men—evidently on an important mission—stepped out purposefully and stood on the sidewalk for a moment, looking up at the house before them. It was, like all the houses on the street, a massive stone structure, three stories tall, set behind an imposing front gate.

Frank Johnson, a police sergeant with the Detective Bureau, led the way to the front door. A maid answered the bell. Yes, Nathan Leopold was at home; he would be down shortly.

Two minutes later the boy was at the door. They had been fortunate to find him at home: Nathan had been on his way out of the house; at three o'clock he was taking a class of schoolchildren on a birding expedition. As Johnson introduced himself, he noticed Nathan's irritation at their presence. Nathan demanded to see their identification. The sergeant bristled at the arrogance in the boy's voice.

"Let me see your credentials," Nathan asked.

Johnson pulled his deputy's star from his pocket: "I am a police officer," he explained, "and they want you at the State's Attorney's office." As the boy turned to get his jacket, Johnson dropped a hint about the purpose of his visit.

"By the way . . . do you wear glasses?"

"Yes."

"Did you lose your glasses?"

"No."

"Have you got them?"

"They are around here someplace."

Johnson realized—too late—that it may have been a mistake to mention the eyeglasses to Nathan. He had thought to save time and have the boy bring along his glasses, but he could not allow Nathan to hunt through the house looking for them—the state's attorney would be annoyed if they were delayed.

"Well, we have to go down to the State's Attorney's office."

"I have got an appointment to teach a class about three o'clock."

"Well, you will have to postpone that appointment."

"Can't you postpone this until some other time?"

"No, you have got to go down now."[2]

Nathan disappeared into the house, leaving Johnson waiting on the doorstep. He reappeared with his eldest brother, Michael, and they joined the three detectives—Frank Johnson, William Crot, and James Gortland—for the ride to the Loop.

In fact, Robert Crowe had requested that Nathan Leopold come to the Hotel LaSalle, a luxury hotel in the downtown business district. Crowe was being cautious; although his men had traced the eyeglasses found at the culvert back to Nathan, he had no reason to believe that the boy was involved in the murder of Bobby Franks and he had little desire to enmesh the Leopold family in the investigation. Media publicity had already confounded the detective work; if Nathan Leopold suddenly appeared at the Criminal Court Building, the newspapers might trumpet the boy as a suspect. Crowe merely wished to hear from Nathan Leopold an explanation for the presence of his eyeglasses near the corpse.

Nathan arrived at the Hotel LaSalle within the hour. Crowe was brisk; he was sure that this matter could be quickly cleared up. To a question about the eyeglasses, Nathan replied that he had possessed a pair of reading glasses for several months; they were, Nathan continued, at his home in the pocket of one of his suits. If it would give the state's attorney peace of mind, he would gladly drive back to Kenwood and retrieve them.[3]

Back at the Leopold home, Nathan made a show of searching his bedroom for his eyeglasses, but he now knew that the state's attorney had one piece of evidence linking him to the murder of Bobby Franks. He soon abandoned the search; his eyeglass case stood on top of the bureau next to his bed, but the eyeglasses were missing. Nathan slipped the case into his coat pocket and went downstairs.[4]

Robert Crowe now had reason to hold Nathan Leopold; his questioning of the boy was no longer casual. Later that evening the police searched Nathan's bedroom and study. They turned up two items; neither connected Nathan to the murder, but both the gun—a Remington .32-caliber automatic repeater—and a letter from Nathan to a second boy, Richard Loeb, were unusual and unexpected.

Nathan had already told the detectives that he carried a shotgun on his birding expeditions, but the Remington was a handgun; it could

not easily be used to shoot small birds at long distances. It was, moreover, an illegal firearm—Nathan had never applied for a permit for it.[5]

The letter to Richard Loeb was also a puzzle. As Crowe read it over
in his office, he could discern that the two boys had quarreled: Nathan
accused Richard of treachery and threatened to kill him but then wrote
of his desire to continue their friendship. The letter was alternately
haughty and pleading, aggressive and submissive; Nathan was angry
with Richard yet desperate that they remain friends. If Richard were to
break off their friendship, Nathan concluded, "extreme care must be
used. The motif of a falling out of cocksuckers would be sure to be
popular, which is patently undesirable, and forms an unknown but
unavoidable bond between us."[6]

There was no clue in the letter as to why Nathan and Richard had
squabbled; nevertheless it was evident that the boys were lovers who
had had a tiff. Perhaps they were part of a homosexual set at the University of Chicago and Nathan was anxious that Richard not publicly
abandon and humiliate him in front of their friends.

Robert Crowe decided to move Nathan from the Hotel LaSalle to the
Criminal Court Building. And he now also wanted to talk to Richard
Loeb. Most probably the second boy—also the son of a wealthy and influential Chicago businessman—knew nothing of the murder, but Crowe could
use Richard to draw out information about Nathan. Crowe had experience
with this form of blackmail: one hint that he would reveal Richard's homosexual secrets, and the boy would sing like the proverbial canary.

IT WAS NOW ONE O'CLOCK in the morning on Friday, 30 May. Crowe
had held Nathan Leopold through Thursday evening but he still had no
firm evidence that Leopold was connected to the killing of Bobby Franks.
Yet he couldn't simply release the boy—the gun, the eyeglasses, and the
homosexual relationship with Loeb all pointed an accusing finger.

Nathan Leopold sat in a chair before him in his office; the assistant
state's attorneys, Joseph Savage and Milton Smith, sat slightly to one
side, also facing the boy; the stenographer, Elbert Allen, had already
begun taking down their conversation in shorthand.

The English teacher at the Harvard School, Mott Kirk Mitchell, was still the most likely suspect. What could Nathan tell them about Mitchell? Nathan had been a pupil at the Harvard School—was there anything to suggest that his former teacher was a homosexual?

"Have you ever heard any stories about Mitchell being queer?"

"Not definitely, no," Nathan replied.

"Well, rumors?"

"I have heard some wild rumors, yes."

"By queer, you mean what?"

"I mean sexually perverted."

"And for how long a time have these rumors been floating around, to your knowledge?"

"Ever since I can remember, almost."

"You have no knowledge as to whether or not the rumors are true?"

"No, sir."[7]

Clearly there was not much mileage to be gained from this line of inquiry; Nathan could not tell Crowe anything he did not already know; and in any case, whatever the boy told him would be hearsay, inadmissible in a court of law.

CROWE TRIED A DIFFERENT TACK. Nathan had failed to find his eyeglasses in his bedroom—he now accepted that the glasses Crowe held out before him were his own. How, Crowe asked, had they come to be found near the body of Bobby Franks?

That was not difficult to explain. Nathan had been birding the weekend before the murder—that would be Saturday, 17 May—and his eyeglasses had probably fallen out of his pocket during the day. Nathan had driven out to Wolf Lake with his friend George Lewis around midday, and almost immediately they had spotted some unusual shorebirds resembling sandpipers. The birds flew west over the Pennsylvania Railroad tracks and alighted in the swamps: "so we both ran over the railroad track into Hyde Lake, crossed on a little log which crosses the little channel there; and after searching around for some time in the swamp, caught up to the birds again; and I fired three shots at them. . . . The fourth shell jammed on me, and the birds flew away."[8]

No wonder his eyeglasses were found near the culvert. Only four days before the murder, he had been near that very spot in the chase after the birds. Crowe was impressed—it seemed an obvious explanation. And Nathan even had a witness who could corroborate his story: George Lewis would back up his account. But, Crowe asked, how close had he been to the culvert?

"How near did you come to the particular spot in this drain where the body was found? How near did you come to that particular spot Saturday?"

"I should say that I passed right over it, probably, about on a level with it. It was as near as . . . I could not exactly say; I should say probably within ten or twenty feet of it, anyhow."[9]

There was no reason not to believe the boy; he told his story in a breezily confident manner, calmly smoking a cigarette as he spoke, occasionally glancing at Crowe's assistants at his side but otherwise looking steadily at the state's attorney. But Crowe was persistent; for his own peace of mind, he wanted to be sure that Nathan was telling the truth. And Crowe had noticed that Nathan had never, in his account of the day out at Wolf Lake, explicitly said he had stumbled; nor, indeed, had he ever given any indication how the eyeglasses had fallen from his pocket.

Crowe held the glasses out before him, just eighteen inches from Nathan's face.

"If you would put your glasses in your pocket, you would put them in what pocket?"

"My left breast pocket."

"Left breast coat pocket?"

"Left breast coat pocket, or possibly left vest pocket."

"Which, generally, would you do?"

"Generally I would put them in my coat."

"Did you stumble or fall at this particular spot at any time?"

"I do not remember."

"You do not remember that?"

"No, sir."

Crowe wondered if Nathan's account was accurate; the boy had been carrying a shotgun that Saturday afternoon out at Wolf Lake. Surely he would recall if he had stumbled while holding a gun? And if Nathan had dropped his eyeglasses by the culvert the previous Saturday—four days before Paul Korff had discovered them—they would have been spattered with mud after lying so long on the ground. But the eyeglasses had been conspicuously free of dirt, as though they had fallen to the ground just a few hours before their discovery. Was Nathan telling the truth when he said that he had lost his eyeglasses on the weekend? The state's attorney motioned to Nathan to take hold of the eyeglasses: "Will you put those in your left breast coat pocket and run and bend, and see whether they will drop out?"

Nathan took a quick drag on his cigarette. He put it carefully in an ashtray on Crowe's desk and reached out for the eyeglasses. He was now a little self-conscious: Crowe and the assistants were watching him intently. The stenographer had stopped scribbling in his notebook; he, too, looked at Nathan, watching the boy as Nathan stepped into the center of the room.

Nathan stepped out, took two paces, and fell forward to the ground, putting out his hands before him. The glasses remained in place, tucked securely in his breast pocket. He repeated the motion—still they remained there; they had barely moved.

"Now, you have fallen to the floor twice?"

"Yes."

"The glasses are still in your pocket?"

"Yes, sir. . . . May I add that Saturday you must remember that I had a pair of large rubber boots that did not fit me, and therefore the probability of my stumbling was greater than if I had been just normal."

"You had a gun in your hand."

"Yes, sir."

"You don't remember falling?"

"No, sir."[10]

IT WAS DISCONCERTING FOR NATHAN that the glasses had failed to behave as he had hoped. But no matter—he had an alibi for the day of the murder. He had gone, as usual, to his classes at the university that Wednesday morning, and around eleven o'clock he had picked up Richard Loeb to drive to the Loop to have lunch at the grill at Marshall Field's department store. Nathan was eager to spend part of the afternoon in Lincoln Park; he had heard from a friend that a heron had been seen there. He had brought his field glasses—would Richard like to come along?

Richard Loeb could not care less about the heron—but although he himself had no interest in ornithology, he tolerated his friend's hobby. Richard was more interested in drinking; there was a pint bottle of gin in Nathan's car. And who knows? Perhaps they could pick up some girls in the park and have a good time.

As the afternoon wore on, both boys, Nathan told the state's attorney, had become "a little bit happy; neither of us was drunk." Nathan knew, however, that he couldn't take Richard home so long as his breath smelled of alcohol; Richard's father was a teetotaler and a supporter of prohibition: he would not be happy that his son had been drinking. They had dinner at the Cocoanut Grove Restaurant and then "drove up and down 63rd Street several times . . . to find a couple of girls with nothing to do."

"And you found them?"

"Yes, sir."

"Then what happened?"

"Then we drove down Garfield Boulevard, almost to Western Avenue, and back up to Jackson Park; parked the car just north and east of the Wooded Island. . . . We sat around in the car and had a few drinks, and couldn't come to an agreement with the girls; so we asked them to leave, and went to go home."

"In other words, the girls . . ."

". . . wouldn't come across."

"And they walked home?"

"That is right, yes."[11]

As Nathan told the alibi to Crowe, Richard Loeb also was now in an office in the Criminal Court Building, telling the same alibi to one of Crowe's assistants. On Wednesday, 21 May, Loeb explained, "between 10 and 11 o'clock . . . Leopold and I started down town. We stopped at

Marshall Field's and had luncheon. Then we . . . started for Lincoln Park. . . . Leopold wanted to spot a migratory bird . . . a heron. . . . We hung around the park for five or six hours, then ducked for Cocoanut Grove. We had something to eat. Got there about 6 o'clock and stayed to have a few drinks. Then we had a few more and beat it."[12]

The alibis presented by the two boys corroborated each other exactly. Richard Loeb also told the tale of the two girls—he remembered their names as May and Edna—and, like Nathan, recounted how he and his companion had made them walk home after the girls had refused to have sex.

Yet the alibi served only to heighten Crowe's suspicions. Crowe had not yet told Nathan that one of his detectives had found the letter from Nathan to Richard indicating that both boys were homosexuals. Why would they want to spend an evening trying to have sex with two girls if they were homosexuals? Richard Loeb might vouch for Leopold's alibi, but Loeb's corroboration now had little value for the state's attorney. Of course, if they could find the two girls, then the alibi was genuine and they would go free. But would they find the girls?

It was now almost seven o'clock in the morning, Friday, 30 May. The state's attorney had questioned Nathan Leopold throughout the night and into the early morning hours, and still the boy had shown no sign of guilt. Richard Loeb was in an adjacent room, also in the Criminal Court Building. The state's attorney decided to keep both boys in custody. They needed to get some sleep; the detectives placed Nathan in a cell in the central police station and took Richard to the 48th Street station.

While the boys slept in their cells that Friday, the press woke up to the realization that Robert Crowe might have caught the murderers. Reporters from the newspapers descended on the Kenwood neighborhood to interview the parents of Nathan Leopold and Richard Loeb.

Both families ridiculed the idea that either boy could be guilty of murder; they had a granite certitude that their sons would soon be released. It was all a terrible mistake—an unfortunate coincidence of circumstances that would soon right itself.

At the Leopold home, Nathan Leopold Sr. invited a small group of journalists into his house to discuss his son's plight. He knew the Franks family personally and was horrified at the kidnapping and murder of Bobby, but he assured the reporters that his son had nothing to do with it: "It is ridiculous. Of course my boy is not involved. I shall do all I can to dispel this notion of the police. . . . We are ready to aid the authorities in every way to solve this murder. . . . But it is ridiculous to suppose Nathan had anything to do with it. . . . I probably could get my boy out on a writ of habeas corpus, but there is no need for that sort of technical trickery. The suggestion that he had anything to do with this case is too absurd to merit comment."[13]

And the discovery of his son's eyeglasses near the body of Bobby Franks? That also was merely a coincidence; his son had been bird-watching the previous weekend close to the culvert: "Nathan has been a student of ornithology for many years and has written numerous articles and papers on the subject. He has contributed to the bird magazine, *The Auk*. There is nothing to this."[14]

The family's faith in Nathan was complete. This trust in the boy's veracity could not be shaken, even in the face of a growing accumulation of evidence that tied him ever more closely to the murder. His elder brothers were also present at the interview with the journalists that Friday; one brother dismissed any possibility of a connection: "The idea of Nathan having anything to do with the Franks boy's death is too silly to discuss. The family is not particularly alarmed for we know just what he did the night the Franks boy disappeared; we know just how he occupied his time, and we know that he can account of himself. If he can help any in solving the crime, so much the better. We know so well where he was that night, we know our brother so well, that we are in no way alarmed at his examination by police."[15]

A few blocks away, at the Loeb house on Ellis Avenue, Anna Loeb was equally convinced that her son was blameless. She faced the reporters that Friday to tell them that neither her son nor Nathan Leopold had anything to do with the murder. "We have absolute confidence that Richard is telling the truth. The implication that either he or the young Leopold are involved in the Franks case is impossible on its face. No matter the circumstances of the spectacles, the idea of connecting them with the crime is absurd."[16]

Ernest Loeb echoed his mother's assurance. There would be no difficulty in providing Richard with an alibi, he told the reporter from the New York *World*, since he was sure that his brother had been in the presence of family members that day. "We know exactly where Dick was every hour of this particular Wednesday and he could not have done the thing the police are charging him with."[17]

The failure of either family to comprehend the gravity of the boys' situation translated into a complacency that over the next forty-eight hours was exposed as astonishing naïveté. Both families expressed a wish to assist the state's attorney in solving the murder, yet neither realized, until it was far too late, that Richard Loeb and Nathan Leopold had become the leading suspects. The families saw no reason to call in their lawyers to go to the Criminal Court Building to advise the boys. As a consequence, Robert Crowe had already had them in custody for almost twenty-four hours without yet making a formal arrest, and without even having to justify their continued detention.

Nathan Leopold's father was self-consciously complicit in the state's attorney's decision to hold his son for questioning. In response to an inquiry from a reporter from the *Chicago Daily Tribune*, he expressed confidence in both the state's attorney's integrity and his son's innocence. "While it is a terrible ordeal both to my boy and myself to have him under even a possibility of suspicion, yet our attitude will be one of helping the investigation rather than retarding it. . . . And even though my son is subjected to the hardships and embarrassment of being kept from his family until the authorities are thoroughly satisfied . . . yet my son should be willing to make the sacrifice, and I am also willing for the sake of justice and truth."[18]

Robert Crowe could scarcely believe his luck. Crowe was now sure that Nathan Leopold and Richard Loeb were the murderers. All the clues pointed to that conclusion. Leopold's handwriting matched that on the envelope enclosing the ransom letter addressed to Jacob Franks; Leopold's eyeglasses had been found near the corpse; the boys were lovers who had concocted an alibi that could not be confirmed; and at that moment, late on Friday afternoon, he was getting news that detectives had discovered typed legal notes belonging to Leopold that matched the typed ransom letter delivered to Jacob Franks the day after the murder.

Yet he continued to hold both suspects for questioning without any interference from either family! Eventually, Crowe thought to himself, one or both families would surely alert the lawyers to the boys' plight.

He had to get the boys to confess before their lawyers could shut their mouths. Neither boy had yet asked for a lawyer; neither boy had refused to answer his questions. How, therefore, could he wring a confession out of them, a confession that would surely send them to the gallows? And could he get that confession before lawyers for the boys appeared with a writ of habeas corpus?

CROWE RECEIVED HELP IN HIS task from an unexpected quarter. Two cub reporters from the *Chicago Daily News*, Alvin Goldstein and James Mulroy, had been following the case from the beginning. Goldstein had been at the morgue on South Houston Avenue after the discovery of the body; Mulroy had driven with Edwin Greshan from the Franks home to check the identity of the boy lying on the undertaker's slab. Both reporters were recent graduates of the University of Chicago; they knew the campus well and still had many friends at the university.

They also knew Nathan Leopold and Richard Loeb. Goldstein was a member of Zeta Beta Tau fraternity, and he and Loeb had become acquaintances during Loeb's postgraduate year at the university. Neither boy was then an undergraduate, but both boys spent time at the fraternity clubhouse, playing cards, swapping stories, and keeping up with fraternity gossip.[19]

Both Goldstein and Mulroy were surprised that Nathan and Richard were in police custody. But if Nathan was a suspect, could they match the typewritten notes for his law classes with the ransom letter sent to Jacob Franks? Alvin Goldstein knew that Nathan had belonged to an informal study group at the law school; the boys in this group met each week to go over legal cases and type up a set of notes for the group. He asked around; sure enough, several boys had copies of the notes.[20]

It did not take Robert Crowe long to confirm the reporters' hunch that one typewriter, a portable Underwood, had been used for both the ransom letter and Nathan Leopold's legal notes. This was one link in the chain of evidence that Nathan would find difficult to break!

But to forge that link, Crowe needed to find the typewriter. If it was in Nathan's study, the case against Nathan would be sealed as tight as a drum.

Forty minutes later, the police were back at the house on Greenwood Avenue. William Shoemacher's men searched again through the study and bedroom. Nathan's aunt was puzzled; the police had taken away Nathan's Hammond typewriter earlier that day; did the detectives not know that it was already at the Criminal Court Building?

Shoemacher explained that he was looking for a second typewriter, a portable Underwood—had any of the staff seen Nathan using a portable typewriter? He questioned the maids—what could they tell him?

Elizabeth Sattler hesitated. She had worked for the Leopolds for four years; she liked her employer and was reluctant to hurt the family; but she had a strong sense of duty and the police captain was persistent. She stepped forward.

"Yes, that typewriter was here."

Shoemacher felt a thrill of appreciation at the words. The link was forged; the net was closing around Nathan. He looked directly at the maid.

"When did you see it last?"

"I seen it two weeks ago."

"Well, what became of it?"

"I don't know, it ought to be around here."[21]

The detectives searched everywhere for the Underwood, but it was not in the boy's bedroom or study; there was no sign of it in the library; there was no trace in any of the other rooms in the house. But Elizabeth's testimony was vital—the police may not have been able to locate the typewriter, but now they knew that it had been in the house only a few days before the murder of Bobby Franks.

. . .

THE QUESTIONING BEGAN AGAIN THAT Friday at 6:30 p.m. Both Nathan and Richard had woken up around three o'clock in the afternoon; the detectives had given them time to wash, to catch a bite to eat, and to prepare for the evening's interrogation before driving them back to the Criminal Court Building.

Joseph Savage, an assistant state's attorney working in Robert Crowe's office, asked Nathan about the portable typewriter. What could Nathan tell him about it? Nathan replied that he remembered having seen a typewriter at his house, but, of course, it was not his; it belonged, no doubt, to one of the boys in his study group.

During the winter and spring quarters at the law school, Nathan had studied with four friends at his house. In preparing for the first-year exams, it was usual practice among the students at the University of Chicago law school to study a number of cases, to winnow the points of law from each individual case, and to classify them. The students even had a slang expression—"dope sheeting"—for this form of study; the law students would customarily discuss the principal points and type up a summary of the points on "dope sheets" for each member of the group.[22]

"The only typewriter other than my own," Nathan explained, "that I ever used in my home was a portable typewriter, what make I don't know, which I had there for a few weeks for the purpose of dope sheeting for law courses."

"Whose typewriter was that?" Savage asked.

"It belonged to one of the boys in the dope section; I am not sure which one."[23]

The five boys usually worked upstairs, in Nathan's study on the third floor, but occasionally they would gather in the downstairs library on the first floor. It was warmer and more comfortable in the library, and the lighting was better. If Nathan's father needed to use the library, then the little group of scholars would make for the third-floor study.[24]

One of his friends, Nathan explained, had brought the portable typewriter into his house. It was necessary because he kept the

Hammond typewriter upstairs in his study and that typewriter was fixed on a special table; it was too cumbersome and heavy to lug up and down two flights of stairs every time they wanted to work in the library.

So the study group had used the portable typewriter in the library. Who had brought it into the house? Again, Nathan was vague; he was not sure, but he thought it might have been Morris Shanberg.

WHILE NATHAN CONTINUED TO ANSWER Savage's questions that evening, Crowe's detectives fanned out through Chicago to bring in the four boys. Shanberg and another student, Lester Abelson, both lived on the North Side of the city; Arnold Maremont and the fourth member of the group, Howard Oberndorf, lived in Hyde Park, near the university.

By ten o'clock on Friday evening, all four were at the Criminal Court Building, waiting in offices adjacent to the state's attorney's rooms. In Crowe's office, Nathan was sticking to his story. In front of him, on a table, the police had placed three portable typewriters: a Corona, a Remington, and an Underwood. He was now sure, looking at the examples before him, that he had used an Underwood, but still he denied ownership—he was certain that the typewriter belonged to Morris Shanberg.

Robert Crowe had been waiting for this moment. He nodded slightly to a sergeant standing on the other side of the room; thirty seconds later, Shanberg, looking nervous, walked into the office. Crowe motioned him to sit down and gestured toward Nathan.

"Sit down, Shanberg. You know Nathan Leopold, Jr.?"

"Yes."

"You and Nathan have always been good friends?"

"Well, always since at school, I met him at school. . . ."

"Shanberg, during your law course at the University of Chicago, you had occasion to go over and work on the dope sheets with Nathan from time to time; is that right?"

"Yes."

Joseph Savage picked up the questioning. Savage had always been a stickler for detail; it was important that there be no ambiguity about the student slang: "By dope sheet, you mean that is preparatory work?"

"Briefing the course as a whole . . ."

"Do you remember at any time, Shanberg, of seeing a typewriter, a portable typewriter over at Nathan's house?"

"Only on one occasion; that was the last time I was there."

"Prior to working on that portable typewriter, you worked with this Hammond typewriter; is that right?"

"Yes."

"And who operated the typewriter?"

"Mr. Leopold, except on occasions when Mr. Leopold went to the phone."

Morris Shanberg glanced cautiously at Nathan. The other boy returned his look and held it; there was a slight smirk on Nathan's face—it seemed almost that he was enjoying this moment.

Shanberg suddenly realized why he was here. It must be that the police had found the typewriter used for the ransom note and Nathan was denying ownership; Nathan was trying to link him to the typewriter and frame him for the murder of Bobby Franks!

Joseph Savage's voice broke his train of thought: "Now, did you ever own a typewriter, Mr. Shanberg?"

"No."

Shanberg's voice was firmer now—less hesitant, less deferential.

"Did you ever bring one over to Nathan's house?"

"No, sir."

"Did you ever know any of the other boys to bring a typewriter over to Nathan's house?"

"No, sir."[25]

The detectives allowed Morris Shanberg to leave. One by one, the three other students entered Crowe's office. Each described in turn the study group, recalled the portable Underwood in the library, and denied any knowledge of its provenance. Howard Oberndorf was the last of the four to speak, and as Oberndorf got up to leave the room, Joseph Savage turned back to Nathan. The assistant state's attorney felt a sense of futility in questioning the boy further—Nathan was sure to stonewall him—but, nevertheless, there was no harm trying. "Nathan, I understood you to say that the typewriter had been taken out again by the boy that brought it in."

"That was my assumption."

"You just assumed that?"

"Yes."

"You don't know whether it was actually taken out or not?"

"No, I do not."

"Or you don't know when it was taken out, if it ever was taken out?"

"No, I don't."

"Do you ever remember the typewriter coming in?"

"I do not."

"Do you remember under what circumstances it could have come into the house? . . . It would hardly come into the house without some comment at the time the machine was brought there; what I mean is, that one would hardly come in and leave a typewriter at your house without saying something about it?"

"I should not think so."[26]

THERE WAS ONE MORE POSSIBILITY. The previous November, he had begun a project with a friend, Leon Mandel, to translate Pietro Aretino's fifteenth-century pornographic novel *I Ragionamenti* into English. This had been a provocative decision on Nathan's part. Aretino's *Dialogues* between two women contained graphic descriptions of sodomy and bestiality; the sensationalism of the narrative overshadowed the work's literary value. Ernest Wilkins, professor of Italian and dean of the undergraduate college at the university, had warned Nathan not to go through with the translation, but Nathan persisted nevertheless. Both Nathan and Leon Mandel hoped to persuade "some friend of ours to publish a very small little edition, two or three hundred copies, or subscriptions to be circulated only among people who had a legitimate interest in the literature of the times," but it was a more demanding task than either had anticipated: they completed fewer than twenty pages before abandoning the translation.[27]

Leon Mandel had, however, frequently come to the Leopold home to work on the translation, and Nathan suggested that he may have brought the Underwood typewriter with him.[28]

But Elizabeth Sattler had told the police that she had last seen the portable as recently as two weeks ago: that is, around the middle of May, just one week before the murder of Bobby Franks. Leon Mandel had been married on 30 April and had immediately sailed for Europe on his honeymoon. One month later, he was still on his honeymoon, so if the maid had seen the typewriter only two weeks ago, then obviously Mandel had not taken it out of the house. So, Nathan, where was that typewriter?

"I don't know."

"If it was Mandel's machine, it would still be there, wouldn't it?"

"Yes."

"These boys say that they never had a machine. Where is that machine? . . . You kept denying, right up until a few minutes ago, that you knew anything about it. . . . It was a machine one of these boys brought in, you didn't know when, where or how, and he took it out, and you didn't know when, where or how."

"Yes."

"Then you were confronted with each boy, weren't you?"

"Yes."

"And after the boy told you you were a liar, you changed your opinion, didn't you? . . . The fact that that letter that Franks got was written on the same machine that some of your stuff was written on, and the fact that experts say that the same person wrote it might be a damned good reason for you in losing that machine."

"Certainly."

"And knowing nothing about it?"

"Certainly."[29]

NATHAN LEOPOLD HAD NOW BEEN in police custody for almost thirty-six hours, from Thursday afternoon through the evening of Friday, 30 May. Yet at the Leopold home on Greenwood Avenue, the family's faith in Nathan's innocence remained unshaken; the entire affair was still, in his father's eyes, an unfortunate mistake that would inevitably be corrected.

Was there anything the family could do to help Nathan in his predicament? Sven Englund, the family chauffeur, told Nathan's father that Nathan could not possibly have abducted Bobby Franks and driven him out to Wolf Lake on 21 May; Englund had spent most of that day working on Nathan's car, fixing the brakes. He remembered the day well; he had been worried over his little girl, his nine-year-old daughter. She had been ill that day, and his wife, Alma, had taken her to the doctor to get a prescription. Englund had worked on the car in the early afternoon, and it had stayed in the garage the entire day.[30]

The family received the news with triumph. Nathan's father, two brothers, and aunt—all gathered that evening at the house on Greenwood Avenue—knew nothing of his alibi, that he had driven to Lincoln Park in his car. They knew only that Nathan was innocent and Sven Englund's testimony proved it; how could Nathan have been driving around Chicago with the body of the murder victim if his car was in the garage all day?

That evening Sven Englund waited on a bench outside the state's attorney's office in the Criminal Court Building. Robert Crowe was busy and could not see him. Could Englund not come back the following day, Saturday? No, it was important—even if he could not speak to Crowe, the chauffeur would like to talk to one of his assistants. Englund was persistent; and eventually he managed to tell his story to one of the assistant state's attorneys.

Englund had been working in the garage at the Leopold house on Wednesday, 21 May, around twelve-thirty in the afternoon. The chauffeur was responsible for five cars: the Leopolds owned a Packard, two Lincolns, a Willys-Knight, and a Wills Saint Claire. The Willys-Knight—Nathan's car—was especially distinctive, a maroon sports model with red disk wheels, nickel-plated bumpers, and a tan top. As Englund looked toward the gate that afternoon, he could see the Willys-Knight approach the driveway with Nathan at the wheel; behind him, a second boy was driving a dark green car.

Nathan stepped out from his car. The brakes had been squealing for several days; could Sven check them that afternoon? He did not need his car that day; he would prefer to have the problem fixed as soon as possible. Nathan and Richard Loeb drove away in the green car.

What make was the second car? Englund tried to remember—he was not sure. Perhaps, he replied, it was a Cadillac.

In recounting his story to the assistant state's attorney, Sven Englund provided convincing detail. On the day of the murder, he had removed the disk wheels from the red Willys-Knight to oil both the brake bands and the brakes; Nathan's car had remained in his garage until ten o'clock that evening.[31]

ENGLUND'S ACCOUNT CAME AS A thunderclap—the chauffeur had smashed the boys' alibi. Crowe broke off his interrogation of Nathan; he realized immediately that both boys had been lying to him about their movements on the day of the murder. Nathan Leopold and Richard Loeb had told him that they had spent Wednesday, 21 May, driving around the city in Nathan's car; yet Sven Englund was now saying that Nathan's car had been in the garage all day.[32]

Crowe had no time to lose. The family had sent Englund on his mission to the Criminal Court Building; perhaps even now, Nathan's father was contacting a lawyer to file a writ of habeas corpus. If Crowe could squeeze a confession out of the boys before the lawyers arrived, he would have a hanging case, but if there was no confession, the killers might yet avoid the gallows.

Which boy was most likely to break first? Should Crowe switch to Richard Loeb or stay with Nathan Leopold? Nathan had denied everything—he had refused to budge an inch. Richard Loeb might be more vulnerable. Loeb did not even know why he was in the Criminal Court Building; throughout his detention, the detectives had held the boy in isolation.

Crowe opened the door. Richard Loeb was leaning forward in a chair with his head resting on his arms on the desk. As the state's attorney entered the room, the boy lifted his head up and slid backward in the chair.[33]

It was almost one o'clock in the morning, and Loeb was very tired. He had slept during the day but only for about four hours. He demanded to know why Crowe was holding him. He knew nothing, and he wanted to talk to a lawyer.[34]

Crowe heard the words but ignored the request. He had been expecting one of the boys to ask for a lawyer—he was surprised it had taken so long. He pretended not to hear; behind him, Joseph Savage, the assistant state's attorney, was entering the room; he was followed by Michael Hughes, the chief of detectives. The stenographer was the last to enter, and as the door closed behind him, Crowe turned to face Loeb.

"Now, Loeb, you told me that Wednesday . . . you drove down town with this young fellow Leopold, in his car, that is a sport model, it is a red car with a tan top, a Willys-Knight?"

"Yes. . . ."

"You had lunch at the grill room at Marshall Field's? . . . Then you went out to Lincoln Park?"

"Yes, sir."

"And that all the driving you did this day was in this car?"

"Yes, sir. . . ."

Crowe had been sitting casually on the edge of the gray metal desk; now he got to his feet and stood in front of Loeb, looking down at the boy in the chair before him. He spoke louder now, in a voice calculated to intimidate the boy, and he moved closer, so close that his physical presence in itself seemed to threaten and menace.

"Isn't it a fact that Wednesday, May 21st, . . . you drove up to that garage, to Leopold's garage, you driving your mother's car, that green Cadillac, he driving the red car . . . and you turned the car over to the chauffeur and got into your car and drove away?"

"No," Richard replied.

"That is not a fact?"

"No," Richard answered again.

Crowe was shouting now. The anger in his voice filled the interrogation room. He wanted that confession so much—he needed Richard to confess—he had to force the boy to break, to admit his guilt to the murder.

"If this chauffeur says so, he is a liar?"

"Yes."[35]

Richard's hands were shaking, and the color had drained from his face. As he slumped down in his chair, the detectives heard him whisper to himself, "My God." He tried to speak, but his words died before they reached his lips. Crowe waited impatiently for the boy to drink a glass of water.

"If the chauffeur took the car in and oiled it up, oiled the brakes and fixed it up, that would make an impression on his mind, wouldn't it?"

"Yes."

"If he says that is a fact, he is a liar or mistaken? . . ."

"Yes. . . . I would say he was still a liar or mistaken."[36]

ROBERT CROWE WAS EXHAUSTED. BOTH boys denied everything; Crowe was discouraged: they were holding fast and he saw no way to break their resistance and force a confession. He stepped out of the office. Perhaps it was time to go home—he badly needed some sleep.

One of Crowe's assistants, John Sbarbaro, remained with Richard Loeb as Crowe talked in his office with Joseph Savage. Twenty minutes passed, then half an hour. There was a sudden bustle in the corridor; Sbarbaro had left the room and was striding, almost running, toward Crowe's office. The assistant state's attorney was breathless as he opened the door. Richard Loeb wanted to talk to the state's attorney . . . there was no time to lose . . . quick, quick, before the boy changed his mind![37]

7 | THE CONFESSIONS

It was really too bad, for the cause of justice, that they were so loquacious.[1]

Robert Crowe, 15 August 1924

AS ROBERT CROWE ENTERED THE interrogation room, Richard wiped a tear from his cheek. Crowe noticed the jerky, staccato movement of the boy's hand. It was, he thought, as if Richard were ashamed that he had been crying, as if he hoped to wipe away the evidence of his panic.

The state's attorney pulled up a chair, making a scraping noise as he dragged the legs of the chair across the concrete floor. As he sat down opposite Richard, the boy spoke through his tears, challenging the state's attorney. "You have no evidence on me. . . . Why are you holding me?"

"Because Leopold is the owner of those glasses—"

Richard looked up, startled; he had not expected this: "My God, is that possible?"

"—because you said you were with Leopold all day on the day of the murder." Crowe continued to list the evidence. "We have been directing our energy in fastening the crime on Leopold. . . . We now have, in addition to his glasses, the fact that you have both lied about being out in Lincoln Park having the red car with you. . . . We know that you had a portable typewriter. . . ."

Richard Loeb had bent over in his chair. He stared at his feet and made a slight rocking movement, back and forth, back and forth, as Crowe continued to talk. Now Richard sat up straight; the tears were streaming down his cheeks; he cried out his terror at having been caught, "My God . . . my God . . . this is terrible. . . ."

There was silence in the room. Crowe waited. The deputies at Crowe's side held their breath in anticipation as they stared at Richard, waiting for him to admit his guilt.

"I will tell you all," Richard suddenly announced.

Crowe clenched his fist in triumph. He had the confession![2]

But the stenographers had gone home for the night. Crowe himself had sent them away only half an hour before. He would now have to send out a police car to bring them back to the Criminal Court Building to take down Richard's confession. And he needed other witnesses to the confession, men outside his command, who would corroborate in court that Richard Loeb had given his confession freely, without duress. Crowe knew that Michael Hughes, the chief of detectives, would want to be present when Loeb made his formal confession; and William Shoemacher also—the deputy captain of police—would certainly not want to miss the occasion.

While his assistants, John Sbarbaro and Joseph Savage, made the arrangements, Crowe resumed his conversation with Richard Loeb. He wanted only the most important details, he told the boy; a full account could come later, once the stenographer had arrived. Richard obliged—he told the state's attorney how he had scouted the Harvard School, and how he had spotted Bobby Franks walking south on Ellis Avenue . . . they had driven out of Chicago on the Michigan City road and had stopped at a roadside cafe for hot dogs and root beer . . . oh, and the culvert by the Pennsylvania Railroad tracks—it had been difficult, Richard remembered, concealing the body in the drainage pipe. . . .

Half an hour later Robert Crowe sat opposite Nathan Leopold in an office just a few doors down the corridor. Nathan was smoking—did Nathan ever, the state's attorney wondered, stop smoking?

Nathan had wanted to speak to Crowe, he said, to ask a hypothetical question. The state's attorney nodded. What did he want to know?

Suppose, Nathan asked, that someone from a wealthy family, a family as rich as his own, had committed this murder—what chance would that person have of beating the murder charges?

Crowe looked at the boy curiously—was Nathan trying to bribe him? Or was he implying in his question that he would try to bribe the jury if he came to trial?

Crowe's answer was abrupt. He was going to give Nathan a chance to find out—he intended to draw up a charge of murder against Nathan for the killing of Bobby Franks.

Nathan smiled. He drew on his cigarette. He knew Crowe was bluffing. This was just a trick to intimidate him. "While you have some few circumstances that point to me," he told the state's attorney, "you haven't sufficient evidence to bring me into court . . . and you won't."

Crowe leaned forward in his chair—did Nathan remember, he asked, the afternoon of the murder, waiting by the car while Richard went around to the back of the Harvard School to find a boy in the school playground? And those hot dogs and that root beer that Nathan had purchased at the Dew Drop Inn after they had killed Bobby? Did he recall those? And what about the trouble he had in concealing the body inside the drainage pipe?

Richard had told him all this detail and had confessed to the kidnapping of Bobby Franks. Did Nathan still think that he could beat the murder charge?

Nathan had stopped smirking. His cockiness had disappeared. Eventually he spoke. His voice was subdued, quiet, almost ruminative. "Well, I am surprised that Dick is talking." Nathan spoke reflectively, as though he were musing to himself. "I thought he would stand till hell froze over."

He thought for a moment. For once, Nathan seemed uncertain, almost lost in his sudden change of circumstances. He looked up. He had realized that Richard might be blaming him for the murder, perhaps even accusing him of wielding the murder weapon.

"Dick is talking." Nathan paused, as though he wanted to make an important announcement. "I will tell you the truth about the matter."

The words came fast now, spilling out one after the other, piling on top of each other, in Nathan's effort to put the blame on the other boy. Richard had wanted to commit the perfect crime, Richard had suggested the kidnapping, Richard had persuaded Bobby to enter the car, Richard had struck Bobby with the chisel . . .

The state's attorney cut him short. He should save his breath until the stenographers arrived. There would be plenty of time later for Nathan to tell everything he knew.[3]

AT FOUR O'CLOCK THAT MORNING, the stenographer, Frank Sheeder, sat waiting alone in an interrogation room. He could hear footsteps echoing along the corridor, making their way toward him, and as they got closer, he could distinguish the voice of John Sbarbaro, the assistant state's attorney. The door suddenly opened. Sbarbaro entered first, and behind him, a young man, good-looking, not much older than twenty, walked shyly into the room. And finally, behind Richard Loeb, the deputy captain of police, William Shoemacher, stepped into the office and closed the door behind him. Sbarbaro introduced Richard Loeb to the stenographer—now that everyone had finally arrived, they could begin.

"State your full name."

"Richard Albert Loeb."

"Where do you live, Mr. Loeb?"

"5017 Ellis Avenue."

"What is your occupation?"

"Student."

"Where are you a student?"

"University of Chicago."

"How old are you?"

"Eighteen."

"You know now that you are in the office of the State's Attorney of Cook County?"

"Yes."

"And you want to make a statement of your own free will?"

"Yes."

"Calling your attention to the 21st day of May, just tell us in your own words if you know of anything unusual relative to the disappearance of Robert Franks."

"On the 21st of May, Leopold and myself . . ."

"What is his full name?"

"Nathan Leopold, Junior . . . and myself intended to kidnap one of the younger boys from the Harvard School. . . . The plan was broached by Nathan Leopold, who suggested that as a means of having a great deal of excitement, together with getting quite a sum of money."[4]

Richard talked about the murder in a matter-of-fact way. He had now decided to pin responsibility for the crime on Nathan's shoulders.

"I drove the car . . . south on Ellis Avenue, parallel to where young Franks was. . . . I told him that I would like to talk to him about a tennis racket; so he got in the car. . . . Just after we turned off Ellis Avenue, Leopold reached his arm around young Franks, grabbed his mouth and hit him over the head with the chisel. I believe he hit him several times. I do not know the exact number. . . . Leopold grabbed Franks and carried him over back of the front seat and threw him on a rug in the car. He then took one of the rags and gagged him by sticking it down his throat. . . . The scheme for etherizing him originated through Leopold, who evidently has some knowledge of such things, and he said that would be the easiest way of putting him to death, and the least messy. This, however, we found unnecessary, because the boy was quite dead when we took him there. We knew he was dead, by the fact that rigor mortis had set in, and also by his eyes; and then when at that same time we poured this hydrochloric acid over him, we noticed no tremor, not a single tremor in his body; therefore we were sure he was dead."[5]

Richard eventually came to the end. He looked around the room, first at Sbarbaro, then at Shoemacher, and finally at the stenographer.

He had recovered his composure. He betrayed no sign of the tears that he had cried only a few hours earlier.

Sbarbaro had only one more question and then they would be done.

"This statement that you have just made has been made of your own free will?"

"Yes." Richard accepted responsibility, but of course Nathan had been to blame; they understood that, didn't they? "I just want to say that I offer no excuse; but that I am fully convinced that neither the idea nor the act would have occurred to me, had it not been for the suggestion and stimulus of Leopold. Furthermore, I do not believe that I would have been capable of having killed Franks."[6]

LESS THAN TEN YARDS AWAY, in an office two doors down the corridor, Nathan also was confessing. Another of Crowe's assistants, Joseph Savage, together with Michael Hughes, the chief of detectives, listened as Nathan told his version of events while the second stenographer, Elbert Allen, scribbled down his words in shorthand.

Savage had already learned that Richard blamed Nathan for the murder. Yet now he was hearing the opposite, that it was Richard who had killed Bobby Franks.

"Richard placed his one hand over Robert's mouth to stifle his outcries, with his right beat him on the head several times with a chisel, especially prepared for the purpose. The boy did not succumb as readily as we had believed, so for fear of being observed, Richard seized him, pulled him into the back seat. Here he forced a cloth into his mouth. Apparently the boy died instantly by suffocation. . . ."

"When Richard hit Robert first, was it down in the tonneau of the car, the bottom of the car, or was it on the seat he choked him?"

"It was on the seat; Robert was sitting on the front seat, Dick was in the back seat."

"Robert was sitting in the front with you?"

"Yes; and Dick sort of leaned over and put his hand over his mouth, like this."

"Did he pull him back in the rear?"

"Not until later."

"After he cracked him on the head, did he fall down then, Robert?"

"No, he struggled."[7]

Each boy blamed the other for the murder—who was telling the truth? Had Nathan or Richard struck Bobby Franks on the head with the chisel?

But in all other respects, their accounts were identical—each prisoner corroborated the other's story. The murder was solved.

Shortly before seven that Saturday morning, Robert Crowe emerged from his office to speak to the journalists waiting in the main corridor of the Criminal Court Building. The air was thick with cigarette smoke; a dozen reporters had spent the night sitting in the corridor, leaning against the walls, waiting for the break in the case. They struggled to their feet as Crowe appeared before them; the state's attorney looked tired, weary from the long hours of interrogation—perhaps, the journalists thought, there was still no result.

Crowe stood in the center of the small group arranged in a semicircle before him. He spoke quietly, just loud enough for his audience to hear: "We have the murderers in custody."

Not one of the reporters was looking at him; they were too busy scribbling down his words in their notebooks. It was a strange scene, Crowe reflected. The end of the murder investigation, and now he was announcing it to this small group of journalists while secretaries, desk sergeants, and clerks walked by him on their way to their offices as they arrived for the day. Surely it should have ended on a more triumphal note?

"The Franks murder mystery has been solved. The murderers are in custody. Nathan Leopold and Richard Loeb have completely and voluntarily confessed. . . . The Franks boy was kidnaped out of a spirit of adventure and for ransom. The kidnaping was planned many months ago, but the Franks boy was not the original victim in mind. . . . He was beaten with a chisel, strangled and then [an] attempt was made to disfigure him with acid."[8]

•   •   •

THE REVELATION THAT ROBERT CROWE had solved the case reached the relatives first. Reporters swarmed into Kenwood to obtain reactions to the news. Jacob Franks came to his front door. The old man was solemn and unsmiling as he spoke to the journalists gathered before him. It was only fitting, he remarked, that two unbelievers had been exposed by a providential mistake: "I understand the two boys boasted they are atheists. I know now they will see there is a God above Who watches all things. It was His providence that caused Leopold's glasses to be dropped near my boy's body—His will that those two boys should pay."

Franks was sorry, of course, for the parents of the killers. "I have known them a great many years," he said, "and for them I have only the deepest sympathy," but the law must take its course. "No punishment would be too severe for them. They are fiends. I can't see how any jury, court or even the President could release them, the act was so atrocious. . . . They ought to hang."[9]

On the opposite side of Ellis Avenue, at the Loeb house, two private bodyguards stood at the front gate to shoo away intruders. Curious spectators had started to gather outside the house; occasionally they could spot Anna Loeb pacing nervously as she awaited more news of her son. A relative of the family did speak to the journalists, but only to deny that Richard had any connection with the murder: "There is no truth to these reports. Just lies, lies, lies! . . . We are not worried about these rumors. . . . He is innocent and confessed merely to get sleep. It can be repudiated when he comes to trial."[10]

Three blocks north, at the Leopold household, Nathan Leopold Sr. bravely denied his son's guilt: "impossible, ridiculous, . . . Nathan—my boy—my boy—I can't believe it. . . . I won't believe it." But as he turned back into the house, a deep frown creased the old man's forehead.[11]

For the close-knit Jewish community in Kenwood, the revelation that the murderers had come from within its ranks was impossible to credit. Acquaintances and friends of the families reacted with shock and disbelief that Nathan Leopold and Richard Loeb had confessed to such an atrocious murder. The attorney Sol Levinson had already heard from the police that Nathan and Richard had eyed his son, Johnny, as a possible kidnapping victim when a reporter from the *Chicago Herald and Examiner* arrived at his home at midday to interview him. Levinson and his wife had had dinner at the Loebs only the previous month. Richard had been present and had "delighted us by his charming personality. I regarded him as one of the finest youths I have ever known. His confession of this awful crime is simply unbelievable to all who know him. I can hardly think it possible that he and young Leopold contemplated harm to my boy."

Adele Harris, the wife of a millionaire building contractor, was equally shocked to learn that the murderers had considered her fourteen-year-old son, Samuel, as a murder victim; she too knew Richard Loeb as "one of the sweetest boys in the world. It was impossible to know him without being fond of him."[12]

Lessing Rosenwald, the manager of the Philadelphia branch of Sears, Roebuck, was baffled that Richard had confessed to the murder. The Rosenwald children and the Loeb boys had grown up together. "Richard Loeb is a fine fellow," Lessing Rosenwald remarked. "I can't understand why he would do a thing like that. If he wanted money all he had to do was to ask for it. . . . I knew Richard as a brother and I can't believe this thing about him."[13]

An acquaintance of the Loeb and Leopold families, speaking anonymously, speculated that the casual attitude of the parents toward religious instruction had allowed Richard and Nathan to fall into bad habits. Both families worshipped at Sinai Congregation, a Reform temple at 47th Street and Grand Boulevard. The rabbi, Emil Hirsch, had been, until his death the previous year, a leading exponent of Reform Judaism, and the synagogue had become an important institution for the affluent German Jewish communities of Hyde Park and Kenwood. But some families had not been as observant as one might expect, and neither Richard Loeb nor Nathan Leopold had been consistently educated in Jewish principles. "Though the father of 'Babe' Leopold is a devout Jew, he failed to make religious influence a part of his son's training. An insistence on an understanding and respect for the father's religion would have made all the difference in the world in that young man's development." And Richard Loeb? His mother, Anna, was a Catholic who had only reluctantly agreed that her sons be brought up in the Jewish faith.[14]

The mayor of Chicago, William Dever, counted Albert Loeb as a personal friend. Dever was careful, in his first public comments on the case, to congratulate the detectives on their swift success: "I am very much pleased with the efficient and vigorous work done by the police in solving this mystery. The case was so mysterious and baffling I was afraid it never would be solved. It was an exhibition of fine work which will be appreciated by all the people of Chicago." Dever knew how quickly anti-Semitism might appear in a scandal that involved the scions of wealthy Jews, and he was careful also to call for restraint: "I have the deepest sympathy for the parents of all three boys. I know Mr. Loeb, whom I regard as a man of splendid character and attainment. It is sad that such a tragedy should be visited upon these people and it invites the sympathy of all."[15]

John Caverly, chief justice of the Criminal Court, promised that he would bring kidnapping and murder charges before the grand jury as soon as possible—most probably on the following Tuesday, 3 June—and predicted that the trial would begin within the next thirty days. There was to be no delay of justice simply because the prisoners came from wealthy families. Robert Crowe welcomed Caverly's announcement. He was ready to go to trial. He was confident, he announced, that he had "a hanging case. . . . I shall present the facts, including the confessions, to the grand jury early in the week."[16]

Crowe had the confessions, but Nathan and Richard could (and probably would) repudiate them. Their lawyers would, no doubt, claim that they had spoken under duress, that the police had beaten them, that Crowe had denied them access to a lawyer.

The state's attorney anticipated such claims. Therefore, he would ask the boys to retrace their steps on the day of the murder—to show him where they had kidnapped Bobby Franks, how they had driven out to Wolf Lake, and where they had disposed of Bobby's clothes.

It was an unusual strategy—but this was an unusual case, unlike anything in Crowe's experience as a state's attorney. Both Nathan and

Richard were cooperating—in that respect, Crowe had no complaints. Neither boy had yet pressed his right to contact a lawyer, and neither the Loeb family nor the Leopold family had yet appeared at the Criminal Court Building to demand access to the boys. It was now nine o'clock on Saturday morning. The Chicago newspapers had already appeared with accounts of the confessions, yet neither Albert Loeb nor Nathan Leopold Sr. had thought to hire lawyers to get the boys out of his custody.

At ten minutes past nine, a cavalcade of seven police cars set out from the Criminal Court Building. Forty detectives—including the deputy captain of police, William Shoemacher, and the chief of detectives, Michael Hughes—accompanied Nathan Leopold and Richard Loeb. In the rear, tagging along behind the seven black sedans, dozens of journalists and photographers followed in their cars.

The procession stopped first at the Rent-A-Car Company at 1427 South Michigan Avenue. The general manager, Walter Jacobs, identified Nathan Leopold as the man who had taken out a dark green Willys-Knight on Wednesday, 21 May.[17]

Where was that car now? Was it in the garage? Could the police, Shoemacher asked, take a look at it? Jacobs checked his records—a customer named Salvatore Sarascio had rented the car the previous day and it was still out, but Jacobs assured Shoemacher that he would make sure to notify the police when it came back into the garage.[18]

They stopped next at the lunchroom at 1352 Wabash Avenue where Richard had waited by the phone to provide a reference for Nathan. Gertrude Barish, the wife of the owner, remembered seeing Richard about three weeks previously—she recalled that he had waited by the telephone booth at the back of the restaurant for almost an hour.

Richard Loeb, surrounded by detectives, stood in the center of the room listening. He had not had a wink of sleep. Richard felt tired and miserable, and then dizzy and light-headed; he heard the woman's voice droning away, and suddenly his legs buckled underneath him and he fell, fainting, to the floor.

Nathan also was exhausted. Even after he had finished giving his confession that morning, Crowe had kept him sitting and waiting,

waiting endlessly in an office in the Criminal Court Building. Now he was in an irritable mood. Nathan had already read the morning newspapers, and he was annoyed that they all painted the murder as the worst crime in the city's history.

Gertrude Barish finally finished talking to the detectives. They left the diner to drive down Cottage Grove Avenue and, in the back of the police car, Nathan gave vent to his indignation.

"I can't understand," Nathan complained, talking to no one in particular, "why the papers say this is such an atrocious murder."

Frank Johnson, the police sergeant who had first brought Nathan in for questioning, turned around in his seat to look at the boy. Johnson had gotten to know Nathan well in the past two days, yet he was as puzzled by the crime as anyone else. How, he wondered, could this slightly shy and rather amiable young man have committed such a callous act?

"Is it necessary," he asked, "that you had to kill the boy?"

"It was," Nathan replied.

"Why?"

Nathan explained that Richard Loeb and Bobby Franks had been second cousins. Bobby knew Richard, and if they had released him, he would surely have identified Richard to the police. "We couldn't afford to take a chance to have him come back and say it was Dick."

But, Johnson replied, "He didn't know you."

"Well, I lived in the neighborhood and it was just a question of time before he would see me."[19]

The police car had been traveling south along Cottage Grove Avenue and now it came to a stop outside a hardware store close to 43rd Street. Albert Hubinger had been the clerk on duty at the store when Richard had purchased the cold chisel and the rope. Yes, Hubinger told the detectives, he remembered Richard well—he could identify him as the man who had bought the chisel and rope.[20]

Two blocks farther on, at a second drugstore at 4458 Cottage Grove Avenue, Aaron Adler remembered selling a pint bottle of hydrochloric acid to Nathan. He had not been likely to forget it, he told the police. He rarely sold such a large quantity of chemically pure acid; it was a very unusual purchase.[21]

The police cavalcade drove north along Cottage Grove Avenue to the Leopold family home on Greenwood Avenue; Nathan had promised to provide the hip boots that he had worn in the culvert. Then it was on to Jackson Park to show the detectives the spot where Nathan had thrown the typewriter into the outer harbor. And then out onto South Shore Drive, stopping briefly at 73rd Street to retrieve the partially burned automobile blanket, before traveling out of the city on the Michigan City Road, turning at Forsyth Avenue and onto Hopp Road, where, Richard told the police, they would find the shoes, belt buckle, and class pin belonging to Bobby Franks.[22]

IN CHICAGO, A SMALL CROWD of onlookers had already gathered at the front entrance of the Criminal Court Building. The spectators never spotted either Nathan or Richard, but they did see, at around two o'clock in the afternoon, four distinguished-looking gentlemen, all dressed in dark suits and with somber expressions, enter the building.

Milton Smith, an assistant state's attorney, met with the four men—the father, Nathan Leopold Sr.; a brother, Michael Leopold; an uncle, Jacob Loeb; and the Leopold family lawyer, Benjamin Bachrach—but was unable to let them see Robert Crowe. The state's attorney was still driving around Chicago with Richard Loeb and Nathan Leopold.

When would they be back? Smith was not sure: sometime that afternoon, perhaps. But in any case, he warned, it was unlikely that they would be able to see either Crowe or the two boys. The state's attorney would release them only on a writ of habeas corpus and the courts would not open again until Monday morning. Whatever else happened, Smith cautioned, both Richard Loeb and Nathan Leopold would remain in police custody until then.[23]

THE NEXT DAY, SUNDAY, 1 June, promised to be bright and sunny. The humidity had dropped and the storms that had broken over the city during the week had now rolled on farther west, across the plains and out toward the Pacific. Ruby Darrow lay in bed, staring up at the ceiling. It was not yet seven o'clock and her husband, Clarence, was fast asleep, snoring contentedly. Ruby turned on her side and lifted herself on her elbow to look across at Clarence. His face was lined, his hair had thinned and had long ago turned gray, and his cheeks now sagged with age, but Ruby thought he was still an adorable man, an immensely comforting and reassuring presence in her life.

Suddenly she heard the ringing of the front doorbell. Who could it be so early on a Sunday morning? They did not expect visitors, and in any case no one would presume to visit at such a time. There it was again! The bell had an urgent, persistent tone, as though the visitor would not be denied.

Ruby climbed out of bed to put on her dressing gown and slippers. The bedroom was at one end of their seven-room apartment, and the front door was at the other end of a long corridor along which Ruby now walked, fastening the cord of the gown around her waist as she made her way toward the sound of the bell.

She opened the door. Four men stood before her. Ruby recognized Jacob Loeb, the former president of the Board of Education, but who were the others? Ruby Darrow had not seen them before.

Jacob Loeb bustled into the apartment. He seemed in a desperate hurry.

"We've got to see Clarence Darrow! Is he here?"

"Mr. Darrow is asleep." In an effort to save her Sunday for herself and her husband, Ruby lied to the interlopers. "He isn't well—he should not be disturbed." But Loeb had already pushed his way past her. He now stood in the hallway; his companions had advanced forward behind him.

Clarence Darrow had made his way along the corridor and now suddenly appeared in the vestibule. His presence electrified the men standing before him. Jacob Loeb rushed across to shake his hand in greeting, and the three others clustered around Darrow in eager anticipation.

"Thank heavens you are here! . . . You must save our two boys."

Darrow had known that Nathan Leopold and Richard Loeb were in police custody, but he had been away from Chicago the previous day, getting into the city late on Saturday night. He had not yet heard that both Nathan and Richard had confessed. Darrow, like everyone else in Chicago who knew the families, found it difficult to believe that they were the murderers.

"But they are not guilty. . . . Their innocence should not be difficult to prove."

"No, no!" Loeb cried out in frustration. "Dickie and Babe confessed. . . ."

"Then what can I do?"

"Save their lives! Get them a life sentence instead of a death sentence. That's all we ask of you." Jacob Loeb clutched at the attorney's arm. "Money's no object. We'll pay you anything you ask. Only for God's sake, don't let them be hung."[24]

WHILE JACOB LOEB WAS IMPLORING Clarence Darrow to save them from the gallows, Richard and Nathan were having breakfast in Daly's Restaurant on 63rd Street. Richard had had another restless night in the prison cell: his eyes were puffy and his face was pale and drawn. He sipped a cup of black coffee moodily—his food lay on his plate, untouched.

Richard stared glumly across the table at Nathan. It irritated him that the other boy was always so chipper; even now, Nathan was laughing and joking, bantering with the police escort, flirting with the blond waitress, and asking for a second plate of scrambled eggs. One would have thought Nathan had not a care in the world.

The chief of detectives, Michael Hughes, had finished his own breakfast, and now he was looking apprehensively at the crowd gathering outside the restaurant—news had obviously spread through the neighborhood that the police had brought Leopold and Loeb there. He looked at his watch—it was already nine-thirty, and Robert Crowe wanted the boys back at the Criminal Court Building by noon. It was time to go. Nathan was now munching a jelly doughnut and drinking a cup of coffee; as soon as he had finished, Hughes announced, they would be on their way.[25]

Crowe had asked Hughes to search for the two pieces of evidence that had eluded the police the previous day: the Underwood typewriter, thrown into the harbor at Jackson Park; and the belt belonging to Bobby Franks, hidden in grass near Hessville. It was only a short drive from the restaurant across to Jackson Park, and Hughes was optimistic that they would pick up the typewriter that morning. He had already directed police divers to the spot where Nathan had thrown it; the divers would be waiting for them at the harbor.

Three thousand spectators waited at the outer edge of the harbor. The crowd stirred when it saw the long cavalcade of black cars pull up; then, as Nathan Leopold stepped out of one car, followed by Richard Loeb from a second car, a roar of recognition flashed around the crowd, a deafening cheer as everyone pointed and waved and shouted at the two murderers.[26]

Nathan leaned over the parapet. He had thrown the typewriter as far as possible—he guessed that it had landed about fifteen feet from the bridge. He pointed to the spot. The diver disappeared into the water, and the crowd waited, but the thick mud at the bottom of the harbor was impenetrable.

Michael Hughes signaled to Walter Sullivan, a reporter for the *Chicago Herald and Examiner*, and to Morrow Krum of the *Chicago Daily Tribune*. The police cars would leave shortly for the drive to Hessville; would they like to ride in the cars with the two prisoners?

The relationship between the police and journalists in Chicago during the 1920s was one of mutual dependence. The reporters would write favorably of the police department in its war against crime, and in return the police would grant access to criminals, supply the newspapers with valuable information, and leak important tidbits about sensational trials. Hughes had known Sullivan and Krum, both veteran journalists, for many years. They were reliable allies who could be trusted to write well of his men.

Michael Hughes knew also that in allowing the reporters access to Nathan and Richard, he might help the two prisoners convict themselves in the court of public opinion. Nathan and Richard had confessed, but those confessions might yet be repudiated. However, if they were to talk of the murder to the reporters, and if their remarks were to be printed in the newspapers, how could their guilt be denied? Nathan and Richard had not yet expressed any remorse for the murder or any regret for the pain they had caused the Franks family. They seemed, rather, to have adopted a cynical, callous attitude toward the killing, as though it were morally inconsequential; all the better, therefore, if their comments about the murder were reported in the newspapers for public consumption.

On the ride to Hessville, a journey of approximately forty minutes, Walter Sullivan sat with Nathan in one car while Morrow Krum traveled with Richard in the other car. It was not long before both prisoners were gossiping about the crime, revealing details about themselves that blackened them irretrievably when Chicagoans opened their newspapers the following day.

AS THE CAR MADE ITS way out of the park, the bell clanging to clear a path through the crowd of onlookers trying to peer into the car window, Walter Sullivan asked Nathan about the murder. Whose idea had it been? And who had wielded the chisel to strike the deathblows? Had Nathan initiated the plan, or had it been Richard's idea?

The mere mention of Richard Loeb was sufficient to send Nathan into a tantrum of anger and indignation. He was still furious that Richard had blamed him for the murder—Richard's treason had been a cruel blow to Nathan's love. "It was all Loeb's idea," Nathan replied, bitterly, "he planned the kidnaping."

The car had now left Jackson Park and was threading its way through the streets of the South Side, out toward the Michigan City road.

"It was Loeb . . . who enticed the boy into the car and it was Loeb who struck him on the head the next instant." Nathan played nervously with the unlit cigarette in his hand, turning it through his fingers. "I could not—it would have been physically impossible for me to have struck the blow that killed Robert Franks. Loeb knows this too. . . . My repugnance to violence is such that I could not have killed Robert. . . .

He thinks that by proving me the actual slayer he will eventually go free."

Nathan paused; he leaned his elbow against the car window and stared at the houses as they passed. It had been a bitter blow, he acknowledged, knowing that Richard was willing to sacrifice him to preserve his own skin.

But his mood lasted only a minute. They passed the South Shore Country Club and then a golf course—what a ridiculous game, Nathan remarked!—and Nathan was soon his old self again, joking and bantering with the reporter. He leaned over and touched Sullivan lightly on the knee and sat back in his seat with a grin on his face,

"Now you're contaminated," he joked. "You've been touched by a murderer."

Sullivan smiled politely. He wondered how Nathan felt about the killing. Granted that Richard had struck Bobby with the chisel, nevertheless, he asked, how had Nathan felt about the boy's death?

It didn't concern him, Nathan replied. He had no moral beliefs and religion meant nothing to him: he was an atheist. Whatever served an individual's purpose—that was the best guide to conduct. In his case, well, he was an intellectual: his participation in the killing had been akin to the desire of the scientist to experiment. They had killed Bobby Franks as an experiment; Nathan had wanted to experience the sensation of murdering another human being. It was that simple.

"A thirst for knowledge," he explained to Sullivan, providing a helpful analogy to the murder of Bobby Franks, "is highly commendable, no matter what extreme pain or injury it may inflict upon others. A 6-year-old-boy is justified in pulling the wings from a fly, if by so doing he learns that without wings the fly is helpless."[27]

IN THE OTHER CAR, Richard Loeb, sitting in the rear seat beside Morrow Krum, talked of his plans after prison; he would serve some time, of course, but eventually he would get out, and then he would make a fresh start. "I'll spend a few years in jail and I'll be released. I'll come out to a new life. I'll go to work and I'll work hard and I'll amount to something—have a career."

"But you have taken a life," one of the detectives interrupted, in surprise. "You've killed a boy. The best you could possibly expect would be a life sentence to an insane asylum."

Richard's hands fluttered nervously; he searched his pockets for his cigarette case. The loss of his liberty was an unpleasant thought, and confinement in an asylum seemed especially grim. Krum asked him a question about Nathan Leopold; Richard answered with a sense of relief at the change of subject.

"Of course he is smart. He is one of the smartest and best educated men I know."

Had Nathan influenced Richard? Had Nathan controlled Richard and led him into the crime?

"Well, I wouldn't say that exactly," Richard paused to reflect on the question. "Perhaps he did dominate me. . . . Leopold suggested the whole thing. . . . I went along with him. . . . Well it was sort of that way after all. . . . I guess I yessed Babe a lot."

What was their relationship? The reporter pressed Richard, fishing for a headline for tomorrow's paper. How close was Richard to Nathan? Did Richard have many girlfriends at the university?

"Girls? Sure I like girls. I was out with a girl on Friday night after the affair. . . ."

"Was Babe a pervert?" Krum interrupted suddenly, using the family nickname for Nathan Leopold.

Richard shook his head indecisively, suddenly cautious about saying too much. "I don't know anything about that."[28]

Twenty minutes later, the cars had reached the village of Hessville. It was only another mile before they came to the spot where the police anticipated finding Bobby Franks's belt. Richard eventually found it, buried under some dirt, in the field adjacent to the copse. It still seemed almost new, a blue belt, with thin red and yellow stripes running down the center and a gold-plated buckle.[29]

· · ·

THAT SUNDAY AFTERNOON, AROUND TWO-THIRTY, Nathan Leopold Sr. met with Robert Crowe at the Criminal Court Building. He was concerned, he told the state's attorney, that his son had confessed under duress. He accepted Crowe's assurances that there had been no beatings, but perhaps the detectives had intimidated Nathan in some other way. Nathan had been in custody since Thursday afternoon—three full days—without access to a lawyer; how could the family be certain that he had received fair treatment?

Crowe could see the agitation on the old man's face. His visitor seemed nervous and confused, and considerably more deferential than Crowe had anticipated. He observed the old man closely. Nathan Leopold Sr.—with his thick salt-and-pepper mustache, his jowly neck and large ears, his watery eyes behind large rimless eyeglasses—bore little resemblance to his son. There was, Crowe decided, scarcely the faintest similarity between father and son.

"Just sit down, Mr. Leopold; I will have the boy brought in."

Nathan seemed in good health; he entered the room confidently and shook his father's hand.

"Hello, Dad."

"Hello, my son." The old man turned to the state's attorney. "Could I talk to this boy myself, privately? . . ."

"Just at this particular time I cannot do it."

"Is that true, Mr. Crowe, that a parent may not have the opportunity to talk to his child?"

"I want to give you an opportunity to . . . ease your mind as to the boy's well-being. . . . He is not being abused . . . but at this particular time I do not think it is proper for me to permit [the] two of you to talk together."

"Mr. Crowe, he may tell me things in my presence that he might be diffident about telling when others are present. In other words, if I ask him of the treatment he got, he might hesitate to answer when these people around here have been working on him, and he might tell me things that might be private in that respect. . . . Of course, you realize, I suppose . . . it is the duty of a parent to stand by his child."

"Absolutely; and it would not be natural that you did not."

"I want him to get every opportunity that everybody else would get under similar circumstances. If he is entitled to counsel, he should have it. If it is not proper for him to talk without counsel, then my advice to him would be not to talk. Is that correct? That is what you would tell a son, isn't it? . . . In other words, if you have constitutional rights, they should be accorded you."

But the state's attorney would not be moved. There was no legal requirement that he allow father and son to converse in private. He would release Nathan only after a writ of habeas corpus had been filed, and that would not happen until tomorrow morning, when the courts opened.

The interview was over, Crowe announced. The old man would have to leave his office. Nathan Leopold Sr. squeezed his son's hand for a brief moment, retrieved his coat and hat from an adjacent chair, and without a word to Crowe, left the room.[30]

CROWE WAS IMPATIENT TO BEGIN the examination. That morning he had found three psychiatrists willing to join the prosecution. He had asked them to come to the Criminal Court Building to examine Nathan Leopold and Richard Loeb.

Hugh Patrick was the first to arrive at Crowe's office. Patrick was sixty-four years old but seemed younger, no doubt because his manner—alert, energetic, and attentive—belied his age. His face was nondescript, neither fat nor thin, nor particularly memorable, save for his luminous blue eyes behind gold-rimmed eyeglasses. His snow white hair had receded but still retained a vestigial presence. He seemed the most amiable of men, someone who managed simultaneously to appear both authoritative and approachable.

Patrick had obtained his medical degree at Bellevue Hospital Medical College in New York; had completed postgraduate studies in Germany, Austria, France, and Britain; and, in 1894, had joined the medical faculty at Northwestern University as an assistant professor of nervous and mental diseases. Within the medical profession, Patrick soon won a national reputation as the founder and first editor of the leading journal for neurology, *Archives of Neurology and Psychiatry*. His affable manner and easy sociability gained him many friends and subsequently ensured his election as president of the Chicago Neurological Society, trustee of the Chicago Medical Society, president of the Institute of Medicine of Chicago, section chair of nervous and mental diseases of the American Medical Association, president of the Mississippi Valley Medical Association, and, last but not least, president of the American Neurological Association. In his spare time, Patrick served as a consultant neurologist to the Illinois Charitable Eye and Ear Infirmary, Wesley Memorial Hospital, St. Anthony Hospital, and the Illinois Eastern Hospital for the Insane at Kankakee. In 1924 he was a leader of his profession, the author of many articles and books, and an emeritus professor at Northwestern.[31]

Patrick introduced himself to Nathan. He looked around Crowe's office: it was a large room but sparsely furnished. There was a heavy oak desk in the center of the room, covered with papers and documents. In one corner there was a watercooler, and scattered around the room were about a dozen chairs, some metal, some wood, but neither one of which resembled its neighbor.

Hugh Patrick and Nathan Leopold chatted together while the stenographer, Elbert Allen, sat to one side, scribbling their remarks in shorthand into a notebook. They could hear a bustle in the outside corridor, but inside the office they were alone; even Robert Crowe had left the room, and none of his assistants were to be seen.[32]

A second psychiatrist, William Krohn, arrived at the Criminal Court Building at five minutes past three; Thomas O'Malley, chief of staff in the state's attorney's office, ushered Krohn into the room.[33]

Krohn was short and stocky, a compact bulldog of a man with a full head of white hair and an aggressive, confident demeanor. He invariably wore a dark bow tie, a crisp white shirt, and a well-cut gray suit. Krohn was fifty-six years old. He had received his PhD in psychology from Yale University in 1889 and, after postgraduate studies in Germany, Switzerland, and Austria, he had eventually secured a position as a clinical psychologist at the Illinois Eastern Hospital for the Insane. Krohn had remained at Illinois Eastern Hospital for seven years, establishing a psychological testing laboratory at the asylum for the evaluation of patients. He had taught successively at Clark University and the University of Illinois, and in 1899 he moved to Chicago to set up a private psychiatric clinic. Krohn simultaneously enrolled as a medical student at Northwestern University, where he studied in the department of nervous and mental diseases. After graduating from Northwestern in 1905, Krohn served frequently as a medical juror and as a member of the insanity commissions of the Cook County Criminal Court.[34]

He was a familiar sight at the Criminal Court, frequently testifying in high-profile cases on the sanity of the defendants. His 1924 textbook *Insanity and the Law: A Treatise on Forensic Psychiatry*, cowritten with H. Douglas Singer, had made his reputation as an expert on the legal aspects of psychiatry. As a consequence, Krohn was in great demand in the Chicago courts as an expert witness.

ROBERT CROWE HAD ASKED THE psychiatrists to the Criminal Court Building to evaluate Richard Loeb and Nathan Leopold. Crowe anticipated that the defense in the coming trial would most probably be a plea of not guilty by reason of insanity; he therefore aimed to counter the defense through an evaluation by the state's psychiatrists that Leopold and Loeb were sane.

So far, everything had worked brilliantly for Crowe; he had used his custody of Leopold and Loeb, first, to extract a confession from both boys; second, to link them irrevocably to the evidence; and third, to enable his psychiatrists to evaluate Leopold and Loeb while both boys were still cooperating with the police.

It would be futile, Crowe believed, for Nathan Leopold and Richard Loeb to deny their guilt on evidentiary grounds. Even if they claimed to have confessed under duress, Crowe had the physical evidence linking them to the murder: the rental car, the rope, the chisel, and, perhaps very soon, the typewriter. Neither Loeb nor Leopold had a credible alibi for the afternoon and evening of Wednesday, 21 May. It seemed impossible for the boys to deny that they had killed Bobby Franks.

A plea of not guilty by reason of insanity also seemed improbable—neither Leopold nor Loeb displayed any sign of mental derangement—but what alternative was there?

It would be difficult even for Leopold and Loeb to claim to have acted under temporary insanity. They had meticulously planned the murder for six months, paying close attention to detail, arranging to collect the ransom while avoiding capture, establishing false identities, and purchasing the necessary items. And after the deed had been done, they had carefully hidden the corpse, disposed of Bobby's clothing, and cleaned the rental car. Clearly the murder was neither an impulsive act nor a crime of passion.

Illinois law followed the British legal system in the determination of insanity. According to the McNaughten rule, adopted in Britain in 1843, an individual was considered insane if he or she had committed the act while not knowing its nature and quality or not knowing that it was wrong. Blame does not attach to the act, and punishment is inappropriate, because insanity deprives the individual of the free will to choose between right and wrong.

But how could one determine that a defendant was incapable of distinguishing right from wrong? Insanity was often not self-evident or obvious; only a psychiatrist with specialized medical knowledge could make that determination satisfactorily.

The defense attorneys would, no doubt, bring psychiatrists into court to testify that the defendants were insane. Crowe, therefore, needed to rebut the defense testimony through expert witnesses who would demonstrate that the defendants could distinguish right from wrong.

All the better, of course, if Nathan and Richard would confess their legal responsibility for the murder in the presence of the state's psychiatrists and the other witnesses. The psychiatrists' task would be facilitated if Nathan and Richard admitted that they were able to distinguish right from wrong and hence that they were legally sane. How could the defense lawyers enter a plea of not guilty by reason of insanity if Leopold and Loeb admitted their legal responsibility?

·   ·   ·

AT HALF PAST THREE, Archibald Church, the third psychiatrist, finally arrived.[35]

Church, fifty-three years old, cut an impressive figure. He took great pride in his appearance and was always meticulously dressed. He habitually had a rather melancholy expression; his large green eyes gazed out from a slightly bulbous face. He was courteous to a fault; indeed, his colleagues at Northwestern University Medical School found Church slightly pompous and aloof.

Church had received his medical degree from the College of Physicians and Surgeons in Chicago in 1884, and after four years' service as the assistant superintendent at the Illinois Northern Hospital for the Insane at Elgin, he had joined the medical faculty at Northwestern. He remained at Northwestern throughout his career as a professor of mental diseases and medical jurisprudence and held joint appointments as professor of neurology at the Chicago Policlinic and consulting neurologist at Michael Reese Hospital. Church was a leader of his profession, with a national reputation for his research in neurology. He had served as vice president of the American Neurological Association and as the section chair on mental and nervous diseases for the American Medical Association. He was the author of many articles and books, most notably the standard textbook in the field, *Nervous and Mental Diseases*, cowritten with Frederick Peterson of Columbia University.[36]

Church nodded a greeting to Hugh Patrick and William Krohn; he sat down with them in the center of the room, a few feet from Robert Crowe's desk. The office was beginning to fill up as more people arrived. Crowe's assistants—John Sbarbaro, Joseph Savage, and Milton Smith—talked quietly among themselves in one corner of the room. Michael Hughes and William Shoemacher sat to one side, waiting. The stenographer was there: Elbert Allen was still transcribing the informal conversations between Nathan and the psychiatrists. George Murray, a detective with the Illinois Central Railroad, had found a chair near the door; John Wesner, a physician, sat by his side, reading some notes from his briefcase; and Thomas O'Malley, the chief of staff assigned to Crowe's office, walked in and out of the room, checking that everything was in order.

Robert Crowe had followed Church into the room. The state's attorney had brought Richard Loeb with him. Now that the psychiatrists had arrived, Crowe prepared to start the examination.

Robert Crowe turned to Richard Loeb first.

"Go ahead and tell the story in your own way. Begin at the beginning."

"Well, I don't remember just exactly when it was." Richard paused to look at Nathan. "Leopold here says it was in November . . . that he first talked to me about this; and I don't remember just how it came about, we had been discussing crimes, and so forth." Richard hesitated again; he was aware that everyone in the room was watching him closely. "We talked it over, and about the possibilities of it. . . . The crime, if it was to be committed plausibly . . . could not be done unless there was some way of getting the money."[37]

Richard began to relax; soon he was speaking more coherently, telling how they had planned the kidnapping, carried out the murder, and disposed of the evidence. Richard claimed that Nathan had struck Bobby Franks; Nathan vehemently denied the accusation, but in all other respects he agreed with Richard's account.

Crowe waited patiently for Richard to finish speaking.

"Let me," Crowe began, "first ask one or two questions. Then we will hear from the other boy. The motive of this, you say, was what?"

"I don't know," Loeb replied hesitantly.

"You had money in the bank?"

"Yes," Loeb replied. "It was a seeking of adventure; money entered into it some, in a way, but I think the main thing was the adventure of the thing, and the—" Richard paused and shook his head indecisively. "Oh, God, I don't know, when I come to think about it."

William Krohn broke in: "Had you made arrangements that you were to divide the money, at all?"

"Yes, the money was to be split up."

"Split even, fifty-fifty?"

"Yes."

"Had you planned how you were to use the money in any way?"

"We arranged that [the] money was not to be used in the city of

Chicago or in this country for a year. Leopold had intended to go to Europe, and it was arranged he could spend the money in Europe if he wanted to."[38]

Richard Loeb admitted that the ransom money was not a sufficient motive for the murder. The ransom had added a element of complexity to the affair, but otherwise it was not important. The murder seemed inexplicable to him now; he had no satisfactory answer as to the motive.

"I feel so sorry. I have asked myself that question a million times. How did I possibly go into that thing?"

Hugh Patrick looked across at Nathan. "You cannot trace the original nucleus of it, can you, Mr. Leopold?"

"Yes, sir, I think I can," Nathan replied, decisively. "I am sure, as sure as I can be of anything, that is, as sure as you can read any other man's state of mind, the thing that prompted Dick to want to do this thing and prompted me to want to do this thing was a sort of pure love of excitement, or the imaginary love of thrills, doing something different; possibly . . . the satisfaction and the ego of putting something over. . . . The money consideration only came in afterwards, and never was important. The getting of the money was a part of our objective, as was also the commission of the crime; but that was not the exact motive."[39]

IF ROBERT CROWE WAS TO win a hanging verdict, he would have to convince the jury that the murder was a rational act. But what possible motive could there be for such a senseless murder? Neither Leopold nor Loeb had any especial reason to kill Bobby Franks. Richard Loeb had disliked his cousin, certainly, but not to any serious extent; Nathan Leopold had not even previously known Bobby.

In any case, both boys had claimed that they had selected Bobby by chance. He happened to be walking south on Ellis Avenue as they had driven by in the Willys-Knight. The victim might have been any one of a dozen boys in the vicinity of the Harvard School.

Could money be the motive for the killing? This, too, seemed implausible. Both Leopold and Loeb received generous monthly allowances. They did not lack money—why would they commit such a grievous crime for a relatively minor sum?

Could the desire for a thrill be the motive for the killing? Was it, as Nathan had stated to the reporters, akin to a scientific experiment whereby they could experience the sensation of killing another human being? But Crowe knew he could not claim that the murderers were sane and, at the same time, ask a jury to believe that they had killed a fourteen-year-old boy solely for the thrill of the experience.

It was, Crowe realized, a serious difficulty for the prosecution. The boys were rational and coherent—they displayed no signs of mental illness—yet they had committed an apparently irrational act. Indeed, the murder seemed to pass so far beyond the expected course of events as to force the conclusion that the perpetrators were insane. No matter how hard one looked, it was impossible to discover a rational motive for the killing of Bobby Franks.

NEITHER LEOPOLD NOR LOEB COULD adequately explain the murder; yet both willingly admitted their responsibility. There was no equivocation or ambiguity in this regard, at least: both had known, when they killed Bobby, that murder was wrong and both admitted that they could distinguish right from wrong.

Archibald Church had said little so far; now he turned to Nathan to ask him about his sense of criminal responsibility for the killing.

"Mr. Leopold, when you made this plan to do the killing, you understood perfectly your responsibilities in the matter?"

"My answer is, yes, sir."

"The criminal act for which certain penalties were provided, and all that?"

"Yes, sir."

Church returned briefly to the question of motive. Perhaps, he suggested, they had wanted to demonstrate their superiority over the Chicago police.

"Were you actuated by a motive to put over some such thing as this without being detected, as it were, to put one over on the detective forces?"

"That I am sure was a large part of Mr. Loeb's attitude, and I think it was a small part of mine. Sort of egotism."[40]

Robert Crowe brought the questioning back to the boys' sense of responsibility; he turned, this time, to Richard Loeb.

"Mr. Loeb, do you know the difference between right and wrong?"

"Yes, sir."

"You think you did the right thing in this particular matter?"

"In the Franks case?"

"Yes."

"Absolutely not."

"And you know it is wrong to kidnap a boy?"

"Yes, sir."

"What is your idea about right or wrong of getting a boy and kidnaping him?"

"It is wrong, sir."

"You know the consequence of this act, don't you?"

"Yes."[41]

The state's attorney could not have hoped for a more satisfying answer. Crowe glanced across at the stenographer as if to assure himself that Loeb's answers had been correctly recorded. Both prisoners had admitted their legal responsibility for the murder! No defense attorney in Chicago could get around that admission! How could they plead insanity now?

As Crowe reflected on his good fortune in having Leopold and Loeb in custody without interference from defense lawyers, William Krohn continued to interrogate Loeb. Krohn was well versed in legal procedure; he, too, could scarcely believe that Leopold and Loeb had so effectively sabotaged their last line of defense: by admitting legal responsibility, they had denied their lawyers any chance of saving them from the gallows.

"Had you," Krohn asked Loeb, "any feeling of detracting or giving up the scheme?"

"No, sir, I don't think so."

16. INSIDE THE STATE'S ATTORNEY'S OFFICE. On Saturday, 31 May 1924, Robert Crowe and members of his staff posed with Richard Loeb and Nathan Leopold in the office of the state's attorney on the third floor of the Criminal Court Building. Seated (from left): Richard Loeb, John Sbarbaro, Robert Crowe, Nathan Leopold, and Joseph Savage.

"You always felt as if you were going to go right through with it?"

"Yes, sir. . . . Yes, I really think I did."

"Didn't want to be called a quitter?"

"Yes, that's just it. I have always hated anybody that was a coward."

"You realize now, though, that you had the power to refrain from doing it?"

"Yes, sir."

"You could have refrained from doing a wrong thing?"

"Yes, sir."

"You had the power of will and choice to decide whether you would do it or not?"

"Yes, sir."

"You had that all the time?"

"Yes, sir. . . ."

"You had full control of doing it?"

"Yes, sir."[42]

IT WAS ALMOST SIX O'CLOCK—TIME, Crowe decided, to conclude the examination. He had obtained everything that he might reasonably have expected. Both Leopold and Loeb had confessed their guilt, a second time, before reputable witnesses, and both had admitted their legal responsibility for the murder; neither had attempted to deny culpability.

The state's psychiatrists had had ample opportunity to evaluate the two prisoners. All three psychiatrists agreed that neither Nathan nor Richard had shown even the slightest sign of mental illness. Quite the opposite: throughout the interview, the boys had been self-possessed, coherent, rational, and lucid. There was no evidence of insanity.

Crowe had learned that the families of the boys had hired Clarence Darrow that morning as the defense attorney. Crowe had not forgotten how Darrow had humiliated him, the previous year, in the trial of Fred Lundin, a prominent Republican politician, on charges of corruption. Now he would exact his revenge; he had a hanging case here: both Leopold and Loeb were going to the gallows, and even that old scoundrel Clarence Darrow—one of Crowe's most bitter enemies—would not be able to save them from the noose.

It would be an epic battle. Darrow and Crowe were polar opposites. Darrow was a determinist. One's actions, Darrow believed, were a consequence of forces that compelled each individual to behave in a certain manner. The criminal did not freely choose wrongdoing; rather, factors outside his or her conscious control acted to determine criminal behavior. There was no such thing as individual responsibility. Imprisonment was futile and even counterproductive; it served no purpose either as a deterrent or as a punishment.

Such views were anathema to Robert Crowe. Could any philosophy be more destructive of social harmony than Darrow's? The murder rate in Chicago was higher than it had ever been, yet Darrow would do away with punishment! Crime, Crowe believed, would decline only through the more rigorous application of the law. Criminals were fully responsible for their actions and should be treated accordingly—it was foolishness to absolve them of blame for their misdeeds.

The trial of Nathan Leopold and Richard Loeb would be a contest between two charismatic individuals—Darrow, who had built his reputation by defending unpopular causes; and Crowe, the most competent and energetic state's attorney in a generation. And there would be a second contest, a contest between opposing philosophies of crime and punishment. Which one would triumph?

PART TWO

THE ATTORNEYS

8 | CLARENCE DARROW

The distinguished gentleman whose profession it is to protect murder in Cook County, and concerning whose health thieves inquire before they go to commit crime, has seen fit to abuse the State's Attorney's office. . . . He has even objected to the State's Attorney referring to two self-confessed murderers, who have pleaded guilty to two capital offenses, as criminals.[1]

Robert Crowe, 26 August 1924

I assume you are intending to practise law when you finish your college-course. It is a bum profession, as generally practised. It is utterly devoid of idealism, and almost poverty-stricken as to any real ideas. Of course, however, there is a lot of chance to do some good in this profession if you can get along without making money your ambition. If you enter the field of law with the idea of helping those who need it most you will have a very interesting life, full of hard work and misunderstandings and misrepresentations,—but you will be able to do something toward alleviating the miseries and sorrows of unfortunates.[2]

Clarence Darrow, 4 November 1933

EUGENE PRENDERGAST HAD PURCHASED the gun earlier that day. Now, as he crossed Ogden Avenue and continued past the Third Presbyterian Church on his right, he touched it once again through the thin lining of his jacket pocket. It was, in 1893, one of the most reliable pistols that one could buy: a Harrington and Richardson top-break .38-caliber revolver. He had carefully oiled it just a few hours earlier. As he turned down Ashland Avenue, toward the mayor's residence, Prendergast felt satisfied that very soon he would have won his revenge for the slights he had endured.[3]

He had worked hard for the mayor's reelection the previous April. The mayor, Carter Harrison, had promised to appoint him corporation counsel; but all his letters to the mayor's office had gone unanswered. Prendergast had no legal training—indeed, he had no qualifications beyond high school—but that was surely irrelevant. He had never even met the mayor; but that too was inconsequential. His plans for the city—ambitious, clear-sighted plans

17. CLARENCE DARROW. In 1887 Darrow moved with his wife and infant son from his hometown of Ashtabula, Ohio, to Chicago. He won notoriety and fame as an attorney for the labor movement, successfully defending members of the American Railway Union and the Western Federation of Miners.

that envisaged the construction of a new streetcar system—were ample qualification for the position of corporation counsel, and yet the mayor had continued to insult him by ignoring his many petitions.[4]

The maid, Mary Hansen, answered the doorbell and ushered the visitor into the hallway. Prendergast waited ten minutes until, shortly after eight o'clock, Harrison, a large man with an affable manner and a distinctive white beard, appeared in the vestibule. Harrison was in a good mood; he had spoken earlier that day at a public meeting to mark the closing of the 1893 Columbian Exposition and his audience had responded enthusiastically, praising his administration for the success of the event.[5]

The two men argued briefly. As Prendergast began to press his demands, Harrison realized that it may have been a mistake to have dispensed with his police bodyguard.

"I tell you," he declared to his visitor, with exasperation in his voice, "I won't do it."

He turned slightly, as though to end their conversation; but before Harrison could step away, Prendergast had pushed the barrel of his revolver against the mayor's waistcoat. His first bullet struck Harrison in the abdomen; his second bullet tore through the mayor's chest, passing slightly above his heart; and the third bullet, fired as Harrison lay bleeding on the ground, wounded him in the left hand.[6]

At his trial later that year, Prendergast, a twenty-five-year-old Irishman with a nervous, agitated manner and no visible means of support, boasted that his action had saved Chicago from certain disaster. He had no regrets over Harrison's death, he explained to the court; the killing had been justified and, just as soon as everyone realized the benefits that would accrue from the mayor's demise, he, Prendergast, would be released from prison and lauded as a hero.[7]

His lawyer's plea was not guilty by reason of insanity. The psychiatrists for the defense explained the murder as a consequence of hereditary insanity—several of Prendergast's relatives had suffered from mental illness. But on 29 December 1893 the jury, after deliberating for less than one hour, returned to the courtroom to declare the defendant guilty and to fix the punishment as death by hanging.[8]

Clarence Darrow was one of several lawyers in Chicago convinced that Prendergast had suffered from a miscarriage of justice. The trial, Darrow believed, had been a travesty. At least one juror knew the mayor as a friend and had concealed that fact from the court. On one occasion, the bailiffs, escorting the jurors to a polling station to vote in the fall elections, had allowed the twelve jurymen to mingle with members of the public. And Prendergast, despite the guilty verdict, seemed, by his eccentric behavior during the trial, oblivious of the gravity of his situation and incapable of distinguishing right from wrong.[9]

DARROW HAD MOVED FROM ASHTABULA, Ohio, to Chicago with his first wife, Jessie, and their infant son, Paul, in 1887. He was twenty-nine years old when he made the move, broad-shouldered, taller than the average man, with a physical presence embodying a determination and ambition that would not be easily turned aside. Nothing in his expression betrayed any hint of self-doubt; nothing in his eyes—brown eyes flecked with green—ever revealed any hesitancy; nothing in his face, with its broad brow and cleft chin, showed anything other than certitude. Even as a young man, Darrow had a presence that commanded respect; and, as he grew into middle age, his ability in the courtroom endowed him with a reputation as an attorney sui generis; there was no one, among the lawyers of the Chicago bar, who could rival Darrow.[10]

Few Chicagoans were as gregarious as Clarence Darrow, and not long after moving to the city Darrow joined the Sunset Club, a debating society for radicals and progressives. He quickly made his mark as a public speaker, participating in discussions on such topics as land taxation and political economy. Darrow had dabbled in Democratic Party politics back in Ohio—he had served as secretary of the Ashtabula County Democratic Convention and had been a delegate to the 1885 state convention at Columbus—and now, in Chicago, he became an active party member, speaking at election meetings, hobnobbing with local politicians, and gradually winning a reputation as an effective speaker and a capable organizer.

He was a disciple of Henry George—Darrow considered *Progress and Poverty* one of the most important and influential books of the time—and, in Chicago, he joined the Single Tax Club, a group of zealots dedicated to the proposition that a tax on the increase in the value of land would eliminate economic inequality. He opposed the tariff and first attracted public attention as a speaker for the Tariff Reform Convention, a group committed to the principles of free trade.[11]

But no single cause was as important to Darrow as the campaign to free the Haymarket prisoners. On 4 May 1886, during a meeting of anarchists in the Haymarket on West Randolph Street, a bomb had exploded, killing one policeman and injuring several others. The police had fired into the crowd gathered around the speakers' platform; gunfire had been exchanged between the anarchists and the police; and by the end of the evening, eight more policemen lay dead. Several protesters also died that day, killed by police bullets, but in the immediate aftermath of the shootings, the Chicago newspapers pinned the blame for the violence on the leaders of Chicago's anarchist movement.[12]

The authorities were quick to take their revenge. At the trial of eight anarchists for murder, the state's attorney was unable to produce any evidence that directly connected the defendants to the Haymarket bombing. But the accused were prominent speakers and writers, and the prosecution, quoting liberally from the anarchist newspapers, was able to convince the jury of the defendants' guilt. Four anarchists died on the scaffold in the Cook County jail; one committed suicide in his cell; and three others received long prison sentences.[13]

Police repression fell heavily on the Chicago labor movement in the months after the Haymarket bombing, but by the end of 1886 the socialist societies and trade unions had regrouped around the campaign for a pardon for the three surviving Haymarket prisoners. Darrow joined the Amnesty Association in 1887, not long after he first arrived in Chicago, and he was quick to take the lead in the organization, traveling frequently to Springfield to petition the governor of Illinois for clemency for the prisoners. The authorities had rushed the anarchists to trial in an atmosphere of hysteria and paranoia, Darrow believed; the newspapers had stoked a vengeful campaign; and the judge and jury had been prejudiced against the defendants from the outset.

Darrow's efforts were eventually successful—in 1893, the governor, citing irregularities in the trial, granted the three prisoners a pardon.[14]

It was the first of many victories in Darrow's lifelong campaign on behalf of the defenseless. The judicial system, Darrow believed, was an institution dedicated to the interests of the capitalist class; it acted in concert with the police and other authorities to deny the poor their constitutional rights. The courts were inherently prejudiced against the impoverished and the outcast, and radical lawyers, such as himself, had an obligation to contest all judgments, at least judgments against their clients, as illegitimate and unjust.

Darrow had an especial hatred of the death penalty as a barbaric anachronism that had no place in American society. Capital punishment, he believed, was a relic of a bygone era; the death penalty was a cruel, brutal, purposeless punishment that failed to deter criminals. It was legal murder by the state, Darrow claimed, and, more often than not, it caught innocent persons in its maw.[15]

THE COOK COUNTY CRIMINAL COURT had scheduled the execution of Eugene Prendergast for Friday, 23 March 1894. But Clarence Darrow had taken an interest in the case, and he intended to save Prendergast from the scaffold. Prendergast was obviously insane; his legal counsel in the original trial had been woefully inadequate; and public feeling toward the defendant had been unremittingly hostile. It would not be right, it would not be just, to stand idly by and let the hangman fasten his noose around the neck of a man so clearly incapable of distinguishing right from wrong.

Prendergast was fortunate to have obtained such a capable lawyer. Darrow was not the most experienced lawyer in Cook County—he had had only limited practice before the Criminal Court in the years since he had moved to Chicago—but he was infinitely resourceful. Darrow knew the law in its intricacy and its complexity and, like every conscientious lawyer, he had no scruples in exploiting the law in the attempt to save his client's life.

Darrow appealed first to the Illinois supreme court for a supersedeas; but the court rejected his petition—it would not stay the decision of the lower court.

Darrow next appealed to the United States District Court for a writ of habeas corpus. The Cook County Criminal Court, Darrow argued, had deprived Prendergast of due process, and the federal court should intervene to safeguard the defendant's constitutional rights. But the District Court refused Darrow also; it was not a matter, the justices declared, that fell within the court's jurisdiction.[16]

Might the governor of Illinois grant executive clemency? John Altgeld, the governor, was traveling outside the state, and in his stead the lieutenant governor, John B. Gill, heard Darrow's petition. But Gill, a politician known for his conservative views, was too canny to risk his career for an unpopular cause—he too rejected Darrow's appeal.[17]

Any other man might have given up hope; but Darrow was too tenacious, too persistent, to abandon Prendergast to the scaffold so easily. He had discovered an obscure clause, buried deep within the Illinois criminal code, that might yet save Prendergast's life. It had lain unnoticed, unseen, and unremarked, for decades; only Darrow's patient reading of the statutes had brought it to light. Now he intended to use it to his advantage.

Section 285 of the Illinois criminal code specified that if a defendant, after judgment and before execution of sentence, should become insane, the court should postpone execution until the defendant had recovered his sanity. Prendergast had become insane, Darrow argued, subsequent to his conviction, and the court should send him to an asylum until he regained his sanity.[18]

So, although, in the original trial, the jury had disregarded the claim of the defense that Prendergast was insane, it seemed that the assassin would have a second opportunity to escape the noose. It was, according to Levy Mayer, a leader of the Chicago bar, an ominous development that threatened to subvert the foundations of criminal justice in Cook County. If Darrow succeeded in winning a second trial in a lower court after the state supreme court had refused to issue a supersedeas to stay the original judgment, would it not mean that a lower court might annul the decision of the higher court? "The only plea of Prendergast," Mayer remarked to the newspapers, "on his trial was that of insanity. Upon that defense the jury found against him. The court rendered judgment and the Supreme Court concurred. . . . Another inquiry as to his sanity is simply an appeal to a lower court from a conviction which has already been confirmed by the highest court. . . . Thoughtful men will consider the precedent thus established with considerable alarm. It adds another to the already too numerous technicalities and obstacles in the way of a prompt and speedy enforcement of the criminal law."[19]

In a more general sense, such critics argued that Darrow's ingenuity threatened to bring the law itself into disrepute. The novelty of the tactic, its application in such a prominent case, and the unfortunate precedent that it would create—all contributed to the public vilification of Darrow as a trickster who would use a loophole in the legal code to postpone judgment indefinitely and thus deny justice. Clever lawyers had already burdened the legal system with technicalities founded on recondite passages in the criminal code—if Darrow now succeeded in saving Prendergast's life by claiming that his client had become insane after sentence had been passed, would not the same tactic be used generally in the Chicago courts to prevent the execution of murderers?

Darrow succeeded in winning a second trial, but he failed to save Prendergast's life. Medical experts testified, again, that Prendergast was a paranoiac; but the jury, after deliberating for ten days, decided that the defendant had the ability to distinguish right from wrong—thus, in a legal sense at least, he was sane. The case had run its course. Neither the state supreme court nor the governor of Illinois responded to petitions from the defense, and on Friday, 13 July 1894, the hangman pulled the trap of the gallows to end Prendergast's life.

THE CASE HAD ENDED BADLY for the prisoner, but for Darrow it had brought a first taste of fame. Some critics viewed Darrow's role as illjudged: he had applied an obscure statute to prolong the life of an assassin who had willfully murdered the mayor of Chicago. Darrow seemed, in this telling, the epitome of the shyster lawyer, concerned less with truth and justice than with abetting an infamous criminal. Other commentators, more sensitive to the constitutional safeguards that ensured due process of the law, commended Darrow for an astute and resourceful defense of his client. The state legislature had provided for the insanity defense when it had revised the Illinois criminal code in 1845; surely no reproof should attach to a lawyer who used the statutes to defend his client.

It never troubled Darrow that he might be accused of manipulating the law in the attempt to save Prendergast from the scaffold. Perhaps he had exploited a loophole in the criminal code—but so what? Was a lawyer not supposed to seek out every possible advantage and use it to the maximum effect to rescue his client? Any attorney who failed to use such tactics, Darrow believed, was remiss in fulfilling his obligation to pursue every possible defense.

And although he had failed, in this case, to save his client, his effort had contributed, nevertheless, to the campaign against the death penalty.

Prendergast's defense was one of many such cases against capital punishment that Darrow undertook—with little prospect of financial reward—in the course of his long career. Typically the defendant would be the author of a heinous crime committed in bizarre circumstances; he customarily suffered from mental illness and failed to comprehend the gravity of the crime. Such clients had limited resources and few friends; they were vulnerable and alone; and from the moment of their arrest they were marked for the scaffold.

Such cases, Darrow believed, illustrated the injustice of capital punishment. The death penalty was born out of hatred toward the criminal. It had no purpose except revenge. There was no evidence that capital punishment was a deterrent to murder. Indeed, Darrow argued, since the taking of a life was an act of violence that corroded sentiments of charity and respect toward one's fellows, it followed that the death penalty cheapened and devalued human life and that it was more an inducement to murder than a deterrent.

If hanging the murderer was meant to serve as a deterrent, why not carry out executions in public before the largest possible audience?

How could hanging serve to deter if it was hidden away, unseen, in a private chamber? And, of course, the death penalty was irrevocable—there could be no reversal. It was a punishment that in its certitude allowed for no mistakes or errors of judgment on the part of the court.

IN HIS OLD AGE, when writing his autobiography, Darrow could recall those occasions when his father, Amirus, had spoken, his voice suffused with regret, of his attendance at a public hanging. Amirus had been one of many hundreds of spectators at the event and he had played no other role in the proceedings, yet many years later, he confessed to his son his shame that he had witnessed the cold-blooded killing of another human being. Amirus's abhorrence of capital punishment had had little impact on his son: as a young man, Clarence, living and working as a lawyer in Ashtabula, had accepted the conventional attitude toward criminality. Crime was the consequence of a deliberate choice on the part of the criminal to commit wrongdoing; it deserved, therefore, the appropriate punishment. Clarence Darrow's belief that each individual exercised free will in choosing good or evil was unexceptional, at least in the small-town atmosphere of Ashtabula where his clients and acquaintances—farmers, businessmen, bankers, and tradesmen—also subscribed to the expectations of conventional morality.[20]

Everything changed for Darrow after he read John Peter Altgeld's *Our Penal Machinery and Its Victims*. A neighbor, one of the local judges on the county court, had lent him the book, and Darrow had devoured it at a single sitting. Altgeld's thesis, that crime is a consequence of social and economic pressures bearing down relentlessly on susceptible individuals, relied on a persuasive combination of statistics and rhetoric. Criminal behavior, according to *Our Penal Machinery*, was less a consequence of free will and deliberation and more a matter of education, upbringing, and environment. The majority of criminals—the overwhelming majority, Altgeld stressed—had grown up in circumstances of dire poverty, in families where one or both parents were absent, and without the benefits of education, schooling, or discipline. Many had never known their parents or had run away from home at an early age; they had drifted to the slum areas of the big cities and had taken up crime as a way to earn a living. Altgeld claimed to have examined the annual reports of all the major prisons in the United States and could assert authoritatively that criminals, almost all of whom had committed their first crime at an early age, are "the poor, the unfortunate, the young and neglected.... To a great extent, [they] are the victims of unfavorable environments. In short, our penal machinery seems to recruit its victims from among those who are fighting an unequal fight in the struggle for existence."[21]

Altgeld's work was as much a jeremiad against the destructive effects of the prison as a dissertation on the causes of crime. Nothing, Altgeld asserted, could be less capable of serving the purpose of rehabilitation than the penal system of the United States. The authorities treated all criminals alike, regardless of their age or the severity of their offense, incarcerating youthful delinquents together with hardened criminals. Conditions inside most prisons were squalid, degrading, and vicious; overcrowding was the rule, rather than the exception; the prisoner spent his or her time either in enforced idleness or in purposeless work; and the prison guards maintained discipline with sadism and brutality. There was, Altgeld concluded, little possibility that anyone would emerge rehabilitated from the penitentiary and little wonder that the rate of recidivism in the United States was so high.

Nothing that Clarence Darrow ever read, either before or since, had as great an impact on his thinking as *Our Penal Machinery*. His former belief that crime was a matter of choice, a willful act freely taken, was now replaced by its opposite, the conviction that environmental circumstances—poverty, unemployment, illiteracy—determined criminal behavior. Indeed Darrow went farther than Altgeld in his determinism. An individual, Darrow believed, could not choose not to commit crime if circumstances dictated otherwise—free will was an illusion and a chimera, and all that mattered was the environment within which an individual had been born and raised.

By 1894, Darrow had achieved renown within Cook County as a clever speaker and an astute lawyer. He had represented the Haymarket prisoners and had defended the assassin of the mayor—his reputation within Cook County as the champion of the weak and defenseless seemed secure. But beyond Chicago, he remained unknown; few people elsewhere, in other parts of the country, recognized his name.

That would soon change: Darrow would quickly become the most famous lawyer in the United States, with a national, and even an international, reputation as a brilliantly resourceful advocate of the rights of labor and the workingman.

Darrow's fame would rest on two pillars: his knowledge of the law and his ability as a public speaker. The first would earn him his reputation within the legal community; the second would win him a degree of recognition unmatched by that of any other lawyer in the country.

Among the lawyers of the Chicago bar, few were as ingenious or as skillful as Clarence Darrow. He was a resourceful attorney whose detailed knowledge of the Illinois criminal code enabled him to win courtroom battles even under the most improbable and adverse circumstances.

It was his skill as a tactician that earned Darrow a reputation among his peers as a formidable adversary, but it was his talent as an orator that brought him more general recognition. In the courtroom, Darrow always seemed to speak as though the cause of his client had become his own cause, and in his appeals to the jury he mixed reason and emotion in a powerful combination that rarely failed to persuade his listeners of the innocence of his client.

Darrow might face overwhelming odds; his case might seem hopeless; his client might seem sure to be convicted. But when Darrow turned to face the jury to begin his concluding speech, always in that low, gravelly voice that rumbled on and on—suddenly something magical would happen in the courtroom. Darrow's eloquence, passion, and conviction would catch and hold his listeners; his emotion, always conveyed at a perfect pitch, would resonate with the jurymen so that they too could understand the justice, the rectitude, and the integrity of his appeal.

It happened again and again—it was as predictable as the summer sunshine and the winter snowstorms. No matter what the odds, Darrow always won his case. His client might be entirely despicable—a murderer and a rapist, perhaps, or a crooked politician, or, more prosaically, a brothel owner and a pimp—yet Darrow was sure to win the defendant the best possible outcome that the circumstances would allow.

IT WAS THEREFORE NO SURPRISE that Eugene Debs, the leader of the American Railway Union, would hire Darrow to defend him against conspiracy charges in connection with a boycott of the Pullman Car Works. Debs had established the American Railway Union in Chicago in 1893 to defend the wages and working conditions of railroad workers, and during its first year, the union had won strikes against the Union Pacific Railroad and then against the Great Northern Railroad.[22]

Flushed with success after vanquishing two of the most powerful railroad corporations in the country, Debs called his members to take action against the Pullman Car Works. The owner of the company, George Pullman, had refused to negotiate with his workers over a pay cut. They had come out on strike, and in June 1894, the American Railway Union, acting in sympathy with the Pullman workers, declared a boycott of all Pullman cars—no member of the union would handle a Pullman car or any train connected to a Pullman car.

It was a step too far—at least according to the General Managers' Association, a powerful federation of twenty-four railroad corporations. The association, now intent on crushing the railroad union, protested to the federal authorities that the boycott was clearly illegal, since it would both obstruct interstate commerce and prevent delivery of the mails. Should the authorities not therefore take action against Debs and his followers?

On 3 July 1894, the United States District Court issued an injunction against the American Railway Union. Debs responded by calling for a general strike against the railroad corporations, and one week later the authorities arrested Debs on charges of conspiring to obstruct interstate commerce and to prevent delivery of the mails.[23]

When the case came to court in January 1895, Clarence Darrow was ready with his defense. The prosecution accused Debs of conspiracy, yet, Darrow explained, no one had been indicted for carrying out the acts that Debs had allegedly conspired to bring about! The real conspiracy, Darrow alleged, was between George Pullman, owner of the Pullman Car Works and the General Managers' Association: a conspiracy to pressure federal authorities to press charges against Debs in order to break the back of the union. He would, Darrow announced to the court, ask for a subpoena for George Pullman to appear in court to testify about his relationship with the railroad corporations and the federal authorities.

It was a brilliant maneuver that caught the prosecution by surprise. Pullman refused to appear in court—he ignored the subpoena—and by a lucky coincidence one of the jurors became ill, forcing the judge to discharge the jury. The judge announced that he would postpone the trial until May, but Pullman's refusal to appear in court had torpedoed the state's case against Debs and the conspiracy charges were quietly dropped.[24]

It was a famous victory—for Debs, of course, and for Clarence Darrow. This had been a bitter contest, an epic battle between capital and labor, and it had captured the attention of the nation. Darrow had rescued Debs from a lengthy prison term, and now Darrow had the fame and renown that he had so much desired. He was no longer merely a Cook County attorney. Darrow was now the most famous lawyer in the United States.

IN SUBSEQUENT YEARS, EACH CASE that Darrow undertook enlarged his reputation; he had become a mythical figure who, through a combination of charisma and guile, always defeated his enemies. His private life was often tempestuous—his first wife, Jessie, had divorced him in 1897, and six years later Darrow married Ruby Hamerstrom—but in public Darrow seemed beyond reproach.

In 1897 he struck at the conspiracy laws a second time, in his de-

fense of Thomas Kidd, the general secretary of the Amalgamated Woodworkers Union. Kidd had organized employees of the Paine Lumber
Company in Oshkosh, Wisconsin, in a strike for higher wages. The local
authorities had charged Kidd with conspiracy. Darrow used the same
strategy that he had employed on behalf of Eugene Debs. The real conspiracy, Darrow claimed in court, was between the Paine Lumber Company and the state authorities to crush the woodworkers' union. Darrow
succeeded a second time: the jury acquitted Kidd of all charges.[25]

Darrow relished such opportunities to defend workers against their
bosses. The cause of the working class was always just, Darrow believed,
and his defense of constitutional rights served to extend the democratic
liberties of all people. And it was a happy coincidence that such labor
trials brought Darrow enormous publicity as the foremost advocate of
the oppressed and downtrodden. Darrow had little patience for the
humdrum business of the law: the accumulation of evidence, the win-
nowing of precedents, and the logical construction of a client's case.
Such tasks constituted a necessary evil, which had to be borne if he was
to make a living. Darrow always carried such burdensome tasks ungra-
ciously, hoping always to make enough money so that he could choose
his clients. Darrow's enthusiasm caught fire only when great principles
were at stake, most typically when he could fight on behalf of the
underdog.

In 1907 Darrow assumed responsibility for the defense of the leaders of the Western Federation of Miners on charges of murder. Labor
struggles between mine workers and the owners had convulsed the
western states for decades and had grown in ferocity year by year. During the previous decade, the miners had successfully organized unions
and had won national support for their strikes, eliciting sympathy and
assistance from the American Federation of Labor.

Nowhere was the struggle more bitter, more protracted, and more
violent than in Idaho. Battles between capital and labor within the state
had lasted for years, and memories of the violence inflicted by both sides
persisted in the mining districts long after hostilities had subsided. In
1899 Frank Steunenberg, the governor of Idaho, had earned the enmity

of the mine workers' unions after using troops to crush a series of strikes in the Coeur d'Alene region. Six years later, long after Steunenberg had left office, a bomb exploded at his residence, instantly killing him.[26]

The authorities quickly found the murderer. Harry Orchard had been in the nearest town, Caldwell, for several days, planning the bombing. After the police discovered explosives in his hotel room, Orchard confessed to the killing of Steunenberg. But, Orchard claimed, he had not acted alone: leaders of the Western Federation of Miners (WFM) had ordered the bombing. One month later the Idaho authorities seized three WFM officials, William (Big Bill) Haywood, Charles Moyer, and George Pettibone, in Colorado and transported them, illegally, without extradition papers, to Idaho.[27]

At the trial of Bill Haywood in May 1907, Clarence Darrow attacked the prosecution's star witness, Harry Orchard, as a liar and a perjurer. Orchard, by his own admission, had lived a rootless, peripatetic existence, drifting through the western states and leaving behind him a trail of mayhem and destruction, including no fewer than nineteen murders. Orchard was not a credible witness, Darrow asserted; he had agreed to testify against Haywood and the other WFM leaders in exchange for a lesser sentence.

Darrow, in his closing speech, mesmerized the jury into acquiescence; the twelve jurymen retired to consider their verdict and returned to declare Haywood not guilty. It was a stunning verdict, received with jubilation by the labor unions. That evening, as the mine workers held a victory parade through the streets of Boise, congratulatory telegrams from around the nation began to arrive, praising Darrow for his magnificent defense of the union officials. The trial of Bill Haywood had been a national event, reported each day by newspapers around the country, and Darrow had consolidated his position as the most famous attorney of his generation.[28]

BUT DARROW'S RENOWN WAS NOT to last. Three years later, on 1 October 1910, a bomb destroyed the *Los Angeles Times* building, killing twenty workers. The newspaper had long been a bitter enemy of the labor unions. Metal trades workers in Los Angeles had been on strike through the summer, and the *Los Angeles Times* had led a campaign to defeat the strike. Soon the authorities had two suspects in custody: John J. McNamara, the secretary-treasurer of the International Association of Bridge and Structural Iron Workers, and his younger brother, Jim McNamara.

Samuel Gompers, president of the American Federation of Labor, declared that the brothers were innocent: no union leader would have countenanced such a destructive and malicious act. Just as the authorities had framed Bill Haywood three years previously for the killing of Frank Steunenberg, so they had now determined to send the McNamaras to the gallows. The frame-up was an attack on the American labor movement, Gompers announced, and the entire resources of that movement would be at the disposal of the defense.

Clarence Darrow arrived in California to take charge of the defense in June 1911. The trial was to be the next round in the battle between capital and labor, and unions from around the country had sent funds to support the defense. The attack on the McNamara brothers was an attack on workingmen everywhere, and with Clarence Darrow at the helm, it was an attack that was sure to be repulsed.[29]

But Darrow soon realized that the brothers had in fact bombed the *Los Angeles Times.* Jim McNamara, the younger brother, had placed the bomb beside some barrels of printer's ink in an alley adjacent to the *Times* building. The massive explosion had caused fatalities that neither brother had either anticipated or desired. The evidence against the brothers was incontrovertible, and if Darrow proceeded with the defense, there was every chance that the court would find them guilty and send them to the gallows.

On 1 December 1911, the McNamara brothers pleaded guilty. For organized labor, the pleas came as a shock—labor had endlessly proclaimed the innocence of the McNamaras and had contributed hundreds of thousands of dollars to the defense fund. Clarence Darrow was the obvious scapegoat. Had Darrow not assured the world that the McNamaras were innocent? The labor movement had accepted Darrow's word; he had taken the unions on a long and expensive ride, confessing the brothers' guilt only after having spent enormous sums of money in preparing a defense. When had Darrow first realized the guilt of the defendants? Had his assurances of their innocence been a means of squeezing the unions for defense funds and thus enriching himself?[30]

Darrow's reputation lay in tatters. He was now a pariah, shunned by the labor unions as unreliable and untrustworthy. And Darrow himself now faced the possibility of a prison sentence: one of his assistants had attempted to bribe a prospective juror, and in spring 1912, the authorities indicted Darrow for suborning bribery. He escaped a prison sentence—in his first trial, the prosecution failed to convince the jury that he had been a knowing participant in the bribery plot; and in a second trial, the jurors had failed to agree among themselves.[31]

Darrow was now free to return to Chicago, yet his career and fame seemed over, damaged beyond repair. He could still practice as an attorney, of course, and he could still earn a living, but he would never again command the national spotlight in defense of the oppressed. Darrow seemed condemned to the fate he had always hoped to avoid: a humdrum law practice.

In 1914 he became a partner with the socialist lawyer Peter Sissman and established the law firm of Darrow, Sissman, Holly, and Carlin, with offices at 140 North Dearborn Street. Despite his association with Sissman, the labor unions and socialist groups in Chicago shunned Darrow. There would be no work for him from that quarter in the aftermath of the crushing humiliation in Los Angeles, and Darrow, cut off from the labor movement, began an association with some of Chicago's less savory characters, including prominent members of the mob. In 1916, after the state's attorney, Maclay Hoyne, began an investigation into illegal gambling, Darrow represented Mont Tennes, a gangster who controlled betting at the Hawthorne racetrack. The following year Hoyne oversaw an investigation into political corruption and caught Oscar DePriest, the sole black alderman, in his net. Hoyne indicted DePriest for bribing the police and for his connections to gambling rings and prostitution rackets within the African-American community, but after a lengthy trial, Darrow won the acquittal of DePriest on all charges. Darrow also secured the acquittal of Charles Healey, Chicago's chief of police, who had been charged with corruption and bribery in 1917.

The entry of the United States into World War I confirmed his friends' suspicion that Darrow had drifted away from radical politics and toward the center. Darrow had become an ardent supporter of American involvement and of Woodrow Wilson, on moral grounds: Germany, an aggressively militaristic power, had violated the neutrality of Belgium. Darrow joined the National Security League, the principal group advocating American participation in the war, and spent several months in 1917 and 1918 traveling around the country speaking in support of the government's foreign policy.

Yet Darrow strongly opposed Wilson's antidemocratic restrictions on free speech at home, and Darrow's efforts on behalf of anarchists, communists, and antiwar protesters helped restore some of his reputation within progressive circles. In 1917 anarchists in Milwaukee fought a gun battle with the police and subsequently received long prison sentences for conspiracy to assault with intent to murder. Eighteen months later, in March 1919, Darrow presented the appeal to the Wisconsin supreme court and succeeded in overturning the convictions.

Darrow also defended members of the Communist Labor Party on charges of violating the Espionage Act. Twenty members of the party stood trial in 1919 in the Cook County Criminal Court. Despite Darrow's best efforts, including a closing speech that attacked the prosecution for trampling on the constitutional rights of the defendants, the jury found the communists guilty of advocating the overthrow of the government.[32]

Darrow thus managed to remain in the public eye throughout the 1910s. His pronouncements and opinions continued to appear in the Chicago newspapers, of course, and occasionally his court cases would attract attention outside Cook County, in cities such as New York, Boston, Philadelphia, and San Francisco. He had reached—and passed—middle age, yet he still retained an uncanny ability as an attorney. He had become a fixture at the Cook County Criminal Court, representing as varied an assortment of clients as one might expect to find in a metropolis such as Chicago: corrupt politicians; bootleggers and saloon keepers; pimps, prostitutes, and owners of massage parlors; embezzlers, gamblers, and gangsters; and, of course, a steady stream of murderers.

No ASPECT OF DARROW'S CAREER before the Criminal Court was as significant in transforming his philosophy of crime and criminal justice as his efforts on behalf of Chicagoans indicted for murder. Until around 1915 Darrow clung stubbornly to the belief that all crime was, in one sense or another, economic crime. Criminals broke the law, Darrow believed, because they were impoverished, uneducated, and destitute; they had been reared in poverty and, deprived of any semblance of education or training, they had no way to make a living by normal means. They had no choice but to engage in criminal activity.

In June 1914, the warden at Joliet Prison invited Clarence Darrow to speak to the prisoners on crime and punishment. Darrow was well known for his opposition to the prison system, and his visit to Joliet was, according to the warden's critics, ill judged and inappropriate. But Darrow had come in support of the warden's inauguration of a more liberal regime at Joliet, and in his talk he endorsed the relaxation of the disciplinary system and urged the inmates to cooperate with the honor system introduced earlier that year. The prisoners, at least, received Darrow's speech with good grace—Darrow absolved them of blame and attributed their incarceration to the effects of impoverishment. "Most all the people in here are poor," Darrow drawled to his captive audience, "and have always been poor; have never had a chance in the world. . . . The first great cause of crime is poverty, and we will never cure crime until we get rid of poverty. . . . Most of the crimes committed, like burglary and robbery and murder, are committed by boys, young people. . . . And they are boys of a certain class; boys who live in a tenement district; boys who are poor, who have no playground but the street; boys [who] . . . gradually learn crime, the same as we learn to be a lawyer, and, of course, after they get started then it is easy."[33]

Yet Darrow's work as a defense attorney in the Cook County Criminal Court often seemed to confound his most fundamental assumptions about the causes of crime. Some defendants seemed to have acted irrationally or, at the very least, in ways that defied easy explanation. Darrow, in his defense of such prisoners, could not make his appeal to the jury in ways that argued an economic motive, and as he took up alternative explanations for such crimes, his philosophy of criminal justice gradually began to adopt a more subtle mien.

Darrow's philosophy of economic determinism could not, for example, account for those murderers who killed in passion and anger. Darrow himself knew that, in order to make an effective appeal to the jury in such cases, he had to abandon his concept of crime as a consequence of economic need.

RUSSELL PETHICK, A TWENTY-TWO-YEAR-OLD deliveryman, was a case in point. On Thursday, 6 May 1915, at ten o'clock in the morning, Pethick stopped at 7100 Lowe Avenue, the house of John and Ella Coppersmith, to deliver groceries. Ella Coppersmith was in the kitchen when Pethick knocked at the door, and her two-year-old son, Jack, was playing in an adjacent room. Pethick unloaded the groceries from his wagon in the alley adjacent to the Coppersmith house and stepped into the kitchen. Ella Coppersmith, alone in the house with her child, offered a ten-dollar bill in payment. There was a dispute over the change; the dispute escalated into an argument; and, as they faced each other, Pethick suddenly reached for the woman's blouse as though to touch her. She responded by striking him in the face with her fist. There was a butcher knife, with a wooden handle and a sharp, serrated edge, lying on the kitchen table. Pethick suddenly grabbed it and lunged at the woman. She fought back, raising her arms to defend herself from the blows, but Pethick struck at her, slashing violently at her abdomen and throat.

As Ella Coppersmith lay dying at his feet, her throat cut, blood streaming out across the kitchen floor, the child, hearing his mother's screams, ran into the room crying. Pethick could not afford to leave behind a witness to his crime—the child might identify him to the police, he thought—and so he grabbed Jack by his shirt, pulled the child suddenly toward him, and slit the boy's throat.[34]

After killing the boy, Pethick ransacked the house, looking for valuables; he then returned to the kitchen, where he sexually abused Ella Coppersmith's body before cleaning his clothes and hands of blood and returning to work.[35]

There seemed to be no mitigating circumstances for the brutal murder of a young mother and her innocent child. At the hearing before the grand jury, several witnesses, including Pethick's employer, John McCrea, testified that Pethick had shown no previous signs of insanity and that he could distinguish right from wrong. The state's attorney, Maclay Hoyne, was confident that he had a hanging case, and he announced that he would seek the death penalty for the double murder.[36]

But according to a diagnosis presented by medical experts, Pethick was mentally ill. Rachel Watkins, a prominent member of the Medical Woman's Club of Chicago, examined him in the Cook County jail. The prisoner, Watkins reported, had "degeneration of the nerve tracts. . . . He is very deficient in memory, reason, and judgment. . . . There is a disturbance throughout the entire emotional field. In general knowledge he is equal to a 5 or 6 year old child; and although he attended public school for eight years, he was unable to pass the third grade."[37]

Psychologists examined Pethick in his prison cell—they agreed with the physicians that Pethick was mentally incompetent. He was unable to perform even elementary tasks, and he had the judgment and intelligence of a young child.[38]

It was exactly the type of case that appealed to Clarence Darrow's humanitarian instincts. Pethick, a young man from a family of modest means, had committed a crime that was extraordinary in its violence. The murders had been entirely out of character. Pethick, according to everyone who knew him, was a reserved, quiet man who never smoked and rarely drank—he had never run wild or behaved indecently but had worked diligently to support his two aged parents.

Darrow had first learned of the case through the Chicago newspapers, and the more he read, the more incongruous it seemed that Pethick should commit such a brutal murder. The killing of Ella and Jack Coppersmith was inexplicable except as a consequence of mental derangement. Russell Pethick had acted from a compulsion to kill. Defects in his mental apparatus, Darrow believed, had removed his ability to choose his actions freely and had compelled him to murder his victims. Pethick was a suitable case for medical diagnosis, and the state's attorney would be better advised to send him to a mental institution than to the gallows.

And if Pethick had not chosen to kill, then what could justify a death sentence? He was not responsible for his actions, Darrow reasoned, and under the circumstances, capital punishment would serve no purpose except to satisfy the bloodthirsty mob. The execution of Russell Pethick would not bring Ella Coppersmith or her son back to life; it would not deter other murderers; and, of course, it would neither redeem nor rehabilitate the murderer.

That summer, as Pethick awaited his trial in the Cook County Criminal Court, Darrow volunteered his services as defense attorney.

George Pethick, astonished that Chicago's most famous lawyer should take up his son's case, quickly consented; and on 24 September, the opening day of the trial, Darrow and his co-counsel, Alice Thompson, stood in front of George Barrett, judge of the Criminal Court, to plead their client's case.[39]

Might Darrow have submitted a motion for a change of venue? Even if Darrow could succeed in moving the trial away from Cook County, he would, he believed, be unable to secure a sympathetic jury. Even the most objective jury would find it difficult to look beyond the brutality of the murders and the intimations of sexual depravity.

There was little chance, moreover, that a jury would find the prisoner not guilty by reason of insanity. The defendant may have been mentally disturbed, but in appearance at least, he presented no obvious signs of derangement. Pethick was lucid and coherent, and the state's attorney would no doubt present a surfeit of witnesses to testify to Pethick's ability to perform everyday tasks in a satisfactory manner.

It would be futile, Darrow realized, to use insanity as a defense. He had a better strategy, a strategy so simple that it caught the prosecution entirely by surprise. On the opening day in court, he said that his client pleaded guilty and asked the judge to consider Pethick's mental condition in mitigation of his punishment. Pethick, Darrow stated to the judge, was capable of distinguishing right from wrong. He did not, therefore, meet the accepted test of insanity. But on the other hand, Darrow insisted, Pethick was suffering from mental illness. This medical condition should be taken into consideration in determining the appropriate punishment.

Pethick, by admitting his guilt, would avoid a jury trial. The judge would first listen to the psychiatric experts present their evidence that Pethick was mentally diseased. On the basis of that evidence, he would then sentence Pethick either to death or to a prison sentence of not less than fourteen years.

Darrow's gamble paid off. H. I. Davis, the former superintendent of the Psychopathic Hospital, testified for the defense that Pethick was subnormal—"His mental capacity is far below par. I wouldn't call him an idiot, but he is feeble-minded"—and that Pethick had a diminished sense of responsibility. Other physicians took the stand to support Davis's assertion that Pethick was mentally diseased.

James (Jimmy) O'Brien, the assistant state's attorney, countered the defense testimony with a reading of the defendant's confession and a recital of the numerous stab wounds found on the victims' bodies, but to no avail. Darrow had saved his client from the gallows. The judge handed down a life sentence in the penitentiary for the murders of Ella Coppersmith and her son.[40]

EVEN WHEN A DEFENDANT CONFESSED that he had acted for the sake of money, Darrow preferred to explain the crime as a consequence of mental derangement. On 5 April 1916, Edward Hettinger, a nineteen-year-old factory worker, had slit the throat of Agnes Middleton after breaking into her apartment looking for money. At his trial later that year, Hettinger denied his guilt and claimed that the police had tortured him to obtain his confession. Hettinger's attorney, Guy Walker, offered a plea of not guilty by reason of insanity, but the jury, after listening to the testimony of the medical experts, found Hettinger guilty of murder and sentenced the prisoner to hang.[41]

Clarence Darrow had played no role in the case. Yet enough had been written about it in the newspapers to convince him that Hettinger was mentally unbalanced. One year before the murder the authorities had committed Hettinger to the Psychopathic Hospital because of his eccentric behavior. The jury had made a mistake, Darrow believed, in sentencing the boy to hang.

Hettinger had a mental ability, according to the medical experts at the Psychopathic Hospital, equivalent to that of a child, and it would be a retrograde step, Darrow protested to the judge, Hugo Pam, to execute a boy with such a low intellectual capacity. "I don't believe any mental defective should be hanged," Darrow stated. "To hang this boy would leave the community cold. It would be a brutal thing to hang him. He is only 19 years old and his mentality is the most important thing to determine what punishment he should get. I believe the jury overlooked those facts."[42]

Pam listened to Darrow's words sympathetically, and a few days later, he announced that he would commute the sentence to life imprisonment, but only if the prisoner confessed his guilt. Hettinger was initially reluctant to concede guilt—he had had nothing to do with the killing, he protested. The police had beaten a confession out of him with their truncheons, and he now repudiated it. But Hettinger, after a long talk in his jail cell with Clarence Darrow, eventually agreed to confess in exchange for a life sentence in Joliet Prison.[43]

THROUGHOUT THE 1910s AND INTO the early 1920s, Darrow defended countless clients on murder charges and avoided the death penalty in every instance. A murder might seem premeditated and deliberate, yet Darrow needed only to bring on the psychiatric experts to explain his client's action for the jury to accept his defense. Most typically the jurymen would accept Darrow's insistence that the defendant was not guilty by reason of insanity. Even on the infrequent occasions when the jurors found the defendant guilty, they refused to hand down a death sentence, specifying instead incarceration in the penitentiary.[44]

Emma Simpson, a wealthy socialite charged with the murder of her husband in 1919, looked to Clarence Darrow as her best hope—her only hope—of avoiding the death penalty. Emma had separated from her husband in 1912 after discovering him in bed with another woman. She had refused a request for a divorce—why should she give him the freedom to marry her rival?—but in February 1919 she filed suit in court charging her husband with infidelity and requesting payments for separate maintenance.

Elmer Simpson regarded his wife's demand as preposterous. She was a wealthy woman, from one of Chicago's most affluent families, he told the judge. He was making a modest living as a telegraph operator. The demand for maintenance payments was fueled more by jealousy and rage than by any need for the money. He taunted his wife, sitting directly across from him, with a cutting remark; but the words were the last he ever uttered. In front of a crowd of witnesses, Emma Simpson drew a revolver from the folds of her dress and fired four shots at her husband. Two bullets struck Elmer Simpson in the face, one lodged in his shoulder, and the fourth went wide, narrowly missing the clerk of the court, Gus Wedemaier.[45]

Emma Simpson had no regrets at killing her husband. As the bailiffs hustled her out of the court, she waved and smiled to a courtroom photographer from the *Chicago Daily Tribune* while he snapped her picture. Later that day, she explained her action to the newspaper reporters as entirely justified: "I took the gun to court with me, but I didn't expect to shoot. He said something to me—something nasty, indicative of his whole nature. It made me boil—I couldn't stand it any longer. . . . I will tell my story to the jury and they will free me. I am perfectly confident of that."[46]

Clarence Darrow announced that he would defend Emma Simpson as a victim of partial insanity—his client, he proclaimed to the newspapers, was rational in all aspects save one. Her husband's philandering, his provocative behavior, his cruel taunts and needling remarks, had driven Emma Simpson into a condition of insanity whenever she contemplated his behavior.[47]

Later that year, at the trial in the Cook County Criminal Court, Darrow produced numerous witnesses to testify to Emma's obsessive neurosis with her husband's infidelity. Ida Will, a close friend of the defendant, related that Emma would talk incessantly about her husband. She had driven all her friends to distraction with her talk. It had caused the dissolution of a card circle—no one could enjoy the card games while Emma complained endlessly about her husband.

Harry McCormick, a business associate of Emma's uncle, recalled the physical changes in Emma's appearance after her troubles began. "She haunted my office asking my aid. . . . She became insane over the subject of her domestic life. I often found her in the office, her hair disheveled, her eyes staring, using violent language."[48]

Medical experts testified also that the defendant suffered from partial insanity. Harold Moyer, a specialist in nervous disorders, believed Emma Simpson to be manic-depressive. She was certainly insane at the time of the killing. Archibald Church, a professor of nervous and mental diseases at Northwestern University, had examined Emma Simpson and found her to display "egregious egotism and lack of self control," both of which, Church concluded, suggested insanity.[49]

In his closing speech, Clarence Darrow focused on Elmer Simpson's raffishly disreputable character. Emma Simpson had married beneath her, Darrow suggested, and she had discovered—too late!—that the man she had wed was an incurable philanderer who cheated on her at every turn. He had married her for her fortune, and just as soon as he had exchanged the matrimonial vows, he had taken up with another woman. No wonder, Darrow continued, appealing to the twelve jurymen, that Emma Simpson had sought to end her misery by shooting her husband—anyone else would have reacted similarly under such provocation! "Does it seem to you, gentlemen, that a person in his or her right mind would pick out a court, a temple of justice, where a dozen persons are gathered, to do a murder? . . . A large number of women, under the same conditions as Mrs. Simpson faced, would go insane."[50]

Darrow's eloquence worked its customary magic. The jury needed only thirty minutes to agree with his diagnosis of partial insanity. The judge committed Emma Simpson to the Illinois Northern Hospital for the Insane, but her confinement lasted less than a year. A few months after her arrival the hospital psychiatrists decided that Emma Simpson had regained her sanity. She was free to return to Chicago and resume her previous life.[51]

BY THE EARLY 1920s, Darrow no longer regarded crime as a consequence of economic circumstances. Darrow now looked to biology—understood in its broadest sense—to explain human behavior. Darrow had an autodidact's awareness of science and scientific theory. His father, Amirus, had an easy familiarity with such nineteenth-century classics as Charles Darwin's *On the Origin of Species* and Charles Lyell's *Principles of Geology* and had transmitted some of that familiarity to his son. In middle age, Clarence Darrow had read Herbert Spencer's *First Principles* and had immediately taken Spencer's evolutionary viewpoint as his own. Darrow was never consistent in his adoption of Spencer's philosophy: he subscribed to the deterministic belief that mind is contingent on matter yet refused to accept the idea that society need make no attempt to ameliorate the lot of the underprivileged. And, although Darrow had never taken courses in science as an undergraduate at Allegheny College, he had, during the 1910s and 1920s, read omnivorously on scientific topics and had kept abreast with the most recent scientific propositions, especially as they touched on criminology. "I have always leaned strongly toward science," Darrow wrote in his autobiography, "and longed to give myself over to its study. I know something of astronomy and geology; I know a good deal of biology and psychology. . . . In that department of science I have spent a great deal of time and labor, and no one can make much of a success of any subject unless he knows a good deal about man himself."[52]

In *Crime: Its Cause and Treatment*, a monograph published in 1922, Darrow attributed criminal behavior to biological determinants. He was, Darrow admitted in the preface, no scientific expert—he had no specialized training in biology or psychology. Yet he had, nevertheless, picked up sufficient science, in the course of a long life, to know that crime was a consequence of biomedical circumstances.[53]

It was obvious, according to Darrow, that each individual differed from every other in mental and physical makeup. Such differences originated in the embryo and were modified only slightly in the passage from childhood to adolescence and into adulthood. The complexity of the nervous system, the capacity of the brain, the strength of the instincts and the emotions—everything found in the adult was potential in the nucleated cell. "There is no exception," Darrow wrote, "to the rule that the whole life, with every tendency, is potential in the original cell. . . . The child is born with a brain of a certain size and fineness. It is born with a nervous system make up of an infinite number of fine fibers reaching all parts of the body, with fixed stations or receivers like the central stations of a telephone system, and with a grand central exchange to the brain."[54]

The metaphor of the body as a telephone system served Darrow's claim that human action was less a consequence of free will and more a result of the effects of external stimuli. Sensory impressions traveled along neural pathways to register their impact on the brain, and knowledge was no more than an accumulation of sensations. "The child . . . feels, tastes, sees, hears or smells some object, and his nerves carry the impression to his brain where a more or less correct registration is made." Each individual operated as a machine might operate; if the machine was defective, then of course it would operate imperfectly. "All of these impressions are more or less imperfectly received, imperfectly conveyed and imperfectly registered. However, he is obliged to use the machine he has. Not only does the machine register impressions but it sends out directions immediately following these impressions: directions to the organism as to how to run, to walk, to fight, to hide, to eat, to drink, or to make any other response that the particular situation calls for."[55]

Science and scientism constituted the core of Darrow's philosophy. Admittedly Darrow's view of science might have seemed, in the 1920s, slightly outdated and old-fashioned. Darrow had come under the spell of positivism and had never abandoned his faith in a thoroughly mechanistic and materialistic universe. The natural world, according to Darrow, alone constituted reality. There was no room within this world for mental processes independent of materialism. The laws of matter and motion governed the world, and nothing, including mankind, could be exempt from their diktat.[56]

Science and technology provided the metaphor of the machine—the telephone system—that supplied an accurate understanding of the human condition. It had become a truism, Darrow believed, that scientific law could account for all phenomena, and there was now no reason to believe that human beings were exempt from the regulations governing the natural world. "That man is the product of heredity and environment and that he acts as his machine responds to outside stimuli and nothing else, seem amply proven by the evolution and history of man. . . . The laws of matter are now coming to be understood. Chance, accident and whim have been banished from the physical world."[57]

Science, Darrow believed, had eliminated free agency in human behavior—how could individuals choose their actions if they were susceptible to natural law? Each new scientific fad seemed to confirm Darrow's faith that an individual acted according to the rules governing the natural world. Endocrinology—the study of the glands and hormonal secretions—was a case in point. The hormones that poured into the bloodstream had a demonstrated effect on human behavior: the proper supply of hormonal secretions seemed to regulate the body precisely as though it were a machine. "Certain secretions," Darrow wrote in *Crime: Its Cause and Treatment*, "are instantly emptied from the ductless glands into the blood which, acting like fuel in an engine, generate more power in the machine, fill it with anger or fear and prepare it to respond to the directions to fight or flee, or to any type of action incident to the machine. It is only within a few years that biologists have had any idea of the use of these ductless glands or of their importance in the functions of life. Very often these ductless glands are diseased, and always they are more or less imperfect; but in whatever condition they are, the machine responds to their flow."

Other sciences also captivated Darrow in the years immediately following World War I. Accounts of the research of Jean-Henri Fabre on instinct and its acquisition by insects and arachnids had recently made their way from France to the United States. Fabre had spent his life in obscurity, patiently observing the insects in the countryside around Sérignan, southwest of Montpellier, and publishing his conclusions in *Souvenirs Entomologiques*. Fabre's predecessors had endowed insects with the ability to reason; but Fabre had demonstrated that their actions were entirely instinctual. The mason bee, the red ant, the dung beetle, the *Sphex* wasp—all caught their prey or provided for their offspring instinctually. Recognition of Fabre's work arrived just before his death in 1915—he had been solitary, reclusive, and impoverished—and it resulted in an avalanche of popular works that brought his research to a general audience for the first time. The American public had to wait until 1921 for the first account of Fabre's work to reach the United States, but that account provoked a torrent of popular articles in the magazines and newspapers in praise of Fabre's work.[58]

In a lecture before the Rationalist Society of Chicago in 1921, Darrow drew his own conclusions from a reading of Fabre's observations of instinct in insects and arachnids. The importance of instinct in the animal world, Darrow stated, provided a clue to its significance in higher forms of life. Human beings believe that they act rationally, but might they not also be subject to instinctual drives? Fabre's research was grist to Darrow's deterministic mill—human beings were no more capable of free agency than the mason bee or the red ant.[59]

Darrow's exegesis remained vague on such questions as the relative significance of instincts vis-à-vis the effects of hormonal secretions. Nor was it apparent that instinct explained human actions comprehensively enough to enable Darrow so casually to dismiss agency and free will. No matter that his account was vague: Darrow seized every opportunity to proselytize his opinion that science had made the concept of choice redundant. Instinct was one more way for him to push home his point. "Human action is governed largely by instinct and emotion. . . . These instincts and emotions are incident to every living machine and are the motor forces that impel the organism. . . .

Instincts are primal to man. He has inherited them from the animal world."[60]

Darrow's philosophy of human behavior was built on the certitude provided by the sciences. This certitude pointed to a conclusion that, to Darrow at least, seemed inescapable. Objective forces compelled individuals to act. Crime was not the consequence of choice, and therefore punishment was inappropriate and futile. "Before any progress can be made in dealing with crime," Darrow declared, "the world must fully realize that crime is only a part of conduct; that each act, criminal or otherwise, follows a cause . . . that however much society may feel the need of confining the criminal, it must first of all understand that the act had an all-sufficient cause for which the individual was in no way responsible, and must find the cause of his conduct, and, so far as possible, remove the cause."[61]

FEW OF DARROW'S CLIENTS CARED one way or the other about his philosophy of behavior. They knew only that he had an extraordinary knack for obtaining the best possible outcome in the courtroom. And so, in May 1924, the parents of Nathan Leopold and Richard Loeb sought out Clarence Darrow to save their boys. Darrow had accomplished miracles in the courtroom—it would take a miracle for their sons to escape the scaffold.

And Darrow would accept the case, not because the defendants were deserving but because it was the opportunity for which he had been waiting. The trial of Leopold and Loeb would capture the attention of the nation. It would be Darrow's chance to prove to the world that crime was less a consequence of free will and deliberate choice and more a result of forces that had compelled the boys to an act of murder. Both families had promised him unlimited resources in the defense; Clarence Darrow would use those resources to make his philosophy of crime and punishment a reality.

9 | ROBERT CROWE

In recent years the American public has been influenced to some extent by an active, persistent and systematic agitation based on an unfortunate and misplaced sympathy for persons accused of crime. This sympathy forgets the life that was blotted out. It forgets the broken hearted left behind. There should be no sentiment about it. Persons whose existence means death and disaster to others who have done no wrong have no claim upon society for anything—not even for life itself. I believe society should have no hesitancy in springing the trap every time the noose can be put around a murderer's neck.[1]

Robert Crowe, 18 February 1928

JANET WILKINSON SKIPPED UP the main entrance stairs of her apartment building at 112–114 East Superior Street. She had golden blond hair, cut in a bob; china-blue eyes, set wide apart; a broad forehead, fair complexion, and firm chin—and she always had a smile on her face. No wonder the six-year-old was the darling of the neighborhood! That Tuesday morning, 22 July 1919, she wore a blue sailor frock with a collar edged with pearl buttons and, on her feet, white cotton socks and a pair of black oxfords. Janet had just come from the public playground on Chicago Avenue; she had forgotten to return the metal identification tag issued by the playground and it hung, attached by a clasp, from the edge of her dress.[2]

Halfway up the stairs, Janet suddenly paused. One of her neighbors, a thin, bespectacled, middle-aged man, was leaning over the banister looking down, watching her intently as she climbed the steps. Janet continued to walk up the stairs, more slowly now. She recognized the man. The previous December he had shown her some comic books in his apartment, and after she had told her parents, her mother had insistently forbidden Janet to speak to him a second time.[3]

Several mothers in the building had complained to the police about Thomas Fitzgerald. He had often befriended children in the neighborhood. On at least three occasions he had exposed himself from the window of his second-floor apartment to girls walking on Superior Street; and a few months earlier, the Morals Court had fined him $100 for indecent behavior.[4]

Now he stood on the landing, still staring down at Janet as she walked timidly up the staircase. Fitzgerald wore rimless glasses over his large brown eyes; he sported a faint mustache under an obtrusive nose, and at that moment his clothes and

18. ROBERT CROWE. After studying law at Yale University, Robert Crowe became assistant state's attorney for Cook County in 1909. He won election as a judge on the Circuit Court in 1916 and served as chief justice of the Cook County Criminal Court in 1919 and 1920.

hair were rumpled and disheveled, as though he had just got out of bed. He was a shy, solitary man with few friends, diffident and awkward in the company of adults. Indeed, everything about his manner expressed a tremulous hesitancy, as though he expected to be contradicted at any moment. Even the few people who knew him well had a disregard for this nervous and vaguely unpleasant man.

Fitzgerald held a box of chocolates in his right hand. Janet looked at the candy, hesitating; Fitzgerald invited her to take one but she silently shook her head. She had remembered her mother's warning—she was not to talk to this strange man.

As she turned away to walk up the next flight of stairs, Fitzgerald suddenly grabbed the girl by the arms. His apartment door was ajar, only a few feet away. He lifted her up as though she were a doll, a blue-eyed, fair-haired doll, and half dragged, half carried her into the apartment, pushing the door behind him with his foot to close it.

Janet was screaming now, crying and kicking. They were in the bedroom and Fitzgerald began to panic: the window was wide open; surely someone in the street below would hear her cries.

He punched the girl hard in the mouth to stop her screams— anything to stop that noise!—and he felt some of Janet's teeth break loose under the impact of his blow. He punched her again and noticed the blood on his hand. Fitzgerald grabbed the girl by the throat and squeezed hard. Soon she had stopped crying; her head fell backward and her limp, lifeless body lay diagonally on the bed; minute specks of blood had spattered over her blue dress.[5]

FOUR DAYS AFTER JANET'S DISAPPEARANCE, Fitzgerald broke down and admitted the killing. He told the police that he had hidden the body in the basement of the apartment building, in the space between the wall and the flue, and buried it with coal lying by the furnace.[6]

The circumstances of Janet's death seemed bad enough. When a rumor spread that Fitzgerald had raped the girl, public anger in the neighborhood reached a crescendo. On Saturday, 26 July, hundreds of men and women waited through the evening outside the East Chicago

Avenue police station for the chance to grab Fitzgerald from his prison cell and lynch him. Even the *Chicago Daily Tribune*, one of the city's more cautious newspapers, could exclaim that Fitzgerald deserved nothing less than the death penalty: "Every circumstance of the crime was horrible, from the motive and the manner to the agony caused by the concealment of it. . . . Fitzgerald is in custody with a clear case against him. . . . There will be a general opinion that he is sane enough to be hanged."[7]

The killing had touched the heart of the city. One week after the murder, on Tuesday, 29 July, more than 1,000 spectators turned out to watch the funeral cortege travel the short distance from Janet's apartment building to Holy Name Cathedral on State Street. Five thousand mourners crammed into the Victorian Gothic cathedral to see the small white coffin carried to the altar by six of Janet's classmates. Banks of flowers, garlands of roses, lilies, peonies, mignonette, poinsettias—red, white, pink, yellow, blue—were massed at the front of the cathedral; the fragrance filled the air of the sanctuary and bore mute testimony to the sorrow of the city for the sudden death of the little blond girl.[8]

ON 21 SEPTEMBER 1919 THE trial of Thomas Fitzgerald began in the Criminal Court. The chief justice, Robert Crowe, left no doubt that, despite Fitzgerald's guilty plea, he was eager to impose a death sentence.

A police physician had diagnosed Fitzgerald as syphilitic and mentally ill—"on the verge of paresis or softening of the brain"—but, nevertheless, Crowe declared, he doubted that there were any mitigating circumstances for such an atrocious killing. Crowe leaned forward over the bench and spat out the words at Fitzgerald standing nervously before him. "If you have any idea," Crowe shouted, "[that] the court would not impose the death penalty, get rid of that notion. . . . If you think the court is chicken-hearted, put that idea aside, too. If the evidence shows that hanging is proper there will be no turning aside."[9]

The next day, the assistant state's attorney, Jimmy O'Brien, argued for the death penalty. It had been a brutal, savage killing, he explained. Several of Janet's teeth had been broken by the force of the blows. The police had discovered spots of blood on the walls of Fitzgerald's bedroom. Most shocking of all, O'Brien informed the court, medical experts had concluded that Janet had still been alive when Fitzgerald had buried her under the coal in the basement.[10]

It was true, O'Brien conceded, that a guilty plea traditionally mitigated the punishment. No one who pleaded guilty had been sentenced to the gallows in Chicago for several decades. Fitzgerald would be the first such case in the twentieth century. Nevertheless, O'Brien continued, the nature of the crime called for capital punishment.

Thomas Fitzgerald cut a pathetic figure as he stood in the dock awaiting sentence the following day. His police guards had beaten him severely in his cell, bruising his face and arms and kicking him in the shins until his legs bled. As he faced Crowe, Fitzgerald's fingers twitched and fidgeted; he shifted nervously from one foot to the other, as though this movement would release him from the terror that he felt at his imminent sentence of death. His eyes seemed to have sunk back into his sockets, and his face was colorless; his forehead shone under the bright lights of the courtroom.

"Have you anything to say," Crowe asked, "before I pronounce sentence upon you for the murder of Janet Wilkinson?"

"I'm sorry. I—I ask forgiveness."

"Is that all?" Crowe demanded impatiently.

"I ask God to forgive me."

"Thomas R. Fitzgerald," Crowe pronounced, in a booming voice that reached the far wall of the courtroom, "I sentence you to be hanged by the neck until you are dead on Monday, October 27, at the Cook County jail."[11]

FOR AN AMBITIOUS POLITICIAN SUCH as Robert Crowe, it was an entirely appropriate verdict, one that bolstered his reputation as a hanging judge. Crowe, in his brief career on the Criminal Court and, in the 1920s, as state's attorney for Cook County, was never reluctant to use such episodes for political gain. Jut-jawed and thin-lipped, with a steady gaze and an intimidating manner, Crowe had always been foursquare for law and order. He was regular in manner and regular in appearance: he dressed conservatively, in a gray business suit, white shirt, and dark bow tie, with his brown hair brushed neatly toward the right. In 1919, he had started to wear brown tortoiseshell eyeglasses to compensate for shortsightedness. In another man, those eyeglasses might have softened the appearance, made him more approachable, less minatory, but with Crowe, there was no appreciable effect, nothing that subdued his appearance of fierce, unbending determination and resolve.

Crowe was still only forty years old—the youngest man ever appointed chief justice of the Criminal Court of Cook County—and already he had a reputation as a formidable presence in the hothouse world of Cook County politics. An intensely competent and precise man who valued punctuality as a cardinal virtue, Crowe was also unscrupulous, cynical, cunning, and devious; he regarded the world with a knowing gaze and judged every situation with cold calculation. He was competitive, charismatic, and clever—as a law student at Yale University, he had quickly risen to leadership in the Republican Club; and on his return to Illinois in 1901, he rapidly made his mark as an attorney with the firm of Moran, Mayer, and Meyer.[12]

His Yale education had given Crowe an intellectual polish and sophistication that distinguished him from his peers. Many attorneys in Chicago at the turn of the twentieth century had attended Kent College of Law or one of the less reputable night schools that flourished in the city. Some had even forgone law school and had entered the profession simply by passing the bar exams after private study. Crowe was different from the rest, and he knew he could never be content with the humdrum, workaday concerns of a law practice. In 1909, at the age of twenty-nine, he wangled himself a position as assistant state's attorney for Cook County.[13]

This was Crowe's first step into Chicago politics. It was a modest beginning—the state's attorney, John Wayman, typically appointed half a dozen assistants each year—but Crowe, during his tenure in Wayman's office, managed to attract the attention of William Hale (Big Bill)

Thompson, a leader of the Republican Party and former member of the City Council. Thompson, a bluff, outspoken, gregarious patrician and accomplished yachtsman, was a brilliant speaker with an appeal that transcended class and ethnic lines. He had served one term as an alderman from the Second Ward but had lost his seat two years later because of redistricting.

In 1915 Thompson won the Republican nomination for the mayoralty. The party bosses had realized that he could attract the middle-class voters, concentrated in the Seventh and Thirty-third wards, with promises of good government, efficiency, and honesty; and they were confident that he could entice the tenement dwellers—Poles in the Sixteenth Ward, Italians in the Nineteenth Ward, African-Americans in the First and Second wards, Russian Jews in the Maxwell Street neighborhood—with vague promises and populist demagogy.

Thompson was just as good on the stump as everyone had hoped. The Republican factions put aside their differences and united around his candidacy. The Democratic candidate, Robert Sweitzer, was a party hack whose German-American heritage and boorish remarks alienated voters and torpedoed his party's chances at the ballot box. On 6 April 1915, Thompson beat Sweitzer by 149,000 votes. It was a stunning triumph for a candidate whose only previous political experience—a two-year term as alderman—had come thirteen years earlier.[14]

Thompson had promised to eliminate the corruption that had characterized Chicago politics for as long as anyone could remember. But his victory had been more a consequence of the West Side machine than a result of his own efforts, and Fred Lundin, the boss of the West Side, was not about to permit the mayor to say and do whatever he wished.

Lundin, tall and gaunt, with a spindly frame, was instantly recognizable. His suit, coal-black and full-tailed, was shiny with age; his newly pressed white shirt had a black four-in-hand tie as its adornment; his large black hat, with a broad rim and a black ribbon, concealed his mass of rumpled, straw-colored hair; and a pair of dark, amber-tinted eyeglasses shaded his eyes from the curious glances of inquisitive strangers. His chalk-colored complexion had a translucent, waxlike pallor, as though he had spent a lifetime indoors. Lundin might have been a mortician—except for that large, expansive, sinister smile which revealed a mouthful of regular, but slightly discolored, teeth.

Lundin—the son of Swedish immigrants—had started modestly; he had begun by selling juniperade, a beverage of his own invention, from a cart and horse, and within a few years, he had amassed a fortune. He entered politics in 1892 as a party worker in the Twenty-Eighth Ward; he served as a state senator from 1895 to 1897; and twelve years later, he won election to the United States House of Representatives. Lundin served only one term in Washington, returning to Chicago in 1911 and establishing himself as the undisputed Republican party boss of the West Side.

Lundin had fixed on William Thompson as his candidate for mayor. Lundin knew the inner workings of the municipal administration better than anyone else in Chicago; and he had no compunction about manipulating City Hall for his own benefit. Lundin was the puppet master who pulled the strings, and Thompson soon fell in with Lundin's scheme to rob the city treasury.

Thompson's election in 1915 ended any hope of reform of the city government, but it served Robert Crowe well. The mayor immediately appointed Crowe to an interim position—attorney to the Police Trial Board (where Crowe was responsible for defending police officers brought before the board on charges of malfeasance)—while he waited for some more lucrative position for his young protégé.[15]

THE REPUBLICAN PARTY HAD BEEN the dominant force in Chicago politics for as long as anyone could remember, and its grip on power endured in the 1910s despite the emergence of three powerful factions within the party. Charles Deneen, a lawyer and former governor of Illinois, was the party boss for the South Side; Edward Brundage, who would be elected attorney general in 1916, commanded the Republican battalions on the North Side; Fred Lundin was the boss of the West Side. Each faction depended for its cohesion on the charisma of its leader and owed its continued existence to his ability to win jobs and patronage for the members. Neither ideology nor policy counted for very much in Republican politics in Chicago during the 1910s; each faction promised good government, an honest administration, and an end to corruption but relied more on the ability of party workers to get out the vote.

In the 1915 elections, the Lundin faction had won overwhelmingly—Thompson's plurality was the largest ever won for the mayor's office by a Republican in Chicago—but factionalism within the Republican Party continued unabated. Too many sources of power and patronage lay outside the control of the mayor's office for Fred Lundin to be able to ever entirely silence the rival factions within the Republican Party.

The disbursement of political power throughout numerous municipal and county agencies foiled Lundin's repeated attempts to crush dissident Republicans who had burrowed deep within the administrative bureaucracy. Warfare within the Republican Party continued unabated as rival politicians ceaselessly battled for the spoils of office. Factional leaders were forever searching for competitive advantage, forming new coalitions and breaking old alliances. Chicago politics was endlessly labile; it offered ample opportunities for a bright, ambitious young politician to fight his way to the top.

In 1916 ROBERT CROWE—WITH the backing of Fred Lundin—secured the Republican nomination for a judgeship on the Circuit Court. In the election later that year, Crowe defeated his Democratic opponent handily. He served as a judge with distinction, becoming chief justice of the Criminal Court in 1919.

In November 1920, voters in Illinois would choose a United States senator, the governor and lieutenant governor, the secretary of state, the auditor, the treasurer, the attorney general, and the clerk of the state supreme court. At the county level, the voters would elect the county judge, state's attorney, recorder, clerk of the Circuit Court, clerk of the Superior Court, three trustees of the Sanitary District of Chicago, ten judges of the Municipal Court, county surveyor, and coroner.[16]

Robert Crowe's reputation as a no-nonsense judge and his effectiveness as an administrator, combined with his fealty to Fred Lundin, made him the obvious choice as the Republican candidate for state's attorney for Cook County. Crowe's decision the previous year to send Thomas Fitzgerald to the gallows for the murder of Janet Wilkinson had been a popular one. Crowe, moreover, could claim that measures adopted during his tenure as chief justice of the Criminal Court had significantly reduced crime in Chicago. He had served as chief justice for only one year, yet during that year, he boasted to a reporter from the *Chicago Daily Tribune*, "more indictments were returned, more tried, more convicted, more hanged, and more sent to penal institutions than in any other year of the Criminal court." For years the court system in Chicago had been notoriously slow and ponderous; criminals had escaped successful prosecution solely because of the length of time it had taken to bring them to court, yet already Crowe had begun to clear up the backlog of cases that had cluttered up the courts. "When I started," Crowe explained, "the Criminal Court was nine years behind in its work and now it is only two years."[17]

Crowe faced anemic opposition in the Republican primary—the Deneen-Brundage nominee, David Matchett, a judge on the Appellate Court, talked loudly about corruption in City Hall but had little else to recommend him. Neither Matchett nor a third candidate, Bernard Barasa, running as an independent without the support of any party faction, had a chance of winning the Republican nomination.

Nevertheless, warfare within the Republican Party reached fever pitch as the September primary approached. The Deneen and Brundage factions had combined forces to present a single ticket in the expectation that a unified campaign would more easily overturn the Lundin group. Whoever won the Republican primary would most probably win the general election, and victory would ensure control of patronage and jobs.

ON THE MORNING OF 15 September 1920, small clusters of city police and deputy sheriffs guarded the polls. Campaign workers stood nearby, watching closely as county officers checked the identity of voters. For three hours the election proceeded peacefully, but toward noon, carloads of men, armed with clubs and revolvers, could be seen moving through precincts on the West Side. Violence broke out first in the Fourth Ward—three carloads of men attacked the polling station on South Lowe Avenue and kidnapped a precinct captain—and spread quickly throughout the city. The police department had too few men to guard every polling place in every precinct, and soon open warfare had broken out across Chicago as armed men fought to take control of the primary.[18]

It was the most violent primary in the history of Cook County. One man, Mike Fennessy, a campaign worker for Al Gorman, a nominee for state senate, died in a shoot-out between police and party workers in the Fourth District. No one else died that day but, across the city, the police, deputy sheriffs, and party workers fought each other in a series of bloody battles that left men beaten, clubbed, stabbed, and shot. Robert Crowe's men were in the thick of it: in one incident a dozen men, armed with clubs, attacked twenty of Crowe's supporters in the Burton & Ascher saloon on Chicago Avenue, but after fierce fighting with blackjacks and knives, the intruders were eventually beaten back.[19]

It was not only the most violent primary in the city's history but also one of the most expensive. The whole affair, wrote the editor of the *Chicago Daily Journal*, was "a disgrace to the republican party, the state of Illinois, and the American people. . . . Close to $2,000,000 was spent by the two republican factions in cutting each other's throats. . . . This money, remember, was not spent to beat the opposing party, but to beat the opposing factions in the same party. Broadly speaking, the principles of the two factions are identical; the really important quarrel between them was over the 'honors,' emoluments and perquisites of office—and does anyone imagine that either side made its outlay without planning to recoup itself in the event of victory? . . . If this be the only fashion in which the people of Illinois can choose candidates for office, the state is in sore straits, indeed."[20]

A disgrace? Perhaps—but Lundin's men had emerged victorious. Candidates on the City Hall ticket won almost every nomination at the state and county levels. Robert Crowe did particularly well, winning the nomination for state's attorney with over 180,000 votes; his closest rival, David Matchett, received 113,000 votes. Crowe's triumph was the more impressive on account of the low turnout. Party registration had fallen since 1916, and even an increase in the vote as a result of women's suffrage had not compensated for the general lack of interest of registered Republicans in a battle between two equally corrupt political factions.[21]

JUST AS SOON AS THE returns had confirmed his victory in the primary, Crowe began the campaign for the November election. His Democratic opponent, Michael Igoe, a graduate of Georgetown University, was an experienced politician who had represented Cook County in the state legislature for four terms. Igoe was the better candidate—he was six years younger than Crowe, yet he had considerably more political experience and was better equipped to serve as state's attorney, having prosecuted several landmark cases while working as an assistant United States attorney for the Chicago district during the 1910s. Two other candidates for state's attorney—William Cunnea of the Socialist Party and John Teevan of the Farmer-Labor Party—were on the ballot, but neither organization now commanded much support within Cook County. The fight for state's attorney would be decided in 1920 in favor of Igoe or Crowe.[22]

Michael Igoe may have been the more qualified candidate, but Crowe was the candidate of City Hall. And factionalism among the Republicans had now subsided—the Deneen-Brundage faction had temporarily given up its attacks on Thompson and Lundin and waited to see how the City Hall ticket would fare in the November elections. Michael Igoe was not so fortunate—he had beaten the incumbent state's attorney, Maclay Hoyne, in the Democratic primary; and Hoyne, furious at having lost the nomination to an upstart, was attacking Igoe in the press as a "fool . . . entirely ignorant of criminal law."[23]

Robert Crowe also attacked Igoe, painting him as a pawn in the hands of unscrupulous enemies of democracy. How, Crowe asked, could Igoe explain his connections to that small clique of corrupt politicians—James (Bull) Dailey, Michael (Hinky Dink) Kenna, and Bernard

(Barney) Grogan—desperate to see Crowe defeated? And why were the corporations, the transportation companies, and the utilities so eager to support Igoe? Why were the criminal gangs, pimps, brothel owners, bootleggers, and saloon keepers all working for Igoe's election? Was it because they knew that Igoe, as state's attorney, would never prosecute their misdeeds and would, in fact, conspire with them to rob the people? "My Democratic opponent," Crowe announced, in a statement released on 16 October, "seems to be imbued with the idea that a candidate for state's attorney can accept political and financial support from the vice lords, the traction barons and the criminal profiteers without the ugly fact coming to the attention of the good men and women of Cook county. I have challenged him to deny his connection with the vice lords and his acceptance of financial support from the interests that bleed the people. He has failed to refute my charges. The real reason for his failure is that he is guilty and he knows it."[24]

Igoe fought back valiantly, accusing Crowe of aligning himself with the most corrupt administration ever to rule the city—"The city hall gang has ruthlessly plundered Chicago. They have invented new schemes of graft and extortion, and that is the reason crime is rampant and criminals more brazen and unafraid than ever before"—but the momentum of victory had already shifted in Crowe's direction.[25]

In his statements to the press, Crowe repeatedly emphasized his record on the bench as a law-and-order judge, reminding the voters that he had sent Thomas Fitzgerald to the gallows and promising to crack down on criminals once he was elected state's attorney. But more significantly, important civic associations and professional organizations—representing realtors, lawyers, insurance brokers, bankers, businessmen, and jurists—endorsed Crowe.[26]

Warren Harding's landslide victory in the 1920 presidential election contributed, no doubt, to the Republican victory in Cook County; but few candidates anywhere did as well as Robert Crowe that November. Crowe's margin of victory—more than 210,000 votes over his Democratic rival—was unprecedented; moreover, it marked him as a man with a bright future. Already there were rumors that Bill Thompson would try for the United States Senate at the next election, and with

Thompson gone, why should Crowe not aim for the mayor's office in his place? Crowe was still a young man with ambition and energy to spare. His election as state's attorney might well be a stepping-stone to the mayoralty, and then perhaps he could try for the governor's mansion.[27]

But before he could think about running for mayor, Crowe would first have to demonstrate his commitment to fighting crime. Chicago was one of the most lawless cities in the nation, and few agencies were more important in the war against the criminals than the office of the state's attorney. It was now Robert Crowe's responsibility not only to put the bootleggers and racketeers out of business but also to reduce the numbers of murders, burglaries, and assaults that plagued the city. In this regard, Crowe, as always, was fortunate, for just a few days after assuming office, he would make a decision that would ensure the conviction of an infamous murderer and raise his personal popularity to new heights.

ON THE EVENING OF MONDAY, 21 June 1920, Carl and Ruth Wanderer strolled home after seeing the movie *The Sea Wolf.* They had been childhood sweethearts: Ruth Johnson had been only sixteen when she had first met Carl in 1915 at a Sunday service at Holy Trinity Lutheran Church. During World War I, Carl had served as a first lieutenant in the Seventeenth Machine Gun Battalion in the Allied Expeditionary Force in France. After Carl's return to Chicago at the war's end, he and Ruth were married on 1 October 1919.

They made a perfect match. Ruth was an attractive woman—men always tried to flirt with her, but she remained faithful to Carl while he was in Europe. For his part, Carl seemed to be the man every mother would want as a son-in-law. He never smoked, or drank, or swore; he attended church regularly; and he, too, ignored opportunities to flirt, claiming that Ruth "was the only girl I ever kissed."[28]

Ruth was in a happy mood that night. She was expecting her first child in two months. She glanced at her husband fondly as they walked home together—Ruth was glad that Carl had settled down after returning to Chicago. He had found work as a butcher in his father's shop, and he, too, seemed content.

As they approached the two-story apartment building at 4732 North Campbell Avenue, Ruth suddenly sensed a man walking behind them. She glanced backward—he seemed very close, just three yards away. He was a young, good-looking man, but dressed in old, dirty clothes, untidy and unkempt, as though he had been sleeping rough, and now he was walking up the path toward their building. Ruth glanced at her husband, but Carl seemed unconcerned. She hurried to open the front door of the building and step inside the darkened foyer.

The first bullet caught Ruth in the thigh as she stepped across the vestibule—she felt the burning sensation as it hit her. The second bullet passed through her body on the left side. Ruth remained conscious . . . more shots came from someone's gun . . . now her husband was kneeling beside her on the blue tiles of the vestibule floor . . . Carl was holding her hand. Her life was leaving her body but she could still see her husband kneeling above her, looking into her eyes.[29]

"Carl, I'm shot." Ruth knew already that the second bullet had passed through her child. ". . . The baby . . . Carl, my baby is dead."[30]

Her husband had shot and killed the tramp. Now, as he tenderly stroked her hair, Carl murmured words of consolation to his dying wife: "I've got him, sweetheart . . . I got him. He won't hurt you anymore."[31]

Ruth's mother, Eugenia, lived in their apartment; Ruth whispered to her husband to call Eugenia.

It was too late. Ruth's eyes closed. Her blood spread slowly out across the floor, forming a dark-red pool around her body.

By the time John Nape, the first policeman on the scene, arrived, a small crowd of neighbors had gathered outside the hallway. The sergeant pushed his way forward into the vestibule. A woman's body lay close to the second doorway—Nape assumed she was the young wife. A few feet away, a tramp lay dead, his shabby brown jacket and cheap cotton trousers stained with blood. Two revolvers lay side by side in the center of the vestibule.[32]

Carl Wanderer explained how the tramp had tried to rob them. His wife had been on the point of opening the inner door when the man had fired two bullets into her, killing her almost instantly. Carl had pulled out his own gun, a .45-caliber army revolver, and had gunned down the assailant.

It seemed a straightforward killing, one of many such murders in Chicago that year.

But the police were puzzled that the tramp would have killed Ruth Wanderer without waiting to rob her. Ruth had not resisted or fought back, according to her husband. It was remarkable also, the detectives realized, that although ten shots had been fired in the narrow hallway, Carl Wanderer had emerged unscathed—he had gunned down his assailant but had walked away from the gunfight without a scratch.

The case soon became even more mysterious.

Ruth Wanderer had withdrawn $1,500 from her savings account a few days before she died. And when the police examined the provenance of the revolver supposedly used by the tramp to shoot Ruth, they discovered that they could trace it back to . . . Carl Wanderer![33]

ON FRIDAY, 9 JULY 1920, Carl Wanderer confessed. He had grown bored with his wife, he explained, and he had a seventeen-year-old girlfriend, Julia Schmitt. It had seemed easy enough to get rid of his wife. He had met the tramp on the corner of Halsted and Madison streets and had promised him a job if he would follow him and his wife home that evening. When they reached the apartment building, Carl first killed his wife and then shot the tramp.[34]

But on the opening day of Wanderer's trial—4 October 1920—for the murder of his wife and the unborn child, Wanderer repudiated his confession. His attorney, George Guenther, protested that the police had beaten his client in a basement dungeon until he confessed. Carl Wanderer, Guenther explained to the jury, was not guilty, by reason of insanity. Guenther presented a brilliant defense: he put several of Wanderer's acquaintances and friends on the stand to describe Wanderer's eccentric behavior.[35]

This defense worked. Some members of the jury believed Wanderer insane but worried that he would be committed to an asylum and released after a few years. Other jurors believed that Wanderer had knowingly and maliciously killed his wife and that he deserved the gallows. But no one wanted a mistrial, and so, after arguing for twenty-three hours and casting five ballots, the jurors came up with a compromise: on 29 October, they decided that Wanderer was guilty and would serve twenty-five years in prison.[36]

The jury's decision provoked an uproar. With time off for good behavior, Wanderer would be a free man in less than fourteen years! The judge, Hugo Pam, could not conceal his dismay at the jury's folly. Immediately after hearing the foreman pronounce sentence, Pam admonished the jury, "A grievous error—you call him a wife murderer and say that he shall pay with twenty-five years imprisonment. A regrettable error."[37]

Jimmy O'Brien, the assistant state's attorney prosecuting the case, was outraged. O'Brien was astonished at the jurors' ineptitude. "They found him guilty of murdering his beautiful young wife, the trusting woman who was about to become a mother. And they gave him twenty-five years. . . . What foolishness! . . . It was an asinine finding, calling for the severest censure."[38]

None of the jurors would admit that he had voted for anything other than life imprisonment or the death sentence, but the damage had been done. Wanderer was jubilant at the result—"I knew they couldn't crack me. . . . I knew I'd never swing"—and, as he listened to the judge discharge the jury and thank the lawyers, a gleeful smirk played across his face.[39]

But Wanderer's trial had coincided with the 1920 elections. On 2 November, just four days after the jury had returned its verdict, Robert Crowe was elected the new state's attorney for Cook County. Crowe had followed the Wanderer trial closely, and now that he was state's attorney, he promised that, despite the jury's decision, Wanderer would eventually swing from the gallows. "One of the first things I will do," Crowe predicted to a reporter from the *Chicago Herald and Examiner*, "will be to force Wanderer to trial a second time. The punishment meted out by the first jury is entirely unbefitting the atrocity of the crime." The murder had been a willful act—it would be a travesty, Crowe declared, if Wanderer were to escape with a prison term.[40]

Carl Wanderer had received twenty-five years for the murder of his wife and unborn child. But what about the tramp? Crowe announced that he would put Wanderer on trial for the killing of the tramp.[41]

The defense attorney at the second trial, W. D. Bartholomew, offered a plea of not guilty by reason of insanity. Psychiatrists for the defense had examined Carl Wanderer in his prison cell and diagnosed his illness as dementia praecox catatonia. William Hickson, the director of the Psychopathic Laboratory of the Municipal Court, had put the prisoner through a series of mental tests and had discovered that Wanderer had been insane since infancy. A psychologist, E. Kester Wickman, testified that Wanderer had the mental age of an eleven-year-old; and James Whitney Hall, president of the Medical Insanity Commission, told the jury that Wanderer suffered from hallucinations and was undoubtedly insane.[42]

But on Friday, 18 March 1921, the jury returned a verdict of guilty and fixed the punishment as death by hanging. The jury had reached its verdict after only twelve minutes. The defense attorney, Bartholomew, complained (justifiably) that the jury had not given the evidence proper consideration.

The prosecution was delighted at the result. Robert Crowe was vindicated; his decision to put Wanderer on trial again might have backfired if Wanderer had escaped the death penalty a second time, but now Crowe was the hero of the moment. Crowe laughed and joked with reporters at the entrance to the Criminal Court Building. He puffed on a large cigar as he gave his comments to the press. "It's a great victory," Crowe exclaimed as he stood side by side with his assistant, Lloyd Heth. "Justice has been done and a great error has been corrected."[43]

CROWE'S SUCCESSFUL PROSECUTION OF WANDERER was an auspicious beginning to his career as state's attorney. Crowe, now one of Chicago's most prominent elected officials, had the responsibility for tackling the crime wave that so troubled Chicagoans during the early

1920s: if he succeeded, he might be the next mayor of Chicago; if he failed, he would be consigned to political oblivion.

Although Chicago was not the most dangerous city in the United States (both St. Louis and New York outranked it in per capita murders and assaults), a series of gangland killings in 1920 had created a perception of the city as the epicenter of the crime wave that swept over the United States after World War I. Murder, robbery, rape, and assault seemed almost routine; and nothing better illustrated the lawlessness of the United States than comparisons between Chicago and other American cities, on the one hand, and comparable cities in Canada and Europe. Thus Chicago, which recorded 352 murders in 1921, had a murder rate approximately fourteen times greater than that of Berlin; Los Angeles, with a population one-tenth that of London, recorded a greater number of murders than were committed in London; there were more murders in New York City in a single year than in Britain and France combined. Only a few hundred miles separated Cook County from Canada; yet the discrepancy in the crime figures was startling: twice as many burglaries, four times as many robberies, and four times as many murders were committed in Chicago as in the whole of Canada.[44]

What could be the cause of such an avalanche of crime? Was it a consequence of economic and social conditions: of poverty, unemployment, and inadequate housing? Was a high level of crime inevitable in a society divided so sharply between the wealthy and the impoverished? Crime was a result of socioeconomic circumstances, reformers argued, and until poverty was eliminated, the crime wave would continue.

Such sentiments had significant support within American society in the 1920s, yet the opposite viewpoint, that crime was less a consequence of impersonal forces and more a matter of free agency and deliberate choice, also had widespread backing. The murderer chose to kill his or her victim; crime was the result of a conscious decision, freely undertaken, and talk of determining circumstances served only to absolve the criminal of responsibility, to undermine the rule of law, and thus to make a bad situation worse.

Those who assumed that crime was the consequence of deliberate choice, malevolence, and evil intent recommended a stricter application

of the law. Punishment was failing to deter only because it was not sufficiently stringent. Too few judges sentenced murderers to death; and
too few death sentences were carried out. Unscrupulous and devious
lawyers exploited loopholes in state constitutions and criminal codes in
order to save their clients from punishment. Delays in the courts and
procedural inefficiency postponed trials for years and allowed criminals to escape punishment. The Eighteenth Amendment against the
sale and manufacture of alcohol was widely disregarded, and in consequence contributed to indifference and apathy among the public toward crime and criminal behavior. The inadequacy of the police and
the courts found its counterpart in the increased competence and organization of criminals. Professional criminals arranged burglary as one
might organize a commercial business—they paid the police to look
the other way; sent stolen goods, often ordered ahead of time, to fences
in distant states; and, in the unlikely event of capture, colluded with
professional fixers, including bondsmen and corrupt lawyers, to fix juries and spirit away witnesses.[45]

To solve such problems, it was necessary, according to those who
believed in free agency, to enforce the law and to apply sufficient punishment to deter the criminal. Remove the loopholes in the law, restore morale in the police force and the judiciary, reestablish respect
for the law among the general public, impose draconian sentences for
wrongdoing—and crime and murder would stop. Punishment acted to
deter, and just as soon as the criminal appreciated the increased probability of arrest and the disadvantages of a lengthy prison sentence, so
at that moment the crime wave would subside.

The idea that impersonal forces had any bearing on crime was, to
Robert Crowe, nonsense. Criminal behavior was no different from any
other type of behavior, Crowe believed; it was freely decided on and
deliberately chosen. To claim that impersonal forces compelled the criminal to act was tantamount to removing the concept of responsibility
from the criminal justice system; it questioned the very foundations of
the law. Crowe's attitude toward deterministic theories of crime was
contemptuous and dismissive—it was not even worth his time, he con-
tended, to argue against such fallacious and erroneous notions.

And in any case, Crowe's political ambitions provided him with little reason to concede ground to a viewpoint that might be interpreted as offering leniency to criminals. He hoped to be mayor of Chicago, and he could best realize that ambition by demonstrating his competence and ability in fighting crime. He had limited resources—the state's attorney traditionally had just forty police officers at his disposal—but soon after taking office he began to use them against the spread of illegal gambling houses. "Gambling in Chicago must stop," Crowe announced in May 1921. "It does not matter whether it flourishes in cigar stores and the back rooms of saloons or in the society residence district; it must be driven out." Crowe's campaign against crime made good copy: each evening, Crowe's men would raid gambling dens, seizing dice tables, slot machines, roulette wheels, tally sheets, and racing handbooks. Most of the raids occurred in the Second Ward, in the area south of the Loop notorious for its black-and-tan cabaret clubs: the Dreamland at 3518 State Street, the Green Mill on the corner of 37th Street and Vernon Avenue, the Stopover on 35th Street, the Excelsior on Indiana Avenue, the Saratoga at 3445 State Street, and the Waiters' and Porters' Club at 3415 State Street. The journalists would follow behind—waiting patiently beside the patrol wagons as the police battered down the doors of pool rooms and gambling houses and filing their reports in time for the morning editions. Crowe zealously cultivated the reporters, feeding them inside information and anecdotes; the journalists repaid the favor, liberally quoting Crowe, praising his administration of the state's attorney's office, and supporting his initiatives.[46]

It was all calculated to win publicity in the media. It was more for show than for effect—how could Crowe's forty constables have any meaningful impact on crime in Chicago?—and Charles Fitzmorris, the chief of police, angrily denounced the state's attorney for interfering with the work of his own department. Fitzmorris had reason to feel aggrieved—the police under Crowe's command were technically on loan from the Chicago police department—and Fitzmorris moved to withdraw them from the state's attorney's office. But Fitzmorris himself was under attack for allowing corruption to spread within the police department—by his own admission, at least half of the men under his command were involved in the liquor trade—and he had little inclination to pursue a confrontation with the state's attorney over the inappropriate use of police resources.[47]

The crackdown on gambling emphasized Crowe's independence and integrity—his war on crime, no matter that it was essentially fleeting and transitory, could only redound to his credit. And it enabled him to lessen his dependence on Fred Lundin and the City Hall machine.

The Harding landslide in November 1920 had swept all of Lundin's candidates into office. Lundin's influence over Cook County politics had metastasized—supporters of City Hall now occupied every significant political position in the county. The City Council, fiercely independent before 1920, had begun to capitulate to the Lundin regime—one by one, the aldermen were throwing their support behind City Hall. And Lundin's reach even extended as far as Springfield; the new governor of Illinois, Len Small, was one of Lundin's closest allies.

Only the judiciary still retained its independence, but now it too came under attack. The courts in Cook County had traditionally been nonpartisan, beyond the reach of party or faction, but tradition was about to be swept aside, or so it seemed. The voters would go to the polls in June 1921 to elect judges to the Superior Court and the Circuit Court; if they pulled the Republican lever, they would elect a pro-Lundin slate that was unashamedly partisan.

But Lundin had taken a step too far. The courts were the last redoubt against the excesses of City Hall, a final bulwark against the hegemony of the Republican Party machine; if Lundin controlled the judiciary there would no longer be any hope of redress against corruption and thievery.

On 6 June the voters turned out en masse and elected a nonpartisan reform ticket—City Hall had lost. It was a stunning defeat for Lundin, his first setback in thirty years. The *Chicago Daily Journal*, the sole Democratic newspaper in a Republican city, crowed that "Napoleon Fred Lundin has met his Moscow. Whether this will be followed by a

Waterloo remains to be seen; but just now the city hall cohorts are trekking back toward the Beresina with a chill in their hearts. . . . Will this be the beginning of the end of the Lundin-Thompson power?"[48]

Such a spectacular failure of the machine to elect its candidates was a sure sign that Lundin had lost his magical touch; association with City Hall might now be as much a liability as an advantage. Over the next eighteen months, Lundin's allies began to desert him, and his enemies became increasingly emboldened. Robert Crowe, now a powerful figure within the Republican Party, split with Lundin in February 1922. Crowe explained to the newspapers that Lundin had been interfering with his duties as state's attorney, but Crowe's departure was as much a bid for leadership of the Republican Party as a sign of dissatisfaction with City Hall.

The decline of Lundin's influence, and the continuing factionalism among the dissident Republicans, provided the Democrats with a rare opportunity to take power. Alfred Lueder, a political novice whose previous experience in public office amounted to a single year as postmaster, was the compromise candidate for the Republicans in the mayoral election in April 1923. Lueder, by his own admission, was a hopeless public speaker who never could arouse much enthusiasm for his candidacy among the electorate. His Democratic opponent, William

19. THE REFORM MOVEMENT. In 1922 dissidents within the Republican Party, led by Robert Crowe, Edward Brundage, and Charles Deneen, united in a campaign to clean up City Hall. The mayor of Chicago, Bill Thompson, left office in 1923, after the Chicago newspapers published details of scandals in municipal government.

Dever, won the election convincingly, receiving almost 400,000 votes.[49]

Dever's victory was less a consequence of Republican disunity than an effect of the corruption scandals that had begun to bubble their way to the surface in 1922. The City Hall machine under Lundin's direction had siphoned millions of dollars from the municipal budget. Corruption was rampant, and no single area of government had been more systematically despoiled than the public school system. The Board of Education had awarded contracts for school supplies to companies—often controlled by friends of Fred Lundin—that sold substandard, shoddy goods at wildly inflated prices. Why had the board paid the Hiawatha Phonograph Company almost $500,000 for 300 phonographs? Patrick H. Moynihan, a member of the City Council, was a part owner of the company—was there any connection? Why had the board spent an exorbitant amount, almost $1 million in 1920, for the purchase of coal? Why had the Apex Supply Company received an unauthorized contract to provide athletic equipment to the Chicago public schools? Edwin Davis, president of the Board of Education, was an uncle of Walter Titzel, an owner of the company—had that relationship influenced the board's decision to award the contract?[50]

In May 1922 Robert Crowe presented indictments against William Bither, an attorney working for the Board of Education, accusing Bither of stealing rents derived from school property. Later that year, in August, Crowe indicted three more officials, on charges of conspiracy to defraud the school system. In September 1922, Crowe charged an additional ten officials with malfeasance and misconduct and conspiracy to defraud.[51]

Crowe had always hoped to connect Fred Lundin to the corruption scandal—with Lundin in the penitentiary, Crowe would face one less obstacle in his drive for the mayoralty—and early in 1923, Crowe announced the indictment of Lundin for conspiracy to defraud. The Board of Education had awarded a contract for steel doors for school buildings to the National Steel Door Company; was it a coincidence that Lundin was president of the National Steel Door Company?[52]

Crowe had enlisted Jacob Loeb, a former president of the Board of Education, as the star witness for the prosecution. Few families played as prominent a role in Chicago's Jewish community as the Loebs: Jacob Loeb had made his fortune as a young man as an insurance broker, and since 1912 he had been president of the Jewish People's Institute; his brother, Albert, was vice president of Sears, Roebuck and a generous contributor to many Jewish charities. Jacob Loeb had been one of Lundin's victims—Lundin had engineered Loeb's removal from the Board of Education—and Loeb willingly agreed to Crowe's suggestion that he testify on the witness stand about the corruption of the public school system by City Hall.[53]

THE TRIAL OF FRED LUNDIN and fifteen codefendants in the Criminal Court began on 5 June 1923. The sixth-floor courtroom was packed; Lundin's friends and supporters had turned out en masse. Lundin himself, dressed in a black frock coat, a white shirt, and a black Windsor tie, sat near the front of the court, his legs stretched out before him, his thumbs in the pockets of his black waistcoat, looking relaxed and untroubled. Lundin had hired Clarence Darrow to defend him. Darrow sat by Lundin's side, reading silently to himself from a sheaf of papers on his lap, occasionally pausing to confer with one of the other defense lawyers seated to his right.

The assistant attorney general, Marvin Barnhart, began his opening statement. Fred Lundin had conspired to appoint trustees to the Board of Education who would acquiesce in the theft of school funds. Lundin himself had profited directly in two instances. In the first, he had arranged for the school board to purchase insurance coverage for school buildings and property from Virtus Rohm & Company, despite a clear conflict of interest: Lundin was a founding partner and director of the firm. In the second, the Central Metallic Door Company, owned by Fred Lundin, had sold hundreds of thousands of dollars' worth of doors and windows to the Board of Education through a noncompetitive contract.[54]

Jacob Loeb took the stand on 7 June. Loeb testified that Lundin had badgered and threatened him to remove incorruptible trustees from the school board. Lundin had contempt for civil service laws, and he had eventually managed to fire those trustees who had refused to bend to his command, replacing them with his cronies. The Public School League, a public interest group that traditionally oversaw appointments to the school board, had protested against the new trustees, but to no effect. Lundin had been successful, Loeb admitted, in evading external supervision of his appointments, and after 1919, when Loeb himself had been removed from the Board of Education, the pilfering of school funds had begun in earnest.[55]

The trial continued through June and into July. The former mayor, William Thompson, interrupted a vacation in Hawaii to testify on behalf of his old friend and to excoriate Jacob Loeb as a "liar and a crook" who had wanted control of the Board of Education for his own purposes. And on 9 July, Lundin himself took the stand to deny everything. Yes, he replied in answer to a question from Clarence Darrow, he knew Jacob Loeb well, but he had never discussed appointments to the school board with Loeb or anyone else—he assumed that the mayor and the City Council dealt with such matters. And that insurance business? Darrow asked. Was there any truth to the allegations that he had sold insurance coverage to the school board? Lundin replied that he had lent a friend some money to start up an insurance firm in 1918, but Lundin himself had never made any money out of it and had had no interest in the firm—the transaction had been a loan to a friend, nothing more. What about the Metallic Steel Door Company, Darrow inquired? Had Lundin been connected with that business? Had he made any money from it? Lundin shook his head. "I had," Lundin testified, "nothing to do with selling. I sold my interest in the National Steel Door company in January 1922 to Blaine Thelin, my nephew. I received $5000. They owed me $20,000 and I took notes which I have since sold. I gave my stock in the Central Metallic company to Titus Thelin, my nephew." His connection with the business had been purely passive, he continued; he had had no knowledge of any sales to the Board of Education.[56]

Clarence Darrow, in his closing speech to the jury, pointed his finger at the prosecution as the real culprit in the case. The accusations against Fred Lundin—"one of the biggest, cruelest conspiracies I ever saw in a court of justice, a conspiracy to imprison a man whom they can't beat in open war"—had been cooked up by Lundin's political enemies in an attempt to send him to the penitentiary. Robert Crowe had dug and dug, looking for evidence to present before the grand jury, finally indicting Lundin for conspiracy; Jacob Loeb, like a lapdog, had tagged along behind Crowe, volunteering to testify on Lundin's supposed influence with the school board, and perjuring himself on the witness stand; and Edward Brundage, the attorney general, had coordinated the prosecution in the courtroom. Everyone knew that each man had an agenda: Crowe sought to become mayor of Chicago; Brundage hoped to be governor of Illinois; and Jacob Loeb looked to revenge himself against City Hall for his removal from the school board in 1919. Crowe and Brundage needed Fred Lundin out of the way for political reasons and, unable to defeat Lundin by fair means, they had resorted to criminal charges to get Lundin into the penitentiary.

The prosecution, Darrow sneered, had failed to find even one scrap of evidence to convict his client. "There never was," he shouted, with ludicrous exaggeration, "a more infamous conspiracy against the liberties of men. Every law distorted, every fact magnified and lied about." Darrow turned to appeal to the jury, holding his hands palms upward, his eyes fixed on the twelve men sitting silently before him. "Gentlemen, they have given you quite a job. Loeb was on record and he had to stick to his story. Therefore we could show it a lie. . . . I have been long in the courts and have never heard such a baseless case brought against any citizen. If it were not a tragedy it would be a joke. What if Lundin did sell insurance and windows? You might as well indict Marshall Field & Co. for selling to the school board."[57]

It was a shameless performance, equal parts bombast and cynicism, by a demagogue who had long ago abandoned the principles that, in Darrow's youth, had earned him a progressive reputation. Darrow was a mesmerizing speaker who could cast a spell over any jury . . . but only if the jury—captivated by the cadence and inflection of his voice—could be lulled into forgetting the facts. Fred Lundin was a political fixer, a backroom operator, who had self-consciously organized the corruption of Chicago politics to a degree unequaled in the history of the city, but in Darrow's telling, he was one part saint, one part sage: "I have met many kinds of men and I will guarantee there is not one in 100,000 with his intelligence . . . his courage, independence, and truthfulness. He might be able to lie. I think he is too proud."

It was in vain that the prosecuting attorney, Hobart Young, in his summation, defended Jacob Loeb as "a man of good standing in this community" and showed again that gouging and price-fixing had become the normative behavior of the Board of Education. The jury deliberated for four and a half hours and acquitted Lundin and his codefendants on all charges.[58]

Lundin's acquittal was a consequence more of Clarence Darrow's guile than of an absence of evidence, according to an editorial in the *Chicago Daily Tribune*. "The defense," wrote the editor, "was in the hands of the shrewdest criminal lawyers of the Chicago bar. . . . As a lawyers' battle, it suggested a fight between Fatty Arbuckle and Jack Dempsey." The Thompson-Lundin ring would revive itself, the newspapers predicted, and there would be renewed bloodletting among the Republican Party factions.[59]

Robert Crowe shared the general disappointment that Fred Lundin had escaped. But Crowe still held the lead position among the Republicans. His faction was unified and cohesive and wielded more influence than any other group within the City Council. His own position also was secure. He was confident of reelection in November 1924. And the mayoral elections were still almost four years in the future; Crowe expected to be a candidate in 1927 and saw no reason why he should not win.

PART THREE

THE COURTROOM

10 | THE INDICTMENT

Of course, dear Mompsie and Popsie, this thing is all too terrible. I have thought and thought about it, and even now I do not seem to be able to understand it. I just cannot seem to figure out how it all came about. Of one thing I am certain tho—and that is that I have no one to blame but myself. . . . I am afraid that you two may try and put the blame upon your own shoulders, and I *know* that I alone am to blame. I never was frank with you—Mompsie and Popsie dear—and had you suspected anything and came and talked to me I would undoubtedly have denied everything and gone on just the same. . . .

I am on a floor of the jail confined entirely to young fellows under twenty years of age. . . . My first cell mate was a clean look-ing young fellow, who was exceedingly nice to me and helped very materially to make things easier. My present 'room-mate' is also a very nice chap—somewhat older than I and with a good high school education. I have managed to get along fine with all the fellows and was, in fact, made captain of the seventh floor ball-team. . . .

The jail authorities have been awfully nice about everything and I seem to get along with all of them splendidly. Upon Mr. Darrow's advice we have not asked for any special privileges, but a number of them have of their own accord gone out of the way to make things easier for me.

Furthermore several of the girls have been awfully nice about visiting me at the jail. Helen, altho her Father did not want her to take the chance of newspaper publicity by coming down here, wrote me a wonderful letter. Buddy Ringer and a couple of the other boys have sent nice messages thru the girls or thru one of the newspaper reporters that I know.

So you see, Mompsie and Popsie dear, that it is not at all hard for me. I intend to be very brave all the way thru and I want you both to know that I will do anything in my power to try and rectify a little the awful thing that I have done. You, dear ones, are always in my thoughts. . . . I shall write again.

Loads of love to Erny, Adele, Jane and Tommy and especially to you two."[1]

Richard Loeb, 28 July 1924

CLARENCE DARROW SEEMED ONE OF the least impressive men that Nathan Leopold had ever met. Darrow sat across from him, in the small windowless room—the lawyers' cage, they called it—where prisoners in the Cook County jail conferred with their attorneys. The air in the cell was stuffy and humid, and Nathan noticed that Darrow was wearing a light seersucker jacket—just about the only kind of jacket one could comfortably wear on such a blisteringly hot day—but it was creased and wrinkled, almost, Nathan thought to himself, as if Darrow had spent the previous night sleeping in it.[2]

Darrow's tie was askew—it had been done up carelessly and it rested awkwardly around his collar. His shirt had not been ironed that morning, and Nathan could see, as he looked more closely, some yellow stains on the front. Were they, Nathan speculated, egg stains left over from Darrow's breakfast? And finally, a pair of red suspenders stretched across Darrow's ample stomach and attached themselves to a pair of baggy gray trousers.

Darrow's face was lined and tired, and a shock of lustreless, mousy, iron-gray hair kept falling over his right eye; occasionally he would brush it back. There was an atmosphere of resignation in Darrow's weather-beaten face, as though Nathan's case were hopeless, doomed before it had even begun.

Nathan was shocked that his father had assigned the defense to such an obvious incompetent. He had heard of Darrow only within the past twenty-four hours and knew only that Darrow had a reputation as a capable, clever lawyer; yet here Darrow sat, looking more like a country bumpkin, an innocent hayseed, than a city lawyer. What could this scarecrow know of the law?[3]

Darrow talked in a quiet, dry voice—there was nothing in his words that suggested urgency. He cautioned Nathan not to say anything further to the state's attorney—both boys had already said a great deal, but their case was not yet entirely hopeless.

The police had now linked Nathan and Richard to other crimes on the South Side. It was important, Darrow warned, to tell the state's attorney nothing which would give Crowe evidence that they had, in fact, committed those crimes.

A twenty-one-year-old cabdriver, Charles Ream, had identified Nathan and Richard as the two men who had kidnapped him one night the previous November at the intersection of 55th Street and Dorchester Avenue as he made his way home after work. One assailant, Ream charged, had held him at gunpoint while the other had rendered him unconscious with a rag soaked in ether. Ream had awoken four hours later. His kidnappers had castrated him and left him, bruised and bloody, on industrial wasteland southeast of Chicago, near 109th Street, not far from the Pennsylvania Railroad tracks and less than one mile from the culvert where Nathan and Richard would later hide the body of Bobby Franks.[4]

The police could also connect Nathan and Richard to the killing of Freeman Tracy, a twenty-three-year-old student at the University of Chicago. On 25 November 1923 Tracy had left a dance late in the evening to walk home alone. Several hours later, shortly before

20. WAITING FOR HABEAS CORPUS. On Monday, 2 June, Clarence Darrow presented a writ of habeas corpus on behalf of Richard Loeb and Nathan Leopold. This photograph, taken that morning, shows the attorneys and relatives of the defendants waiting for the judge's decision. Seated in front (from left) are Michael Leopold (brother), Benjamin Bachrach (attorney), Nathan Leopold Sr. (father), Jacob Loeb (uncle), and Clarence Darrow.

three o'clock in the morning, a passerby had discovered his body lying near the intersection of 58th Street and Woodlawn Avenue, close to the university. There had been no robbery; his wallet was untouched. But his assailants had killed Tracy with a single gunshot to the head, and the steel-jacketed bullet, according to the police, matched the automatic revolver found in Nathan's bedroom.[5]

There was also the abduction of Louise Hohley, a forty-five-year-old housewife and mother of three. Hohley had identified Nathan and Richard as the two men who had kidnapped her one evening in February in front of the Riviera Theater on Lawrence Avenue. Hohley claimed that they had beaten her and, after raping her, had driven her to the outskirts of the city and thrown her from their car.[6]

Finally, there was the mysterious disappearance, on 7 April 1924, of

Melvin Wolf, a young man who had vanished after leaving his uncle's house at 4553 Ellis Avenue to mail a letter. Was it a coincidence that Wolf had last been seen in Kenwood, less than three blocks from the spot where Nathan and Richard would kidnap Bobby Franks?

On 8 May, one month after the disappearance of Wolf, the police had found his badly decomposed body floating in Lake Michigan. Could Wolf's death have been a suicide? But Wolf had been a happy, carefree young man, at least according to family members, and he had shown no signs of depression or melancholy. Had kidnapping and murder resulted in his death? Were Nathan Leopold and Richard Loeb the culprits in this case also?[7]

CLARENCE DARROW WAS SKEPTICAL ABOUT Nathan and Richard's involvement in the kidnapping of Louise Hohley. Both boys strenuously denied the accusation, and even the state's attorney doubted Hohley's truthfulness; it remained to be proved that Nathan and Richard were connected with the castration of Charles Ream and the deaths of Freeman Tracy and Melvin Wolf.[8]

In any case, Darrow was too preoccupied with winning Nathan and Richard their constitutional rights. His clients, he protested to the chief justice of the Criminal Court, had been in the custody of the state's attorney for more than three days and only now, on the morning of Monday, 2 June, had they obtained access to legal counsel. He had presented petitions for writs of habeas corpus earlier that morning asking that Robert Crowe relinquish the prisoners and remand them to the custody of the sheriff.

CLARENCE DARROW, REPRESENTING THE LOEB family, and Benjamin Bachrach, the attorney for the Leopold family, stood in front of the chief justice, John Caverly. They listened in silence as Robert Crowe spoke to the judge, urging that he, Crowe, be allowed to keep Leopold and Loeb in his custody, at least until after the inquest into Bobby Franks's death.

"That's a most extraordinary request," Darrow exploded angrily. "What an astonishing proposition!" he continued. "I never heard the like of it in court before. These boys are minors and under the constitution entitled to more than ordinary protection from the court . . ."

"A cold-blooded, vicious murder," Crowe interrupted, almost shouting at the defense attorney, "and these boys have confessed to it."

"It matters not how cold-blooded the murder was," Darrow shouted back, "citizens have rights. There is but one place for them to be held, in the county jail, in the custody of the sheriff. That question is not debatable and the matter of an indictment has nothing to do with it."[9]

John Caverly agreed. He would place Leopold and Loeb in custody of the sheriff. Both the defense attorneys and the prosecution would have access to the boys and would be able to question them further before the start of the trial.

The following day, Tuesday, 3 June, John Caverly impaneled the twenty-three members—all men—of the Cook County grand jury. LeRoy Fairbank, an assistant state's attorney, had prepared two indict-

ments: one for murder and the second for kidnapping for ransom. Both indictments carried the death penalty in Illinois.[10]

Grand jury proceedings were customarily brief, especially in a

21. LEOPOLD AND LOEB ENTER COOK COUNTY JAIL. After Clarence Darrow presented a writ of habeas corpus, Leopold and Loeb were put in the custody of the sheriff of Cook County and transferred to the Cook County jail. From left: Nathan Leopold, Richard Loeb, David Edfeldt (deputy sheriff), and Hans Thompson (assistant jailer).

case such as this, where the corpus delicti—the facts necessary to establish the commission of a crime—were not in dispute. Nathan Leopold and Richard Loeb had confessed and there was a mass of evidence to affirm their statements—the grand jury would surely not need long to decide that the evidence warranted formal charges against the prisoners.

But Crowe intended to use the grand jury proceedings as a record of the evidence. The Leopold and Loeb families had enormous resources—many millions of dollars—and perhaps they would use their money to postpone and prolong the trial indefinitely. Witnesses might change their minds or, if the trial were to stretch on for several months, might even die. The families of the prisoners might conceivably use their money to fix the result and to bribe witnesses to change their testimony.[11]

Crowe would call the witnesses now. They would testify to the grand jury, and if any witnesses subsequently changed their testimony, Crowe announced, he would prosecute them for perjury.[12]

And so, that Tuesday afternoon, the witnesses began their testimony. Jacob Franks appeared first: he wept as he described the clothing Bobby had worn to the Harvard School on the morning of 21 May. Then Tony Minke took the witness stand to tell the grand jury how he had discovered Bobby's body in the culvert by the Pennsylvania Railroad. Paul Korff told how he had found the eyeglasses lying a few feet from the culvert. Sven Englund also testified that first day, telling the grand jury that Leopold's red Willys-Knight had remained in the garage the entire day.[13]

On and on it went, a succession of witnesses—seventy-two in total that week—all linking Nathan and Richard to the crime and providing an unbroken chain that fastened them to the murder of Bobby Franks.

MICHAEL HUGHES, THE CHIEF OF detectives, had never known a case like it; he could not imagine that the accused could escape the gallows. The evidence was overwhelming.

"We have unearthed too much corroborative evidence . . . to permit them to escape," he confided to a reporter from the *Chicago Daily*

Journal, "I am certain they will receive the death penalty." It was ironic, Hughes thought, that Nathan and Richard had—directly or indirectly—provided much of that evidence themselves. "The police knew only that young Franks had been murdered and that a pair of tortoiseshell eyeglasses and one of young Franks' stockings had been found. We had nothing else. Guided entirely by Leopold and Loeb, we were led to the place where they buried Franks' belt and buckle, and these we recovered. On their information . . . we also located the blood-stained automobile in which the boy was murdered and found the robe which they wrapped around his body. We now also have the tape-bound chisel with which young Franks was beaten over the head, and the boy's shoes. We have been led by Leopold and Loeb to the drug stores from which they made their telephone calls to the father of the Franks boy."

Of course, Hughes had heard the rumor that the fathers of the boys were preparing to spend millions of dollars in defense of their sons—but how could their wealth stand against such an accumulation of evidence? "They talk about 'millions for defense,'" Hughes said, "but I don't believe all the money in the world could save these boys."[14]

Thomas Marshall, an assistant state's attorney, explained to the same reporter the precautions taken by the state in drawing up the indictments. There was, for example, some ambiguity over the cause of death. Had Bobby Franks died from the blows to the head or from asphyxiation when Richard had jammed the rag down his throat? Or perhaps the murderers had poisoned the boy with the hydrochloric acid. The coroner's physician, Joseph Springer, had determined that asphyxiation was the cause of death, but Robert Crowe was taking no chances: the indictments for murder and kidnapping had to be sufficiently broad to cover all possible challenges from the defense.

Marshall's final draft of the murder indictment contained eleven counts: the first count charged murder with a chisel; the second, murder with a club; and the third, murder by smothering with a bandage. Other counts included smothering with a piece of cloth; murder with chisel, club, and smothering; smothering with hands; smothering with hands and a cloth gag; killing with deadly poisons; and poisoning with unknown ingredients.[15]

The second indictment, charging Leopold and Loeb with kidnapping for ransom, contained sixteen counts: seizing and confining for the purpose of extorting money; inveigling, decoying, and kidnapping for ransom; seizing and confining for $10,000; inveigling to extort $10,000; and so on. Each count repeated the same charge, albeit in different phrases.[16]

By the end of the week, the jurors had heard enough evidence; they would now vote on the indictments. Frederick Hoffman, the foreman of the grand jury, announced that the jurors had endorsed both indictments; the state's attorney had indeed demonstrated that the evidence warranted the prosecution of Nathan Leopold and Richard Loeb.[17]

IT WAS A PREDICTABLE OUTCOME, of course: no one had expected the grand jury to refuse the indictments. Robert Crowe was satisfied with the result and boasted to the press that it was "the most complete case ever presented to a grand or petit jury. The evidence against the two undoubtedly constitutes a hanging case." But did not Crowe's case, one reporter asked, rest on the confessions? What if Leopold and Loeb repudiated the confessions? And if the judge excluded the confessions because the police had obtained them by duress, how would Crowe's case stand then?

"When this murder trial is called," Crowe replied, "I shall place on the stand the three stenographers from the state's attorney's office who alternated in taking the statements from Leopold and Loeb. . . . The stenographers will be backed by attorneys, police officers and other witnesses who were present when Leopold and Loeb declared they had kidnaped and murdered young Franks. I am confident that . . . we will be able to get the two youths' statements before the jury in the event they repudiate their confessions and plead not guilty of the crime."[18]

It was not true that his men had tortured the prisoners. "They were not given 'goldfish' treatment or kept in 'goldfish' rooms," Crowe asserted, using the slang term for a beating by the police. "Because of kindness mixed with firmness, we were able to obtain the confessions, which were voluntary and given without fear. . . . No one ever laid a hand on them or spoke a harsh word to them."[19]

Crowe reminded the reporters that he also had handwritten notes that Leopold and Loeb had made on each other's account of the slaying. Each had recounted the killing in Crowe's office on Sunday, 1 June, but the boys' versions of the murder had differed in certain details—most significantly, each had accused the other of striking the blows with the chisel—and the state's attorney had helpfully suggested that each boy make notes on the other's version of events.

They had complied, willingly, even enthusiastically, not realizing that their notes might be used by the state's attorney as evidence against them. Crowe had now secured those notes—he had locked them away in a safe in his office—and he intended to use them to convince a jury, first, that the prisoners had given their confessions voluntarily; and, second, that both of the accused were aware of the nature of their crime and hence were, in a legal sense, sane.[20]

Crowe's optimism that his evidence against the boys was sufficient to send them to the gallows found an echo among other, less partisan, legal observers. Nevertheless, it was cause for concern that Clarence Darrow might exploit some technicality to free his clients; he had done it in the past and he might do it again. Leopold and Loeb were guilty, of course, but would they therefore necessarily receive the appropriate punishment? Or would their lawyers find some loophole that would allow the accused to get off lightly?

John Clinnin, a former district attorney, was cautiously optimistic that justice would prevail but warned, nevertheless, that Crowe should zealously watch for any tricks from the defense. "I am certain," Clinnin remarked, after the grand jury had voted on the indictments, "that Mr. Crowe will prosecute this case to the full extent of his power. . . . But the people are watching the case with very suspicious eyes because of the money involved. The state must be on its guard at every point of the legal conflict."

Julius Smietanka, a member of the Board of Education, agreed with Clinnin that Crowe should be on guard. Smietanka urged that the trial "be expedited in every possible way. Public feeling is running high and there will be no toleration of unnecessary delay. . . . The full penalty of the law should be invoked."[21]

Leopold and Loeb had already confessed; there were no mitigating circumstances; a jury would surely find them guilty; and the sentencing would quickly follow. Any delay would, therefore, assist the defense: public feeling would die down and the atrocity of the murder would be forgotten. Edmund Jarecki, a judge on the County Court, wondered why the United States "should not follow the example of England in expediting its trials in criminal cases and particularly in a case like this one. I am sure," Jarecki continued, "that the state will not lose any time in satisfying the public demand that justice be done in this case."[22]

Constitutional rights seemed beside the point in a case such as this. The killers had confessed and had substantiated their confessions by revealing physical evidence of their crime to the police. What more needed to be said? Of course, Nathan Leopold and Richard Loeb did have the right to a trial, but there was not much more that the law should grant them, at least according to the editor of the *Chicago Herald and Examiner*: "For every reason this is a case for steady judgment and not for the introduction of technicalities. The remaining right of the young men who have confessed is for such a trial. . . . The people of this city, whom this thing has shaken with its horror, have a right to immediate procedure. This is not a case the details of which anybody cares to cherish in his memory. . . . Delay can serve no purpose of justice. The evidence is at hand; there is not need to wait for distant witnesses or to search for hidden testimony. . . . The quick, firm action of investigation calls for equally quick and firm action in prosecution!"[23]

Already, rumors were circulating that the families were prepared to spend as much money as was necessary to free the boys. Albert Loeb had, according to one report, paid Clarence Darrow a retainer of $25,000 and had provided Darrow with $1 million to spend on the defense.

The grand jury had recommended that Leopold and Loeb be held for trial without bond, but now a second rumor, that the defense would attempt to have the prisoners released on bail, had appeared in the newspapers. And would Darrow seek to move the trial out of

Cook County, thus incurring additional delay, arguing that the notoriety of the case made it impossible to obtain an unprejudiced jury in Chicago?

Public opinion had never favored the murderers of Bobby Franks, and now, as it appeared probable that Darrow would use some subterfuge to evade justice, public sentiment hardened in favor of the death penalty for Leopold and Loeb. Chicagoans who had previously opposed capital punishment wrote to the newspapers demanding that the murderers be sent to the gallows. Both Leopold and Loeb had confessed their guilt and had yet to express any remorse for the killing; why, therefore, should they be spared the noose?[24]

On Friday, 6 June, Albert Loeb and Nathan Leopold Sr. issued a joint statement denying their intention to influence the result by using their wealth. Their sons would expect the same treatment in a court of law that every American was entitled to receive—nothing more and nothing less—and rumors that the fathers would use their fortunes to evade justice were unfounded: "the families of the accused boys . . . have not the slightest inclination or intention to use their means to stage an unsightly legal battle with an elaborate array of counsel and an army of high-priced alienists in an attempt to defeat justice. Only such defense as that to which every human being is entitled will be provided for their sons.

"They emphatically state that no counsel for the accused boys will be retained other than those lawyers now representing them, with the possible, but not probable, retention of one additional local lawyer. There will be no large sums of money spent either for legal or medical talent. The fees to be paid to medical experts will be only such fees as are ordinary and usual for similar testimony.

"The lawyers representing the accused boys have agreed that the amount of their fees shall be determined by a committee composed of the officers of the Chicago Bar association.

"If the accused boys are found by a jury to be not mentally responsible, their families, in accordance with their conscious duty toward the community, agree that the public must be fully protected from any future menace by these boys. In no event will the families of the accused boys use money in any attempt to defeat justice."[25]

The letter was eminently reasonable, calculated to appeal to the better instincts of Chicagoans. All of Chicago's newspapers printed the statement, and most also published editorials praising the fathers and supporting their sons' right to a fair trial. The *Chicago Daily Tribune*, which considered itself the highest-minded of the city's newspapers, expressed itself satisfied with the fathers' statement and confident that the lawyers would conduct the defense on its merits: "Undoubtedly there was a very general assumption in the public mind that money would be used without stint to retard, complicate, and, if possible, defeat the ends of justice and the public good. The American public has had too much reason to fear such procedure. It sees year in and year out the escape of offenders through the meshes of the law, in cases where the accused has fewer resources of evasion than the accused in this case possess. . . . The determination of the families concerned in the coming trial to regard their duty to the community as well as the legitimate rights of the accused, should ease public disquiet."[26]

ON WEDNESDAY, 11 JUNE, at ten o'clock in the morning, Richard Loeb and Nathan Leopold stood before the judge's bench in the sixth-floor courtroom in the Cook County Criminal Court. Anticipation had been mounting throughout the week; hundreds of spectators had been standing outside the building at seven o'clock that morning, hoping to gain entrance; hundreds more had descended on Austin Avenue in the interim; and now the courtroom was packed. Peter Hoffman, the sheriff, had been caught unawares; he had ordered a special detail of fifteen deputies, in addition to the customary guard, but it had been inadequate to control the thousands of Chicagoans who tried to enter the building. The crowd, in its initial surge to enter the courtroom, had torn one of the heavy oak doors off its hinges, and now a line of bailiffs stood in the doorway, nightsticks drawn, ready to repel a second invasion of the courtroom.

Inside the courtroom, hundreds of spectators squeezed into every available space. Some sat, precariously, on the windowsills; others stood in the aisles or leaned against the walls; and others stood on temporary benches at the rear of the room, craning their necks over the heads of the crowd for a glimpse of the accused.[27]

John Caverly, chief justice of the Criminal Court, peered down from the bench at the crowd in front of him. The previous day, Caverly had announced that he would be the trial judge. Frederic Robert De-Young, a judge on the Superior Court, would normally have presided over the trial (since he was first in sequence), but he was to ascend to the Illinois supreme court on 19 June. Since DeYoung might hear the case on appeal, Caverly had decided that he himself would be a better choice.[28]

Caverly's decision had pleased Darrow. Caverly was a liberal judge. During his three years on the Criminal Court, he had sentenced five men to death, but in each case he had merely been giving formal utterance to a decision of the jury. And on the one occasion when Caverly might have sentenced a prisoner to hang—when Sam Rosen pleaded guilty to the brutal murder of his wife, Jennie—he had handed down a life sentence instead.[29]

Caverly waited patiently for the crowd to come to order. On his left, just a few feet away, Robert Crowe sat with his assistants—John Sbarbaro, Joseph Savage, and Thomas Marshall—at the prosecution table. Caverly could see Samuel Ettelson, representing the Franks family, sitting immediately behind Crowe; at Ettelson's side, Caverly noticed the wan figure of Jacob Franks, wearing a coal-black suit, white shirt, and black necktie, his eyeglasses dangling from a black ribbon attached to his waistcoat.

Across the aisle from Crowe, on Caverly's right, Clarence Darrow sat next to Benjamin Bachrach. Nathan Leopold and Richard Loeb, each accompanied by a guard, sat directly behind their attorneys. Bachrach was a familiar figure in the Criminal Court and a celebrated attorney in his own right. He had graduated from the University of Notre Dame, and, after studying at Columbia University, had returned to Chicago to receive his law degree from the Kent College of Law in

22. JOHN CAVERLY. After studying law at Lake Forest University, Caverly was elected city attorney of Chicago in 1906. In 1910 he won the election for judge of the Municipal Court. He served on the Municipal Court until 1920, when he was elected to the Circuit Court. Caverly served as chief justice of the Cook County Criminal Court in 1923 and 1924.

1896. Bachrach had a magical touch in the courtroom, winning acquittals for prominent and wealthy clients charged with murder, embezzlement, conspiracy, and fraud.[30]

Bachrach, like Darrow, had made his reputation in a series of sensational trials, most notably in his defense of Jack Johnson, the black heavyweight boxing champion. Johnson, a flamboyant extrovert who had outraged public opinion by marrying a white woman, had paid the train fare for a woman friend to visit him from Pittsburgh. Unfortunately for Johnson, his friend also happened to be a prostitute, and federal authorities could thus charge Johnson with violating the White Slave Traffic Act, legislation that banned the promotion of prostitution across state lines. Bachrach doggedly fought Johnson's case through the courts, and eventually the charges were dismissed in the Circuit Court of Appeals in April 1914. It had been an unpopular cause—Johnson, by far the most prominent black Chicagoan at the time, had become the most visible target for white hostility and racism in the city—yet Bachrach, in his defense of Johnson, had made his reputation as a methodical and persistent lawyer capable of successfully defending a client who had seemed destined for the penitentiary.[31]

Darrow and Bachrach constituted a formidable defense team and a striking sartorial contrast. Whereas Darrow dressed carelessly, never bothering greatly about his appearance, Bachrach was impeccably dressed in a conservative business suit, white shirt, and expensive necktie. He was almost too meticulous, too careful about his appearance—journalists covering his cases occasionally poked fun at a fastidiousness that bordered on self-absorption.

JOHN CAVERLY BROUGHT THE COURTROOM to order. The clerk of the court, Ferdinand Scherer, read the indictments and then turned toward the accused: "On June 6 the grand jury returned indictments, charging both of you with murder. Do you plead guilty or not guilty?"

Richard Loeb answered first: "Not guilty, sir." Leopold, standing slightly behind the other boy, repeated the same phrase.

"On June 6 the grand jury returned indictments charging you two with kidnaping for ransom. Do you plead guilty or not guilty?"

"Not guilty."

The photographers maneuvered among the spectators at the front of the court, stepping around the bailiffs to get the best position; a dozen flashbulbs popped and hissed and crackled.

Caverly motioned to Clarence Darrow and Benjamin Bachrach for the defense and Robert Crowe for the state to step forward.

"This case," Caverly began, "will be assigned to Branch No. 1, my own court. Have you gentlemen any objections?"

Neither the defense nor the prosecution had any reason to protest against Caverly as the trial judge.

"Have you gentlemen agreed upon a date for trial?" Caverly asked.

"No, your honor," answered Bachrach, "we haven't had a chance."

"I would suggest," Crowe interrupted, "that your honor follow out the procedure you have been adopting in murder cases and set this for an early date. July 15 would give the defense a month and a half for trial."

"This case is not in the class with other murder cases." Darrow brushed his hair away from his eyes impatiently. "There isn't a man in Chicago who would say we could get a fair trial within a month. We are as anxious as anyone to get ready, but we must have a fair trial."

"That is a very short time in which to prepare the case," Bachrach added, a trace of anxiety in his voice. "The state must know the defense can not get ready within that time. Your honor must be aware of the public feeling arising from the statements in the newspapers. According to the newspapers, Mr. Crowe has boasted he'll hang the boys. . . ."

"I've made no such statement. I am not responsible," Crowe snapped back angrily, "for the articles in the press. . . . It has been the policy of judges to speed up murder trials. I don't see why this case should be handled any differently."

"The defense is anxious to get through with the case as soon as possible," Darrow spoke now, pleading with the judge to allow them more time, "but I believe it will be impossible to obtain a fair trial if the trial is held immediately. It will take a large amount of preparation to get the defense side of the case ready. We need time to prepare the case and time," he added meaningfully, "for public sentiment to die down."

Caverly listened patiently to the attorneys. He had a characteristic pose on the bench, seated forward, away from the back of his chair, peering through wire-rimmed glasses, a pen in his right hand, ready to scribble notes on a pad before him.

He turned to look at a calendar on the wall behind him, and as the attorneys waited for his decision, he silently counted out the days and turned back to face the court.

"I will set the case then, for July 21. All motions will be disposed of on that day. I will then set the trial for August 4."

Darrow relaxed. Perhaps, he suggested to the judge, the defense would require an adjournment, some additional time to prepare; if so, he added, the defense might present a motion for a continuance on 21 July.

Caverly nodded. He would hear the motions then, he repeated, and he would assuredly consider any request from the defense to delay the opening of trial. "Of course," Caverly replied, "if anything occurs that makes a continuance necessary, the motion can be heard."[32]

The judge gathered up his papers, as if to leave the room. The crowd began to drift away, melting back down to the street outside, to the bright sunlight that flooded Austin Avenue as Richard and Nathan, each handcuffed to a guard, exited through a side door to cross the bridge that connected the Criminal Court Building to the Cook County jail.

Robert Crowe bustled about purposefully for a few minutes, conferring with the sheriff, Peter Hoffman, before leaving for his office on the third floor. A small retinue of assistants—five or six, perhaps more—trailed along in his wake, to prepare for a conference later that day in the state's attorney's office.

Clarence Darrow also lingered in the courtroom. He murmured some words to Benjamin Bachrach, and then turned to greet Richard Loeb's brother Allan. Neither Albert Loeb nor Nathan Leopold Sr. had been in court that morning, but Darrow expected to talk with them later that day to discuss his strategy. In five weeks, he reminded Bachrach, they would be back in court to present motions to the judge; there was no time to lose!

11 | THE SCIENTISTS ARRIVE

Science and evolution teach us that man is an animal, a little higher than the other orders of animals; that he is governed by the same natural laws that govern the rest of the universe; . . . that free moral agency is a myth, a delusion, and a snare.[1]

Clarence Darrow, March 1911

THE TWENTIETH CENTURY EXPRESS from Boston pulled into LaSalle Street Station at noon on Friday, 13 June. A small-statured, narrow-shouldered middle-aged man, with thin lips, large ears, and tortoiseshell eyeglasses, and wearing a black porkpie hat, opened one of the train windows as the express slid to a halt along the side of the platform. Clarence Darrow had promised to meet him at the station. The man leaned out of the window and scanned the platform anxiously, trying to recognize the attorney, but the sudden maelstrom of passengers—spilling from the train, collecting belongings, greeting friends and relatives—had created a whirlwind that, for the moment at least, rendered Darrow invisible.[2]

He had read of the murder of Bobby Franks in the Boston newspapers, of course; the entire country seemed to be talking about this sensational killing in Chicago. He knew that two killers—both wealthy teenagers—had confessed to the murder. But he had never anticipated that Clarence Darrow would ask him to join the defense team—what did he know of the law? Nevertheless, once Darrow had explained the defense strategy, he had immediately consented to travel to Chicago.

Karl Bowman, chief medical officer at the Boston Psychopathic Hospital, looked up and down the platform. Suddenly Bowman saw Clarence Darrow, walking casually in his direction, looking left and right, pushing his way through the crowds. He recognized Darrow instantly—who could not recognize the most famous lawyer in the country?—and he waved from the window, hoping to catch the attorney's attention.

Darrow watched expectantly as Bowman descended the steps to the platform. They shook hands enthusiastically, as if they had both been waiting a long time for this encounter, and Darrow turned to introduce Benjamin Bachrach, the lawyer representing the Leopold family in the case.

Bowman was amused at the contrast between the two men. Darrow was dressed in a slovenly manner, in an inexpensive jacket, a slightly grubby shirt, and a frayed necktie. Bachrach was dressed impeccably in a well-cut, expertly tailored, dark business suit—his shoes gleamed, his white shirtfront dazzled, his cuff links sparkled, and his colorful yet tasteful silk necktie bespoke a man with expensive tastes. If he had not known better, Bowman realized, he would have assumed that Bachrach was the lead attorney.

As they drove to the Cook County jail, Clarence Darrow explained that he had hired Harold Hulbert, a neuropsychiatrist in private practice, to assist Bowman in the examination of Nathan Leopold and Richard Loeb. Hulbert was still in his thirties, Darrow confided, yet he already had considerable experience in the treatment of psychiatric disorders. After postgraduate work in nervous and mental diseases at the University of Michigan, Hulbert had worked in Tennessee under a grant from the Rockefeller Foundation, examining mental defectives in the state prisons, before serving in the war as a psychiatrist in the United States Navy. He was a pleasant young man, Darrow mused, tall, good-looking, with an open, honest appearance; Darrow was sure that he would be an asset to the defense team. He continued to talk as Bowman listened in silence and Bachrach, absorbed in his own thoughts, stared out at the lunchtime crowds thronging LaSalle Street. They reached the swing bridge stretching across the Chicago River, continued north on LaSalle, turned right onto Austin Avenue and left onto Dearborn Street, and finally stopped in front of the Cook County jail.[3]

The warden, Wesley Westbrook, ushered the visitors into the room on the second floor set aside for the examination. Bowman looked around with satisfaction. Everything was as it should be; the room perhaps was a little small, but, importantly, it was isolated within the prison so that there would be no possibility of interference or disturbance from the other prisoners. A table stood in the center of the room with chairs arranged along one side; there was a sink in one corner with faucets for hot and cold water, and a metal frame bed with a mattress ran along one side of the room. It was, Bowman remarked, much better than he had expected, and now that he had reached his destination, he was eager to begin his examination of the two prisoners.[4]

THE KEY TO MENTAL HEALTH, Bowman believed, lay within endocrinology, the study of the secretions of the endocrine glands: once researchers understood the effect of the hormones on the body, physician-psychiatrists would be able to eliminate mental illness.

No science was more fashionable in the 1920s than endocrinology. It was one of the youngest scientific disciplines, yet already it promised to deliver new therapies for disease. Scientists could now explain the workings of the body, and soon, perhaps, they would be able to control and determine the body through manipulation of the glands. Endocrinology, some scientists speculated, might even join with eugenics to transform American society. Endocrinology, in concert with such novel sciences as psychoanalysis and behaviorism, would allow the scientist to go beyond surface appearances to a discovery of the interior self, which was otherwise hidden. Science would thus arrive at a new level of understanding of human action.[5]

In 1916, endocrinologists meeting at the annual convention of the American Medical Association had established a professional organization, the Society for the Study of Internal Secretions, and in January 1917 the journal *Endocrinology* made its first appearance. Scientists had already mapped the positions of the endocrine glands in the body and had begun to understand the action on the body of the hormones that poured from each gland into the bloodstream. Each hormone acted as a chemical messenger that, in ways yet unknown, regulated physiological action and helped maintain health.

The thyroid gland—consisting of two lobes, one on each side of the larynx—secreted a substance, thyroxin, that regulated the body's metabolism. An excess of thyroxin in the bloodstream—a condition known as hyperthyroidism—correlated with an abnormal enlargement of the thyroid, visible as a swelling of the neck, and resulted in excessive metabolism, an irregular pulse, anxiety, restlessness, and an abnormally rapid heartbeat. A decrease in thyroxin (hypothyroidism) had equally dramatic consequences: the patient became dull and lethargic, gained excessive weight, suffered from hair loss, and had thick dry skin. In extreme cases, the condition resulted in cretinism in children and myxedema in adults.[6]

The pituitary gland, located in a bony cradle-shaped cavity, the *sella turcica*, at the base of the brain, secreted pituitin, a hormone that regulated growth and development. A deficiency of pituitin might result in dwarfism; other symptoms included obesity, lethargy, and sexual dysfunction. The skin of a patient suffering from hypopituitarism was often fine, smooth, and hairless; his or her behavior was often capricious, childish, and uninhibited. An excessive amount of pituitin, on the other hand, might result in, inter alia, exaggerated growth, leading to acromegaly and gigantism.[7]

Other glands also were linked to physical and mental symptoms of ill-health. Disease of the pineal gland manifested itself as excessive sexual activity, the premature development of secondary sex characteristics, and an abnormal mental precociousness. Disturbances in the adrenal glands were linked to symptoms of listlessness and nervous disability, discoloration of the skin, and abnormal secondary sex characteristics. The removal of the interstitial sex glands led to decreased sexual virility and the failure of secondary sex characteristics to appear. The malfunction of the thymus gland resulted in the persistence of a child-like, irresponsible personality into adulthood.[8]

The endocrine glands were no doubt significant in understanding health and disease, but how significant? Had physicians in the 1920s sufficient knowledge of the glands to treat physical and mental ailments? Or were the therapeutic effects of glandular extracts and surgical operations on the glands merely a chimera, more a hope than a reality?

The relationship between the endocrine glands and mental health was especially intriguing. Researchers at the Michigan Institution for the Feeble-Minded had found that twenty percent of the inmates suffered from glandular disorders, most commonly either hypothyroidism or hypopituitarism. Physicians at the Massachusetts State Psychiatric Institute had found from postmortem examinations that seventy-four percent of patients had suffered from diseases of the glands. Nolan Lewis and Gertrude Davies, two researchers at the Government Hospital for the Insane at Washington, D.C., had discovered that in more than 200 patients mental illness went hand in hand with glandular dysfunction. Therapeutic intervention, they concluded, was most effective when it combined psychotherapy and the administration of glandular extracts to the patient.[9]

The association of mental disease with endocrine pathology promised a means of determining the presence and character of mental illness. Glandular disturbances in the body manifested themselves through measurable effects on the urine, blood, pulse, blood pressure, and metabolism. Thus the thyroid gland controlled metabolism—the rate at which the body oxidizes food. Any deviation of the metabolic rate from the norm was evidence of a diseased thyroid—too much thyroxin from the thyroid elevated the body's metabolism; too little thyroxin caused a lowering of the metabolic rate. Similarly, the pancreatic glands regulated the amount of sugar in the blood—an excess of sugar in the bloodstream was a sure sign of the failure of the pancreas.

Any correlation between glandular dysfunction and mental illness might pinpoint a particular gland as the cause of a specific psychiatric disorder. Yet Karl Bowman's own research had been inconclusive. In 1921 Bowman had examined 229 patients at the Bloomingdale Hospital—a group that included patients with manic-depressive psychoses, dementia praecox, melancholia, paranoia, senile dementia, and psychoneurosis. A blood analysis of each patient— including readings of nonprotein nitrogen, dextrose, uric acid, and chlorides—had revealed nothing abnormal.[10]

A more detailed study that same year on ten patients suffering from dementia praecox was equally inconclusive. Bowman measured the blood count, conducted a urine analysis, estimated the metabolism, and determined the quantity of sugar in the blood but found nothing unusual—the metabolism of some patients was low, but not consistently so. There was, Bowman concluded, "nothing to confirm a simple dysfunction of a single endocrine gland and a constant condition in dementia praecox."[11]

A third study, in 1923, of fifty mental patients at the Boston Psychopathic Hospital revealed that twenty-seven had a metabolism well below the normal range, indicating a lack of thyroid activity. Was a disease of the thyroid gland a cause of mental illness? Bowman was pleased that he had found the correlation—"a low basal metabolism in cases of mental disease is of importance and merits consideration in formulating our theories as to etiology and treatment"—yet he remained reluctant to make any grand claim that might subsequently be disproved: "we do not feel that any conclusions are justifiable as yet."[12]

Little evidence existed to link the dysfunction of a specific gland with an identifiable psychiatric illness. Perhaps in the future, endocrinologists might establish such a relationship, but for the moment at least, the connections between psychiatry and endocrinology remained vague and uncertain. Yet for Clarence Darrow, the idea that glandular disease could cause mental illness was irresistible. Each individual was akin to a machine, Darrow believed; consciousness had a strictly materialist basis, and human action was entirely a consequence of external stimuli acting on the organism to produce predictable results. Endocrinology provided the somatic content for Darrow's philosophy of behavior—nothing could be better suited to Darrow's worldview than the idea that the action of the glands regulated human behavior.

The murder of Bobby Franks was inexplicable, according to Darrow, unless one assumed that Nathan Leopold and Richard Loeb were mentally ill. Each boy's psychiatric disorder was hidden from view—indeed, on casual acquaintance both Richard and Nathan seemed entirely normal—but an analysis of their endocrine glands would surely, Darrow believed, reveal the somatic basis of their mental disorders and lay the groundwork for an explanation of the killing of Bobby Franks.

ON SATURDAY, 14 JUNE, at nine o'clock in the morning, Karl Bowman, accompanied by Harold Hulbert, arrived back at the Cook County jail. Two physicians, J. J. Moore and Paul Dick, walked with them into the jail; Moore carried a portable oxygen tank and Dick held a metabolimeter.[13]

Richard Loeb, still limping after hurting his leg in a baseball game two days previously, appeared in the examination room to greet Bowman and Hulbert. He had followed their instructions not to eat breakfast that morning; now he listened attentively as they outlined the procedure. He noticed a machine—it was a Jones metabolimeter, an apparatus for calculating metabolic rate—on one side of the room, and as he lay on the bed, the doctors clamped the mouthpiece to his face and attached the tube to the apparatus.[14]

Richard remained lying on the bed for an hour, breathing into the apparatus, staring up at the ceiling. The scientists waited expectantly and then measured his body temperature, pulse, respiration, and blood pressure. Richard's metabolic rate—minus seventeen percent—was unusually low, so low that it could be explained, according to Bowman, only by the assumption of glandular dysfunction.[15]

Later that morning, Bowman and Hulbert repeated the procedure with Nathan. He too lay supine on the bed for one hour, while they waited for the result. But Nathan's measurements fell within the expected range; his metabolic rate—minus five percent—was slightly lower than expected for a boy of his height and weight but not abnormally so.[16]

Other tests followed. On the following Monday, Bowman and Hulbert used a plethysmograph, an instrument for measuring variations in blood volume during emotional stimulation, to record the emotional capacity of Nathan and Richard. Both boys were intellectually precocious, far superior to their peers. Could the same be said for their emotional ability, or were they emotionally stunted? Had an inability to experience emotions contributed to their desire to murder another human being?[17]

On Tuesday, 17 June, technicians delivered a Victor X-ray machine to the jail. Edward Blaine, a researcher from the National Pathological Laboratory, and Carl Darnell and Edward Philleo, experts in X-ray photography at the Victor X-ray Corporation, were present, hired by the defense to witness the examinations.[18]

Might X-ray images reveal physical pathology in Richard Loeb and Nathan Leopold? If so, they would constitute scientific evidence that the state's attorney would find hard to dismiss. Ever since the turn of the twentieth century, judges had granted X-rays a privileged position as courtroom evidence: the Illinois supreme court, for example, had ruled in 1905 that X-rays were admissible. Other forms of visual representation—diagrams, maps, drawings, photographs—were deemed only illustrative of the testimony of a witness and, as such, had no independent evidentiary value. X-rays were different: they seemed to allow direct access to facts that might otherwise be disputed and, as a consequence, their status in the American courtroom went unchallenged.[19]

It was necessary, nevertheless, to demonstrate to the court that the X-rays had been produced faithfully and accurately. As the scientists took X-ray images of Nathan and Richard, therefore, Harold Hulbert carefully examined each structure directly through a fluoroscope, comparing the image on the fluorescent screen with the X-ray image, ensuring also that each image carried the appropriate identification marks.[20]

Nothing was amiss in Richard Loeb's X-rays. His cranial bone

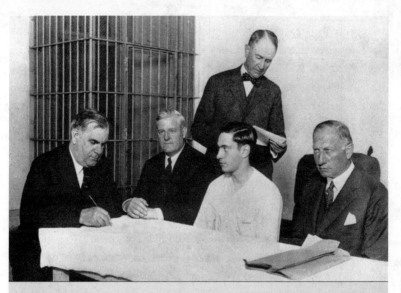

23. PSYCHIATRISTS FOR THE DEFENSE. The defense attorneys employed over a dozen psychiatrists to evaluate Nathan Leopold and Richard Loeb. From left to right: James Whitney Hall, William Hickson, Sanger Brown (standing), Nathan Leopold, and Benjamin Bachrach (attorney).

structure—in density and thickness—was about as normal as it could be, as were his facial bones. X-rays of the thorax showed that his heart was slightly more centered that one might expect, but the difference had no pathological significance; and the bones of the forearms, wrists, hands, and fingers showed no symptoms of disease.[21]

Nathan Leopold also seemed healthy. X-rays of the thorax revealed nothing unusual. His forearms, wrists, hands, and fingers were normal, and his facial bones and the bones and joints of the upper spine showed no irregularity. But Hulbert could see that some of the suture lines in Nathan's skull were obliterated, indicating osteosclerosis, or hardening of the cartilage. Osteosclerosis in the skull typically occurred in middle age, between ages thirty and forty-five—it rarely occurred in anyone nineteen years old. Hulbert also noticed, as he studied the X-ray more closely, that the pineal gland, an endocrine gland located at the base of the skull, had prematurely hardened and calcified. This, too, was unexpected. The calcification of the pineal gland customarily took place at thirty years. The pineal gland had several functions, including the inhibition, in Hulbert's words, of "the mental phase of one's sex life." Its premature calcification in Nathan Leopold surely indicated glandular dysfunction, with implications for his sexual development.[22]

THE DISCOVERY OF PATHOLOGICAL INDICATIONS in both Nathan and Richard was welcome news for the defense, but it did little to ease a growing concern that the scientific results would not easily translate into an argument sufficiently lucid to persuade a jury that the boys were mentally diseased. Richard Loeb had an abnormally low metabolism and Nathan Leopold had a pineal gland that had prematurely calcified, but so what? Even if the expert witnesses could prove that these pathologies did in fact exist, would a jury be sufficiently knowledgeable to understand the science? And how could the defense convince the jury that the physical abnormalities indicated glandular disorders, which had in turn caused mental illness in Richard and Nathan? And what was the nature of that mental illness? How had it contributed to the murder of Bobby Franks? The chain of cause and effect would be difficult to prove and, under withering cross-examination from the state's attorney, difficult to maintain.[23]

Nor did it help matters that, one week into the examination, Nathan resented the scientists' control over his body and detested the impression conveyed by the Chicago newspapers that he was mentally ill. On 18 June Nathan hinted to a reporter from the *Chicago Herald and Examiner* that he would repudiate his confession and thereby force the state's attorney to prove that he had committed murder. He was not insane, Nathan protested to the reporter; if he were insane, how would he be able to discuss the details of his defense? "I'm not insane," he remarked to the journalist, "and I'm not going to be made to appear insane. I'm sane—as sane as you are." For someone who imagined himself a genius, it was doubly humiliating: the examinations in the Cook County jail, the subject of much speculation in the newspaper columns, had given the impression both that he was mentally ill and that he was merely an experimental object, a plaything of the scientists. "From reading the newspapers," he complained, "I would infer that Loeb and I are being trained like fleas to jump through hoops just to entertain the curious."[24]

Nathan had encouraged the public perception that he was a precocious intellectual, far in advance of his years. Yet he had failed to foresee that his claim to be a genius would, in the public mind, at least, confer on him the role of mastermind in the murder of Bobby Franks. Nathan had frequently claimed to be extraordinarily clever and astute—surely, therefore, he was responsible for inveigling Richard Loeb into a complex scheme that had ended in the death of their victim. "I've been pictured in the public mind as the Svengali, the man with the hypnotic eye, the master mind and the brains," Nathan protested bitterly to a reporter from the Chicago Evening Post. "I've been made out the man who schemed, planned and executed this thing. I've been described as the devil incarnate. But Dicky Loeb, on the other hand, seems to have won the sympathy of the public."[25]

Toward the end of June the atmosphere within the jail tightened; it seemed as if all Chicago had focused its gaze on the dilapidated, shabby gray stucco building on Dearborn Street. The warden, Wesley Westbrook, resented the attention paid to his two celebrity prisoners and grumbled at the demands that their care placed on his staff. Westbrook had learned that a small group of prisoners planned a jailbreak—the scheme relied on guns smuggled into the prison and the theft of keys from one of the guards. The ringleaders planned to escape from their cells, release all the prisoners in the jail, and, in the ensuing commotion, escape unseen. Nothing ever came of it; it appeared to be no more than a rumor. But Westbrook acted anyway, revoking visiting privileges and transferring seven prisoners (including Nathan's cell mate, Ed Donkar) to the Boys' Reformatory at Pontiac.[26]

KARL BOWMAN AND HAROLD HULBERT completed their examination of the defendants on 30 June. Each report—one on Nathan, a second on Richard—included a physiological and endocrinological analysis, along with a detailed life history, including sections on each boy's childhood and adolescence. Both Nathan and Richard had volunteered information on the kidnapping of Bobby Franks, limning their individual contributions to the planning and execution of the murder. Both had talked of their fantasies, Nathan saying that he imagined himself as a powerful slave and Richard saying that he envisaged himself as a master criminal.

Darrow proclaimed himself satisfied with the report: Bowman and Hulbert had done everything he had asked—he had no complaints on that score. But their report constituted only one part of the defense that Darrow expected to present in court—a second part would be provided by the psychiatrists who, only now, at the beginning of July, were arriving in Chicago to meet with Darrow and Benjamin Bachrach.

William Alanson White arrived in Chicago on Tuesday, 1 July. He was an imposing man whose physical presence matched his status as the leading American psychiatrist of his generation. His jet-black eyebrows formed a striking contrast with a shock of gray-white hair that swept back toward one side of his head to reveal an expansive forehead. Pale blue eyes peered through gold-rimmed glasses balanced on an aquiline nose; his large mouth turned downward in an ungenerous grimace. His very presence seemed to demand acquiescence; his bearing exuded authority; his attitude—imperious, impatient, and urgent—indicated a man who brooked no equivocation or hesitation.[27]

White, at age fifty-four, had reached the height of his profession. After attending Cornell University on a scholarship, he had obtained

24. COOK COUNTY CRIMINAL COURT AND JAIL. The Cook County Criminal Court (left) occupied a Romanesque-style building on the northwest corner of Dearborn Street and Austin Avenue (now Hubbard Street) from 1894 to 1929. Prisoners called to trial would pass over a bridge connecting the Cook County jail (right) with the Criminal Court Building.

his medical degree in 1891 from Long Island College Hospital in Brooklyn, New York. His first appointment, as a physician at Binghamton State Hospital, gave him an opportunity for clinical research in psychiatry; he spent twelve years at Binghamton before moving to Washington, D.C., in 1903 to become the superintendent of the Government Hospital for the Insane.[28]

The hospital, established in 1855 by Dorothea Dix, had never been anything other than a custodial institution that provided psychiatric care for employees of the federal government, members of the armed forces, and residents of the District of Columbia. White, during his tenure at St. Elizabeths Hospital (as it was subsequently called), transformed the institution into a leading center of medical research. Under White's leadership, the hospital expanded, caring for some 6,000 patients at any one time. White also recruited a cadre of ambitious young physician-psychiatrists to the sprawling campus east of the Anacostia River with the promise that the hospital would focus as much on scientific research as on therapeutic care. White himself was a prolific author, publishing twelve research monographs by 1924, editing the *Psychoanalytic Review*, translating classic works from French and German, and writing scores of articles and reviews. By the early 1920s, he was the best-known psychiatrist in the United States, and in June 1924 the psychiatric profession acknowledged his leadership by electing him president of the American Psychiatric Association.[29]

WHITE FIRST MET WITH RICHARD LOEB on 1 July. Richard spoke hesitantly at first, telling White of his plans, necessarily in abeyance, to write his graduate thesis on John C. Calhoun and the question of states' rights. Richard also talked of his studies at the University of Michigan, mentioning the zoology course taught by the geneticist Aaron Franklin Shull. Richard confessed his agnosticism; he had read Richard Swann Lull's *Organic Evolution* in college and felt certain that Darwinism could account for the origins of mankind.[30]

Walter Bachrach sat silently listening as White, scribbling notes on a pad, continued to ask questions. As the morning wore on, White

probed more intently, interrogating Richard about his childhood, in-
quiring about Richard's governess, questioning him about his teachers
at University High School, searching for clues that might explain the
murder of Bobby Franks. Richard began to relax and, as he talked,
more details emerged to offer a glimpse into his psyche. He had always
desired to be famous, he confessed; he had imagined himself as a football player, handsome, athletic, strong; on other occasions, he had
thought of himself as an explorer, brave and adventurous, tracing out
new paths in the West; and most frequently he had pictured himself as
a master criminal capable of carrying out the perfect crime. He had a
recurrent fantasy of himself in a jail cell, half-naked, being whipped
and abused by prison guards, as a crowd of spectators, young girls for
the most part, looked on with a mixture of admiration and pity.

Had he ever imagined, White suddenly asked, that he might rape a
girl? Richard shook his head. No, that was not something he would
do—Nathan Leopold had demanded that they kidnap and rape a young
girl but Richard had vetoed the suggestion; it had never been part of his
plan. He had always been gentle with his girlfriends, Richard insisted,
kissing them only if they consented. What about sexual fantasies? Did
Richard imagine, White asked, himself having sex? He could picture
himself with a girl, Richard replied, undressing and caressing her, but
nothing further usually happened. His sexual imagination went only
so far and never reached the point where he might have sexual inter-
course. But what, Richard countered, did sex have to do with the murder of Bobby Franks? He had kidnapped Franks in order to show that
he could commit the perfect crime—there had been nothing sexual
about it.[31]

White also interrogated Nathan Leopold that week, seeing him for
the first time on Wednesday, 2 July. That afternoon, as White listened
to Nathan talk about his studies at the University of Chicago, he came
to appreciate the difference between the two boys. Richard had seemed
diffident in talking about himself at first, revealing his thoughts only
with reluctance. Nathan was garrulous from the outset, proclaiming
his competence as a philologist, his aptitude for study, his intellectual
brilliance—he was unique, he informed White, in his ability to learn

languages. The more obscure a language, the better; he had learned Umbrian, for example, not because he might need to speak it or read it—it was an extinct language, originally spoken in a region of central Italy—but because it emphasized his status as an individual elevated above the rest of humanity.[32]

White noticed that there was nothing altruistic in Nathan's attitude toward others. He had no regard for his companions, for his classmates, or even for members of his own family except as their existence contributed to his own welfare. He lived only for his own advantage, Nathan admitted, and he considered others only insofar as their actions worked to promote his pleasure. He was a Nietzschean who stood above the law, above morality, someone whose actions were uninhibited by conventional behavior; he did not recognize any obligation to society—he could do whatever he wished.

Nor did Nathan have any qualms about killing Bobby Franks. He regretted only that they had failed to carry the killing off successfully; what tremendous satisfaction it would have given him to have collected the ransom and evaded capture! But regrets? No, he had no regrets—murder was a small thing to weigh in the balance against the pleasure that he might gain from the act. Would he do it again, White asked, if he knew that he could escape detection? Yes, Nathan replied, without hesitation—why not?

Nathan talked knowingly of sex—he claimed to have had many sexual experiences—but he admitted that sex was truly pleasurable only if he experienced it as a violent, forceful, sadistic act. Nothing was more enjoyable than compelling another person to submit to his desire. Nathan had often imagined himself as a German officer in the Great War raping a girl. Sex with Richard Loeb had always been enjoyable, of course, especially when Richard pretended to be drunk and incapable of resisting; Nathan would then forcibly remove his clothes and rape him.[33]

As Nathan continued to talk, White realized that the intensity of each boy's fantasies and Nathan's overwhelming desire for Richard had created a potent combination between the two boys that seemed to ensure some violent catastrophe. Richard imagined himself as a master criminal; Nathan was Richard's obsequious companion, eager to do anything the other boy desired. Their relationship was pathological, based on fantasies that, in both boys, had supplanted reality; and the murder of Bobby Franks had been the consequence. White, in his final report, emphasized the boys' detachment from reality, writing that Richard, especially, had never developed the sense of social awareness that characterized the passage from childhood to adulthood: "normally the child, from being a purely instinctive, selfish individual, controlled solely by the desire to gain pleasure and avoid pain, develops into a social individual with a desire to make his conduct conform to socially acceptable standards. . . . To the extent that this knowledge of right and wrong is deficient, to the extent that it is only on the surface and has not become a part of a well-integrated personality, [Richard Loeb] is lacking in those standards of character and conduct which we think of the normal person as possessing." Nathan, also, lacked the capacity to transcend an immediate need for gratification; he, too, had never developed the ability as a social individual of adjusting his own desires in accordance with the wishes of others.[34]

ON FRIDAY, 4 JULY, the prisoners in the Cook County jail could hear the firecrackers exploding in the street outside in celebration of the holiday. The warden had arranged a chicken dinner to mark the occasion, but otherwise there was a subdued atmosphere inside the county jail. No visitors were allowed that day; Nathan and Richard spent the holiday reading in their cells, emerging occasionally to chat briefly with each other and to watch a baseball game in the yard.[35]

The following day, William Healy, a tall, slender, soft-spoken man with thinning auburn hair and a deferential manner, arrived at the Cook County jail to begin his examination of Nathan and Richard. Healy now lived in Boston—he was the director of the Judge Baker Foundation, a research agency for the study of adolescent crime—but he knew Chicago well, having graduated from Rush Medical College in 1900 and having served until 1917 as the director of the psychiatric clinic attached to the Cook County Juvenile Court. Healy had first made his mark with *The Individual Delinquent*, a monograph, based on his work for the Juvenile Court and published in 1915, that emphasized the unique character of each individual criminal and the importance of early childhood influences in determining adult behavior. It was an innovative and original work—the first by an American author to contest the notion of a criminal archetype. There was no pattern to criminality, Healy believed, and it was idle to imagine that criminals displayed characteristic features or behavior. There was an endless diversity to criminality: the motives and causes of crime varied according to individual circumstances.[36]

Few criminologists had as extensive experience as Healy in the treatment of adolescents, yet even he was surprised by the emotional detachment of Nathan and Richard. They could discuss the murder casually, in a matter-of-fact way, without any apparent emotion or feeling. The details of the crime, its planning, and its execution were plainly spoken by both boys; there was neither any hint of remorse in their words nor any regard for the grief that they had caused the Franks family.

Could the dichotomy between their intellectual ability and their emotional retardation provide evidence for a psychological interpretation of the crime? Was the boys' affective incapacity one of the factors that had provoked the killing? Would it be possible, perhaps, to measure their intellects through the use of standardized tests? Intelligence testing—the application of standard procedures to quantify mental ability—had grown to maturity during the previous decade in response to the widespread belief that delinquency and deviance were consequences of mental impairment. The feebleminded, the mental defectives, were predisposed to prostitution, alcoholism, pedophilia, antisocial behavior, and criminal activity; if scientists could measure an individual's intelligence, it was argued, they could determine which individuals were subnormal and hence likely to break the law. During the 1910s, psychologists, on the basis of their training and expertise, had self-consciously claimed the authority to determine mental ability and thus to assert professional autonomy. As psychologists had expanded their reach to claim that intelligence testing could be used for pedagogical and vocational purposes, such testing had become ubiqui-tous in American society.[37]

William Healy regarded mental defect as one, among many, of the causes of crime. Healy had been a member of the American Association for the Study of the Feeble-Minded during the 1910s and was familiar with the psychological tests used to measure mental ability. What, Healy wondered, might such tests reveal about Nathan Leopold and Richard Loeb? Would they demonstrate that each boy did in fact have exceptional intelligence? Might the tests allow the scientists to show that each boy's intellect was so far in advance of his emotional capacity as to constitute a type of derangement?

Throughout the second week of July, Healy used a series of tests to measure each boy's intelligence. Nathan demonstrated a remarkable ability to complete each test successfully within the allotted time; he effortlessly completed the Monroe Silent Reading Test, the Kelly-Trabus Test, the Thurston Syllogism Test, the Cryptogram Test, and the McAlly Cube Test. He did less well on the Judgment Test, and his answers to the Kent-Rosanoff Association Test revealed, according to Healy, that, con-trary to appearances, Nathan did have some affective capacity.[38]

Richard Loeb was less conspicuously intelligent, demonstrating ability appropriate for an eighteen-year-old. He performed well in the Thurston Syllogism Test, answering almost all twenty questions cor-rectly, but failed the Monroe Silent Reading Test. He successfully com-pleted the Cryptogram Test within the allotted period but did only moderately well on the Kent-Rosanoff Association Test. Healy's exami-nation had produced no clear result except that Nathan was exception-ally intelligent. It was not evident, even to Healy, that the results of the intelligence tests might contribute to the defense case.[39]

A THIRD PSYCHIATRIST, BERNARD GLUECK, arrived in Chicago on Tuesday, 8 July. After graduating from Georgetown University, Glueck had trained as an intern in psychiatry at St. Elizabeths Hospital under the tutelage of William Alanson White, and in 1910 he had secured an appointment as medical officer in charge of the criminal division at the hospital. In 1916 Glueck left St. Elizabeths to become director of the psychiatric clinic at Sing Sing prison in New York state. Crime, according to Glueck, was more a consequence of social maladjustment than a result of deliberate choice. At Sing Sing, in concert with the prison authorities, he initiated a regimen that emphasized rehabilitation and reform. Glueck's research, funded by the Rockefeller Foundation, demonstrated the pervasive character of mental illness among the prison population. Crime was a consequence, more often than not, of mental defect: sixty percent of the inmates at Sing Sing displayed symptoms of mental disease and almost twenty percent were dangerously psychopathic. The many forms of mental illness among the prison population, Glueck asserted, rendered the legal test of insanity applied in the courtroom entirely inadequate. Psychiatric causes lay behind criminal behavior, and only the psychiatrist, treating the individual delinquent, could satisfactorily solve the problem of crime. By the early 1920s, his research at Sing Sing on criminality and deviance had earned Glueck a national reputation in penology, and in 1921 he moved to New York City to take up a joint appointment as director of the Bureau of Children's Guidance and professor of psychiatry at the New York Postgraduate Medical School and Hospital.[40]

Glueck's research at St. Elizabeths and at Sing Sing had made him familiar with as diverse a range of criminal behavior as one might expect, yet like Healy he was surprised that both Richard and Nathan showed so little affect. It was as though, within each boy, an emotional deadening had extinguished all empathy and affection. There was a sad, melancholy air about Richard, Glueck thought, as he listened to Richard confess that he, not Nathan, had wielded the chisel on the afternoon of the murder. Nathan had been driving the automobile, Richard explained. Bobby Franks had climbed into the front passenger seat, next to Nathan, and Richard had first clubbed him from behind and then asphyxiated him by stuffing a rag down his throat.[41]

Richard suffered from an overwhelming sense of his own inferiority, Glueck decided. Everything in Richard's life had conspired to multiply his feelings of impotence and inadequacy: the demands of his governess, his attendance at university at fourteen, his sexual immaturity—all contributed to reinforce in Richard's mind that he was not capable of meeting the exigencies of everyday life. And to compensate for his feelings of inferiority, Richard had immersed himself in a fantasy universe in which he was a master criminal capable of planning devious and complex crimes. There was little doubt, Glueck concluded in his final report, that the murder of Bobby Franks was linked to Richard's need to compensate for his feelings of inadequacy. "The impelling motive," Glueck wrote, "in the defendant's criminal career was the motive of compensating through criminal prowess for his feelings of inferiority." The compensatory urge acted almost as a compulsion; Richard craved "to reach perfection, completeness, potency, and compensation for his sense of inferiority."[42]

Nathan Leopold, also, had retreated into a fantasy life. Yet, Glueck decided, Nathan's retreat was a consequence not so much of an inability to deal with everyday demands as of perverse sexuality. Nathan had constructed a cynical, aloof intellectualism that enabled him to turn aside his self-disgust at his sexual aberrancy. It had not been possible for Nathan to reconcile himself to his homosexuality, and he had been incapable of forming emotional connections on such a basis. He had, Glueck concluded, an "overwhelming desire to negate and repudiate whatever was part and parcel of his real nature beneath the crust of cold-blooded intellectualism." Nathan could feel comfortable with his sexuality only within the relationship with Richard Loeb; the sexual connection had cemented the bond between the two and had compelled Nathan to go along with Richard's criminal misdeeds. Nathan's "complete self-realization as a homo-sexual was made possible only in connection with his association with Richard Loeb."[43]

BEFORE 1900, NEUROLOGY—THE STUDY of the brain and the nervous system—had dominated Americans' intellectual understanding of mental illness. According to the neurologists, psychiatric illnesses were a consequence of such somatic disorders as, for example, lesions of the brain; psychiatry, at least in the United States, was synonymous with biological psychiatry. By the first decade of the twentieth century, psychoanalysis—the idea that neuroses were a consequence of unconscious conflicts over traumatic events—had made its initial bid to replace neurology as an alternative way of understanding mental illness. Neurology could (and did) offer a diagnosis of the causes of mental illness but was less effective in devising a cure. Psychoanalysis provided an alternative to neurology, an alternative, moreover, that would allow psychiatrists to break out of their professional role as asylum superintendents and enable them to assume greater social and cultural authority as experts on a wide range of social and cultural problems.[44]

Such psychoanalytic interpretations as those advanced by the defense psychiatrists to explain the murder of Bobby Franks paid homage to the influence of Freudian ideas within the American psychiatric community. Experiences in childhood shaped and determined adult behavior; psychosis in the adult was rooted in infantile sexuality; and conflicts within the unconscious found expression in seemingly irrational behavior. Few American psychiatrists, however, accepted Freud's ideas unreservedly; the leaders of the American Psychiatric Association, a group that included William Alanson White, Bernard Glueck, and William Healy, adopted an eclectic approach that borrowed as much from Jung and Adler as from Freud.[45]

Their group identity, however, relied less on a set of shared ideas and more on a common program of professional values developed in an attempt to broaden the cultural influence of the psychiatric movement. American psychiatry traced its nineteenth-century origins to the care of patients in the institutional setting provided by the mental asylum. The asylum superintendent—the forerunner of the twentieth-century psychiatrist—concerned himself with the administrative management of large numbers of patients. Therapeutic efficacy—the cure and treatment of mental illness—was a secondary concern. Psychiatry was a profession, at least until the end of the nineteenth century, that interacted only casually with medical science and research.[46]

After 1900, psychiatry moved away from the restrictive role imposed by the asylum setting and began to diffuse itself more generally within American society. Psychiatrists could still be found in their traditional administrative roles, but increasingly they established and organized alternative institutions: outpatient clinics, psychopathic hospitals, and private practice. As a corollary of the shift away from the asylum, psychiatry concerned itself less with the custodial care of acutely ill patients and more with the psychopathology of everyday life and its attendant problems: alcoholism, pauperism, prostitution, delinquency, and crime. In this novel manifestation, psychiatry could align itself effortlessly with the Progressive Era and its glorification of the scientific expert; psychiatrists, with their specialized knowledge, could assert the cultural authority to deal with a wide range of social problems.[47]

No one was more active in promulgating an enlarged role for psychiatry than William Alanson White. The psychiatric perspective necessarily assumed that deviant behavior was a medical phenomenon; from this standpoint, which was adopted by White and his colleagues, science had demonstrated that human agency was a fiction—actions were never freely chosen, and the concept of individual responsibility was meaningless. All behavior, according to White, was a result of antecedent circumstances, usually rooted in the patient's childhood and adolescence. It was necessarily futile, therefore, to punish individuals for deeds for which they bore no responsibility; a more appropriate and more satisfactory response to criminal behavior, one that promised a permanent solution, would be found in psychiatric diagnosis and medical treatment in a psychopathic hospital.[48]

The denial of free will and evil intent and the rejection of punishment as a response to crime necessarily assumed a radical revision of courtroom procedure. All three of Darrow's psychiatrists—White, Healy, and Glueck—subscribed to a medicalizing ideology; all three hoped to extend and expand the influence of psychiatry within the courtroom in a way that would challenge the authority of the legal profession. The legal framework that determined the judicial process in the American courtroom was, according to White, hopelessly outdated; it relied on nineteenth-century concepts and methods that, because they took no heed of modern science, were entirely unsuited to the present day.[49]

White's animus toward contemporary legal procedure found its focus in the concept of insanity. The court customarily could find a defendant not guilty by reason of insanity; in the American courtroom, the accepted definition of a defendant's insanity was the inability to distinguish right from wrong. But insanity, according to White, was solely a legal concept; it had no basis in medical science. Moreover, this legal concept took no account of the complex character of mental illness. According to medical science, the dichotomy between sanity and insanity simply did not exist; an individual might have any one of an infinite number of degrees of mental illness, all of which lay on a continuum.[50]

In a legal sense, neither Nathan Leopold nor Richard Loeb was insane. Both had been able to distinguish right from wrong when they murdered Bobby Franks; both had been aware, at the time of the murder, of the character of their act; both had known that it was wrong. Yet to admit their sanity was not to preclude the possibility that both Nathan and Richard were mentally diseased.

To claim that crime was a medical phenomenon, and then to replace punishment with diagnosis and treatment, would necessarily expand the authority of the psychiatrist within the courtroom. It was not possible, White argued, for a lay jury, possessing neither scientific nor medical expertise, to diagnose the medical causes of a crime. Only a psychiatrist, as an objective expert, could make such a diagnosis; and only the psychiatrist, moreover, was capable of recommending an appropriate course of treatment. The jury still had a role, albeit circumscribed, in determining that a criminal act had occurred, but in all other respects its place in the courtroom was no more than vestigial.[51]

Would the defense psychiatrists find an opportunity to publicize their agenda through their participation in the trial of Nathan Leopold and Richard Loeb? Certainly, in one sense, the circumstances were about as auspicious as one could expect. Clarence Darrow had promised to provide the defense experts with unlimited access to the defendants, of course, and nothing would be spared in the effort to diagnose their mental condition. There would be ample opportunity for the psychiatrists to proselytize—to present their belief that criminal behavior was a medical phenomenon best interpreted by scientific experts. Newspapers across the country would send the psychiatrists' courtroom testimony into every household in the land. It was an opportunity not to be missed—William Alanson White fully expected to be able to use the courtroom to broadcast his reforms of the judicial process; the defense psychiatrists would find an unprecedented audience for their program through the newspapers.

White's expectations remained high as the trial date approached, but his ability to persuade a national audience that legal procedures in the American courtroom were outdated rested, in some measure, on the cooperation of the state's attorney. White was anxious, for example, to avoid an adversarial contest in the courtroom between two rival sets of psychiatrists. Typically, in such cases, each set of psychiatrists flatly contradicted the other even when both sides agreed on the facts. It was an embarrassment to the psychiatric profession, White believed, that the psychiatrists rarely agreed to produce a joint report analyzing the mental condition of the defendant. Would Robert Crowe allow the state's psychiatrists to participate in such an endeavor? Probably not, Darrow advised, though it would be possible, of course, to raise the issue in court.

BUT COOPERATION WITH THE PROSECUTION seemed unlikely. Even now the state's attorneys were maligning the defense, portraying Darrow and his colleagues as dishonest. Joseph Savage, an assistant state's attorney, publicly complained that the defense had recruited more than a dozen scientific experts. Was Darrow hoping to tie up the court in technicalities? Did he hope to delay the proceedings by introducing procedural questions that would lengthen the trial by months, perhaps years? And what had happened to the promise made by Albert Loeb and Nathan Leopold Sr. just a short time before, that they would not spend exorbitant amounts in defense of their sons? The experts were each receiving as much as $1,000 a day for their services; did the defense hope to purchase the boys' acquittal?[52]

Savage, in his remarks to the *Chicago Sunday Tribune*, reminded the reporter that Harry Thaw, the murderer of the New York architect Stanford White, had used an insanity defense to evade punishment.

Thaw had shot and killed White in 1906 before dozens of witnesses. But he was wealthy—the son of a Pittsburgh railroad baron—and his lawyers had hired psychiatrists to testify to his insanity. Their strategy had succeeded; after spending several years in the Matteawan State Hospital for the Criminally Insane, Thaw had eventually regained his freedom.[53]

But, Darrow countered, no one was advocating that Nathan Leopold and Richard Loeb be released from confinement. Harry Thaw had used the insanity defense to win acquittal, but no one wished to see either Nathan or Richard free. "Many persons compare the cases of Leopold, Jr., and Loeb to the Harry K. Thaw case," Darrow stated. "In one vital respect the Franks murder case is different. Every possible means of securing Thaw's acquittal or release was attempted while in this case there is no one who wants to see the boys freed. . . . The parents are not seeking the acquittal of the boys. They do not want this at all. Convinced now of the truth of their confessions, they are afraid to have them freed. They believe their sons should be committed to an asylum." Nor was there any truth in the rumor, Darrow continued, that the families intended to use their wealth to purchase freedom for Nathan and Richard. No one on the defense team was receiving an exorbitant payment for his participation in the case. The Chicago Bar Association would set the remuneration for the lawyers, and the American Medical Association would determine the fees for the psychiatrists; how, under such circumstances, could the prosecution accuse the families of using their wealth to thwart justice? And, in any case, the defense psychiatrists stood at the top of their profession; they had no need to testify for financial gain. "There is not a doctor," Darrow announced, "who has been called into this case who would think of charging an exorbitant fee in consideration of the wealth of the parents of the accused. They have ascended to such heights in their profession that matters of fee are beyond their consideration."[54]

In his statements to the press, Darrow hinted that the plea would be not guilty by reason of insanity. On Saturday, 12 July, Darrow explained that the psychiatrists had discovered evidence of insanity in other members of the defendants' families. "We have found insanity in both the families of Leopold, Jr., and Loeb," he remarked. "I can not specify at this time how far back, or on which sides of the families the insanity has been traced. Neither may I assert just yet whether this evidence will be used in the trial."[55]

Other members of the defense team also dropped hints that some form of insanity would be presented to the court. The psychiatrist James Whitney Hall, in an interview with a Canadian journalist, explained that in Illinois an insanity defense did not necessarily involve showing that the defendant was unable to distinguish between right and wrong. "We will not claim," Hall stated, "that these boys did not, when the act was committed, know the difference between right and wrong." It might be possible to show that Nathan and Richard acted under a compulsion to commit the murder; if so, then, according to the legal definition, they would be insane. "But when it comes to the point," Hall concluded, "as to whether . . . these accused were possessed also of the power to choose between what was right and what was wrong, we will show that they did not possess such ability."[56]

Would Darrow use the insanity defense? Despite his assertion, the psychiatrists had found no evidence of hereditary insanity, yet everyone nevertheless assumed that he would use insanity as a defense at the coming trial. It was difficult to imagine any jury finding the defendants insane—both Nathan and Richard seemed rational and coherent, fully capable of distinguishing, and choosing between, right and wrong—yet what alternative did Darrow have? He surely could not plead simply not guilty—both Nathan and Richard had voluntarily confessed to the murder and had provided the police with evidence to corroborate their confessions.

Any man other than Robert Crowe might have been complacent—surely the jury would sentence Leopold and Loeb to hang!—but Crowe was too experienced, too watchful, too cautious to imagine that he could defeat Clarence Darrow so easily. Crowe regretted now that the psychiatrists for the prosecution had not had more time to question Leopold and Loeb—already, even before the trial had begun, Darrow was sneering at the brevity of the state's examination of the defendants and contrasting it unfavorably with the lengthy analysis undertaken by the defense psychiatrists. It was important, at least, that the prosecution anticipate the intricacies of an insanity defense, and so, during the hot summer days of early July, Crowe arranged for the state's psychiatrists to educate his staff on the ramifications of an insanity plea.[57]

Also that summer, in preparation for the trial of Leopold and Loeb, three of Crowe's assistants traveled to Geneva, forty miles west of Chicago, to attend the deliberations of Kane County Circuit Court on the sanity of Warren Lincoln, a confessed murderer. Lincoln, a lawyer practicing in Aurora, had surprised his wife, Lina, having sex with her brother, Byron Shoup. Enraged by the sight of his wife in an incestuous relationship, Lincoln had gotten his revolver from the greenhouse and, returning to the bedroom, had killed first his brother-in-law and then his wife.[58]

Nothing so bizarre as the double killing of Lina Lincoln and Byron Shoup had ever previously occurred in Kane County. Shortly after his arrest, Lincoln confessed that he had decapitated both victims and had encased their heads in a block of concrete, placing it underneath his back porch. Lincoln claimed that the murders constituted justifiable homicide, but his lawyers, less optimistic that a jury would agree, had petitioned the court to find him insane. Robert Crowe had decided that no better opportunity would present itself for learning about the insanity defense and had therefore sent three of his closest associates—Joseph Savage, Milton Smith, and John Sbarbaro—to attend the insanity hearing at Geneva.[59]

In Chicago, Crowe worked to influence public opinion against leniency for Leopold and Loeb. In interviews with the Chicago newspapers in the days before the start of the trial, Crowe predicted the failure of an insanity defense. It was preposterous, Crowe asserted, to claim that the defendants were insane; no jury would believe it. "The report that Leopold and Loeb are insane is nothing more than propaganda sent out by the defense to throw dust into the eyes of men who may be called to serve on the jury." And what of the psychiatrists? Would any psychiatrist be either so foolish or so corrupt as to testify to their insanity? "No reputable alienist," Crowe continued, "would testify the two murderers are insane. If any of them do, it will be because they were either fools who were duped by the defendants or knaves who have profited by their gold."[60]

WHILE ROBERT CROWE AND CLARENCE Darrow each argued his case in the pages of the Chicago newspapers, a novel proposition, one that neither side had anticipated, suddenly elbowed its way into the discussion about the coming trial.

The trial would be held in the principal courtroom in the Criminal Court Building, yet the demand for seats would clearly outstrip the available supply. Every major newspaper in the United States planned to send at least one reporter to cover the trial, and inquiries had already been received from press agencies in Cuba, Argentina, Canada, Britain, Italy, and Australia. The courtroom could accommodate only 200 spectators, and few seats would be available for members of the Chicago public who wished to observe the trial. Why not, therefore, broadcast the proceedings on the radio so that everyone in Chicago could hear the testimony as it unfolded in court?

The publishers of the *Chicago Daily Tribune* owned station WGN. On 17 July, in a front-page editorial, the newspaper proposed that the trial be broadcast in its entirety. Would not such a step serve to educate the public in the workings of the criminal justice system? The more the general public knew about civic affairs, the better. Political corruption and malfeasance would have few opportunities to flourish if an educated populace felt a keener sense of public responsibility. "It is bromide among persons occupied in civic affairs," the editor of the *Chicago Daily Tribune* wrote, "that the public should be more interested than it is in events of social importance. . . . It has been the attitude of English and American law that the greater the degree in which the people enter into the enforcement of the law, the more publicity given to trials by law, the greater the degree of justice."[61]

But not everyone subscribed to the view that broadcasting the Leopold-Loeb trial would serve unambiguously as a civics lesson. Nor was it evident that radio was a suitable medium for the transmission of such a sensational and lurid event as this trial. In 1924 radio was in its infancy—not even a majority of American households owned a radio set—and, unlike the movies, radio had yet to become a mass medium. Only the more prosperous families had a radio, and as a consequence radio was still an exclusive phenomenon. The movies and the tabloid newspapers catered explicitly to plebeian audiences; the radio, in contrast, served a patrician listenership that valued the evening programs as a source of cultural uplift. And radio was more intimate and more personal than either the newspapers or the movies; the speaker's voice directly entered the family circle and carried its message to each listener as though he or she alone constituted the audience.[62]

In the early 1920s, social commentators assigned various roles to radio, but none of those roles meshed easily with the broadcast of a sensational murder trial. Evangelical leaders hoped that radio could be used to promote religious sentiment; high-minded politicians expected that radio would foster thoughtful debate on the issues of the day and help eliminate demagoguery. Others saw radio as a way to prevent war—if people were better able to communicate with each other, surely nations could more easily avoid the type of general conflagration that had engulfed the world just a few years earlier.[63]

Chicagoans were divided over the desirability of transmitting the trial on the radio, yet a sufficient number—a majority—expressed such forceful opposition to the idea that even the *Tribune* conceded it might do more harm than good. John Owen, an attorney with the First National Bank, warned that "some of the testimony may be objectionable. . . . The case would be a show instead of a trial." Robert Calkins, a police officer, cautioned that many children and teenagers owned a crystal set; was it wise to transmit the details of a murder to such a susceptible audience? "It's a bad example," Calkins explained, "for the children to listen to such a trial. They are the most eager radio fans." P. J. Halldorson, the secretary of the Ravenswood Kiwanis Club, announced that the members had voted unanimously against the proposal as giving "undue publicity to a crime which is abnormal and not

25. RADIO TRANSMISSION. Would the trial be broadcast on the Chicago station WGN? In this cartoon the *Chicago Daily Tribune* imagines the possible consequences.

representative." O. A. Danielson, a builder from Evanston, deplored the idea as "yellow journalism . . . I'll take music and other things on the radio, but I believe the newspapers can give us a good enough account of the trial." William McCall, a realtor, insisted that "the radio should be used for entertainment, music, and literature, not for scandal and murders . . . I don't want my family to listen all day to such facts as doubtless will be heard in this Franks murder trial." And Beatrice Vahle, a stenographer, demanded that "the radio . . . [be] a source of enjoyment and not for scandals and murders . . . I'm very much against broadcasting the trial."[64]

Not everyone was ready to give up on the idea—Charles Dunham, a real estate agent, was one of many Chicagoans who believed that "the radio broadcasting of the Loeb and Leopold case would result in a great benefit to the public. The more publicity given this, the direst of all known murder cases, the less chance of its being repeated"—but public opinion was overwhelmingly opposed to radio broadcasts of the trial. Chicagoans had learned enough about the murder to realize that Nathan and Richard were lovers and that either one or both of the killers might have abused the corpse. No parent could reliably prevent his or her children from learning the sordid, vulgar details if the trial were broadcast, and as a consequence, the *Tribune*, to its surprise, was put on the defensive. The newspaper belatedly explained that a censor would prevent the transmission of salacious testimony: "there will be no filth. . . . A man with an electric push button, sitting in the courtroom while the trial is in progress, will accomplish this result. A movement of his finger tip will cut the microphone from the sending apparatus"—but organized opposition from civic organizations and religious congregations grew to a crescendo. Pearl Hart, the president of the Women's Bar Association of Illinois, reported her members' opposition; Benjamin Cox, a prominent scoutmaster with the Wilmette troop, warned that the broadcasts would degrade his boys; Asa Ferry, pastor of the Edgewater Presbyterian Church, complained that far too much information about the murder had already been made public; Francis Wilson, a judge on the Circuit Court, claimed that the law would be brought into disrepute; and F. C. Erselen, president of the Garrett Biblical Institute, lambasted the *Tribune* for its irresponsible suggestion.[65]

A regional meeting of the Methodist Church, at Des Plaines, northwest of Chicago, adopted a resolution against transmission of the trial. Thomas Holgate, the president of the Chicago Church Federation, an influential alliance of denominations in Cook County, issued a statement condemning the proposed radio broadcasts as immoral: "Our homes should not be placed under the necessity of protecting themselves against the demoralizing influences certain to follow such an exposition of youthful depravity. . . . It is not in the public interest that the details of a trial should go before all the people, and especially before the children in our homes. It is sufficient that the court and the jury hear the evidence and that the public should know the verdict."[66]

On 18 July, Clarence Darrow announced his opposition to the proposal as prejudicial to the interests of his clients and hinted that he would appeal an unfavorable verdict if the microphone was allowed into the courtroom. Influential members of the Cook County judiciary endorsed Darrow's position the following day. Phillip L. Sullivan, a judge on the Superior Court, stated that allowing broadcasters to transmit the trial would be tantamount to presenting the proceedings as entertainment. The *Chicago Daily Tribune* had argued that radio broadcasts of the trial would give the public an enlarged respect for judicial authority. The *Tribune* had also claimed that the public would gain an awareness of the constitutional intricacies of the criminal law and, through an appreciation of courtroom procedure, would put a greater value on the legal system. But, Sullivan countered, it was more probable that the radio broadcasts would have the opposite effect. Legal wrangling in the courtroom was not always as dignified as one might suppose—theoretical disquisition on abstract points of law was often conspicuously absent; crude banter between opposing attorneys was a more typical feature of the proceedings. Public familiarity with the courtroom, Sullivan believed, would breed contempt, and to present the proceedings in a medium—radio—customarily associated with entertainment would invite disrespect for the law. Any judge who allowed the microphone into his courtroom, Sullivan predicted, would bring on himself the censure of the state supreme court. "The Illinois Supreme Court has already reversed the decision in one case where a judge converted a trial into a show.... How much more true if broadcasting of the proceedings were permitted?"[67]

Not even the *Chicago Daily Tribune* could ignore the groundswell of opposition. On 19 July, the newspaper quietly abandoned its plan. There would be no broadcast on station WGN or on any other radio station.

PUBLIC DISCUSSION OF THE UPCOMING trial now shifted once more to a debate over the defense strategy. John Caverly would convene his court on Monday, 21 July, to listen to the attorneys argue motions that they wished to present. Would Clarence Darrow then submit a motion to the court? Was it certain, for example, that Darrow's clients would plead not guilty by reason of insanity? Darrow had stated several times in public that Nathan and Richard were insane. Did such pronouncements reliably indicate the defense strategy, or was Darrow preparing to spring a surprise on the court?

He might, for example, plausibly argue a motion to exclude evidence on the basis that it had been illegally obtained. Nathan and Richard had confessed to the murder during their first weekend in the custody of the state's attorney, and perhaps Crowe had obtained the confessions through intimidation or violence.

Darrow could also ask the judge to appoint a special commission to determine that the defendants were insane. The results of an insanity hearing might abrogate the need for a trial; if the commission decided that Nathan and Richard were insane, Caverly could, on his own initiative, send them to an asylum.

It was also possible, but unlikely, that the defense would ask the court to try each defendant separately. But Darrow had already expressed his belief that the killing was a consequence of each defendant's influencing the other; an idiosyncratic combination of two individuals had produced the murder. There was no indication, therefore, that the defense would argue for a severance.

Nor was it likely that Darrow would ask the judge to delay the opening of the trial beyond 4 August, the assigned starting date. Caverly's term as chief justice of the Criminal Court would expire at the end of August. If the defense requested a continuance, the new chief justice, Jacob Hopkins, might assign a different judge to hear the case. But Caverly was one of the more liberal justices on the court; he had never voluntarily sentenced a defendant to death; and it would be foolish for the defense to request a delay that might remove him from the case.

Darrow might also present a motion to remove the case from the Cook County Criminal Court. Almost immediately after the kidnapping, Nathan had driven the rental car across the state line into Indiana. Perhaps Bobby Franks had died outside Illinois; and perhaps, therefore, the murder did not fall within the jurisdiction of the Cook County court. But Darrow had already declared that he would not ask for a change of venue, and Crowe, in any case, could still charge Leopold and Loeb with kidnapping, a capital offense in Illinois, and hope to obtain a hanging verdict.[68]

ON THURSDAY, 17 JULY, three men met with Darrow in his office downtown. Walter Bachrach was the only one of the three to know the purpose of their meeting; James Whitney Hall, a consulting psychiatrist on the defense team, was curious to learn what Darrow had to say; and Jacob Loeb also wondered why Darrow had suddenly convened their meeting that evening in his rooms on Dearborn Street.

Darrow swore all three to secrecy. His strategy depended for its success on its surprise. Not one word should reach the state's attorney's office.

The insanity defense would not work, Darrow explained. They could never obtain a jury that would find Nathan and Richard insane; it would be futile to make the attempt. They would go down to certain defeat. Nor would he attempt to delay the trial by a procedural motion—any attempt to challenge the validity of the confessions would certainly fail, and a motion for a change of venue would only postpone the inevitable. It would be futile also to ask the judge to convene an insanity hearing, Darrow continued; neither Nathan nor Richard was legally insane.

But there was one strategy that might work. Perhaps it would succeed in saving the boys' lives—perhaps it would fail—but it was certainly the only chance they had. He had used it only once before, nine years earlier, and on that occasion he had won a life sentence for his client.

Darrow spoke quietly, softly, and with conviction. The four men remained talking until late in the evening, debating and discussing Darrow's proposal, trying to predict the response of the state's attorney, wondering if the judge would provide them with the leeway necessary for success. Finally they adjourned—departing separately, each finding his way home in the evening twilight. Jacob Loeb was the last to leave; he paused in the doorway to shake Darrow's hand. He had known

Darrow for many years—not always as a friend, more often as an enemy—but on this occasion he recognized Darrow's genius as a strategist. Jacob Loeb had never been optimistic that they would save Nathan and Richard from the scaffold, yet now, for the first time, he could see how they might succeed.[69]

12 | MITIGATION OF PUNISHMENT

MONDAY, 21 JULY 1924–THURSDAY, 31 JULY 1924

I wish, at this time, to emphasize the difference between a mental disorder or a mental disease, and insanity. Now, there are certain forms of . . . mental diseases which do not constitute insanity. . . . Epilepsy is a form of mental disease which does not constitute a defense to a charge of murder or any other crime. . . . We have other forms of mental diseases such as deliria, melancholia and mental defects of various kinds, all of which constitute mental disorder and mental disease which fall far short of constituting insanity.[1]

Walter Bachrach, defense attorney, 31 July 1924

NATHAN HELD OUT HIS HANDS before him and studied them absentmindedly, turning them slightly in a circular motion. He had scrubbed them vigorously that morning, as part of his preparations for his first day in court, but the orange-brown nicotine stains on his right hand still remained, blemishes on his index and middle fingers. He had wanted to make a good impression, of course; his hair, carefully pomaded, lay slicked backward across his head—not a strand was out of place. He had dressed conservatively for his first appearance before the public; his dark blue suit had been pressed the previous evening and his brown-tan shoes, white shirt, and black four-in-hand tie completed the picture that he was about to present to the court.[2]

Nathan could hear, on the other side of the door leading to the courtroom, a voice, muffled and indistinct, speaking for several minutes, interrupted occasionally by other voices, equally indistinct. He strained to catch the words. Was that Darrow's voice—now interrupting the first—and speaking at a slightly lower pitch?

Nathan nudged Richard Loeb, sitting beside him on the wooden bench, smoking his third cigarette of the morning, looking down at his legs stretched out in front of him. Richard also had taken care with his appearance; he too was dressed in a dark blue suit. He wore a white shirt and a blue bow tie with white polka dots; his black shoes, carefully brushed and polished, looked as good as new.[3]

He couldn't tell, he answered in reply to Nathan's question, if that voice belonged to Darrow—it was too indistinct.

The bailiff spoke now, telling Richard to extinguish his cigarette, warning that they would soon walk from the antechamber into the courtroom. The judge had been speaking to the photographers, telling them that once the proceedings had begun, they should not use their flashbulbs.

26. RICHARD LOEB ENTERS COURT. A guard escorts Richard Loeb along the corridor from the Cook County jail to the Criminal Court Building.

Soon the bailiffs would receive the signal to bring Nathan and Richard into court.

The door to the courtroom swung open. The sheriff, Peter Hoffman, entered first. His deputy, David Edfeldt, followed close behind, along with two guards. Richard followed immediately afterward and Nathan Leopold stepped out behind him, trailed by more guards. The room was silent. Richard looked curiously around the courtroom and noticed that all eyes were on him; the crowd had turned in a single motion—as though choreographed—toward the right-hand side of the court, to gaze at the prisoners as they walked into the room.[4]

As Nathan and Richard took their seats behind him, Clarence Darrow gave them a reassuring smile, before turning to the front of the court to address the judge.

"Your honor, in the case of general number 33623 and 33624, where the defendants, Nathan F. Leopold, Jr., and Richard Loeb, are indicted for murder and kidnaping, these cases are set for this morning for any motions we might wish to make."

Darrow paused. It was still only quarter past ten in the morning, but already the summer heat was building relentlessly. Perspiration had gathered on Darrow's brow; he wiped it away with a single motion of his thumb across his forehead.

"Of course it is unnecessary," Darrow continued, "to say that this case has given us many perplexities and sleepless nights. Nobody is more aware than we are of what this means and the responsibility that is upon us. . . . No one . . . will doubt for a moment that we have the deepest sympathy for every one of the three families involved.

"Of course, this case has attracted very unusual attention on account of the weird, uncanny and terrible nature of the homicide. We have meant to consider it from the standpoint of the defendants, but we must also consider it first of all from the standpoint of their families—and by the families I include all three—and from the standpoint of the public, who are rightfully interested in this proceeding. . . .

"We want to state frankly here that no one in this case believes that these defendants should be released. We believe they should be permanently isolated from society and, if we as lawyers thought differently, their families would not permit us to do otherwise.

"We know, your honor," Darrow continued, "the facts in this case are substantially as have been published in the newspapers and what purports to be their confession, and we can see we have no duty to the defendants, or their families, or society, except to see that they are safely and permanently excluded from the public. . . ."[5]

Behind Darrow, listening to his words with an air of intense concentration, Nathan Leopold had moved forward in his seat as though to hear the attorney more clearly. Richard Loeb, seated adjacent to Nathan, seemed not to be paying attention—his eyes wandered around the courtroom until he caught the gaze of his brother Allan.[6]

"After long reflection and thorough discussion . . . we have determined to make a motion in this court for each of the defendants in each of the cases to withdraw our plea of not guilty and enter a plea of guilty. . . ."

Robert Crowe sat bolt upright in surprise as he heard the words. He stared across the aisle at Darrow, motionless, his lips parted, waiting to discover the import of Darrow's words.

"The statute provides that evidence may be offered in mitigation of the punishment and we shall ask at such time as the court may direct that we may be permitted to offer evidence as to the mental condition of these young men, to show the degree of responsibility they had and also to offer evidence as to the youth of these defendants and the fact of a plea of guilty as further mitigation of the penalties in this case.

"With that we throw ourselves upon the mercy of this court and this court alone."

There was a momentary silence in the room. Then a low buzz of conversation came from among the spectators. Was Darrow saying that Leopold and Loeb were insane? But why, then, plead guilty? Would the judge sentence the prisoners now, or later?[7]

At the rear of the room, reporters stumbled over chairs in their haste to get to the telephones and read their reports to their editors in time for the midday editions. Crowe and his assistants were on their feet, looking first at Darrow and then at the judge, seeking somehow to retrieve an initiative that had slipped from their grasp.

And, sitting among the spectators, Nathan Leopold Sr. had a stricken look, his face twisted in anguish, as he realized that the guilty plea left only a slender hope that Nathan might now escape the gallows.[8]

Crowe had immediately realized the implications of Darrow's maneuver. Illinois law mandated that an insanity plea be heard before a jury. If the plea had been not guilty by reason of insanity, Darrow would have had to argue his case before a jury—an impossible task. How could any jury have found the defendants insane?

But by changing the plea to guilty and arguing that their mental condition—along with their youth and their guilty plea—should be considered a mitigating factor in determining their punishment, Darrow had cleverly avoided a trial by jury. There would now be no trial. John Caverly would instead preside over a hearing to determine the punishment, which might range over several distinct possibilities from the death penalty to a minimum of fourteen years in prison. Caverly was a liberal judge, and clearly it was preferable for Darrow to argue his case before a single judge than before twelve jurors susceptible to public opinion and to Crowe's inflammatory rhetoric.

Darrow had turned the case on its head. He no longer needed to argue insanity in order to save Leopold and Loeb from the gallows. Now he needed only to persuade the judge that they were mentally ill—a medical condition, not at all equivalent or comparable to insanity—to obtain a reduction in their sentence. And Darrow needed only one reduction—from death by hanging to life in prison—to win his case.

Crowe's long-standing antipathy toward Darrow could not prevent him from acknowledging his adversary's brilliance. Darrow was using the insanity defense yet pretending it was something else. Moreover, he was introducing it by a back door so as to avoid confronting a jury.

JOHN CAVERLY GESTURED TO THE defendants to approach the bench. Both Nathan and Richard stood before the judge, their faces pale, Richard chewing nervously on his lower lip, Nathan looking directly ahead at the judge.[9]

"Nathan Leopold Jr.," Caverly began, "if your plea is guilty, and the plea of guilty is entered in this case, 33623, the court may sentence you to death; the court may sentence you to the penitentiary for the term of your natural life; the court may sentence you to the penitentiary for a term of years not less than fourteen. Now, realizing the consequence of your plea, do you still desire to plead guilty?"

"I do."

"Let the plea of guilty be entered, Mr. Clerk, in indictment number 33623, charging Nathan Leopold Jr. with murder. . . .

"Now, Nathan Leopold, in indictment number 33624, in which you are charged with kidnaping for ransom, the court desires to inform you that if you plead guilty, the court may sentence you to death, to the penitentiary for the term of your natural life or for a term of years . . ." Caverly paused, puzzled that he could not remember the statute. "What is the minimum in kidnaping?" he asked the clerk, Ferdinand Scherer.

"There is," Robert Crowe called out, "no minimum, your honor."

Caverly continued, ". . . any term up to life. Now, realizing the consequences of that plea do you now wish to withdraw your plea of not guilty in that case and plead guilty?"

"I do."

"Mr. Clerk, let the record show that Mr. Nathan Leopold, Jr., in indictment number 33624 charging kidnaping for ransom, desires to withdraw his plea of not guilty and have a plea of guilty entered, after being warned by the court of its consequences."

Caverly read the same cautions to Richard Loeb. Did he understand that his guilty plea might result either in death by hanging or in a prison term not less than fourteen years? Yes. Richard—still nervous, still chewing on his lower lip—acknowledged the judge's warning.

Caverly conferred with the attorneys. He would begin the hearing on Darrow's motion—to consider evidence in mitigation of punishment— in two days, on Wednesday, 23 July.[10]

Benjamin Bachrach rose to speak. The psychiatrists for the

defense—"men of science, of high standing, well known," he began—had investigated the mental condition of Nathan Leopold and Richard Loeb and would report their findings to the court as evidence in mitigation of the punishment. He understood that the prosecution had also hired psychiatrists to rebut and answer the defense presentation. Would it not be better, Bachrach asked, for defense and prosecution to present a joint report on the mental condition of the defendants?

Psychiatric evidence was typically submitted in a partisan manner, with the psychiatrists on one side contradicting those on the other side, and, as a consequence, "the ordinary hearing of insanity in criminal trials," Bachrach continued, "is much in the nature of a vaudeville show. It looks like high-class arguments, bickerings, denials, one set of alienists say one thing, another set of alienists say another thing." It brought disrepute on everyone involved. Each set of psychiatrists impugned the honesty of the other; psychiatry was regarded by the public as a laughingstock, less a serious science than an exercise in charlatanism and buffoonery, and the attorneys—never reluctant to purchase testimony from expert witnesses to say whatever served their purpose—were damned in the public eye as corrupt and venal.

A joint report by both sets of psychiatrists not only would save everyone the customary embarrassment that accompanied such proceedings but would ensure that the salacious details of the relationship between Nathan and Richard would not appear in the newspapers. Before the hearing begins, Bachrach explained, there must be "a joint conference of the alienists of the defendants and the state . . ."

"Now, just a minute," Robert Crowe interrupted.

"Well, before . . ."

"Just a moment," Crowe interrupted again. "Is there a plea of guilty entered here by two sane men or is the defense entering a plea of guilty by two insane men? . . ."

"Now, I ask counsel not to interrupt until I finish . . ."

"I know, but what I want to know is whether the contention is here the boys are sane or insane?"

Crowe's implication was obvious. The defendants had pleaded guilty. By their plea they admitted responsibility for their actions. If they admitted responsibility, they admitted their sanity. Why would the defense present evidence on their mental condition if the defendants had admitted their sanity?

"I am not to be sidetracked," Bachrach replied testily, glancing across the aisle to look at Crowe, "we ask counsel for the other side to assume that we are in good faith. . . . What we desire to do is to determine the degree of mental responsibility of the defendants. When the court hears all of the evidence it is his duty to fix the penalty. I think it comes with bad grace for the state's attorney to try to shut me off at this time. . . . What these alienists that we have talked to want to do is to meet with the alienists of the state and talk it over with them and see if they can iron out whatever differences there may be among them. Maybe our alienists will be won over to their side; maybe it will be the other way, but at any rate they want to present a joint matter."[11]

It seemed a futile proposal, which Crowe would certainly disdain. Crowe had nothing to gain and everything to lose. Any hint that the defendants were insane necessarily reduced their responsibility for the murder. And if the defense could argue that the defendants were insane, why, then they would be committed to the asylum. Crowe had boasted, again and again, that he had a hanging case. Why would he torpedo his own case by agreeing to a joint report on the defendants' mental condition and, by implication, conceding to the defense that Leopold and Loeb suffered from mental illness?

"Well, the court," Caverly interjected, "of course . . . has no power to require the state's attorney to do that."

And if anyone had any doubts about the matter, Crowe answered Bachrach's petition with as definitive a statement as it was possible for him to make.

"The state's attorney," Crowe declared, "is in a position to prove by evidence beyond all reasonable doubt that these boys are not only guilty, but that they are absolutely sane under the law and should be hanged, and the state will introduce its evidence beginning Wednesday morning to that effect."

"All right," Caverly banged his gavel on the bench to conclude the proceedings. "We will suspend, gentlemen, then, until Wednesday morning at 10 o'clock. All be here promptly at ten."[12]

NATHAN AND RICHARD, BACK INSIDE the Cook County jail, chatted with the reporters in an outside corridor. Richard was in a giddy mood. He had a sense of nervous relief, now that his first court appearance was behind him. How much coverage would they get in the evening newspapers, he wondered? Would they make the front page?

A reporter for the *Chicago Herald and Examiner* asked if Darrow had surprised them by entering a guilty plea. Or had they known beforehand?

"We're not allowed to say," Nathan spoke rapidly, trying to cut Richard off before he said something foolish. "Ask us something else."

"I bet we're all over the front page," Richard gloated. His moment in the spotlight had left him light-headed—it had given him a sudden rush of adrenaline. "I wish I had the papers. There certainly was a commotion when Mr. Darrow moved to plead guilty . . ."

"Better not talk about that," Nathan interrupted, angrily.

"What is it that the judge says when it's all over," Richard continued. "The court finds you . . ."

"Shut up!"[13]

IN HIS OFFICE ON THE third floor of the Criminal Court Building, Robert Crowe insisted to the reporters that Darrow's plea would not save Nathan and Richard from the gallows.

"The fact that the two murderers have thrown themselves upon the mercy of the court does not in any way alleviate the enormity of the crime they committed."

Darrow's case was a contradiction in terms, Crowe argued. How could Darrow introduce psychiatric evidence showing insanity and simultaneously introduce a plea of guilty? An insane person did not know the difference between right and wrong, could not be responsible for his or her actions, and was therefore not guilty of the intent to commit a crime.

"The defense is not permitted to introduce any insanity testimony because the law states that a plea of guilty to a fact automatically presumes the defendant to be sane.... For the defense to say they attempt to introduce alienists to testify regarding the mental condition of the two slayers would be going clearly outside the rules of evidence. There can be no insanity for a person who pleads guilty.... There is but one punishment which will satisfy the prosecution," Crowe concluded. "We will demand they be hanged."[14]

Clarence Darrow was in a reflective mood when he, too, met with the Chicago reporters after the adjournment. "I think we did the best thing we could for these two boys.... We have thrown ourselves upon the mercy of the court because I firmly believe that nowhere in this broad land could there be gotten together a fair-minded and impartial jury to try the case." There was no trickery about it, he insisted; there was no intent to have them released into society again. Most certainly they would spend the rest of their days in prison. The reporters repeated Crowe's assertion that the defense could not introduce psychiatric testimony, but Darrow was not concerned. If Crowe tried to prevent their testimony, the judge would assuredly rule in favor of the defense. "We can go as far as we want to go with insanity evidence, and we probably will."[15]

27. THE DEFENSE TEAM. The defense attorneys confer together before court convenes. From left: Walter Bachrach, Benjamin Bachrach, and Clarence Darrow.

•   •   •

CROWE HAD PROMISED TO SPARE no effort in his crusade to send Leopold and Loeb to the gallows, and on Wednesday, 23 July, at the opening of the hearing, he began to make good on his promise. A large steel filing cabinet, its drawers locked and sealed, stood close to the wall on the right-hand side of the courtroom; it contained exhibits that Crowe intended to show in evidence to the court. In other respects, the scene was a replica of the proceedings two days earlier. Darrow and Benjamin Bachrach sat at the defense table on the left; Crowe and his assistants sat on the right.[16]

The bailiffs had opened the twelve high windows, and the long white curtains stirred in the morning breeze. It promised to be another stiflingly humid day. The sheriff, Peter Hoffman, had thoughtfully placed a large metallic fan on the judge's desk, facing the audience. It stood still, for the moment, but soon one of the bailiffs would reach forward to turn the switch and send its loud hum into the well of the courtroom.[17]

Flora Franks—her mouth turned downward, her eyes red from weeping, her lips pressed tightly together—took the stand. She glanced occasionally toward her husband, seated on the right, among the spectators, but averted her gaze from the other side of the court where Leopold and Loeb sat two rows behind the defense attorneys.[18]

Sympathy for the victim's mother seemed almost tangible—it hung heavy over the silent courtroom. Even Richard Loeb seemed regretful. There was a sorrowful expression on his face, and his demeanor was attentive. Nathan Leopold stared at the floor; he seemed too ashamed even to look at the witness.

Robert Crowe had decided to make it brief. He held up Bobby's brown shoes, then the black-and-white patterned sock that had fallen by the culvert. Flora Franks identified both items: yes, they had belonged to Bobby, and she also recognized the class pin as well as the belt buckle that Crowe showed her.[19]

Later that morning, Jacob Franks took the stand. The old man stumbled slightly as he climbed the steps; he clasped and unclasped his hands nervously, gripping his fingers, as he waited for Joseph Savage, the assistant state's attorney, to begin asking questions. He, too, could identify Bobby's shoes, his stocking, belt buckle, and class pin. He recalled his son's disappearance on May 21 and recounted waiting for the kidnapper to call with instructions for the ransom money.[20]

Thirteen more witnesses took the stand that day. Edwin Greshan, Bobby's uncle, described how he had identified the body at the morgue; Joseph Springer, the coroner's physician, explained the cause of death as asphyxiation and listed the bruises and scratches on Bobby's body. Employees at the Rent-A-Car Company told how Nathan took out the dark green Willys-Knight; cashiers and tellers at the Hyde Park State Bank remembered Nathan opening a bank account in the name of Morton Ballard; and the clerks at the Morrison Hotel recalled that Richard Loeb had taken a room there.

In eight days, the state called eighty-two witnesses.

Clarence Darrow protested that this proceeding by the state was redundant: the facts were not in dispute; the defendants had confessed to the crime. Crowe had boasted of his intention to pile up the evidence to show the magnitude of the crime, its planning, and its premeditation; but, Darrow countered, there was only one reason to call so many witnesses. Crowe intended, Darrow continued, to whip up public opinion against the defendants and thus to create such a vengeful and vindictive atmosphere that Caverly would, despite himself, sentence Leopold and Loeb to death. Darrow appealed angrily to Caverly not to allow the state's attorney to proceed with his long list of witnesses: "the court should not permit for the pure purpose of rehearsing again to this community—to stir up anger and hatred— . . . details which have nothing to do with this case upon a plea of guilty and of which the community is already aware." It was, Darrow continued, nothing more than a "lurid painting in this courtroom . . . made for nothing excepting that a hoarse cry of angry people may somehow reach these chambers."[21]

But even if Caverly had agreed with Darrow that Crowe intended to inflame the public with graphic testimony, he could not have done anything about it. The state had as much right as the defense to present its evidence. The state would present evidence in aggravation of punishment; the defense would then present evidence in mitigation.

•   •   •

WOULD THE DEFENSE CALL NATHAN and Richard to the stand? The court had heard all the evidence from the state, and now, on Wednesday, 30 July, the defense was ready to present its witnesses.[22]

There was an air of expectation in the court. Either Nathan or Richard might sit in the witness box today; who could say? But the early-morning crowd gathered at the Criminal Court Building, waiting for the doors to open, knew that Clarence Darrow at least would be on the stage that day. Darrow had been largely silent during the presentation of the state's evidence during the past week. Since he did not dispute the facts and since he was reluctant to prolong the prosecution testimony any more than necessary, neither Darrow nor Benjamin Bachrach had bothered to cross-examine any of Crowe's witnesses. But now it was Darrow's turn and a throng of spectators had turned out to see the old lion perform.[23]

Darrow typically paid no attention to his wardrobe, but today he had made an effort. His hair no longer fell haphazardly across his forehead but had been slicked back into place. Ruby Darrow had sent out her husband's gray suit to be pressed; on this occasion there were no wrinkles or creases. She had also bought Clarence a new powder-blue shirt.[24]

Darrow was impatient to begin. He had listened to Crowe's witnesses for a week, occasionally grumbling at the redundancy of the proceedings, and now he was eager to present the defense testimony to the court.

The defense called William White to the stand. The psychiatrist took his place in the witness box. He carried a black leather briefcase in one hand, and as he sat down, he drew out some typewritten papers and placed the briefcase by his side. White wore a gray suit, tightly buttoned. He seemed aged, older than his fifty-four years; and his eyes burned with impatience—he was ready to begin.[25]

Walter Bachrach rose to his feet. Until now, he had deferred to Darrow and to his elder brother, Benjamin, but now, as the defense attorney with an expert knowledge of psychiatry and the law, he was about to take center stage.

28. CROWD OUTSIDE THE CRIMINAL COURT. Each day hundreds of spectators gathered across from the entrance of the Criminal Court Building on Austin Avenue, hoping to gain admittance to the courtroom.

"Will you please state your name?"

"Dr. William A. White."

"And your place of residence?"

"Washington, D.C."

"What is your profession?"

"Physician."

"What is your age, Doctor?"

"Fifty-four."

"Will you please state your professional connections, both present and past."

"Just a moment." Robert Crowe was on his feet, waving a paper in his hand. "I object to that, if your Honor please."

Caverly straightened his back and stiffened in his chair; he peered down from the bench at the state's attorney. "Why?"

"It is incompetent, irrelevant, and immaterial."

"Why?"

"The only purpose of it," Crowe explained, "would be to lay a foundation for him to testify as an expert on the question of the sanity or insanity of the defendants. On a plea of guilty your Honor has no right to go into that question. As soon as it appears in the trial, it is your Honor's duty to call a jury."[26]

Crowe had seen his chance, and now he was ready to take it. Clarence Darrow had decided not to offer a defense. Darrow's clients had pleaded guilty. Yet here was a psychiatrist on the witness stand, about to argue that Leopold and Loeb were mentally ill. It was illegitimate, Crowe believed, for the defense to introduce insanity into the hearing. How could they plead guilty and simultaneously offer an insanity defense?

And, Crowe continued, the law contained no ambiguity on the matter. The Illinois supreme court had ruled that any decision on the sanity of a defendant must be heard before a jury—it could not be decided by a judge acting alone. Therefore, just as soon as the defense introduced psychiatric testimony, Crowe argued, the judge should dissolve the hearing and call a jury to determine the defendants' sanity.

"I want to be heard on that, your Honor," Crowe insisted, "because if there is any testimony introduced in this trial as to the mental condition of these boys, any act or any order that your Honor enters in the case is a nullity. In other words, if your Honor, at the conclusion of this trial, after having gone into the sanity proposition, should sentence these boys to hang, your judgment would not be worth the paper that it was written on. The Supreme court would set it aside."

Suppose Caverly allowed the defense to present evidence on the boys' mental condition without calling a jury. Then if Caverly subsequently sentenced them to death, Clarence Darrow would appeal the judgment to the Illinois supreme court, contending that the psychiatric evidence should have been presented to a jury.

Crowe stepped forward. He rapped the documents table angrily with his knuckles. "What is the purpose of entering a plea of guilty and then maintaining that you have a defense and you have a right to hear it, when the law says that that defense has got to be decided by twelve men? What is the defense trying to do here?"[27]

Crowe's intent was clear. If he could persuade Caverly to call a jury, then the state would certainly be able to hang Leopold and Loeb.

Caverly listened patiently as the state's attorney continued to argue his case. He was willing to hear Crowe out, he said, but where were Crowe's authorities on the matter? Had the Illinois supreme court ruled, in fact, that psychiatric evidence should be heard before a jury and not before a judge? Were there any precedents?

"Have you," Caverly inquired, "got any authorities sustaining your position?"

"I have got the Geary case, your Honor."

"The Geary case isn't in point," Caverly replied. "I know the Geary case. . . . But that is not on all fours with this case. That was a trial for insanity, in which counsel waived the constitutional rights of the defendant to a trial by jury, and the Supreme Court said, 'you must go back and try the insanity case with a jury.' There was no question about that."[28]

Robert Crowe had good reason to remember the trial of Eugene Geary. In July 1920, as a judge on the Criminal Court, Crowe had presided over the arraignment of Geary for murder. It had been a notorious case. The trial and subsequent appeals of Geary, one of Chicago's most violent and dangerous gangsters, had scandalized the public and created important precedents under Illinois law regarding the insanity defense.

_____

On Thursday, 27 May 1920, at ten o'clock in the evening, Eugene (Gene) Geary, a gangland enforcer working for Maurice (Mossy) Enright, entered the Horn Palace Saloon at 4165 South Halsted Street. As he walked up to the bar, Geary almost collided with another man, Harry Reckas, who had been about to leave the saloon. Reckas had never seen Geary before, but as they passed each other, their eyes met and they stared each other down. Reckas caught the smell of whiskey on the other man's breath—he was obviously drunk.

Geary spoke first; his voice was coldly menacing. "Who are you looking for?"

"Nobody." Reckas gestured toward a friend standing by his side: "We are going home."

The bartender, David Ruse, sensed trouble; he moved cautiously up behind Geary and spoke quietly into his ear: "Gene, these men are friends. . . . You're not looking for them."

It was too late. Geary's hand reached for his weapon, the bartender ducked for cover, and the loud report of the gun echoed around the saloon as Reckas fell dead with a bullet through his left side.[29]

Geary had killed Reckas on behalf of Rex Bain, leader of a South Side whiskey ring. Geary had a notorious reputation as a hired gun: only six months earlier, he had killed a cabdriver, Leonard Tripple, in the Cadillac Cafe at 2134 South Wabash Avenue and had been charged with murder, but he had been acquitted.[30]

One week after the murder of Harry Reckas, detectives from the office of the state's attorney captured Geary in an apartment on the South Side. At his trial, later that year, the plea was not guilty by reason of insanity and his lawyers, Thomas Nash and Michael Ahern, spoke of his paranoia. He was syphilitic—he had had syphilis for nineteen years—and was an alcoholic who consumed copious quantities of gin and whiskey. Geary suffered from hallucinations: he saw sand flies and bugs crawling on his food. He never allowed anyone to turn off the lights if he was in the room, and he believed that drivers of yellow cabs were out to kill him.[31]

The jury was unmoved by his lawyers' plea and sentenced Geary to hang.

But Illinois law gave particular consideration to the constitutional rights of the insane. The criminal code stipulated that if after conviction and a sentence of hanging, the prisoner were to become insane, the court should then postpone the punishment until the prisoner had regained his or her sanity.[32]

Since his conviction and sentencing, Geary had become ever more violent, fighting with other prisoners, threatening the guards, setting his mattress on fire, and attempting suicide.[33]

His lawyers petitioned for a sanity hearing. Geary had become insane, they argued, since his sentencing. He was entitled to a hearing to determine his mental condition. If he was indeed insane, the court should commit him to an asylum.[34]

Their petition for a hearing was successful. On 19 May 1921, Charles McDonald, chief justice of the Criminal Court, announced the appointment of a commission of three psychiatrists—Archibald Church, Hugh Patrick, and Douglas Singer—to examine Geary to decide if he had become insane. Ten days later, the psychiatrists returned their verdict: Geary was sane. He would face the hangman's noose on 17 June.[35]

But now the Illinois supreme court intervened. It had not been legitimate, the court decided, for McDonald to have impaneled a commission of psychiatrists to decide on Geary's sanity. The statute was unambiguous: only a jury could rule whether a prisoner was sane or insane. McDonald's commission of three psychiatrists had no provision in law and therefore violated the prisoner's constitutional right to appear before a jury: "he was entitled to a trial by a jury of the question whether or not he had become insane or lunatic after the original sentence of death.... A jury trial in such cases is imperative.... Such question, when so raised, cannot be legally tried otherwise."[36]

Geary was fortunate to have such resourceful lawyers. On 23 September 1921, a jury deliberated for less than an hour and declared that he was insane. Amazingly, he had escaped the hangman. The court committed him to the Illinois Asylum for Insane Criminals at Chester.[37]

The decision provoked outrage. The Illinois criminal code, with its many safeguards against the punishment of the insane, seemed to favor the murderer.

The editor of the *Chicago Daily Tribune* denounced Geary as "one of the worst men who ever lived in Chicago and one of the most dangerous who possibly could be allowed at large." It was, he continued, a travesty of justice that such a notorious, cold-blooded killer should escape punishment: "Geary is not a gibbering idiot or a raving maniac.... Gene Geary should be hanged."[38]

The Geary case, Crowe explained, had established the precedent. Only a jury could decide the sanity or insanity of a defendant. If Caverly were to allow psychiatrists to testify to the mental condition of Leopold and Loeb, he would be usurping the role properly allotted to a jury.

Crowe had now finished giving the court the details of the Geary case and had completed reading the decision of the Illinois supreme court.

"Can language be more explicit, more mandatory and more direct than the language that I have just read?"

Crowe turned slightly, to his left, to indicate the defendants seated behind their attorneys. "But here is a cold-blooded murder, without a defense in fact, and they attempt, on a plea of guilty, to introduce an insanity defense before your Honor, and the statute says that is a matter that must be tried by a jury."

Caverly leaned forward to interrupt, gesturing toward the defense attorneys: "Has anybody said that they are going to introduce an insanity defense?"

"Well," Crowe answered, "what is the purpose of putting an expert on the stand?"

"They have a right to, in my opinion."

"Aren't they going into his mental condition?"

"Well, suppose they do?"

The court had not yet heard the psychiatric testimony, Caverly explained. Were the psychiatrists on the stand to show that Leopold and Loeb were insane? The court had not yet heard a single word of White's testimony, and until he heard the testimony, he could not determine what it would be. "The defense hasn't said they are going to put on alienists to show that these men are insane, and I don't think that they are going to attempt to show that they are insane."

"Well then what is the evidence for, what are they going to show?"

"You will have to listen to it."

Crowe remained obdurate. He intended to push his point as far as it would go. He repeated his contention: only a jury could hear testimony regarding mental illness.

"Will you cite one authority?" Caverly asked.

"I have cited, Your Honor, and I believe they are in point."

"The Geary case?"

"The Geary case and the statute itself, your Honor."

"If you are relying on the Geary case you might as well end the argument. The Court will overrule you. . . ."

"Your Honor misses the real point. You have not the power to determine whether the evidence that has been introduced constitutes insanity or not. Just as soon as evidence of a mental condition is brought in the case, that is a question, as the Courts have stated, peculiarly for a Jury."

"They never said it."

"We just read it to you," Crowe replied, exasperated that Caverly could be so obtuse.[39]

Caverly shrugged. He was not convinced, he answered. Clarence Darrow was not introducing psychiatric testimony in order to show that the defendants could not distinguish right from wrong and were thus insane; he was presenting the testimony to demonstrate that Leopold and Loeb suffered from a medical condition. The defense asked for mitigation on account of that medical condition.

And, in any case, Caverly asked, suppose he were to exclude the psychiatric testimony. Would the defense not then have grounds for appeal? The statutes mandated a judge to hear evidence from both sides, one in aggravation of the punishment, the other in mitigation.

Caverly indicated to the clerk of the court to pass him a copy of the Illinois statutes and began thumbing through the pages. He started reading from the criminal code.

" 'It shall be the duty of the Court to examine witnesses as to the aggravation or mitigation of the offense.' " Caverly paused in his reading; he looked up from the book to address the state's attorney. "Now, then, under that wording of the statute . . . the Court permitted eighty witnesses to testify to every detail to show an aggravated murder; and after the State is through the defense come in and . . . they wish to put on certain evidence to show a mitigation of the crime. Now then, supposing I were to say no, and then should impose the extreme penalty. Would not the Supreme Court say that if the Court had listened to mitigating circumstances then he would not have imposed the death penalty? . . . Would not the Supreme Court say that I should have listened to what the defendants had to say rather than have made an arbitrary ruling and sentenced them to whatever it might be?"

Crowe had been hoist with his own petard. He had insisted on presenting testimony from eighty witnesses to persuade the judge to send the defendants to the gallows. How could he deny the defense the right to produce evidence that might reduce the punishment?

BUT, CROWE ASKED, WHAT SORT of evidence did the defense intend to produce? The defendants, according to Darrow, were not insane, and there was no evidence that they were insane. But Darrow's claim that they were mentally ill could be based only on the fact and the character of the crime. The nature of the crime, the boys' callous disregard for Bobby's life, the mutilation of the body, the random choice of the victim—all led the defense to argue backward from the crime to infer mental disease.

But the Illinois supreme court had already deliberated on the admissibility of such evidence—in a case decided three years earlier—and had ruled such evidence to be inadmissible.

It was Friday, 4 April 1919, a bright, sunny spring day, when John Bachman strolled down the main street of the town of Carmi, Illinois, and met an old friend, Frank Lowhone, walking toward him. Lowhone was doing well: he told Bachman that he was no longer a farm laborer; he had found better pay as a coal miner near Benton in Franklin County. A third friend, Mack Nottingham, passed by, and the three men gossiped for fifteen minutes on the sidewalk. Nottingham had not much to do that day, and after Lowhone left, he and Bachman walked on together, talking. Soon Bachman also departed and Nottingham drifted over to the front of Hubele's Store. There was a bench facing the store; Nottingham hoped to meet friends, to catch some town gossip, and to while away the afternoon chatting.

Suddenly a shot broke the stillness. Nottingham looked up—the report had seemed very close. To his right he could see Frank Lowhone running along the sidewalk toward him. Lowhone had a gun in his hand, and as he approached, a second shot rang out. Both shots had missed their intended target but now Lowhone was almost on him, taking aim to fire a third shot in his direction. Nottingham rose up off the bench and darted around the side of the store, but his assailant was close behind. As Lowhone turned the corner in pursuit, he fired a third shot. The bullet tore through Nottingham's chest. As blood spurted out onto the ground, Lowhone emptied his revolver into Nottingham; two more bullets hit their target.

The town sheriff, Charles Gibbs, and another man, Frank Martin, had been in the courthouse when they heard the gunfire. They both ran out to the street. Lowhone was walking toward them, his head down, intent on reloading the gun. They cautiously approached him and reached him as he placed the final bullet in the chamber. Lowhone glanced up and relaxed; as he handed over his weapon, he addressed the sheriff.

"Here it is; I meant to give myself up."

Why had he fired his gun? asked Martin.

"Oh, they have been running over me around here; trying to run me out of town and one thing and another."

"Did you kill him?"

"I hope I did, the damn son of a bitch."[40]

Was Lowhone insane when he killed Mack Nottingham? Or was the killing a rational act, the decision of someone able to distinguish right from wrong? There was no obvious motive for the killing; there had never been any animosity between Lowhone and Mack Nottingham. On the contrary, the two men had known each other for many years and had become close friends. At Lowhone's trial, relatives and workmates testified to his eccentric behavior and his antipathy toward some residents of Carmi, but up until the moment of the shooting, there had been little to suggest that Lowhone was insane.

Was the fact of the murder itself evidence that Lowhone was insane? It had been a bizarre killing, no doubt, one that defied explanation. Yet on appeal, the Illinois supreme court ruled that neither the lack of a motive nor the suddenness of the attack nor the satisfaction expressed by Lowhone after the shooting could be the basis for a judgment that Lowhone was insane. Lowhone was an alcoholic who had had previous brushes with the law, but this fact too was insufficient evidence to conclude that he was insane. The court's decision left no room for doubt—"depravity of character and abandoned habits are not in themselves evidence of insanity. Neither is the commission of an unnatural crime"—and it affirmed the lower court's decision that Lowhone was guilty of murder. Frank Lowhone was hanged on Friday, 15 April 1921.[41]

Just as Frank Lowhone was unable to claim insanity on the basis of the unnatural character of his crime, so, Crowe argued, it was not possible for Nathan Leopold and Richard Loeb to argue mental illness as mitigation when evidence of their mental illness arose solely from the commission of the crime.

Clarence Darrow had listened attentively to Crowe's exegesis, but now even he had lost the thread of Crowe's logic. Darrow was losing patience. The defense had listened to Crowe for three days. Crowe's arguments had become repetitive and flat and increasingly threadbare. If he were now saying that the defense could not introduce psychiatric testimony because it was the wrong kind of evidence, then just what would he allow?

"The State's Attorney," Darrow called out, sarcastically, "ought to tell us what we could offer in mitigation. What kind of evidence would be in mitigation? . . ."

"I don't think you have any evidence here," Crowe replied, calling back across the aisle.

"Well, is there any such evidence in any case in the world?"

"Yes."

"What?"

"Evidence," Crowe responded, "that grows out of the transaction itself. In other words, as I explained yesterday, after a murder has been proved, it is competent, in order to mitigate the punishment, to show, for instance, that the man who was killed had seduced the daughter or the wife, that is mitigating evidence."

"Why," Darrow called out, "would that be competent?"

"Because it is in mitigation."

"Why?"

"Because the law would not hold a man who had a reason in morals . . ."

"Oh, that is nonsense," Darrow interrupted.

". . . for killing," Crowe continued, "for the same strict accountability that the law would hold a man who had absolutely no justification in morals."[42]

Mitigation, according to Crowe, was to be found only in the external circumstances of the case, not in the mental condition of the defendants.

But was not mental condition, Walter Bachrach replied, one feature of a case such as this? Crowe himself had claimed, when he had presented his witnesses in aggravation of punishment, that the murder was undertaken in cold blood and that it therefore demanded the extreme penalty. But did not that claim require an assessment of the defendants' state of mind?

"He says," Bachrach explained, pointing to the state's attorney, "he was trying to show that it was a cold-blooded murder. Upon what does a cold-blooded murder depend if it does not depend upon the mental condition of the man who is committing the murder? How are you going to tell whether it was a cold-blooded murder if you don't know what the mental condition of the person was who committed it?"[43]

JOHN CAVERLY SAT TWIRLING a pencil in his hand, looking first at the defense and then at the state as each side presented its case. To his left, still on the witness stand, William White waited patiently for the judge's decision. If Caverly agreed with Darrow that the psychiatric testimony was admissible, White would continue with his testimony; if Caverly sided with Crowe and denied the evidence, Darrow's gamble would have failed. The defense had wagered everything on the psychiatric evidence—withdraw that, and Darrow's case would collapse.[44]

Caverly had been very patient—he had listened to arguments on this point for three days—but now, on Friday, 1 August, he seemed ready to draw the debate to a close and announce his decision. It was, everyone realized, a crucial moment—would he decide for the defense or for the state?

13 | PSYCHIATRISTS FOR THE DEFENSE

[Richard Loeb] is still a little child emotionally, still talking to his teddy bear. . . . He is infantile. I should say somewhere around four or five years old, perhaps a little older. . . . [Nathan Leopold] also is the host of a relatively infantile emotional aspect of his personality but . . . he has reacted by a defense mechanism, which has produced the final picture of a marked disordered personality makeup in the direction of developing feelings of superiority.[1]

William Alanson White, superintendent of
St. Elizabeths Hospital, 1 August 1924

The development of their ideas of criminality, the planning and carrying out of their deeds, seems to be only possible because each of them had already abnormal characteristics.[2]

William Healy, psychiatrist, author of
The Individual Delinquent, *4 August 1924*

[Richard Loeb] is suffering from a disordered personality. . . . The nature of this disorder is primarily in a profound pathological discord between his intellectual and emotional life. . . . [Nathan] Leopold is . . . a paranoid personality in which are the elements of a pathological exaggeration of his ego and . . . a profound judgment disorder.[3]

Bernard Glueck, professor of psychiatry, New York Postgraduate School and Hospital, 5 August 1924

THE COURTROOM WAITED EXPECTANTLY. "UNDER that section of the statute," Caverly announced, speaking in a slow drawl, "which gives the court the right, and says it is his duty to hear evidence in mitigation, as well as evidence in aggravation, the Court is of the opinion that it is his duty to hear any evidence that the defense may present, and it is not for the court to determine in advance what it may be." Caverly halted briefly. The pause lent his words dignity. "The Court will hear it and give it such weight as he thinks it is entitled to. . . . The objection to the witness is overruled, and the witness may proceed."[4]

NATHAN AND RICHARD SMILED AS they heard Caverly's decision. Nathan leaned forward slightly; he touched Darrow's arm in congratulation and then turned in his seat to look in triumph at his relatives. His elder brother, Michael, seated two rows behind him, returned his smile; and, by Michael's side, his father breathed a heavy sigh and wiped his forehead with his handkerchief. Richard's uncle, Jacob, turned to Allan Loeb, seated beside him, and whispered a few words to his nephew before turning his attention once more to the front of the court.[5]

Jacob Franks had sat impassively, listening to Caverly's decision. Now he rose from his seat and walked down the aisle, past the defendants and their guards, through the crowd of spectators, retreating to the corridor for a cigarette. The reporter from the *Chicago Daily News* caught up with him outside the courtroom and, as Franks reached for his cigarette case, asked him about Caverly's decision to allow the psychiatric evidence. Was the judge's ruling a setback for the prosecution?

"This particular decision," Franks replied, "makes very little difference to me. I feel sure justice will be done."

"Do you mean," the reporter pressed, "that you feel sure the boys will be hanged—is that what you mean by justice?"

"No," Franks answered enigmatically, pausing to light a cigarette, "I'm not sure hanging would be justice. . . ."

"Do you mean you have faith in Judge Caverly's making a just decision?"

Franks smiled. "I have faith in the state's attorney," he replied.[6]

IN THE COURTROOM, WILLIAM WHITE, still on the witness stand, reached into his briefcase. As he glanced through his papers, he settled himself more comfortably in his chair. Walter Bachrach stepped into the well of the court.

"From the result, Doctor, of your examination and observation of the defendant, Richard Loeb, are you able to form and have you formed an opinion as to his mental condition at the present time and on the 21st of May 1924?"

29. WILLIAM ALANSON WHITE. In this photograph, taken on 1 August, the psychiatrist William White is seated on the witness stand, waiting to give testimony on the mental condition of the defendants. White was president of the American Psychiatric Association and superintendent of St. Elizabeths Hospital.

Richard Loeb, White replied, had had the misfortune, as a young child, to have had Emily Struthers as his governess. This virago had hounded young Richard into submission, preventing his association with his peers, gradually separating him—emotionally, at least—from his parents and siblings, and placing such inordinate demands on him that he had no recourse except in lying.[7]

"She pushed him tremendously," White explained, "in his school work, was apparently very ambitious with regard to him and stimulated and pushed him ahead, further than he would have gone without that sort of stimulus."

Emily Struthers had propelled Richard Loeb onto his path of crime. Her demands—her outrageously extravagant demands, White suggested—had forced the young boy into a habit of lying and deceit. It had become pathological. Richard lied on every occasion, even when there was no apparent need to deceive.

"For example, in college he lied about his marks. He lied about all sorts of things. He lied to Babe Leopold, his comrade, about his attendance in college. While his marks were on the whole pretty good he made them a good deal better. . . . He was continually building up all sorts of artificial situations until he himself says that he found it difficult to distinguish between what was true and what was not true."[8]

It was but a short step, according to White, from Loeb's habitual lying to the creation of a fantasy life that had entrapped and overwhelmed him. He now imagined himself as a master criminal, so brilliant that he could outwit any detective sent to catch him, so clever that he could coordinate the activities of dozens of other criminals, and so cunning that he could eternally elude his enemies.

"He considered himself the master criminal mind of the century, controlling a large band of criminals, whom he directed; even at times he thought of himself as being so sick as to be confined to bed, but so brilliant and capable of mind . . . [that] the underworld came to him and sought his advice and asked for his direction, and so he directed this whole group of criminal conspirators from his sick bed."[9]

Richard was emotionally infantile, White suggested; he remained trapped by fantasies that a five-year-old might entertain. Yet as far as his intellect was concerned, Richard was entirely normal, slightly superior to his peers, but not extravagantly so. The divergence between his emotional experiences on the one hand and his intellectual ability on the other was so pronounced as to seem pathological and, White concluded, boded ill for the future. His infantile emotional makeup, so discordant with his intellectual ability, could lead only to a splitting of his personality and, as a consequence, severe mental deterioration.

"In a well-rounded, well-integrated, well-knit personality, emotion and intelligence go hand-in-hand. . . . Dickie is in a stage which if it goes on further is capable of developing that kind of very malignant splitting."[10]

"DOCTOR," WALTER BACHRACH ASKED, "will you now address yourself to Nathan Leopold, Junior, and state what you have obtained as a result of your examination of him?"

Nathan's pathology, the psychiatrist replied, had begun in early childhood. His classmates at the Douglas School had teased him relentlessly; his estrangement from his peers had begun when he was seven or eight years old and had continued through his time at the Harvard School and into the present. Nathan had always been a lonely, unhappy child, ever the outsider, and to protect himself from further pain and hurt, he had retreated into an inner world where emotion counted for nothing and intellect was all.

Nathan, like Richard, was trapped inside a world of fantasy. Nathan imagined himself as a slave, subservient yet physically powerful, who had saved the life of his king and had thereby earned the king's gratitude. It was an elaborate fantasy, played out in innumerable ways, yet it always allowed Nathan to imagine himself as superior.

"Babe fancies himself as being a slave," White explained, looking at Walter Bachrach, turning occasionally to his right to glance at the judge, "in which case he has saved the king's life, and the king is very grateful, and the king wants to recompense him by giving him his liberty, which he refuses. However, he is a very unusual slave. He is not an ordinary every-day slave. He belongs to the social grade of slaves, to be sure, but he is very powerful, physically powerful. The various kings, when they are in dispute with one another, if they want to settle their differences, each pick out one of their slaves to fight in single-handed combat. He is always the one that is picked out. He always wins. Some times, he says, he has found himself fighting many, many men in his phantasies, to save the king. At times it was getting where he was fighting a thousand men, single-handed; and then the thing would get so utterly ridiculous that he would shake himself out of the phantasy and perhaps begin over again."

White paused; he looked down at the notes in his lap; there was silence in the courtroom as White shuffled through his papers.

"Now," Bachrach prompted, helpfully, "what findings did you arrive at . . . with reference to each of the defendants in combination with the other?"

Nathan and Richard complemented each other, White replied. Richard needed Nathan's applause and admiration in order to confirm his sense of his own self.

But Nathan also needed Richard to play a role; Richard took the role of a king who was simultaneously superior and inferior. Richard had suggested the murder and had taken the initiative in its planning—in that sense, White suggested, he had been the king. But at crucial moments, when Richard had appeared to falter, Nathan had assumed command. For example, on the day following the murder, Thursday, 22 May, Richard had wanted to abandon the ransom attempt as soon as they had learned of the discovery of the body—"Dickie would have let it gone by"—but Nathan had insisted that they call Jacob Franks one more time in order to secure the ransom: "Babe . . . insisted upon sending the last telephone message and taking such chances to bring the whole thing to a successful combination."[11]

It was a peculiarly bizarre confluence of two personalities, each of which satisfied the needs of the other. Nathan would never on his own initiative have murdered Bobby Franks. Nathan had confessed feeling a degree of pleasure from planning the murder and in undressing the boy—to have someone in his power, he had admitted, was sexually arousing—but there was no indication that without Richard's suggestion, he would have committed murder.[12]

As for Richard—his suggestion would never have been carried into effect without the encouragement provided by Nathan's participation.

"I can not see how Babe would have entered into it at all alone because he had no criminalistic tendencies in any sense as Dickie did, and I don't believe Dickie would have ever functioned to this extent all by himself, so these two boys with their peculiarly interdigitated personalities come into this emotional compact with the Franks homicide as a result."[13]

"As a result," Bachrach asked, "of your examination and observation of the defendant Richard Loeb have you formed an opinion as to his mental condition on the 21st of May, 1924?"

"Yes, sir."

"What is that opinion?"

"He was the host of anti-social tendencies along the lines that I have described; he was the host of an infantile make-up which was a long way from the possibility of functioning harmoniously with his developed intelligence. . . . The main outstanding feature was his infantilism. I mean by that these infantile emotional characteristics. That is the outstanding feature of his mental condition. He is still a little child emotionally, still talking to his teddy bear. . . ."

"Now, have you an opinion as to the mental condition of Nathan Leopold, Jr., on the 21st of May, 1924?"

"Yes."

"What is your opinion?"

"Well, he also is the host of a relatively infantile emotional aspect of his personality but . . . he has reacted by a defense mechanism, which has produced the final picture of a marked disordered personality make-up in the direction of developing feelings of superiority, which places him very largely out of contact with any adequate appreciation of his relations to others."[14]

Walter Bachrach turned, away from the witness, to address the prosecution: "You may cross-examine."[15]

•   •   •

IT WAS FUTILE, CROWE REALIZED, to debate psychoanalytic theory with the witness. To dispute White's analysis of Richard and Nathan— Were they emotionally retarded? Did their fantasies indicate mental illness?—would be to play into the hands of the defense. Crowe had little or no understanding of psychiatry, and he could not expect to defeat White in a debate over Freudian theory. The defense had placed the murder within a psychoanalytic framework, using psychoanalytic concepts and theories, and if Crowe accepted that framework, he would surely lose the debate.

Better for the state to demolish the framework than to accept it. There was no advantage for Crowe in discussing the extent or character of the defendants' mental condition—and, in any case, both Nathan and Richard, he believed, were entirely rational.

But how best to demolish the psychoanalytic framework? White was the leader of his profession, with awards and honors to prove it. His credentials—president of the American Psychiatric Association, author of almost twenty books, editor of a prestigious psychoanalytic journal—gave his pronouncements authority and legitimacy. How could Crowe, an obscure state's attorney, unknown outside Cook County, hope to vanquish the acknowledged leader of the psychiatric profession?

"Now, how many persons—," Crowe paused, seeking to rephrase his question. "From how many persons did you get any information in reference to Nathan Leopold, Jr. that you base your opinion on? . . ."

"I did not," White replied, "get any information from anybody except Nathan Leopold, Jr. . . . I beg pardon. I want to supplement that. I had read—There is one other thing I did have. I had read the so-called Bowman and Hulbert report."[16]

Karl Bowman and Harold Hulbert had based their report on interviews with Nathan—so, in essence, White's analysis was based in its entirety on conversations with Nathan. But how, Crowe continued, had White known that, in those conversations, Nathan had been telling the truth? And if he had not been telling the truth, did White's psychoanalysis have any value? Or was it merely a preposterous chimera, fabricated to exculpate the murderers of Bobby Franks?

"Do you think that Nathan Leopold would attempt to mislead you?"

"I don't think he did. . . ."

"He has not lied to you at all?"

"I don't remember any particular instance," White replied, cautiously, "at this moment where I believe Nathan lied to me. I think he was frank, as frank as he could be."

"You are satisfied that he has been absolutely truthful, that is, Nathan has, with you all the way through? . . . Don't you think it is strange that he lies to Loeb and he lies to everybody else except you? . . . The fact that Nathan Leopold has lied to every other person that he has talked to except you, doesn't make any impression on your mind at all? Does it?"[17]

What was White to say? It would be impossible to demonstrate the truthfulness of Nathan's statements. Perhaps, after all, Nathan was incapable of telling the truth—he was a proven liar who lived in a fantasy world, and it was in his own interest to assist the psychiatrists in their diagnosis that he was mentally ill. Why would anyone take Nathan's statements to be true?

But if Nathan had lied to the psychiatrists, then their reports were worthless, their analysis had no value, and the defense case would be without merit.

Crowe reminded White that in his testimony under direct examination, he had spoken of the defendants' antisocial behavior as evidence of their mental deterioration. Could he provide examples of such behavior? Crowe inquired. What exactly had Nathan and Richard done? What were those crimes?

"They set fire to several buildings. Three instances I think they gave me of having set fires. . . ."

"Now tell us what Loeb told you about these fires? . . ."

"Well, this shack was set on fire, this particular one . . ."

"When and where was it?" Crowe interrupted.

"I don't know where it was."

"Didn't you ask them?"

"It was out in the middle of a lot somewhere."[18]

"Can you give us any information that will enable me to check up and show whether this actually happened or whether they had just imposed on you?"

"No, I can't give anything to satisfy you. . . ."

"If you were able to tell me the date on which it happened and the location don't you think I would be able to obtain proof as to whether or not they were lying to you or telling you the truth?"

"You probably would be able to tell whether such a thing happened in the city," White answered, grudgingly.

"And your conclusion depends entirely upon the fact that you believe what these boys told you? . . . If they have fooled you and consistently lied to you then your conclusion isn't worth anything, is it?"[19]

White, so self-assured a few hours earlier, now seemed flustered. Crowe continued to pepper him with questions delivered staccato at a pace so rapid that even the stenographers had difficulty keeping up with him. White's eyebrows knitted in a frown. He struggled to find a way out of the trap that Crowe had prepared for him; and as he searched for the answers that would turn back Crowe's attacks, he seemed confused and uncertain. He hesitated; and to the onlookers it seemed as if his dignity had evaporated under the insistent demands of the state's attorney.[20]

Crowe continued to batter the witness all day, but he had already won his point. White's testimony was a fake defense with little or no relationship to the facts—a defense manufactured solely to defeat justice. Perhaps the attorneys had instructed Nathan and Richard to deceive the psychiatrists; or perhaps the psychiatrists had willingly colluded in the scheme, Crowe suggested. But such speculation, he stated, was irrelevant. The defense testimony relied on the truthfulness of the defendants and, as such, it was rotten to the core.[21]

Clarence Darrow listened to Crowe's cross-examination in silence. Darrow sat in a slouch, his eyes fixed on the floor, one side of his head resting against his right hand. He seemed not to pay any attention to White's testimony; he appeared sunk in gloom at this unexpected course of events. Benjamin Bachrach, at Darrow's side, followed the proceedings with a worried, anxious look, his pen in his right hand, his eyes closely monitoring the drama playing out a few steps in front of him.[22]

Perhaps the next witness would put on a better show. Crowe was flushed with victory and eager to deal out the same treatment to all the defense witnesses. "I intend," he announced, with relish, "to submit every defense alienist to the same sort of cross-examination I gave Dr. White."[23]

William Healy, a tall, thin man with sandy-colored hair and a nervous expression, first took the stand on Monday, 4 August. Healy had brought a clutter of documents—papers that showed a series of graphs and tables—but for the moment they lay unnoticed on the document table in front of the bench.[24]

Clarence Darrow took up the questioning of the witness, prompting Healy to tell the court his observations on the relationship between the boys. Healy talked in a quiet, soft voice; spectators at the back of the courtroom had to strain to make out his words.

"As far as I can find out from the account given by the boys themselves and from their relatives," Healy said, "their association began at fifteen years of age. They just barely knew each other earlier, but that is the time they first came together. It is very clear from the study of the boys separately that each came with peculiarities in their mental life. . . . Each arrived at these peculiarities by different routes; each supplemented the other's already constituted abnormal needs in a most unique way. And in regard to the association I think that the crime in its commission and in its background has features that are quite beyond anything in my experience or knowledge of the literature. There seems to have been so little normal motivation, the matter was so long planned, so unfeelingly carried out, that it represents nothing that I have ever seen or heard of before. . . . In the matter of the association, I have the boys' story, told separately, about an incredibly absurd childish compact that bound them. . . . For Loeb, he says, the association gave him the opportunity of getting someone to carry out his criminalistic imaginings and conscious ideas. In the case of Leopold, the direct cause of his entering into criminalistic acts was this particularly childish compact."

Crowe was suddenly attentive—here was something new!

"You are talking about a compact," he interrupted, "that you characterize as childish. Kindly tell us what that compact was."

"I am perfectly willing to tell it in chambers but it is not a matter that I think should be told here."

"I insist that we know what that compact is," Crowe replied, "so that we can form some opinion about it. . . . Tell it in court. The trial must be public, your Honor. I am not insisting that he talk loud enough for everybody to hear, but it ought to be told in the same way that we put the other evidence in."

John Caverly motioned to the attorneys, from each side, to approach the bench. He called the stenographers to join the small group gathered in front of him. William Healy would testify sotto voce, he directed, so that no one outside the small semicircle could hear. These matters were to remain private, Caverly warned; the attorneys and stenographers were not to break the confidence of the court. The public should never learn the words that Healy was about to divulge.

Healy lowered his voice, almost to a whisper. "This compact," he murmured, "as was told to me separately by each of the boys . . . consisted in an agreement between them that Leopold, who has very definite homosexual tendencies . . . was to have the privilege of—," Healy paused, and turned, hesitating, toward Caverly: "Do you want me to be very specific?"

"Absolutely," Crowe interrupted, with whispered urgency, "because this is important."

"—was to have," Healy continued, "the privilege of inserting his penis between Loeb's legs at special rates; at one time it was to be three times in two months, if they continued their criminalistic activities together . . . then they had some of their quarrels, and then it was once for each criminalistic deed."

Caverly glanced toward the back of the courtroom. The crowd sat still, unable to distinguish the words that Healy was speaking to the attorneys, waiting impatiently for the testimony to be resumed in open court.

"I do not suppose," Darrow reminded the judge, indicating some reporters who had crept closer in an attempt to overhear the testimony, "this should be taken in the presence of newspapermen, your Honor."

"Gentlemen," Caverly shouted, "will you go and sit down, you newspapermen! Take your seats. This should not be published."

"What other acts, if any," Crowe asked, "did they tell you about? You say that there are other acts that they did rarely or seldom?"

"Oh, they were just experimenting once or twice with each other," Healy replied diffidently.

"Tell what it was," Darrow prompted.

"They experimented with mouth perversions. . . . Leopold has had for many years a great deal of phantasy life surrounding sex activity. . . . He has phantasies of being with a man, and usually with Loeb himself. . . . He says he gets a thrill out of anticipating it. . . . Loeb would pretend to be drunk, then this fellow would undress him and he would almost rape him and would be furiously passionate. . . . With women he does not get that same thrill and passion."

"That is what he tells you?" Crowe asked doubtfully, glancing over his shoulder at Nathan and Richard sitting next to their guards behind the defense table.

"Surely. . . . That is what he tells me," Healy replied. "Loeb tells me himself . . . how he feigns sometimes to be drunk, in order that he should have his aid in carrying out his criminalistic ideas. That is what Leopold gets out of it, and that is what Loeb gets out of it. . . . When Leopold had this first experience with his penis between Loeb's legs . . . he found it gave him more pleasure than anything else he had ever done. . . . Even in jail here, a look at Loeb's body or his touch upon his shoulder thrills him so, he says, immeasurably."

Healy sat back in his chair, relieved that he had broken the taboo in private, trusting that his revelations would never reach the public eye.

Caverly looked at the attorneys, inviting them to ask the witness further questions, but both Crowe and Darrow indicated that they had heard enough.

"I think," Crowe muttered, "that is all."

Caverly sent the stenographers to their places, on the far side of the courtroom, but held Crowe and Darrow back, indicating that he had some more words to say to them alone. He spoke rapidly and—it seemed to the crowd, watching the three men whisper together at the front of the courtroom—with urgency. He was perhaps seeking their agreement to some proposal, and requesting their acquiescence, and eventually both Crowe and Darrow—tight-lipped and solemn—returned to their seats.[25]

Although Healy remained on the witness stand one more day, there was never anything as controversial in the remainder of his testimony as his revelations about the defendants' sexual relationship. He took up the charts on the documents table to explain the results of the intelligence tests and explained how they revealed Nathan Leopold's exceptional ability ("He answered them all very well and correctly") and Richard Loeb's competence ("I found him to be a fellow of certainly not more than average intelligence"). The tests also demonstrated, according to Healy, the gulf between the boys' emotional capacity and their intellectual ability. Both Nathan and Richard were emotionally infantile.[26]

THE PSYCHIATRISTS HAD REPEATEDLY EMPHASIZED the significance of the disparity between emotion and intellect, Crowe asked on cross-examination; but just how credible was this claim that Nathan and Richard were emotionally infantile, and what did it have to do with the murder? The defendants had demonstrated remarkable foresight and preparation in the commission of the crime, qualities difficult to reconcile with the claim that they were infantile. They had meticulously planned the killing six months in advance, making elaborate plans to kidnap a victim, to obtain a ransom, and to dispose of the body. The assertion that Nathan and Richard were emotionally infantile was spurious, Crowe asserted, and in any case had little or nothing to do with the killing.

"When Leopold began to plan with Loeb this murder," Crowe asked, ". . . what was acting then, his intellect or his emotions?"

"His intellect," Healy replied, "but always accompanied by some emotional life, as it always is . . ."

"Which was in control, the intellect or the emotions, at the time they planned to steal the typewriter, so that they could write letters that could not be traced back to them?"

"I think the intellect was the predominating thing there probably."

"And when they rented the room in the Morrison Hotel, intellect was still walking in front?"

"Yes."

"And so on through all the details of this murder?"

"Yes, sir."

There was nothing, Crowe concluded, about this murder that revealed the actions of two children. It was a preposterous defense—without any merit—designed solely to bamboozle the court.

CROWE'S SKEPTICISM WAS ECHOED OUTSIDE the courtroom. The murder of a child for a thrill by two wealthy, college-educated teenage lovers seemed to signal the moral collapse of Western civilization or, at the very least, the corruption and degeneracy of the modern age. The evangelical preacher Billy Sunday, passing through Chicago on his way to Minnesota, warned that the killing could be "traced to the moral miasma which contaminates some of our 'young intellectuals.' It is now considered fashionable for higher education to scoff at God. The world is headed for Hades so fast no speed limit can stop it. Precocious brains, salacious books, infidel minds—all these helped to produce this murder."[27]

Arthur Kaub, pastor of Winslow Park Evangelical Lutheran Church in Chicago, deplored the sentimentality that denied the murderers' responsibility for their actions. Christian beliefs were fully congruent with the death penalty, he asserted, and the killers of Bobby Franks should not escape their just deserts.

"When notorious criminals," Kaub preached to his congregation, "are found guilty of atrocious crimes deserving the death penalty, a host of sympathetic people intercede for them, urging pardon or a lesser sentence. . . . We must not shirk responsibility. . . . Neither must we condone sin because of sympathy with the parents or the criminal. We must have the law upheld, justice meted out and proper punishment executed upon the evildoer."[28]

Certainly, it was difficult for the majority of Chicagoans to understand why, since the murderers had admitted their guilt, there should be such a protracted and elaborate hearing. The proceedings would cost the state alone almost $100,000, and if the defense appealed the verdict, the expense might exceed $500,000. Why should the taxpayer have to bear such a burden for two murderers who had yet to express any remorse for their actions?[29]

Edward Gore, a former president of the Chicago Association of Commerce, speaking to a meeting of the Central Lions Club on 5 August, criticized the hearing as "an example of the slowness of our judicial procedure" and appealed for a quick resolution—"Why are two confessed murderers permitted to take up the time of our criminal courts?"—in order to demonstrate the resolve of the Chicago courts to end crime. Thomas R. Marshall, a former vice president of the United States who had served in Woodrow Wilson's cabinet for eight years, added his voice to the chorus of criticism, complaining that "high-minded men have been pouring into the ears of the public the idea that in reality there is no such a thing as crime. It is just disease, they have been arguing, and ought to be treated as such."[30]

The less one knew about the case, it seemed, the more likely one was to criticize the hearing as a waste of time and money. Harry McDevitt, a judge on the Common Pleas Court of Philadelphia, knew only what he had read in the Philadelphia newspapers yet he confidently asserted of the defendants that "their alleged 'split mentality' and their much talked-about superior intellect had little to do with the crime. . . . They are the personification of conceit, vanity, and asininity. They manifested no respect for the law of God or man and have a contempt for the conventions of reality. . . . Were the case being tried in Philadelphia, I am confident a jury would return a verdict of murder in the first degree. It wouldn't take long to reach a conclusion."[31]

Such comments indicated that the murder of Bobby Franks seemed sui generis in its depravity. It appeared unique, set apart from crimes of passion and anger, and elevated above other killings by its deliberate character. Yet when viewed as symbolic of the times, it seemed to reveal much about the United States in the 1920s that many white Protestant Americans found deeply troubling. Sometime within the past few years—perhaps immediately after the war—the country had experienced a sudden shift in public morality that had entirely overthrown Victorian conventions. Women now bobbed their hair, smoked cigarettes, drank gin, and wore short skirts; sexuality was everywhere and young people were eagerly taking advantage of their new freedoms; a flood of new consumer goods poured onto the market while advertisers beckoned and cajoled with subversive messages; and the predictable failure of Prohibition had transformed formerly respectable Americans into habitual lawbreakers. The traditional morality, centered on work, discipline, and self-denial, had evaporated and in its place there was a culture of self-indulgence. There were no longer any social restraints; each individual now sought self-fulfillment and self-realization in an unceasing pursuit of pleasure. The United States, prosperous throughout the 1920s, was now a society that valued a species of hedonistic self-absorption.[32]

What single event could better illustrate the dangers of such a transformation than the heinous murder of Bobby Franks? The two killers had cheerfully confessed their motive: the killing had been done solely for the experience, for the sensation, for the thrill of murder. Neither Leopold nor Loeb had yet uttered a single word of remorse; neither had expressed contrition. The worship of youth, the rejection of morality, the obsession with sex and sexuality—all eloquently described in the novels and short stories of Scott Fitzgerald—had found their ultimate expression in this perverted act by Nathan Leopold and Richard Loeb. Fitzgerald, in his books and in his personal life, had discarded traditional morality and had consequently found himself trumpeted as the spokesman of the Jazz Age, but the abolition of restraint had now produced a callous and cynical murder that far surpassed anything in fiction.

. . .

No organization was more hostile to the licentiousness of the 1920s than the Ku Klux Klan. The abrupt revival of the Klan in the early 1920s, after several decades of quiescence, centered less on white supremacy and more on Protestant fundamentalism. The Klan was still violently opposed to blacks, of course, but now other groups in the Klan's worldview also threatened traditional morality: Catholics, Jews, and immigrants.

It was predictable, therefore, that the Klan would add its condemnation to the critical comments of the politicians and clergymen who remarked so freely on the courtroom proceedings. The Klan had experienced remarkable growth in Chicago in the early 1920s. In 1922, for example, it had enrolled more new members in Chicago than in any other comparable urban center in the United States, and the City Council, fearful of the Klan's rapidly growing influence, had voted not to hire known Klan members as municipal employees. The Klan, never reluctant to blame marginal groups as the cause of all social problems, portrayed itself as the guardian of public morals and, in that role, was eager to see two Jewish homosexuals sent to the scaffold for the murder of a child. "I can tell you," an official of the Klan confided to a reporter from the *Chicago Evening Post* on 5 August, "that members of the organization are in the court every day. They are determined to see that justice is done."[33]

Members of the Klan not only attended the court sessions but also sent threatening letters to the judge and occasionally telephoned him in the middle of the night to demand that he hang Leopold and Loeb. The Klan persisted in its campaign of intimidation throughout the hearing, earning the organization welcome publicity in the newspapers. In July the Klan burned a fiery cross, fourteen feet high, on a vacant lot not far from the Loeb family home. On another occasion, toward the conclusion of the hearing, Klan members left a human skull and bones near the Loeb house along with a note that promised a lynching of the two defendants.[34]

The threats of the Klan, along with the comments of the clergymen and politicians, viewed as attempts to influence the judge, were in contempt of court. Public sentiment might demand the death penalty for Leopold and Loeb, but Caverly was resolute, nevertheless, in his determination to give the defendants their constitutional rights. "This sort of thing," he announced, "is wholly out of order, whether it is a bloodthirsty demand, purporting to come from the Ku Klux Klan, or a plea for mercy from a clergyman. In either case, the writer not only displays poor taste but is actually violating the law. . . . The fact of the matter is, I have not yet made up my mind as to what is to be done with these boys. I am still listening to the evidence." Yet Caverly's statement was not enough to quiet the complaints of Clarence Darrow that the comments of influential politicians, businessmen, and religious leaders were harming his clients' opportunity for an unprejudiced hearing and might influence the judge to truncate the proceedings prematurely and hand down the death penalty. "If the boys hang," Darrow fumed, "the United States might well vote murder indictments against the unjudicial agencies, many of them far removed from Chief Justice John R. Caverly's courtroom, who are trying to 'fix' public opinion." There was only one reason, Darrow explained, for the intense public interest in the case; it was the wealth of the defendants' families that caused the mob to shout for the death penalty. If the defendants had been poor, unknown, of humble origin, no one would have paid the slightest attention to the case.[35]

THERE WAS NOT A GREAT deal in Bernard Glueck's testimony, either on his first day in the witness box—Tuesday, 5 August—or on the next, that had not already been said by the two other psychiatrists. Glueck, also, remarked that he had found Richard's emotional detachment unusual. Indeed Richard Loeb lacked any emotional or affective response to the killing.

"I then took up with Loeb the Franks crime," Glueck responded, in answer to a question from Benjamin Bachrach, "and asked him to tell me about it. He recited to me in a most matter of fact way all the grue-some details of the planning and execution of this crime, of the disfigur-ing and the disposal of the body, how he and Leopold stopped with the body in the car to get something to eat on the way. He spoke to me in a most matter of fact way about his doings and movements immediately following this act. As his recital proceeded, I was amazed at the abso-lute absence of any signs of normal feeling, such as one would expect under the circumstances. He showed no remorse, no regret, no com-passion for the people involved in this situation, and as he kept on talking . . . there became evident the absolute lack of normal human emotional response that would fit these situations, and the whole thing became incomprehensible to me except on the basis of a disordered personality. . . . In the course of my conversation with him he told me how his little brother . . . passed in review before him as a possible vic-tim of the kidnapping and killing. Even in connection with this state-ment, he showed the same lack of adequate emotional response to the

situation."

"In the conversation with Ri-chard Loeb," Bachrach asked, "did he say anything about who it was that struck the blow on the head of Robert Franks with the chisel?"

"He told me all the details of the crime, including the fact that he struck the blow. . . ."

"If you have reached any con-clusion with reference to his mental condition, you may now state it."

"My impression is very definite that this boy is suffering from a disordered personality, that the

30. CLARENCE DARROW.

nature of this disorder is primarily in a profound pathological discord between his intellectual and emotional life."[36]

"Now then, doctor, are you ready to begin with your examination of the defendant Nathan F. Leopold, Jr.?"

"Yes."

"You may proceed. . . ."[37]

"I started out with him by asking him to tell me about the Franks murder. . . . He argued with me that for many years he has cultivated and adhered to a purely hedonistic philosophy that all action is justified if it gives pleasure; that it was his ambition and has been for many years to become a perfect Nietzschean and to follow Nietzsche's philosophy all the way through. . . . He told me of his attitude toward Loeb and of how completely he had put himself in the role of slave in connection with him. He said, 'I can illustrate it to you by saying that I felt myself less than the dust beneath his feet.' . . . He told me of his abject devotion to Loeb, saying that he was jealous of the food and drink that Loeb took, because he could not come as close to him as did the food and drink. . . . Nathan F. Leopold, in my estimation, is a definitely paranoid personality, perhaps developing a definite paranoid psychosis. I have not seen a definite psychosis of this sort in as young a person as he is. His aberration is characterized primarily by this abnormal pathological transformation of his personality and by the delusional way of thinking."[38]

Throughout the hearing, Robert Crowe had repeatedly asked how two boys, supposedly suffering from mental illness, could have planned and prepared a murder so meticulously; their attention to detail, their intelligence and perspicacity, could not, Crowe had asserted, be reconciled with mental disease.

Benjamin Bachrach now prompted Glueck to respond to Crowe's assertion. Could such qualities associated with the preparation and planning of a crime coexist with mental illness?

"Doctor," Bachrach asked, "from your experience in dealing with persons of disordered mind, state whether or not it is common and ordinary to find in such persons a high degree of intelligence existing at the same time as the abnormality or diseased condition?"

"If I should give an answer to this question in a general way," Glueck replied, "I should say that it is quite characteristic of paranoid individuals to have along with their disordered mental state a highly developed intelligence. . . ."

"Have you observed among other such persons under your care the ability to plan like ordinary intelligent people without abnormality?"

"I have observed the most ingenious and great capacity to plan among paranoid patients. . . . Patients suffering from mental disorder—and 90 percent of my patients in private practice do suffer from mental disorder—carry on their activities while they are under treatment for their mental disorder."

Benjamin Bachrach indicated that he had completed his questioning. "You may take the witness," he told Robert Crowe.

THE CROSS-EXAMINATION WAS BRIEF. Crowe, once again, poured scorn on the notion that Nathan and Richard were emotionally stunted and, once again, demanded to know what, in any case, that might have to do with the murder. But the state's attorney seemed temporarily to have run out of steam; he spared Glueck the inquisition that he had meted out to William White and William Healy, and by half past two, just two hours after he had begun, he had ended his cross-examination of the witness.[39]

Glueck lingered in Chicago, before taking the train back to New York City, just long enough to sit for an interview with Maurine Watkins, a reporter for the *Chicago Daily Tribune*. Watkins had asked Glueck, as an expert on juvenile delinquency, to give advice to the parents of Chicago's children, and Glueck was only too happy for the opportunity to impart progressive, modern ideas on bringing up children. His philosophy was one of tolerance and understanding; parents should encourage their children to talk out problems and concerns; they should eschew discipline, especially over trivial matters; and they should talk frankly on sexual matters. "This tragedy," Glueck said, referring to the murder of Bobby Franks, "may do great good: if it makes parents know that contact with their children must be psychological as well as physical, and that children can't be kept to their own devices."[40]

Glueck's statement was intended as the antidote to those critics who claimed that the murder defied explanation. Glueck identified himself with the child guidance movement, a coalition of experts on the proper upbringing of children that explained deviant behavior as a consequence of dysfunctional relationships between parent and child. Child psychiatrists asserted that all behavior was a product of its environment and that delinquent behavior in the child could best be avoided, therefore, by providing affection, love, education, recreation, and wholesome advice. There was, according to the child guidance experts, no divide separating normal and abnormal behavior—everything could be explained in terms of familial relationships.[41]

That analysis seemed plausible, perhaps even unexceptional, except that it demonstrably failed to account for the murderous behavior of Nathan Leopold and Richard Loeb. There seemed to have been nothing dysfunctional about either the Loeb family or the Leopold family. On the contrary, both sets of parents had provided their sons with a familial environment that, in appearance at least, had lacked for nothing. Glueck's philosophy of child guidance might account for deviancy in some cases, perhaps—but its precepts could not be applied to Richard Loeb and Nathan Leopold. The question still remained: why had two highly educated, wealthy, intelligent young men sought out a random victim for murder?

ON FRIDAY, 8 AUGUST, Walter Bachrach called Harold Hulbert to the witness stand. Hulbert seemed impossibly young—he looked more like a graduate student than a learned expert—and the air of innocence that he conveyed reinforced the general impression that he had somehow blundered his way into the witness box by error. He carried a thick loose-leaf binder of typewritten notes under his right arm; as he settled himself into the chair, Hulbert opened it gingerly—taking care not to allow some loose sheets of paper to fall to the floor—and placed the binder on his lap.[42]

Harold Hulbert was an important witness. His evidence, Darrow believed, would be unimpeachable. Hulbert's testimony—a summation of the endocrinological examinations—rested on the hard objectivity of rational science and relied for its persuasive power on quantification and measurement. White, Healy, and Bernard Glueck had presented the psychoanalysis of Leopold and Loeb, but such evidence, by its nature, was open to question and liable to dispute. Hulbert would present the endocrinological evidence, evidence obtained through physical examination and expressed mathematically—how could Robert Crowe dispute such objective testimony?

In preparation for his appearance on the witness stand, the defense attorneys had spent considerable time coaching Hulbert. Crowe would attempt to discredit the endocrinological results by questioning the reliability of the evidence. The defense attorneys had no way to know just how or where Crowe would attack; yet, for all that, they were confident that Hulbert would be a capable witness.

Walter Bachrach began by asking Hulbert to list the physical tests that the scientists had employed in their examination of Richard and Nathan. What were the specific results? Bachrach asked Hulbert to begin with Richard Loeb.

"As I understand you, you say you took his blood pressure?"

"Yes."

"Tell us the result of that test."

"Systolic, 100; diastolic, 65. Blood pressure, 35. Pulse rate, 88 to 92. . . ."

"Did the result of that test in any way indicate a deviation from the normal, as far as blood pressure is concerned?"

"It is below normal," Hulbert replied.[43]

"You said you took a basal metabolism test. State what that is and its purpose."

"The basal metabolism test is a chemical test to determine the rate at which the body tissues oxidize the food which the body has ingested, and gives us an indication of the vital forces of the body. The test is done in a technical way by having the patient appear without any break-fast and lie quietly for an hour in loose clothing, breathing into an apparatus which has been clamped to the mouth, the nose having been shut tight, to measure the carbon dioxide of the breath."

It was a routine test, Hulbert explained, commonly used to search for glandular disease; it served as a reliable method to pinpoint endocrinological disorders. "This has all been carefully tabulated in thousands of cases. . . . We are able to contrast the results obtained in any one patient with what would be normal for that patient considering his age, weight, etc. The metabolism test, in the case of Richard Loeb on June 14th, taken under ideal circumstances, was minus seventeen percent, which is abnormally low."

"What," Bachrach prompted, "does such an abnormally low basal metabolism result signify . . . ?"

"A disorder of the endocrine glands and the sympathic nervous system," Hulbert replied. "It is one phase of medical evidence to indicate that there is such a disease of the endocrines and sympathetic nervous system."[44]

Hulbert continued to read off the results of his tests on Richard Loeb, occasionally consulting the loose-leaf binder spread across his knees. The Wassermann test for syphilis had been negative; the sugar tolerance test had been slightly high; the blood physics test had shown Loeb to be slightly anemic; the blood chemistry test had revealed a slight excess of nonprotein nitrogen in the blood; and the urine examination had been normal—the urine showed "clear transparency and amber color," Hulbert replied, "no albumin, no sugar, no indican . . . but there was mucus present, and a few epithelial cells. . . ."

"That," Crowe interrupted sarcastically, grinning at his quip, "throws considerable light on this murder, does it not? . . ."

"I object," Bachrach shouted angrily, "to counsel interrupting!"[45]

Bachrach turned back to the witness.

"Did you make an X-ray examination of Richard Loeb?"

"We did," Hulbert replied, indicating several X-ray photographs, along with charts and diagrams, lying on the documents table in front of the bench. Hulbert explained that the scientists had taken X-ray photographs of the skull, face, wrists, and thorax. There was no pathology, he concluded; the X-rays revealed extensive dental work, but in all other respects Richard Loeb was normal.[46]

THE SCIENTISTS HAD EXAMINED NATHAN Leopold also, Hulbert continued. Measurement of Nathan's metabolism had produced a result of minus five percent, well within the normal range; the Wassermann test for syphilis had been negative; and the blood physics test had shown that Nathan was only slightly anemic. His blood pressure reading had been low; the sugar tolerance test had revealed that Nathan did not metabolize sugar properly; and a chemical analysis of his blood had revealed premonitory signs of kidney disease.[47]

Hulbert continued to read from his notes. He had a flat, emotionless voice and his matter-of-fact recitation of the tests scarcely hinted at their significance. Crowe no longer bothered to interrupt the witness with objections or sarcasm, and even the reporters seemed to have lost interest. One by one, the stenotypes stopped clicking. The reporters merely listened, without bothering to record the testimony for their readers, until eventually only a solitary Caligraph machine, recognizable by its enormous keyboard, remained in operation, quietly clacking away as an accompaniment to Hulbert's voice.[48]

Walter Bachrach pointed to the X-ray photographs lying on the documents table. Had the X-rays revealed anything unusual, he asked, with respect to Nathan Leopold?

The clerk of the court, Ferdinand Scherer, stepped across to the documents table to hand the X-rays to the witness. Hulbert had stopped speaking; he was now looking through the photographs, holding each to the light in order to make his choice.

"The X-ray of the skull," he began, "revealed the most pathology. The tables of the skull, the bony tables of the skull, are of normal thickness, but the union between the various bones of the skull has become firm and ossified at the age of 19."

"What in normal life," Bachrach asked, "is the time at which such ossification takes place?"

"It varies, but usually at full maturity or when a man is in his prime."

"In terms of years when does that usually take place?"

"I would say from thirty to thirty-five."[49]

As John Caverly leaned across to look at the photograph, Hulbert rose slightly from his chair, holding the X-ray in his right hand, and pointed to a slight shadow at the base of the skull. The photograph showed that the pineal gland had calcified prematurely, he explained, as Caverly looked on; in a normal individual, the pineal gland did not calcify until thirty years of age.[50]

"The pineal gland," Hulbert explained, "in this x-ray throws a definite shadow, typical of a calcified pineal gland."

"What is the pineal gland?" Bachrach asked. "What is the function of the pineal gland so far as it is known to science?"

The pineal gland had two functions, Hulbert replied. It acted as a brake on sexual desire, serving to inhibit the libido, and it stimulated mental development.[51]

Nathan displayed other indications of glandular pathology. His thick, dry skin and his coarse hair; the early appearance of his primary and secondary sexual characteristics; his low blood pressure, low body temperature, and slight anemia—these were signs that Nathan had previously suffered from an abnormal thyroid gland.[52]

Nathan's medical history during childhood and early adolescence— his lack of resistance to disease, including such skin infections as urticaria—indicated a disorder of the adrenal medulla.[53]

X-rays of Nathan's skull had shown that the *sella turcica*, the bony cradle at the base of the skull enclosing the pituitary gland, was smaller than one might have expected, and its small size would have the effect of congesting and crowding the pituitary gland. Other indications of hyperpituitarism, according to Hulbert, included Nathan's sexual development and activity, his inability to metabolize sugar at a normal rate, and his coarse, heavy hair.[54]

Finally, Hulbert concluded, Nathan's sex glands were undoubtedly diseased. Nathan possessed an abnormally high sex drive and both his primary and his secondary sexual characteristics had appeared prematurely.[55]

Nathan, sitting immediately behind Clarence Darrow, whispered an occasional remark to the attorney, while listening to the witness. Hulbert paused in his testimony and Nathan turned slightly in his seat to see Richard Loeb, sitting to his left, grinning mischievously. As Nathan turned toward him, Richard murmured in his ear that it looked as if he, Nathan, were in a bad way—and both boys laughed quietly at the joke.[56]

Walter Bachrach sought to lead his witness to the conclusion toward which he had been heading. That Nathan suffered from glandular disease, there was no doubt; but how was this relevant to the murder of Bobby Franks?

"What relation," Bachrach asked, "is there between the abnormal functioning of his endocrine glands and his mental condition?"

"The effect of the endocrine glands on the mental condition is definitely established in the minds of medical men in certain points and is still a matter of dispute in others. . . . I would say that his endocrine disorder is responsible for the following mental findings. His precocious mental development, his rapid advance through school, his ease of learning, are of endocrine origins. . . . The early development and strength of his sex urge is obviously of endocrine origin. His shallow mood and his good bearing are of endocrine origin and particularly his mental activity and early mental development are of endocrine origin. . . ."

"What would be the effect of that upon him, where there was not a corresponding maturity of his emotional life and judgment?"

"The effect of the intellectual drive of endocrine origin . . . and [his] emotional shallowness is that he now has mentally a decided degree of discrepancy, a diseased discrepancy, between his judgment and emotions on the one hand and his intellect on the other hand. . . ."[57]

"What, if any, effect," Bachrach asked, "did the diseased mental condition of Leopold on May 21st, 1924, have in connection with the Franks kidnaping and homicide?"

"A very great deal. . . . His mental condition or disease at that time would not primarily have caused him alone to have carried out any such kidnaping or homicide. It caused him to ignore the ordinary re-

31. A JOKE IN COURT. Testimony on the witness stand gives the defendants cause to smile. From left: Nathan Leopold, Richard Loeb, and Nathan Leopold Sr.

straint which individuals impose upon themselves because of their consciousness of their duties they owe to society; it caused him to react in the non-emotional way he did at that time and subsequently; caused him to justify his own actions to himself, so that he is uncritical of them; and his mental condition at that time is one of the predominating factors in this homicide and kidnaping."

"Would Leopold on May 21st, 1924, have been able to commit the Franks kidnaping and homicide but for the presence of such mental disease?"

"He could not have done it."

"State whether the diseased mental condition of Richard Loeb on May 21st, 1924, entered into the Franks homicide and kidnaping?"

"It did."

"Will you tell us how?"

"The mental condition of Richard Loeb on that date was a direct factor. . . . He was impelled by motives which had been nourished in his subconscious mind, his judgment was childish and uncritical and did not restrain him. . . . His emotions are definitely immature and childish, and he had only an academic realization of what he owed to society, his feeling on the matter being too slight to bind him or modify his conduct and his mentally diseased condition at that time based on his experiences and based on his constitution was a definite factor in this kidnaping and homicide."

"Could Richard Loeb but for the existence of the mental disease existing in him on the 21st of May, 1924, and which you have described in your testimony, had committed the Franks kidnaping and homicide?"

"He could not."[58]

JUST AS, ONE WEEK EARLIER, it would have been foolish for Robert Crowe to have challenged William White on his knowledge of psycho-analysis, so it would now be reckless for the state's attorney to confront Harold Hulbert on his knowledge of endocrinology. Crowe had no scientific training or expertise, and he knew nothing about endocrinology. Perhaps an abnormally low metabolism did indicate glandular disorder; perhaps a calcified pineal gland was a sign of mental illness; perhaps a diminutive *sella turcica* was a cause of hyperpituitarism—who, apart from the experts, could say? No, Crowe decided, there was nothing to be gained from disputing endocrinological theory with the witness.

Clarence Darrow, at least, could not see how the state could easily overthrow Hulbert's testimony. It relied on scientific evidence—tangible evidence in the case of the X-rays—that could not be disputed. The scientists had found that Richard had an abnormally low metabolism; that finding was consistent with mental disorder. And the X-rays of Nathan Leopold's pineal gland showed that it had prematurely calcified; that also was a sign of mental disease. The defense had proved its point: neither Richard nor Nathan was insane, but both clearly suffered from mental illness. Surely the evidence of their mental illness would be sufficient to save them from the gallows?

Darrow had supposed that the endocrinological data were impervious to attack; but Crowe soon forced him to reconsider. Crowe went straight to the heart of the matter—he questioned both the metabolic reading for Richard and the X-rays of Nathan's skull.

The science, Crowe asserted, was not at all as objective as the defense liked to pretend. The scientific results were not identical with reality but stood as a representation of it, a representation mediated through the scientific apparatus. The scientists had obtained a reading for the metabolism of Richard Loeb—minus seventeen percent—that, they claimed, indicated mental disease; but this reading was accurate only insofar as the apparatus was reliable. And, Crowe might have added, the reading, of course, possessed only the meaning conferred on it by the scientists; Crowe could also challenge that assigned meaning.

Crowe began his cross-examination—on Monday, 11 August—with a question about the tests for metabolism,

"Who made the basal metabolism test?"

"Dr. Moore, Dr. Bowman and myself," Hulbert replied. "On Leopold we repeated the test three times, and took the average of the three, and on Loeb we took the test twice, and took the average of the two. Those tests were continued one right after the other."

"Don't you know," Crowe asserted, "you have no machine in Chicago that can accurately make this test?"

"I was quite satisfied with the machine we used."

"What kind was it?"

"A Jones," Hulbert answered.[59]

Hulbert had too much confidence in his knowledge of the test to allow Crowe's assertion to rattle him. And, in any case, Crowe was wrong. In 1924 there were several types of apparatus for measuring metabolism, and most of them were in use in hospitals and laboratories in Chicago. Hulbert had used the Jones metabolimeter, a machine designed by Horry Jones, a medical professor at the University of Illinois, and he knew it as a reliable and trustworthy apparatus that would give accurate results.[60]

"Is it not a fact," Crowe demanded, "that there is no machine that can accurately take this test, but they take a great many and average them in order to arrive at some conclusion?"

"I don't know whether there is a perfect machine or not. Now, this machine was good enough."

"If it was not perfect, then the result would not be perfect?"

"It might or might not. . . ."

"If it is not a good reliable test, it is not of any use, is it?"

"I would not use an unreliable test," Hulbert replied, confidently.[61]

Crowe had chosen the wrong angle of attack. He was no expert on the measurement of metabolism, and whatever gleanings on the subject he had picked up in the previous month were no match for Hulbert's expertise. Perhaps he would have better luck asking Hulbert about the X-ray examinations.

"Describe the X-ray apparatus," Crowe asked, "and the techniques by which these x-ray pictures were taken. . . ."

"The apparatus we used was a portable machine furnished by the Victor X-ray people, one of the largest X-ray manufacturers in America, brought to the jail by Dr. Blaine, of the National Pathologic Laboratory, former radiologist at Cook County Hospital for a number of years, and by Dr. Darnell, research pathologist of the Victor Company. . . . Triplicate films were taken in all cases. The parts of the body pictures were studied by me through the fluoroscope for the purpose of identification, and the films were identified with my Veterans of Foreign Wars insignia, which I wear, so that there would be no doubt as to their identity. The pictures were carried to the laboratory by the technicians in the same taxi with me; they were never out of my sight. I went into the dark room at the time they were developed, and stayed there talking with Dr. Blaine while they were being developed."[62]

There was enough detail in this account, surely, to satisfy even the most skeptical inquisitor! But Crowe was relentless. Hulbert had relied on others to take the X-rays, so how much did he know of the process? His training and education had fitted him to be a psychiatrist—who was he to testify on the reliability of the X-rays?

"Do you know," Crowe asked, "the name of the machine you used?"

"A Victor portable."

"What kind of a current, direct or alternating?"

"I don't know."

"What kind of a tube?"

"All I know is, it was a new tube suitable for the portable machine, a Victor tube."

"What transformer was used?"

"I don't know."

"Where was the transformer located on the machine? . . ."

"I don't know."[63]

Previously, under direct examination, Hulbert had made much of his observation, through a fluoroscope, of the bones of the skull as the technicians had taken the X-ray photographs. But once again, Crowe attacked Hulbert's testimony as flawed. How much had he seen through the fluoroscope, and what was the value of his observations?

"Is it possible to see a calcified pineal gland through a fluoroscope?"

"It may be."

"Did you see it?"

"I did not."

"Did you ever see one through a fluoroscope?"

"I don't think so. . . ."

"Can you see the sella turcica through the fluoroscope?"

"Yes, sir."

"Did you?"

"I did."

"Did you use cassettes in taking these films?"

"I beg pardon?"

"Did you use cassettes in taking these films?"

"I don't know what you mean."

"If you don't know what I mean, then you would not know who furnished them, would you?"

"If I don't know what you mean, I don't know what you are talking about."

"What screens were used, do you know?"

"I don't know, sir."

"Was the Bucky diaphragm used?"

"I am not a radiologist."[64]

It was a devastating attack. In vain, Hulbert protested that Crowe's questions were irrelevant. He might not know the physical characteristics of the X-ray machine, admittedly, but that, Hulbert retorted, did not invalidate his claim that the X-rays showed indications of glandular disorder.

Crowe, by exposing Hulbert's ignorance of technical detail, had called the witness's authority into question. If he did not know whether a Bucky diaphragm had been used, then what value were his explanations of the X-rays?

Crowe kept Hulbert on the witness stand the entire day and into the next, not allowing him to leave until midday on Tuesday, 12 August.

HE HAD REASON TO BE pleased with his performance. None of the defense experts had emerged unscathed from his cross-examination, and on various occasions, Crowe had compelled the witnesses either to admit ignorance or to contradict themselves. The scientific evidence had been Darrow's strongest suit and now it lay in a state of disrepair. Soon Crowe would put his own expert witnesses on the stand, but his witnesses needed only to claim that Nathan and Richard were normal. Crowe had ridiculed his opponent's evidence; would Darrow be able to do the same?

14 | PSYCHIATRISTS FOR THE STATE

TUESDAY, 12 AUGUST 1924–TUESDAY, 19 AUGUST 1924

There was no evidence of any mental disease.[1]

*Hugh Patrick, emeritus professor of
nervous and mental diseases, Northwestern University,
12 August 1924*

There was no mental disease of any character.[2]

*Archibald Church, president of the Chicago
Medical Society, 13 August 1924*

There is nothing . . . that would indicate mental disease.[3]

*Harold Singer, professor of psychiatry,
University of Illinois, 15 August 1924*

They are not suffering from any mental disease.[4]

William Krohn, psychologist, author of
Insanity and Law, *18 August 1924*

NATHAN LEOPOLD HAD COMMITTED SUICIDE!
No one could say for sure how or where the rumor had begun, but by mid-afternoon on Sunday, 17 August, it had taken hold of the city. Huge crowds began to gather outside the Cook County jail, thronging the sidewalks, spilling into the street, and peering expectantly at the cell windows on the sixth floor of the grimy, gray building on Dearborn Street. The strain had finally taken its toll on Nathan, the rumor went, and now that the hearing was in its final stage and he was facing either life in prison or the scaffold, he had hanged himself in his cell.[5]

Nathan, oblivious of the commotion in the streets outside, spent that afternoon playing the piano in the jail's recreation room. As a child, he had attended symphony concerts with his mother and had learned the piano with her encouragement. He knew the notes and could read the music but he was not a musician, he insisted to the visiting journalists. "I get intellectual pleasure out of playing," he remarked, "and particularly in my sense of mastery over the instrument. . . . The thing that determines my taste is chiefly the interest which the composer arouses in me from a scientific or mathematical view. I am interested in the problem which the composer sets for himself." He was fond of the works of Bach and Beethoven, less interested in the compositions of Richard Strauss and Claude Debussy, and almost entirely ignorant of such contemporary composers as Igor Stravinsky and Darius Milhaud. Who was his favorite composer? the reporters inquired. Nikolay Rimsky-Korsakov, Nathan replied—his favorite composition was Rimsky-Korsakov's symphonic suite *Scheherazade*. "I like him for his precision and finish," Nathan explained, "rather than for his emotional qualities."[6]

Wesley Westbrook, the warden of the county jail, issued denials of Nathan's suicide, but to no effect. The rumor seemed appropriate, after all; the crowd outside might well imagine Nathan sitting alone in a gloomy prison cell, depressed and melancholy, brooding despondently over his fate and deciding to end his life. Westbrook, anxious to protect his career against the effects of a prison suicide, no matter how improbable, announced that he was doubling the guard on the sixth and seventh floors that evening. A guard would check both Nathan Leopold and Richard Loeb every ten minutes and report their condition to the warden's office.[7]

Eventually the crowd dispersed, filtering through the streets in the twilight, cheated by Nathan's selfish refusal to provide the spectators with the sensational news of his suicide. But the court hearing would end soon, perhaps within the week, and the adventure that had held Chicago in its grip for three months would end dramatically enough.

THAT SUNDAY, THE CITY'S MINISTERS and other religious leaders, sensing that soon they would no longer have the courtroom revelations as a moral text, thundered from the pulpit on the perils of spiritual delinquency and religious indifference. James Durand, the rector of Wesley Methodist Episcopal Church, in a reference to the atheistic beliefs of Nathan and Richard, warned his congregation that religious skepticism led eventually to self-doubt, confusion, and bewilderment. "The life without God is the limited life," Durand cautioned. "The individual who places self on the throne of life is certainly not in harmony with God's plan for him. He has no clue to the mysteries of life. He sees confusion and darkness; history seems to be little more than a fairy tale and life's battles, convulsions, and revolutions are apparently without aim."

Monsignor William O'Brien, of St. John's Roman Catholic Church, tied religious belief to patriotism, parental discipline, and moral choice in a text that had

32. SUICIDE WATCH. A guard stands watch outside the cell of Nathan Leopold in the Cook County jail. Leopold occupied cell 604 on the sixth floor, facing onto Clark Street. Richard Loeb occupied cell 717 on the seventh floor, facing east onto Dearborn Street.

been repeated endlessly, in one form or another, in press and pulpit over the previous three months. The murder of Bobby Franks, O'Brien suggested, was a consequence of irreligion, parental failures, and malign influences: if Nathan and Richard had received correct guidance, they would never have sought thrills in the abduction and killing of a small boy. "Faith in God and charity in our fellowman must be inculcated in the youth of our land if we are to adhere to the principles that made our country great. . . . If the laws of our land are being disregarded today by our American youth, the only explanation of it lies in the lack of the exercise of parental authority in the days of childhood. It is indeed to be regretted that the age of the slipper and the hair brush has passed by."[8]

THE FOLLOWING DAY, MONDAY, 18 August, William Krohn took the stand as an expert witness for the prosecution. Krohn had testified as an expert witness in many criminal cases, most memorably in the trial of Gene Geary for the murder of Harry Reckas in 1920. His extensive experience as an expert witness was evident to the spectators in the courtroom. Krohn looked relaxed, even nonchalant, as he sat on the witness stand, waiting for the assistant state's attorney, Joseph Sbarbaro, to begin his questioning. Ten weeks earlier, on Sunday, 1 June, Robert Crowe had called Krohn to the state's attorney's office to interrogate Nathan and Richard. Krohn remembered how willingly both boys had talked about the murder and how they had agreed in every particular—except that each boy had accused the other of striking the blows that had ended Bobby's life. Krohn remembered how assuredly each had accepted responsibility for the crime and had acknowledged his ability to distinguish right from wrong. Neither had shown any symptoms of neurological disease—there had been no signs of mental illness that afternoon.[9]

Joseph Sbarbaro began by asking Krohn if he had diagnosed any signs of mental disorder in the two boys. What about Richard Loeb, for example—had he shown any symptoms of mental disease?

"In my opinion," Krohn replied, "as a result of that examination, he was not suffering from any mental disease, either functional or structural, on May 21st, 1924, or on the date I examined him."

"Will you give your reasons?"

All of Richard Loeb's faculties, Krohn answered, seemed to be in order. His senses—hearing and eyesight—were unimpaired. His memory was excellent: Loeb had been able to recall every detail of the killing including the origin of the scheme six months before the time of the murder. Loeb's judgment was balanced and appropriate; there were no instances when Loeb displayed poor judgment.

"Furthermore," Krohn continued, "the stream of thought flowed without any interruption or any break from within. There was not a single remark made that was beside the point. The answer to every question was responsive. There was no irresponsive answer to any question. There was abundant evidence that the man . . . was perfectly oriented as to time, as to place, and as to his social relations." Loeb's ability to reason was also entirely normal; he was able to group together instances and to argue inductively to a logical conclusion. "Not only that, there was excellence of attention. . . . There was not a single evidence of any defect, any disorder, any lack of development, or any disease, and by disease I mean functional as well as structural."

The other boy, Nathan Leopold, also appeared to be perfectly healthy. There were no signs of neurological disease. An impairment of the nervous system might manifest itself as a jerking of the limbs, as an awkward unsteady gait, or as tremors of the body, but neither Nathan nor Richard had displayed such symptoms.

"There was no defect of vision, no defect of hearing, no evidence of any defect of any of the sense paths or sense activities. There was no defect of the nerves leading from the brain as evidenced by gait or station or tremors."

The Argyll-Robertson pupil, Krohn explained, was a sure sign of neurological dysfunction. The pupil of the eye was capable of focusing on objects placed at either a short or a long distance, but in patients afflicted with neurological disease, the pupil failed to react to light. In this condition, the Argyll-Robertson pupil indicated a lesion of the dorsal nerve fibers that subserved the pupil's response to light; the ventral nerve fibers, by contrast, remained unaffected and functioned normally. Neither Nathan Leopold nor Richard Loeb displayed the characteristic symptoms associated with the Argyll-Robertson pupil; in this respect, also, they were normal.

"There was no evidence of any organic disease of the brain," Krohn testified, expanding on his analysis of Nathan's mental health, "as would have been revealed by the Argyll-Robertson pupil. . . . There was no evidence of any toxic mental condition resulting from any toxicity of the body, because the pulse and the tremors that would have been incidental thereto were absent at this examination."

Nathan Leopold had a remarkable memory; he too had been able to recall innumerable details of the murder. His reasoning was intact, and Nathan had been able to argue logically and coherently during the examination in the state's attorney's office. And finally, Krohn concluded, "he showed remarkably close attention, detailed attention; he showed that he was perfectly oriented socially as well as with reference to time and space."[10]

There was nothing about the behavior or appearance of Leopold and Loeb in the courtroom, Krohn added, to indicate mental disease. There were "none of the modifications of movement that come with certain mental disorders." Neither defendant displayed those "slowly resisting movements . . . that come in certain conditions that are known as mental disorders; . . . the gait and the station showed form and ease; . . . in the attitude, sitting, there was no staring, no gazing fixedly, none of the positions that are characteristic of certain mental diseases."[11]

OTHER WITNESSES AGREED WITH KROHN'S conclusion that both Richard and Nathan were free of mental disease. Hugh Patrick, emeritus professor of nervous and mental diseases at Northwestern University, testified that he too had found no signs of psychiatric illness in the defendants. Patrick also had extensive experience on the witness stand as a psychiatric expert and he had cultivated a relaxed, easygoing manner that commanded respect and admiration. On his first day as a witness for the prosecution he wore a light blue homespun suit and a high starched white collar; his unruffled amiable presence, the twinkle in his eyes, and his inoffensive manner made even the arcane scientific minutiae that he presented somehow seem more palatable.[12]

Patrick stated, in response to Joseph Sbarbaro's inquiries, that there was nothing significant in the testimony presented by the defense witnesses. The Bowman-Hulbert report, Patrick asserted, was full of inconsistencies and contradictions. Evidence supporting the defense claims was either faulty or nonexistent. Consider, for example, the defense statement that the small size of the *sella turcica* at the base of Nathan's skull had affected his pituitary gland and was, therefore, an indication of mental illness. It sounded plausible, perhaps, but Patrick had read the X-ray report submitted separately—and there had been no mention in that report of a diminutive *sella turcica*! And in any case, would the size of the *sella turcica* necessarily have a relationship to mental health? Not at all, Patrick asserted; "a small sella turcica ... does not mean there is any abnormality necessarily in the pituitary at all."[13]

The Bowman-Hulbert report, Patrick claimed, was full of statements that, on closer examination, were so vague as to be meaningless. Nathan, it was claimed, responded to pain by sweating, weakness, and fainting; but to what degree of pain had he been subjected? A sufficiently high degree of pain might cause anyone to faint—by itself, the statement proved nothing; and, in any case, Nathan's alleged reaction was not evidence of mental disease.[14]

Nor was there was anything exceptional, Patrick claimed, in the fantasies of Nathan and Richard, and certainly there was nothing that would have compelled them to murder. The defense had represented personality quirks as psychoneuroses. Nathan's imagination was slightly outré, perhaps, but fantasies of power and domination were not uncommon or extraordinary—everyone fantasized to an extent. And Richard's desire to be a master criminal? It showed merely that he possessed a criminal mind and that he was ambitious. There was no evidence for the defense claim that Nathan was on the verge of dementia praecox or that Richard suffered from a split between his intellect and his emotions. Patrick had carefully read the Bowman-Hulbert report and had found no symptoms of pathological behavior in either boy.[15]

Only the crime itself might be evidence of mental illness, and even that was not certain. There was no basis for asserting that the defendants were mentally diseased "unless," Patrick concluded, "we assume that every man who commits a deliberate, cold-blooded, planned murder, must, by that fact, be mentally diseased. There was no evidence of any mental disease . . . in any of the statements the boys made regarding it. . . . There was nothing in the examination; there were no mental obliquities or peculiarities shown, except their lack of appreciation of the enormity of the deed which they had committed."[16]

ARCHIBALD CHURCH, CHAIR OF THE department of nervous and mental diseases at Northwestern, agreed with his colleagues' diagnosis. Church—tall, broad-shouldered, and meticulously dressed, with a military bearing—was an authoritative presence on the witness stand. He, too, remembered both Nathan and Richard as free from mental disease when he had interviewed them in the state's attorney's office on 1 June.

"Have you an opinion, doctor," Sbarbaro asked, "from your observation and examination, as to whether the defendant, Richard Loeb, was suffering from any mental disease on that day, at that time? . . ."

"The young man," Church replied, "was entirely oriented. He knew who he was and where he was, and the time of day and everything about it. His memory was extraordinarily good; his logical powers as manifested during the interview were normal, and I saw no evidence of any mental disease."

"Now, doctor, have you an opinion from your observation and examination of Nathan Leopold, Jr., as to whether he was suffering from any mental disease at that same time?"

"I have."

"What is that opinion?"

"There was no evidence of any mental disease."

"Will you state your reasons again, please?"

"Because he was perfectly oriented, of good memory, of extreme intellectual reasoning capacity, and apparently of good judgment within the range of the subject matter."[17]

Nor, Church continued, did the scientific findings presented by the defense have any significance. Clarence Darrow had claimed that the fantasy life of each boy had contributed to creating a symbiosis between Leopold and Loeb, but the defense experts had failed to demonstrate how the fantasies—either separately or conjoined—had compelled the killing of Bobby Franks. The supposition that each defendant fantasized was interesting, perhaps, but trivial in its relationship to the murder. The psychoanalytic evidence was not sufficient ground for any mitigation of punishment.

"Phantasies," Church stated, "are day dreams. Everybody has them. Everybody knows they are dreams. They have an interest in relation to character and conduct, but they do not compel conduct nor excuse it."[18]

The witnesses for the state were unanimous in their verdict: the defendants displayed no signs of mental illness.

IT WAS REGRETTABLE, OF COURSE, that each set of psychiatrists—one for the state, the other for the defense—had contradicted the other. Few observers noticed that each side spoke for a different branch of psychiatry and was, therefore, separately justified in reaching its verdict. The neurologists, witnesses for the state—Krohn, Patrick, Church, and a fourth expert, Harold Douglas Singer—had found no evidence that any organic trauma or infection might have damaged either the cerebral cortex or the central nervous system of either Nathan or Richard. Neurologists assumed the somatic origins of psychiatric illness, and there were no symptoms of organic disease in either defendant. The conclusion reached by the neurologists was, therefore, a correct one—there was no mental disease.

The psychoanalytic psychiatrists—White, Glueck, and Healy—could assert, with equal justification, that according to their understanding of psychiatry, an understanding informed by psychoanalysis, the defendants had suffered mental trauma during childhood that had damaged each boy's ability to function competently. Nathan and Richard had each experienced abuse at the hands of a governess: in Richard's case, Emily Struthers had imposed a set of demands that had distorted his perception of reality; in Nathan's case, Mathilda Wantz had seduced him when he was still a child. The damage inflicted on each boy at an early age had resulted in compensatory fantasies that led directly to the murder.

Most commentators, however, were unaware of the epistemological gulf that separated neurology from psychoanalytic psychiatry. The expert witnesses all claimed to be psychiatrists, after all; and it was, everyone agreed, a dark day for psychiatry when leading representatives of the profession could stand up in court and contradict each other. If men of national reputation and eminence could not agree on a common diagnosis, then could any value be attached to a psychiatric judgment? Or perhaps the experts in each group were saying only what the lawyers required them to say—for a fee, of course. But if psychiatrists, leaders of the profession, no less, were so avaricious as to hire themselves out as mercenaries for a few hundred dollars, then of what value was the psychiatric profession?

It was an evil that contaminated the entire profession, thundered the *New York Times*, in an editorial similar to dozens of others that appeared at the same time. The experts in the Leopold-Loeb hearing were "of equal authority as alienists and psychiatrists," apparently in possession of the same set of facts, who, nevertheless, gave out "opinions exactly opposite and contradictory as to the past and present condition of the two prisoners. . . . Instead of seeking truth for its own sake and with no preference as to what it turns out to be, they are supporting, and are expected to support, a predetermined purpose. . . . That the presiding Judge," the *Times* concluded sorrowfully, "is getting any help from those men toward the forming of his decision hardly is to be believed."[19]

DARROW HAD LISTENED PATIENTLY as Joseph Sbarbaro asked Archibald Church questions about the mental condition of Nathan and

Richard. Now it was his turn. The neurologists had had only one op-portunity to examine the boys, Darrow began, and they had come into court arguing that their examination—on Sunday, 1 June, in the office of the state's attorney—allowed them to claim that neither boy suffered from mental disease. But how, Darrow asked, could they have exam-ined Nathan and Richard under conditions that were far from ideal? Darrow himself had been in the anteroom to Crowe's office that Sun-day afternoon, trying to get access to the boys; he had seen for himself the to-and-fro of the police sergeants, the stenographers, the psychia-trists, and various functionaries. How had it been possible to have de-termined the boys' mental condition under those circumstances?

"Now, there were," Darrow asked Church, "some fifteen people in the room while you were talking to these boys?"

"I think," Church replied cautiously, "hardly that many, but there were many, I know that."

"Too many," Darrow suggested, "for a thorough consultation?"

"Too many," Church admitted, grudgingly, "for an ideal consulta-tion."

"You never had anybody bring you a patient to treat where you called in any such number of people as that, did you?"

"Occasionally it is very difficult to keep all the members of the family out."

"I asked you a specific question," Darrow responded tartly, his voice rising slightly.

"No, I never treated a patient in private practice—" Church paused, reluctant to concede Darrow's point; "—examined a patient before as many people."

"You have laid down the rules yourself as to how a private exami-nation should be conducted, have you not?"

"Well, I control the situation under those conditions."

"Did you ask any questions?"

"Yes."

"Who did most of the questioning?"

"Really, there were very few questions asked," Church glanced mo-mentarily toward Hugh Patrick and William Krohn, sitting behind the state's attorney and his assistants. "Dr. Patrick asked a few and Dr. Krohn asked a few and Mr. Crowe asked a few, but most of it was continuous narrative on the part of Mr. Loeb and some questions asked him by Leopold and some back and forth conversation between them. . . ."[20]

"Did you ask any questions to find out evidence of mental disease?"

"No."

"Did anybody else that you know of?"

"Well, all of the questions and conversations were for the purpose, as far as I was concerned, of determining their mental status."[21]

In other words, Darrow concluded, the examination had been entirely superficial, so superficial as to render it worthless. There had been perhaps fifteen people in Crowe's office during the examination—could it even be properly called an examination? he wondered—and yet the state's witnesses persisted in saying that they had evaluated Nathan and Richard! The examination had lasted a mere three hours, and none of the neurologists, according to Church, had even asked questions designed to elicit evidence of mental disease!

Had Darrow known, he could have asked whether Church had carried out the routine tests that neurologists customarily used when evaluating defendants. By the 1920s, physicians had devised well-known procedures for determining lesions of the nervous system. Church could have used an esthesiometer, a needlelike instrument designed to measure tactile sensibility and to test for damage to the peripheral nervous system. He could also have used a dynamometer, an instrument for measuring muscle strength and movement, useful in detecting signs of decreased muscle tone (hypotonia), symptomatic of cerebellar lesions. And even if the state's experts had not had such instruments at their disposal during the examination, it would have been possible for them to have tested for ataxia (a loss of balance due to lesions of the cerebellum) by requiring Richard and Nathan to perform simple walking and standing exercises.

Roentgenology also had become an accepted procedure in neurological diagnosis. It had become possible, as early as 1910, to map the central nervous system by X-rays; and by the 1920s, physicians had learned to detect tumors of the spinal marrow with the aid of X-rays.

The lumbar puncture—the insertion of a fine needle into the lumbar interspace of the spine to collect a sample of cerebrospinal fluid—enabled neurologists to calculate pressure measurements of the cerebrospinal fluid and to draw off a sample for biochemical and serological analysis. By 1924, the lumbar puncture had become the most common diagnostic technique favored by neurologists to test for tabes dorsalis, a form of syphilis that results in the degeneration of the dorsal columns of the spinal cord.[22]

That Darrow knew nothing of such diagnostic procedures and their use in neurological examination did not prevent him from pushing forward his attack on the state's testimony. Church had been a coauthor, with Frederick Peterson of Columbia University, of the textbook *Nervous and Mental Diseases*, long the standard work on neurological disorders and their treatment. Darrow had a copy of the most recent edition, the ninth, on the table before him. He picked up the book, a heavy volume with black covers, and turned toward Church to read his words back to him. "This is your latest on this subject," Darrow began "and you have said here: 'The examination of a patient with mental disorder is a much more complex process than that of a case of physical disease. . . . For it is necessary in the former not only to ascertain the present physical condition, as with ordinary patients, but also to investigate the mental state, which involves the employment of unusual and new methods and brings us into contact with a novel series of psychic phenomena, and moreover to attain our end we need to study the whole past life of the patient, his diseases, accidents, schooling, occupation, environment, temperament, character; nor can we stop here; for it is of the greatest importance to inform ourselves as to conditions among his antecedents to determine the type of family from which he sprung, and the presence or absence of an hereditary taint. There is therefore much to learn even before seeing the patient in person.' "[23]

Darrow paused. He looked from the book to the witness. "And you did not learn that before seeing them, surely?"

"I did not," Church replied, "have the opportunity."

Church explained that the state's attorney had called him at mid-day on 1 June. He had not had the time to prepare for the examination. And in any case, Church continued, his coauthor, Frederick Peterson, had written the words that Darrow had quoted. The preface, Church explained, stated that Church had been responsible for the sections on neurology and that Peterson had contributed the second section on psychiatry.

It was an evasive response. Darrow pointed out that Church would not have put his name to a book if he had disagreed with the contents. Did he agree with the words that Peterson had written on the procedure for a psychiatric examination? "Doctor, don't you think," Darrow asked, "you share in the responsibility, when you let nine editions go out? . . . And you would not question what I have been reading as being correct, would you, that is, as being proper in the examination of a patient, would you?"[24]

But Church refused to concede Darrow's point. Frederick Peterson had written the words quoted by Darrow—and he, Church, was not responsible for that section of the book.

"Just a moment," Robert Crowe interrupted, appealing to the judge. "I object to cross examining upon a textbook, a portion of which—and the portion that he is being cross-examined on—he did not write, and disclaims any responsibility for. . . . You can only cross-examine him on something that he has based his opinion on in this case." How could Darrow cross-examine the witness on something that Church had not written? And, in any case, Crowe continued, the words that Darrow had quoted had not been introduced into testimony on direct examination.[25]

It was an inconclusive argument. But Darrow had already made his point. Church had had insufficient opportunity for a proper examination of the defendants. He could not plausibly assert that Richard and Nathan were free of mental disease.

OTHER WITNESSES FOR THE STATE had no recourse but to concede that the inadequacy of the examination was the weakest link in the state's case. There had been insufficient time on 1 June for the psychiatrists properly to evaluate the mental condition of Nathan Leopold and Richard Loeb. Benjamin Bachrach, in his cross-examination of Hugh Patrick, pushed the witness to accept the same inevitable conclusion: that the brevity of the examination, along with the conditions under which it had taken place, nullified any judgment the state's psychiatrists might make. There had been at least fifteen people in the room at the time of the examination—how could any analysis of any value be obtained under such conditions?

Just how many people, Bachrach asked Patrick, had been in the room that afternoon? Ten? Fifteen? Or perhaps as many as seventeen?

"I suppose," Patrick answered cautiously, "there were about ten people there or something like that. There may have been more."

"Don't you think," Bachrach responded, "there were about fifteen?"

"No, I shouldn't think there were fifteen, but it was possible."

"Let us count them," Bachrach spoke decisively, armed with the confidence that came from knowing the answer to his question. "There were the state's attorney and three assistants. That is four."

"Four, and the two prisoners make six," Patrick agreed.

"Six."

There had been three psychiatrists and one physician present as well as several police officers—perhaps there had been as many as fifteen persons in the room.

"And four doctors are ten," Patrick conceded reluctantly. "Well it might go to fifteen. . . ."

"And two stenographers?" Bachrach demanded impatiently.

"Yes, two stenographers. I guess it would reach—"

"About seventeen?"

"Well, I don't think so, but I don't know."

Bachrach smiled, flushed with victory. "Did you ever in your life," he asked with mock incredulity, "make an examination of any person, as to his mental state, under circumstances of that kind before?"

"I think not."[26]

•   •   •

Harold Douglas Singer, professor and chair of psychiatry at the University of Illinois, succeeded Patrick on the witness stand. Singer, a tall, gangly man with a distinctive British accent, had studied medicine at St. Thomas's Hospital in London before moving to the United States in 1904 to become an associate professor of neurology at Creighton University. Singer had stayed in Nebraska only three years before moving to Illinois as director of the State Psychopathic Institute. He had taken up his present position at the University of Illinois in 1919.[27]

Singer had read the Bowman-Hulbert report and had met briefly with Nathan and Richard in the state's attorney's office; he had been a constant presence in the courtroom and had heard the evidence presented by both sides. There had been nothing in the testimony, he stated in reply to a question from Milton Smith, assistant state's attorney, that would indicate mental disease in Leopold and Loeb. Indeed, the evidence presented in court argued against the presence of mental illness. The planning of the murder, the preparation of the alibis, the disposal of the body—all showed that Nathan and Richard had had sufficient mental acuity to calculate and to organize, and in that sense they were normal.[28]

What about the psychoanalytic evidence introduced by the defense psychiatrists? Did Richard's fantasy that he was a master criminal have any significance in assessing the character of the crime? Fantasy, Singer replied, was a means of satisfying wishes that could not otherwise be fulfilled. "The phantasy life of an individual," Singer explained, "represents the striving of certain longings or appetites for expression, being prohibited by the social conditions under which he lives, more or less. The phantasy life, therefore, represents the dreaming of his longings as being fulfilled. It is a way of meeting desires which is permissible in society because it will not lead to difficulties." Richard's fantasy—a career as a master criminal—indicated merely a desire for excitement. Nathan's fantasy—as a powerful slave to a grateful king—represented, according to Singer, homosexual desire.[29]

Clarence Darrow listened attentively. There was a book on the table in front of him, and occasionally, as Singer continued to talk, Darrow thumbed through it absentmindedly. It was a copy of Singer's *Insanity and Law: A Treatise on Forensic Psychiatry*, cowritten with William Krohn and published earlier that year. Darrow had read the book and prepared his questions; soon he would begin his interrogation of the witness.

Milton Smith had now finished his examination; he had no further questions. Darrow, his left hand hooked behind one gallus as though to prevent it from snapping back, approached the witness stand, holding his copy of Singer's book in his right hand. Was it not true, Darrow began, that Singer had written in *Insanity and Law* that mental illness often lay dormant, unseen, until precipitated into visibility by the stress of circumstances? Some individuals coped successfully with the demands of everyday life; in such cases, mental disease might never reveal itself. Others, according to Singer, succumbed to external conditions in ways that revealed what had previously been hidden.

Darrow started to read from *Insanity and Law*, glancing occasionally at the witness. "'It would,'" Darrow began, reading back to Singer, "'be a mistake to assume that every person with a schizophrenic trend is going to develop a psychosis or become insane. Very many never do so at all, possibly because the complexes that are split off do not involve a very large part of the man's personality, or because the conditions under which he has to live do not make demands that he cannot meet

THE BATTLE OF THE ALIENISTS

[Copyright, 1924, By The Chicago Tribune.]

33. THE BATTLE OF THE BOOKS. The alienists (psychiatrists) for the defense and for the state supported competing psychiatric theories. Here the cartoonist for the *Chicago Daily Tribune* imagines the courtroom as the scene of a battle between the two sets of psychiatrists.

sufficiently well. . . . One of the subgroups of dementia praecox comprises such individuals under the name of dementia simplex. They do not often come under the observation of the psychiatrist and have but little importance. . . . It is readily intelligible, however, that the outbreak of a psychosis is especially liable to occur when special demands in the way of responsibility and direct contact with the real world are made. One such period is that of leaving school and emancipation from home control.' "[30]

Singer had described latent schizophrenia and had characterized the conditions under which the schizophrenic patient might become psychotic—did not his description apply accurately to Richard Loeb? Singer had also described the onset of psychosis; it manifested itself, according to *Insanity and Law*, in a series of violent acts, apparently random and unforeseen, for which the psychotic individual showed neither remorse nor regret.

Darrow resumed reading from the book he held in his right hand: " 'The outbreak is sudden, unexpected, . . . and apparently without motive; a truly impulsive and unconsidered act. The man's attitude toward the deed after its accomplishment is devoid of remorse. It is almost as though he fails to accept authorship, he is not a free agent, and he apparently often experiences considerable relief after the act is performed.' " Was that not also an accurate description of the murder of Bobby Franks? Neither Richard Loeb nor Nathan Leopold had had any reason to kill a fourteen-year-old boy; and the murder had been unexpected and unforeseen; and neither Richard nor Nathan had expressed any remorse for their deed. On the contrary, both boys had adopted a cocky, dismissive attitude toward the murder.[31]

Darrow had hoped to force Singer into a contradiction—between, on the one hand, the analysis presented in *Insanity and Law* and, on the other, the claim that both boys were free of mental illness—but the attempt could not be sustained: the terms of the debate were too imprecise. Singer always managed to find some qualification that helped shift the meaning of his words; and, in any case, too little was known of the defendants to match description with reality. Neither the experts for the state nor those for the defense had been able, in their descriptions on the witness stand, to capture the essence of those two inscrutable boys. Darrow's psychiatrists had spent weeks examining Nathan and Leopold, yet their inner characters seemed as elusive as ever. Crowe's experts had resolutely persisted in proclaiming the normality of the defendants, but how could such claims be sustained when neither boy felt regret for such a crime?

Darrow had undoubtedly undercut the state's claim that Nathan and Richard were normal; it was apparent that the state's experts had conducted a superficial and largely meaningless examination. Yet Darrow had won no concessions from the state; none of the witnesses had conceded any sign of mental illness in the defendants.

Now the hearing had reached its conclusion. Each side had presented its evidence. The defense had demonstrated the character and extent of the mental illnesses that inflicted Nathan Leopold and Richard Loeb. It would not be just for the judge to exercise the extreme penalty of the law on two defendants so clearly afflicted with mental disease.

The state had made its case also. It would be preposterous to mitigate the punishment on the grounds of mental illness. The defendants were entirely rational. They had shown no signs of impairment either before or after the crime, and now, inside the courtroom, they appeared normal. Capital punishment was entirely appropriate in such a case.

It remained only for the judge to hear the closing statements from each side. It seemed that both defense and prosecution had already said all they wanted to say—there was surely nothing new to add. But Robert Crowe was to give the final summation, following immediately after Clarence Darrow, and Crowe had prepared a surprise that would catch the defense unawares. And Crowe had the final word—it would not be possible for the defense to rebut his allegations.

15

CLOSING STATEMENTS

The penalty under the laws of the State of Illinois for aggravated, deliberate murder, is death. . . . If this is not an aggravated deliberate murder on the facts as they are before the court, if this is not a murder of the extreme type on the facts, then of course a lesser penalty can be invoked; but when, as here, the greatest turpitude, months of detailed planning, careful execution of every detail, a money motive, a kidnaping for ransom, the deliberate murder, the cruel blows of a sharp steel chisel, the gagging, the death and the hiding of the body all appear as they do in this case, the malice and deliberation take the crime out of the scale of lesser penalties and prescribe death.[1]

> *Thomas Marshall, assistant state's attorney*
> *for Cook County, 19 August 1924*

I want to say, your honor, that if we do not hang these two most brutal murderers, we might just as well abolish capital punishment, because it will mean nothing in our law. . . . Murder must stop, and the only way you will stop murder is by hanging the murderers; and if your honor hangs these two murderers, it will set an example to the others, if we have any of them among us, that justice is swift, and that justice is sure, and that if they fail to live up to the letter of the law they will receive the extreme penalty of the law.[2]

Joseph Savage, assistant state's attorney for
Cook County, 21 August 1924

WALTER KRAUSER WAITED AT THE corner of Halsted and West 47th streets. It was a cold December morning, just one week before Christmas 1922, and Krauser could feel the wintry chill penetrating his thin jacket. He stamped his feet in a futile attempt to keep warm and cursed his friend, Bernard Grant, for his want of punctuality.

Both boys—Krauser was nineteen; Grant, eighteen—lived in Back of the Yards, a notorious slum area, in dilapidated ramshackle terrace houses built at the turn of the century for the stockyard workers. Both boys had criminal records: Krauser was a petty thief, known to the police for a string of burglaries; Grant had been arrested a dozen times already, once in connection with the murder of Frank McGurk, a police sergeant shot during a payroll robbery. Both boys were unemployed and looking for work, but even at the height of the Christmas season, there were no jobs for two unschooled illiterate teenagers.[3]

The second boy finally appeared, and they started south, down Halsted. It was still only seven o'clock, too early in the morning to be looking for work; the storekeepers had not yet begun to unlock their shutters and open for business.

They drifted haphazardly from street to street. There was no plan; they did not, if truth be told, even know how to begin looking for work or where to find it.

The streets were still relatively deserted in the morning darkness; dawn had just broken and only now were the storekeepers throwing up the blinds and shutters. Krauser touched the revolver in his jacket pocket and ran his index finger down the barrel. Perhaps, he thought, it would be easier to rob a store than to find a job.

Krauser stopped his companion in front of the Atlantic and Pacific Tea Store at 5361 Morgan Street. Through the front of the store, they could see the manager, Daniel Glass, moving around behind the counter, stepping up and down a short ladder, stacking cans on the shelves above him.

Krauser and Grant peered again into the store, more intently this time, to look beyond Glass into the interior of the store, to see if he was alone. Grant nudged his accomplice with his elbow; the store was empty. As they passed through the doorway, Krauser drew his gun from his jacket and held it in his right hand.

They had no intent to kill; they only wanted the cash in the register. Krauser held Glass at gunpoint while Grant searched for the money in the cash drawer. Krauser ordered the manager to the back of the store—if they could find some rope in the storeroom, they would tie him up and make good their escape.

Inside the storeroom, unaware of the drama that was making its way toward him, Ralph Souders sat reading the morning newspaper. There had recently been a rash of robberies of A&P stores in the area. Souders, a probationary policeman, was about to begin the morning shift guarding the store. His gun lay on a chair beside him; his right hand held a cigarette.

As Krauser entered the storeroom, he suddenly saw the policeman. Grant was following close behind. Krauser barked out a warning to his accomplice, "Get the copper's gun!"

Souders looked up in surprise. His cigarette fell to the floor as he jumped up, away from his chair. The policeman grabbed for Krauser's gun; the three men struggled together in the middle of the room and suddenly there was a loud explosion—the gun had gone off, and two more shots were fired in rapid succession.[4]

Ralph Souders, who was killed, left behind a young widow, Mary, with one young child and a second expected the following April. Detectives picked up Krauser and Grant that evening, and within hours both had confessed to the murder of the young policeman.[5]

The court sentenced both boys to hang, but appeals to the Illinois supreme court delayed their execution. By August 1924, twenty months after Souders's death, Krauser and Grant still waited on death row for the final disposition of their cases.[6]

ON TUESDAY, 19 AUGUST 1924, Thomas Marshall, assistant state's attorney for Cook County, stood in front of John Caverly in the sixth-floor courtroom in the Criminal Court Building. The hearing on Nathan Leopold and Richard Loeb was almost concluded; the state had questioned its last witness, and now Marshall was presenting his closing statement on behalf of the state.

What sort of justice, Marshall demanded, would prevail in Chicago's courts if Krauser and Grant went to the scaffold while Leopold and Loeb escaped with a prison sentence? The Criminal Court had sentenced Walter Krauser and Bernard Grant to death for the killing of a young policeman, but there had been no forethought, no premeditation, in their act. Neither Krauser nor Grant had been aware that Ralph Souders was on the premises; they had intended merely to rob the store. The shooting had been incidental to the robbery. "There was," Marshall explained, "no deliberate original intention to commit the murder of that police officer. There was no thought of the murder of that police officer."[7]

And what, Marshall asked, of Leopold and Loeb and the murder of Bobby Franks?

Nathan Leopold and Richard Loeb had plotted and planned the murder for six months. They had been meticulous in their preparations, preparations that had included the use of alibis and false identities and the rehearsal of the scheme to obtain the ransom. There had been nothing impulsive about the killing of Bobby Franks. Few crimes in the history of Chicago, Marshall stated, had shown as detailed preparation and premeditation as the murder of this fourteen-year-old boy. Yet Darrow dared to ask for mitigation of punishment!

At the time of the killing, Krauser and Grant were both young men—nineteen and eighteen years old, respectively—but, apart from their youth, they were as unlike Leopold and Loeb as one could imagine.

Krauser and Grant had grown up in the squalid slum district known as Back of the Yards, west of the meatpacking plants on the South Side. They had known only poverty and destitution; both had come from broken homes; they had had no schooling worth the name; both were illiterate. Their original crime, the robbery of the A&P store, Marshall suggested, had been born almost of necessity, and the murder of the policeman had been an unseen consequence.

What a contrast, Marshall exclaimed, with those pampered, wealthy, self-indulgent killers, Nathan Leopold and Richard Loeb! Leopold and Loeb had breezed through life, with all the advantages that money could buy. Their parents had showered them with all the luxuries they could desire.

Bernard Grant had not even fired the gun that had sent the bullets into Ralph Souders. And yet now he sat in his cell, awaiting execution on 17 October. How, Marshall exclaimed, could the court not give Leopold and Loeb the same sentence—death by hanging—that Grant had received?

"Shall Grant, who killed a police officer in a struggle in a robbery in that store . . . go to the gallows . . . when men of the same age, of greater education, of better opportunity, can deliberately plan and scheme a murder and kidnaping for ransom for months and months, carry it into execution and by any possibility escape that penalty? Grant . . . committed an atrocious crime, but in comparison the crime at bar revolts whereas Grant's crime can be understood."[8]

Darrow had asked that his clients' age mitigate the punishment. But many youths in Cook County—some younger even than Nathan Leopold and Richard Loeb—had received the death penalty for murder, and none had killed with comparable deliberation.

David Anderson, a nineteen-year-old executed for murder in 1908, was a case in point, Marshall explained. Anderson had been present when a companion, Albert McGagg, had shot and killed a plainclothes detective on the street. At his trial, the state had failed even to show that Anderson had drawn his revolver. Nevertheless, the court had found Anderson guilty of murder and had sentenced him to death, a verdict later upheld by the Illinois supreme court.[9]

Nicholas Viani, a member of the Cardinella gang, was only seventeen years old when he killed Andrew Bowman, a saloon keeper, during the robbery of a restaurant on Canal Street, near the factory district. Perhaps, Marshall suggested, a clever and resourceful lawyer might have appealed in that case for mitigation of punishment, just as Darrow had. Salvatore Cardinella, a thirty-nine-year-old Sicilian, had initiated Viani into a life of crime. Cardinella was a notorious fagin, infamous for his ability to manipulate young boys; Viani, who ended his life on the scaffold, was one of the less fortunate boys drawn into Cardinella's spiderweb. How, Marshall demanded, could one compare Viani's crime—a bungled robbery that turned, in a moment, without premeditation, into murder—to the deliberate and calculated killing of Bobby Franks?[10]

Marshall continued to read from his list of men executed by Cook County for murder. Thomas Schultz, nineteen years old; Thomas Errico, nineteen; Leonard Crapo, nineteen; William Yancey Mills, twenty-one; Dennis Anderson, twenty-one; Andrew Williams, twenty-two; John (Smiling Jack) O'Brien, twenty-two; Frank Camponi, twenty-two; John Henry Riese, twenty-two. All had ended their lives swinging from the beam of a scaffold in the Cook County jail, yet none of them, not one, Marshall emphasized, had planned his crime with as much deliberation as Leopold and Loeb in the killing of Bobby Franks.[11]

If Leopold's and Loeb's youth did not mitigate the crime, then what of Darrow's plea that their mental condition should save them from the gallows? Marshall reminded the court that the defendants had pleaded guilty to the murder. Both, therefore, had admitted responsibility. But responsibility for an action was not divisible; in law, a defendant was either responsible or, alternatively, bore no responsibility at all. The defense had admitted responsibility and, with its admission, had conceded that Leopold and Loeb were eligible for the penitentiary. And if they were eligible for the penitentiary, they were equally eligible for the gallows.

The court, Marshall argued, should impose its sentence not in consideration of the mental condition of the defendants—"their fate is determined not by weak mind or phantasy, delusion, or mental disease"—but with regard to the gravity of the offense.[12]

Murder was punishable in Illinois by a sentence of death, by life in the penitentiary, or by a prison sentence not less than fourteen years. The state legislature allowed judicial discretion in the determination of punishment. But that discretion, Marshall reminded Caverly, should give effect to "the will of the law, not the will of the individual. . . . By judicial discretion is meant sound discretion guided by law, not an arbitrary discretion, never exercised for the purpose of giving effect to the will of the judge, always for the purpose of giving effect to the will of the legislature, or, in other words, to the will of the law."[13]

And in the case now before the court, the crime was so flagrantly willful, so deliberate and premeditated, that Caverly, if he were to give effect to the law, had little choice but to impose the death penalty. The killing of Bobby Franks was unique, Marshall claimed, in the degree of preparation and forethought that had preceded it; and the callousness of the act, an act committed more as an intellectual exercise than as a crime of passion, gave the murder an especially horrific aspect. There were no mitigating circumstances; there were abundant aggravating circumstances; and both defendants, moreover, had confessed their guilt and admitted responsibility! The murder cried out for the death penalty; any other sentence would be a travesty.

"A fourteen year old helpless school boy lured by deceit into the automobile, by two stout robust young men, bent upon murder, bent upon kidnaping for ransom, for Ten Thousand Dollars in old bills; lured into that car, seated in the front seat to talk about a tennis racket with his friend, whom he had known for a long time; and while he is facing forward in that car, talking about a tennis racket, he is beaten upon the head with a steel chisel, and his life crushed out at the hands of two strong young men,—a helpless boy."

Marshall had already spoken for almost two days—his voice was hoarse—and now he had almost finished. "There is nothing in Illinois jurisprudence that compares with it. It cannot be found on the books. . . . And so upon the whole of the record, compare all of the Illinois cases I have cited from the beginning down to this moment, and nowhere in any of them will you find the premeditation, the deliberate malice, the cunning plans, the months of preparation, the thought, the science, the ability. . . . There is only one sentence that can be imposed upon these vile culprits. . . . Any lesser penalty than the extreme penalty of the law under such circumstances and upon the record in this case, would make a mockery of the law itself."[14]

WALTER BACHRACH, IN HIS RESPONSE for the defense, replied that Thomas Marshall was wrong to say that the defense had advanced mental illness to dilute the responsibility of Nathan and Richard for the murder. Bachrach seemed to have a calming influence on the court-room; his manner, as he stood before the bench, was thoughtful, even scholarly; his sentences, precise and neat, seemed designed to dissect Marshall's erroneous logic; and his voice, smooth and silky, drifted through the warm, moist air of the courtroom, lulling his audience into agreement. The defense admitted full responsibility for the crime, Bachrach stated; what other conclusion could one draw from a plea of guilty? And responsibility was not, of course, divisible; one could not be partially responsible for an action.[15]

But the judge, Bachrach continued, had a duty and a right to con-sider the circumstances of the murder when deliberating on the appro-priate punishment. The Illinois legislature had provided the court with discretion in fixing the penalty for the crime. It expected the court to examine the condition of the murderer in sentencing him. A man who had killed the seducer of his wife might, for example, have acted in a jealous rage, out of sudden anger; surely, under those circumstances, the court would take into account the mental condition of the mur-derer when determining punishment.[16]

Age, also, was a mitigating circumstance; a child had not the same judgment, knowledge, or experience that one would expect to find in an adult. There was not, therefore, the same degree of deliberation in the action of a child as in the action of an adult, and as a consequence the court would determine on a lesser punishment.[17]

Was not an individual suffering from mental illness comparable to a child? Both lacked the ability to comprehend the effect of their ac-tions on others; both lacked knowledge and experience in successful social relations; and both lacked, therefore, awareness and understanding of moral behavior. The defense had demonstrated mental illness in Nathan and Richard, but this was not an attempt to evade responsibility, Bachrach explained. Just as their youth was an aspect of the case that called for a lesser punishment, so their mental condition also mitigated punishment.[18]

And, of course, there was no doubt that both Nathan and Richard were mentally ill. Nathan was a paranoiac. He displayed all the symptoms of someone suffering from a paranoid psychosis: delusions of grandeur, self-satisfied superiority, disregard of others, and exaggerated self-importance. Nathan, in letters to Richard Loeb and in comments to classmates at the University of Chicago, had repeatedly represented himself as a superman who had no need either to behave according to the law or to conform to social convention. His philosophy was an individualistic hedonism that held others in contempt; whatever gave him pleasure or satisfaction determined his daily course of action.

Walter Bachrach paused and glanced briefly across the aisle to look at the cluster of psychiatrists sitting behind the prosecution lawyers. He smiled briefly—almost imperceptibly—as he noticed William Krohn seated directly behind Robert Crowe. Bachrach now leaned forward slightly to pick up a book that had been lying on the table before him. He began, with steady deliberation, as the courtroom waited to hear his words, to leaf through its pages. He resumed speaking. The symptoms of a paranoid psychosis, so conspicuous in Nathan Leopold, were, Bachrach stated, elegantly described by William Krohn and Douglas Singer in their recent book, *Insanity and Law: A Treatise on Forensic Psychiatry*. Bachrach turned to page sixty-eight and started to read: "'The essence of the paranoid personality is an exaggerated appreciation of self. Everything that happens is considered in relation to the effects it has on the self, and there is a corresponding diminution in the sentiments of altruism and gregariousness. . . . The man is a dominant aggressive person, anxious to be in the forefront and careless of the feelings and interests of others. He takes life seriously, works hard, and with purpose.'" Was that not an accurate description of Nathan? asked Bachrach. "'He is always sure of himself, is satisfied with his own views and constantly endeavors to impose them on others. . . . Naturally, he is not popular and he does not make friends though he may have many acquaintances. . . . He prides himself on his intelligence and control of emotions, and, as a matter of fact, reasons logically and connectedly.' "[19]

William Krohn, in his testimony for the state, had claimed that Nathan had shown no evidence of mental disease during the examination in the office of the state's attorney. Nathan had expressed himself in a logical and coherent manner with no long pauses or inappropriate gestures such as one might see in a person suffering from neurological disease. Yet—Bachrach now asked—was such external normality in speech and gesture necessarily a sign of mental health; or could a mentally ill individual nevertheless speak and talk in an apparently normal manner? Bachrach turned to page seventy-four and began to read, again, from Krohn's description of a paranoid personality: " 'Throughout, the intelligence remains intact; perception is clear and there is no disorientation in the narrower sense of this term. Memory is good, in spite of the falsifications in meaning and context that have been mentioned. The man remains in contact with reality, active, alert and interested and there is no tendency to deterioration or dementia. Hallucinations are unusual, though they may occur during periods of marked excitement.' "[20]

Once again Bachrach looked briefly across the courtroom at Krohn. He then turned, with a slightly supercilious expression, to look directly at the judge. "Now there, if your honor please," Bachrach said, "you have a statement of Drs. Singer and Krohn which in effect destroys their testimony as given here in the court; the testimony of Dr. Krohn that he based his judgment as to the absence of mental disease of Leopold, upon his memory, his logical processes and his orientation, and his senses, are all shown by his own book to be no evidence that a mental disease did not exist at all."[21]

The state's claim that Nathan was normal was contradicted by the diagnosis of paranoid psychosis presented in *Insanity and Law*. And what about Richard Loeb? Was the state's evidence with regard to Richard also undermined by Krohn's book?

Richard was a schizophrenic, Bachrach explained. During his puberty and adolescence, Richard had displayed a progressive loss of contact with reality, a failure to function in everyday life, and a disintegration of personality. He believed himself to be a master criminal, capable of leading other criminals in the organization of perfect crimes. The fantasy was deeply rooted in his psyche; it had been a feature of his everyday thoughts for at least six years—perhaps longer—and showed no sign of diminution. On the contrary; Richard had attempted to translate his wish into reality, stealing cars, burning down outhouses, robbing private homes, and finally killing a fourteen-year-old boy. Even now, Bachrach continued, he was obsessed with the image of himself as a criminal, standing alone in a prison cell, while spectators looked on with a mixture of pity and admiration.

William Krohn, testifying as a witness for the state, had denied, of course, that Richard suffered in any degree from mental illness. The boy was intelligent, lucid, and coherent in his manner and expression and could not be mentally diseased. But what, Bachrach asked, as, once again, he picked up the book that lay before him on the defense table, had Krohn written in *Insanity and Law*? "'The intelligence of schizophrenic persons,'" Bachrach read, "'is usually good and is often above the average.... Typically, perception and the formation of memories with clear grasp and orientation are fully up to the average.... The trouble lies not in the quality of the intellectual tools, but in the use that is made of them.... In school he often does extremely well so far as scholastic acquisitions are concerned. He is liable to be absorbed in books and especially in topics that are philosophic and abstract rather than those that would bring him into dealing with the real and the concrete. Often the school successes give rise to hopes of a brilliant future, incapable of realization because of the impossibility of effectively meeting reality.'"[22]

Was that not also, Bachrach asked, an accurate description of Richard Loeb? Richard was outwardly normal; but that, according to Krohn's own statements in *Insanity and Law*, would be consistent with a diagnosis of schizophrenia.

The failure of the state psychiatrists to discover mental illness in

Richard and Nathan was a consequence of the abbreviated examination in the state's attorney's office on Sunday, 1 June. Whom should the court believe: the state psychiatrists or the defense psychiatrists? The former had examined the defendants for three hours on a Sunday afternoon in a crowded office; the latter had examined the defendants over several weeks in an isolated, secure room equipped with the necessary scientific equipment. Only one side had presented any credible scientific evidence in this hearing, Bachrach explained, and that evidence led inexorably to the determination of mental illness in Richard Loeb and Nathan Leopold. "Now, how can the testimony," Bachrach concluded, exasperated that there remained any doubt about the matter, "of men like Drs. Singer, Krohn, Patrick, and Church be mentioned in the same breath with the testimony of the experts of the defense?"[23]

WALTER BACHRACH FINISHED SPEAKING SHORTLY before noon on Friday, 22 August. During the recess for lunch, hundreds of Chicagoans began to converge on the Criminal Court Building. Clarence Darrow, scheduled to speak directly after Bachrach, had hinted that the Leopold-Loeb hearing would be the last court case of his career. It was the final opportunity to hear Darrow speak in a criminal trial, the last chance to hear the most famous lawyer in the United States!

By two o'clock that afternoon, 2,000 Chicagoans stood before the doors of the Criminal Court Building in the bright sunshine flooding Austin Avenue. They were packed into a tight knot, a semicircle, in front of the narrow entrance. The crowd seemed to get larger every minute; it had brushed past the line of police guarding the street entrance and already it had forced its way into the entrance hall, up the staircase on the left, winding its way up six flights of stairs. A line of bailiffs, stern and imposing in their dark brown uniforms, their nightsticks ready, stood at the top of the stairs, but the crowd smashed its way through, sweeping aside the thin line, and surging forward down the corridor that led to the courtroom of the chief justice.[24]

A dozen women had fainted in the crush; two persons had been trampled by the crowd; and a bailiff, seriously hurt, had been driven away in an ambulance. Police reinforcements had now arrived in Austin Avenue. Squads of blue-jacketed constables rushed forward, their nightsticks smashing first left, then right, as they fought to regain control of the building. Mounted police charged their horses at the mob, seeking to split it away from the entrance. For ten minutes, Austin Avenue was a battleground as the crowd fought back against the police; but eventually the constables won control of the street. They could now turn their attention to clearing the corridors and stairways of the Criminal Court Building.[25]

Inside the courtroom, Clarence Darrow had started speaking. He wore a loose-fitting gray suit, a blue shirt, and a white wash necktie of a kind that had been fashionable twenty years earlier. His hair, thinning and gray, fell over his forehead; his wrinkled face, punctuated by his shining brown eyes, expressed resolve; and his hands moved eloquently, in synchronicity with his words. The courtroom was full to overflowing—it would have been impossible to squeeze even one more person into the room—and all eyes were focused on Darrow standing in the small space in front of the bench. The afternoon heat was almost unbearable—the thermometer had already reached eighty-two degrees—and Darrow, holding a pair of eyeglasses in one hand and a handkerchief in the other, was mopping the perspiration from his forehead as he addressed the court.[26]

"It has been almost three months," Darrow began, "since I first assumed the great reponsibility that has devolved upon me and my associates in this case, and I am willing to confess that it has been three months of perplexity and great anxiety. A trouble which I would have gladly been spared excepting for my feelings of affection toward some of the members of one of these families. It is a responsibility that is almost too great for any one to assume that has devolved upon me. But we lawyers can no more choose than the court can choose."

The spectators at the rear of the room leaned forward, but it was impossible for them to hear Darrow's words above the racket coming from the hallway. Outside the courtroom, in the corridor, the crowd pressed forward, pushing and shoving at the sheriffs barring the way; punches were thrown and blows were exchanged. Inside the courtroom, muffled shouts and screams could be heard coming from the other side of the thick oak doors.

"Your Honor," Darrow said, speaking above the din, "I think I had better wait."

"Is that hall filled outside there?" Caverly called out to a bailiff standing at the back of the room. "Officers," he instructed a group of sheriffs, "clean out that hall, please and if you have not got enough men, get fifty more. Put everybody out of the building except those in the room now."

The crowd eventually retreated down the corridor and back down the stairs to the fifth floor. Curses and shouts could still be heard, but they came more faintly now; within five minutes the scuffling outside the courtroom had ended.[27]

Robert Crowe's demand for the death sentence, Darrow began, speaking in a quiet, subdued voice, was solely a consequence of the wealth and prominence of the defendants' families. Take away the Loeb fortune; take away the Leopold fortune; take away the Franks fortune—and would anyone be interested in the case now before the court? The newspapers had devoted countless articles, many thousands of words, day after day, to the courtroom hearing—but, if the defendants had been unknown, obscure, and penniless, would anyone apart from the immediate families have cared about the murder of Bobby Franks? It had not even, Darrow continued, been a particularly bloody or violent murder, and if one were to compare it with some of the cases that had previously appeared before the Criminal Court, it would seem unremarkable.

But the wealth of the defendants, together with the random nature of the killing and the absence of any motive for the crime, had transformed the case into one of the most sensational crimes in the history of Chicago. And, of course, Darrow remarked, with bitterness in his voice, the state's attorney had done everything possible to elevate the notoriety of the murder, portraying it, falsely, as the worst such act in the history of Illinois. "I have heard"—Darrow's voice was sharper now, less subdued—"nothing but the cry for blood. I have heard raised from the office of the State's Attorney nothing but the breath of hate."

In any other case, the prosecution would have been content with a life sentence for a guilty plea from two teenagers; but the wealth of the families had barred them from the customary consideration that Robert Crowe would normally have extended.[28]

Both Nathan and Richard had pleaded guilty—yet Crowe demanded the death penalty! Nathan and Richard had been minors, nineteen and eighteen years old, respectively, when they killed Bobby Franks—yet Crowe demanded the death penalty! Did the court realize, Darrow asked Caverly, that it would be an unprecedented act to execute defendants so young on a guilty plea?

Darrow stepped across to the defense table and picked up a single sheet of paper containing a typewritten list of executions in Cook County. There had been ninety hangings in the history of Chicago, he continued; only three of those ninety persons had been hanged on a guilty plea; and none of those three had been younger than age twenty-nine. Julius Mannow, thirty years old, had pleaded guilty to murder with robbery and was hanged in 1895; Daniel McCarthy, twenty-nine years old, was executed on a guilty plea in 1897; and Thomas Fitzgerald, forty-one, the murderer of six-year-old Janet Wilkinson, had received the death sentence on a plea of guilty in 1919.[29]

There was no precedent, Darrow exclaimed, for Crowe's demand that the court hang two defendants who had not yet reached their majority. Capital punishment on a guilty plea—just three cases in the history of Cook County!—was so infrequent that its imposition seemed unjust and unwarranted. Moreover, recent decisions of the Criminal Court made the death penalty appear even more archaic. Since 1914, 350 people had pleaded guilty to murder in Cook County, but only one, Thomas Fitzgerald, had received the death penalty. And it was no coincidence, Darrow remarked, pointing directly at the state's attorney, that Robert Crowe had been the judge who sentenced Fitzgerald to death.[30]

There was no justification, according to precedent, for the death penalty in the case before the court; it would be an unprecedented act to hang Nathan Leopold and Richard Loeb. Nor, continued Darrow, was there even any justification in the circumstances of the act. The murder had neither motive nor purpose; it had been a senseless, random action that could be explained only on the basis of mental illness. The prosecution had hinted that the boys had killed Bobby for the ransom, to pay off their gambling debts, but this seemed too far-fetched to contemplate seriously for more than a moment. Both Nathan and Richard had as much money as they could possibly desire; each boy received a generous allowance from his father. The state, moreover, had provided scant evidence that either Nathan or Richard had gambled for high stakes. There had been one witness—one witness!—who had testified that he had seen Nathan and Richard play cards but the amount wagered had been derisory, a total of ninety dollars. Crowe was desperate, no doubt, to find a motive for the killing, but he was clutching at a weak reed if he hoped to establish the ransom as a sufficient motive for the murder.[31]

The state's attorney had claimed that this was the worst murder in the history of Illinois. But where was the motive? The killing had been "a senseless, useless, purposeless, motiveless act," Darrow challenged. "There was absolutely no purpose in it all, no reason in it all, and no motive in it all. . . . What does the State say about it? In order to make this the most cruel thing that ever happened, of course they must have a motive. And what, do they say, was the motive? . . . 'The motive was to get ten thousand dollars' say they. These two boys, neither one of whom needed a cent, scions of wealthy people, killed this little inoffensive boy to get ten thousand dollars." But Richard Loeb had $3,000 in his bank account and had not even bothered to collect the interest on three Liberty bonds that he owned. Nathan Leopold had been about to go on a European vacation that summer, a vacation paid for by his father. Why, Darrow asked, was there any need for them to risk their freedom, and even their lives, in a scheme to kidnap a boy for ransom? "Your Honor," Darrow appealed to the bench, holding out his hands before him, as though in supplication, "I would be ashamed to talk about this except that in all seriousness—all apparent seriousness—they are asking to kill these two boys on the strength of this flimsy foolishness."[32]

It was futile, Darrow exclaimed, to seek a rational motive for so bizarre a crime. The crime was inexplicable unless one assumed that both Nathan and Richard were mentally ill. And each boy's mental condition was a consequence of the forces that had determined him. "Science has been at work," Darrow stated, with his customary self-assurance; "humanity has been at work, scholarship has been at work and intelligent people know that every human being is the product of the endless heredity back of him and the infinite environment around him. He is made as he is and he is the sport of all that goes around as applied to him. . . . Under the same stress and storm, you might act one way and I might act another."

It was a comforting assumption, but it remained just that—at least in Darrow's account. Heredity and environment had shaped each boy's conduct, but how, exactly? Darrow claimed, once again, an emotional deficiency in the boys' reactions to the murder—all the psychiatrists had remarked the contrast between each boy's advanced intellect and his stunted emotional capacity. But beyond some vague statements on "the emotional life . . . the nerves, the muscles, the endocrine glands, the vegetative system," Darrow was unable to give any more complete account.[33]

Darrow's reluctance, in his closing speech, to use the testimony of his scientific experts was nothing less than an admission of failure. He could not rely on the scientific evidence, because the evidence did not demonstrate that either boy had acted under compulsion in committing the murder. William White's psychoanalysis, William Healy's intelligence tests, and Harold Hulbert's endocrinology—none of it, either separately or in combination, was sufficient to explain the murder; and Darrow, compelled to abandon the scientific evidence, had only his homespun philosophy of extreme determinism to fall back on. "I know," Darrow continued, speaking of Richard Loeb, "that one of two things happened to this boy; that this terrible crime was inherent in his organism, and came from some ancestor, or that it came through his education and his training after he was born. I do not know what remote ancestors may have sent down the seed that corrupted him, and I do not know through how many ancestors it may have passed until it reached Dickie Loeb. All I know is, it is true, and there is not a biologist in the world who will not say I am right."[34]

But if Richard's mental condition was a consequence of the hereditary and environmental forces that had determined him, then where could one fix responsibility? Richard, in Darrow's account, was a plaything of impersonal forces, some stretching back over many generations; and in this rendering, Richard bore no responsibility for his actions. But if one extended the argument, was not everyone shaped by such forces? Therefore, was anyone ever responsible? There was, in Darrow's world, no such thing as individual responsibility, and there was no purpose in a legal system that assigned responsibility and determined punishment. Indeed, Darrow was explicit in his rejection of the concept of individual responsibility. With a characteristic shrug of his shoulders, his left hand buried in his trouser pocket, his right hand gesturing vaguely at the bench, Darrow expelled the concept of blame from the courtroom. "Is Dickey Loeb to blame because out of the infinite forces that conspired to form him, the infinite forces that were at work producing him ages before he was born, that because of these infinite combinations he was born without [emotional capacity?] . . . Is he to blame for what he did not have and never had?" Darrow pushed back a lock of hair from his forehead and half-turned toward the spectators. "Is he to blame that his machine is imperfect?"[35]

Nathan Leopold also was blameless. Nathan too suffered from emotional incapacity; he too had an excess of intellect and a deficit of emotion. Nathan was "just a half boy," Darrow continued, "an intellect, an intellectual machine going without balance and without a governor, seeking to find out everything there was to life intellectually; seeking to solve every philosophy, but using his intellect only."[36]

The metaphor of the machine was the intellectual kernel of Darrow's philosophy. Crime was a consequence of imperfections in the machinery—a loose cog here, a missing governor there—and just as the concept of responsibility was inapplicable to the machine, so individuals were blameless for their conduct. Neither Nathan nor Richard was responsible for the killing of Bobby Franks. If responsibility had to be assigned for that event, then, Darrow argued, blame society for the killing and refrain from punishing Nathan and Richard. "I protest,"

Darrow cried, "against the crimes and mistakes of society being visited upon them."[37]

It was the Great War that, more than any other single event or factor, had contributed to the murder of Bobby Franks. The killing of human beings had become so commonplace, so casual and routine, that society now had a bloodlust which, almost inevitably, had found its way into Nathan and Richard. "It is due to the cruelty that has paralyzed the hearts of men growing out of the war. We are used to blood, your honor." Darrow held his right hand out before him, his forefinger pointing upward. "We have not only had it shed in bucketfuls, we have it shed in rivers, lakes and oceans, and we have delighted in it, we have preached it, we have worked for it, we have advised it, we have taught it to the young, encouraged the old, until the world has been drenched in blood, and it has left its stains of blood upon every human heart and upon every human. . . . For four long years the civilized world was engaged in killing men, Christian against Christian, barbarians uniting with Christians: anything to kill. . . . I need not tell your honor this, because you know; I need not tell you how many upright, honorable young boys have come into this court charged with murder, some saved and some gone to their death, boys who fought in this war and learned how cheap human life was. You know it and I know it."

Darrow had now droned on for three days, interminably rambling his way down rhetorical paths in a disorganized, chaotic mess of a speech. There was little structure to his remarks; he habitually veered off on a tangent at the slightest provocation. Despite its length, his summation contained little of substance; Darrow scarcely even mentioned the scientific testimony introduced during the hearing. His audience fidgeted and yawned yet listened respectfully; and it was only toward the conclusion of the speech, when he indulged in his customary theatrics, that the spectators saw and heard the Darrow of legend.

The path of progress, Darrow argued, led inexorably to the abolition of the death penalty. Society looked back in horror at the barbaric punishments inflicted in previous centuries for petty crimes; and 100 years from now, in the twenty-first century, society would recoil at the

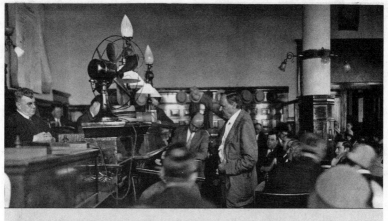

34. CLARENCE DARROW IN COURT.

realization that capital punishment had been a part of the penal code in the United States. Would John Caverly side with the barbarism of the past or align himself with the steady march of progress? Would he conspire with the forces of reaction? Or would he stand with the enlightenment of the future? "If your honor can hang a boy 18, some other judge can hang him at 17, or 16, or 14. Some day, some day, if there is any such thing as progress in the world, if there is any spirit of humanity that is working in the hearts of men, some day they will look back upon this as a barbarous age which deliberately turned the hands of the clock backward, which deliberately set itself in the way of all progress toward humanity and sympathy, and committed an unforgivable act."

Hanging Nathan and Richard would be a futile act of revenge, only a gesture, an appeasement of the mob; in all other respects, it would accomplish nothing. It would not bring Bobby Franks back to life. It would not deter crime, as the state had claimed; but it would be a savage act, certainly, an act that would add its measure of violence to society and diminish man's capacity for understanding, love, and charity. "I know the future is with me and what I stand for here; not merely for the lives of these two unfortunate lads, but for all boys and all girls; all of the young, and as far as possible, for all of the old. I am pleading for life, understanding, charity and kindness, and the infinite mercy that forgives all. I am pleading that we overcome cruelty with kindness and hatred with love. I know the future is on my side. Your honor stands between the past and the future. You may hang these boys; you may hang them by the neck till they are dead. But in doing it you will turn your face toward the past. . . . I am pleading for a time when hatred and cruelty will not control the hearts of men. When we can learn by reason and judgement and understanding and faith that all life is worth saving and that mercy is the highest attribute of man."

Perhaps two-thirds of the spectators were women; Darrow's seductive voice caught at their emotions, and as he spoke of the hanging that might await Nathan and Richard, some women quietly began to cry. There was a oppressive mood in the courtroom; Darrow's reflective, somber words spoke of the tragedy of two wasted lives. Neither Richard nor Nathan had a future—even if each boy escaped the scaffold, he would spend many years shut up between the walls of a harsh and unforgiving prison cell.

The crowd sat still. There was a breathless silence in the courtroom, broken only by the sound of Darrow's voice, and from Dearborn Street, six stories below, the faint screech of trolleys grinding along their metal tracks. Darrow was both solemn and mournful; he no longer waved his arms at the judge or brandished his eyeglasses or strummed his galluses; his posture seemed more erect and his demeanor more dignified. He seemed to be speaking as much to the spectators behind him as to the judge before him as he ended his speech in a resolute voice that appealed for understanding and compassion, not so much for Nathan and Richard as for those many other boys, less privileged, who would be judged in years to come. "If I can succeed, my greatest award and my greatest hope and my greatest compensation will be that I have done something for the tens of thousand of other boys, for the other unfortunates who must tread the same way that these poor youths have trod, that I have done something to help human understanding, to temper justice with mercy, to overcome hate with love."[38]

There was a momentary silence in the courtroom as Darrow finished speaking, just a few minutes before four o'clock. The silence lasted a minute, relieved only by the sound of Darrow shuffling together the papers that lay before him.

"If your honor please," Benjamin Bachrach broke the silence, glancing at his watch to check the time, "will you adjourn at this time?"

"We will suspend now," Caverly replied, "until tomorrow morning at 10.30 o'clock."[39]

How, Robert Crowe wondered as he listened to Darrow's final words, had the old man managed to fool so many people? Darrow was a mendacious windbag, a charlatan, who lulled his audience with empty sentiments and meaningless phrases. He had replaced the progressive principles of his youth with an eagerness to represent anyone, no matter how corrupt or vicious, for the right price. It was a puzzle, Crowe admitted to himself, that the American public continued to regard Darrow as a secular saint whose eccentric philosophy only added to his charm. For many Americans, Darrow could do no wrong; he was the most visible reminder of the heyday of Progressivism; he seemed, with his humanitarian pronouncements, just as utopian and radical as the young lawyer who, thirty years earlier, had championed Eugene Debs in his fight against the railroads.

But Crowe knew better. Darrow was irreligious and irresponsible, an attorney whose deterministic and atheistic philosophy justified and excused crime; Darrow's beliefs had no consequences for himself, of course, but they encouraged murder, violence, and depravity. Darrow seemed a kindly old man, with his calls for mercy and understanding, but he espoused a dangerous philosophy, a philosophy that would remove legal and judicial restraints and leave society vulnerable to the forces of mayhem and chaos.[40]

The next morning Crowe rose to his feet to address the court. It was now his turn to speak. He had changed his shirt shortly before entering the courtroom, but already there were faint patches of perspiration on his shirtfront; in his futile protest against the intolerable heat, Crowe mopped the perspiration from his face with his white handkerchief.

It was ridiculous, Crowe began, for Darrow to say that the notoriety of the killing was on account of the wealth of the families; and it was false to claim that he, Crowe, refused to treat this murder like other murders and agree to a plea bargain because of the wealth and reputation of the families. The kidnapping of a child was the source of the notoriety; it was a crime that had touched the heart of everyone in the city; and it had been the topic of every conversation in Chicago throughout the week after the murder, before anyone had known the identity of the killers.

"There is something," Crowe shouted, angrily, pounding his right fist into his left palm in emphasis, "in the nature of the crime itself that arrests the attention of every person in the land. A child is stolen. The heart of every father, the heart of every mother, the heart of every man who has a heart, goes out to the parents of the child." Crowe turned in the direction of Nathan and Richard sitting behind the defense attorneys. "Their wealth in my judgment has not anything to do with this except it permits a defense here seldom given to men in the criminal court. Take away the millions of the Loebs and the Leopolds, and Clarence Darrow's tongue is as silent as the tomb of Julius Caesar. . . . Clarence Darrow once said that a poor man on trial here was disposed of in fifteen minutes, but if he was rich and committed the same crime and he got a good lawyer, his trial would last twenty-one days. Well, they got three lawyers and it has lasted just a little bit longer."[41]

And Darrow's assertion that there was no motive for the killing? That also was false, Crowe continued. There was the ransom, of course; he would talk about that later. But one motive, certainly, was Nathan's desire to rape a young child. Why had the killers removed Bobby's trousers three hours before disposing of the body in the culvert by the Pennsylvania Railroad tracks? Bobby's shirt and jacket had remained on his body until they had arrived at Wolf Lake. Only then had Nathan removed the boy's remaining clothing before pouring acid on Bobby's face and genitals.

"How," Crowe demanded, staring directly at Nathan as he spoke, "do you undress a child? First the little coat, the collar, the tie, the shirt, and the last thing is their trousers. Yet, immediately after killing this poor little boy, his trousers alone came off, and for three hours that dead little boy, without his trousers but with all his other clothes on him, remained in that car, and they did not take the balance of the clothes off until after they pushed the body into the culvert. You have before you"—Crowe indicated it to the judge—"the coroner's report, and the coroner's physician says that when little Robert Franks was examined, his rectum was distended that much," Crowe held his thumb and forefinger one inch apart, "indicating almost the size of a half-dollar."

"If the court please." Benjamin Bachrach was suddenly on his feet, signaling for the judge's attention. "I take exception to that statement. The coroner's report said there was no sign of recent dilation."

"Your honor has the report," Crowe shouted in reply. "I want to call Your honor's attention to the fact that this little naked body lay in the water all night long with running water going over it, and that is why there wasn't any other evidence." The coroner had found no traces of semen—it had been taken away by the water passing through the culvert—but the rectum was distended beyond its normal size. One of the killers—most probably Nathan—had raped Bobby.

"This is the first time," Bachrach protested, "it has been charged in this case that the committing of a sexual act was the purpose of this crime upon the boy. . . ."

"I think I know," Crowe sneered, with heavy sarcasm, "what the evidence was in this case and I think all my arguments are based on facts and not on dreams or phantasies. . . . The Coroner's report says that he had a distended rectum, and from that fact, and the fact that the pants were taken off, and the fact that they are perverts, I have a right to argue that they committed an act of perversion. That is the extent of my argument. I do not contend that the coroner's report states that an act of perversion was committed. It merely says that the rectum was distended. There was no evidence of semen, but it was washed away, I contend."[42]

There was only one way to settle the dispute. Had there been an enlarged rectum or not? What did the coroner's report say?

"Let the coroner's report be read," Caverly ordered. He looked out across the courtroom. The audience, mesmerized by Crowe's sudden revelations, stared back at him expectantly, waiting for the reading of the report. "The women will leave the courtroom," Caverly commanded, "and we will put the report into the record."[43]

A few dozen women rose reluctantly to depart, but the majority—at least 100, perhaps more—remained seated, silently defying the judge's order. Amused laughter from the men murmured its way around the room. No one among the bailiffs could recall another time when so many spectators had so brazenly challenged a judge's authority.[44]

"I have asked the ladies to leave the room," Caverly repeated angrily. "Now I want you to leave. If you do not, I will have the bailiffs escort you to the hallway. There is nothing left here now but a lot of stuff that is not fit for you to hear." Caverly rapped his gavel on the bench as four bailiffs moved among the crowd, encouraging the women to leave the courtroom. "Step out into the hallway!" he ordered.[45]

An elderly reporter, a woman from one of the city's newspapers, approached the bench. "Does that mean that even us—?"

"It means that all of you ought to go!" interrupted Caverly, waving his arm imperiously at the cluster of female reporters standing before him.[46]

A reading of the report was inconclusive—perhaps. On the one hand, the coroner's physician had concluded that his postmortem had shown "no evidence of a recent forcible dilation." Yet on the other hand, he had written that "the rectum was dilated, [and] would easily admit one finger." Crowe would not back down—after all, the physician had examined the corpse more than twenty-four hours after the murder, and, in the interim, Crowe claimed, other evidence, traces of semen, for example, would have disappeared.[47]

But did Crowe have corroborative evidence of sexual assault? The physician's report, argued Walter Bachrach, favored the defense, and if Crowe wanted to prove rape, he had to provide more substantial evidence that such an attack had indeed occurred. And, if Crowe could not show that either Nathan or Richard had raped the boy, then where was the motive for the crime?

"Before the State's Attorney would be entitled," Bachrach argued, "to draw any inference that there was any evidence of mistreatment of the body in the sexual way, there would have to be some evidence upon which he could base such an argument or from which he could draw such an inference. . . ."

"Oh, no," Crowe interrupted, "there is other evidence."

"Pardon me—?"

"The evidence is that these two defendants are perverts, and when they took the body of the boy in, the first thing they took off was his trousers."[48]

Neither defense nor prosecution, Caverly chided, was able to prove its case. Crowe had made the claim and he had provided his evidence— he had the right, in his closing speech, to summarize his case without interruption from the other side.

"May we have a recess now," Crowe appealed to the judge, "until tomorrow morning?"

"There is nothing further," Caverly asked, "you have now that you want . . . ?"

"I am through with that argument now anyway," Crowe replied.[49]

Robert Crowe returned to court the following day, Wednesday, 27 August, with more revelations. He had caught the defense by surprise the previous day with his accusation that the defendants had sexually assaulted Bobby Franks; now, on the second day of his summation, Crowe once again had come to court prepared to reveal new secrets about the murder.

There was, he claimed, something mysterious about the relationship between the two killers. How had they become locked together in their mutual embrace? Their supposed fantasies, Crowe argued, were fabrications, constructed after the murder, all part of an elaborate scheme to fool the judge into believing that Nathan and Richard were mentally ill. Before the day of the killing, no one had ever heard Nathan mention his desire to be the powerful slave of a beneficent king; nor had Richard ever confided to anyone—apart from Nathan—his wish that he might be a master criminal capable of committing the perfect crime. Because the fantasies had been conjured into existence only after the murder, Crowe argued, those fantasies could not, as the defense had claimed, explain the relationship between Nathan and Richard.

One passage in the Bowman-Hulbert report, the secret report prepared by the defense but leaked to the newspapers, had caught Crowe's attention. Richard had mentioned four crimes—denoted by the letters A, B, C, and D—to the scientists. What were those crimes, Crowe wondered. No one knew; the defense psychiatrists had decided not to ask Richard about them. Did anyone know the deeds Richard claimed to have committed? Yes, replied Crowe, in answer to his own question; there was one person who did know. Nathan Leopold knew, and Nathan had blackmailed Richard Loeb into a sexual relationship. "I will tell you, your honor, and I think I will demonstrate it beyond the peradventure of a doubt," Crowe explained, "that these four episodes, that these four crimes, were known to Leopold, and he blackmailed Loeb, he threatened Loeb with exposure if he did not submit to him, and Loeb had to go along with Leopold. . . . Loeb had committed major crimes, four of them, that he would not even tell his lawyers about, that he would not tell the doctors about, and they concluded it was a bad thing to make inquiry about. . . . Leopold knew about these. . . . Loeb was afraid of Leopold. . . . He contemplated killing him so that he would not be in his power."[50]

The defense had not intended that the Bowman-Hulbert report be made public, but it had found its way to the state's attorney's office nevertheless. Crowe waved his copy triumphantly in his right hand as he addressed the court. What, Crowe asked, as he prepared to read from the report, had Richard Loeb said to the psychiatrists about his companion, Nathan Leopold? "Let us see what the evidence is on that. . . . 'In a way, I have always been sort of afraid of him. He intimidated me by threatening to expose me . . . and I could not stand it.'" Richard had been terrified that Nathan would spill his secrets, terrified enough to contemplate killing Nathan. "He was afraid," Crowe continued, "of Leopold; he was afraid that Leopold might tell of A, B, C and D. 'I could not stand it. I had often thought of the possibility of shooting him.'"[51]

There had been a reason, a very good reason, for Richard's insistence that they kill Bobby Franks by strangulation, each boy pulling on the end of a rope tied around the victim's neck. As soon as Nathan pulled on that rope, he too would be guilty of murder and would no longer be able to blackmail Richard into a sexual relationship. Richard Loeb, Crowe explained, was "to pull one end and Leopold the other; and the reason he wanted that done was [that] . . . Leopold had something on him. Leopold knew about the crimes A, B, C and D, and in this murder he was going to make Leopold pull the rope so he would have something equal on Leopold."[52]

The newspapers had spoken of the search for excitement, a thrill, as a motive for the killing. Two teenagers with too much time on their hands, perhaps, looking for a new sensation. But the Bowman-Hulbert report indicated that Richard Loeb had been a quiet, studious boy. Crowe picked up his copy of the report. "What does Bowman and Hulbert say about it? 'He never appeared to crave a thrill or excitement, but was rather quiet in his conduct.'" Nor, according to the report, had either Nathan or Richard derived any pleasure from the thought of murder. On the contrary; each boy had approached the task with revulsion and apprehension. It was not true, Crowe continued, that the killing had provided Nathan and Richard, as the defense had claimed, with "the thrill that they tried to make you believe. 'They anticipated a few unpleasant minutes.' Not pleasant minutes; not the thrill and the delight and the fast beating heart that they tell you Dickie Loeb has, if he has got a heart at all. 'They anticipated a few unpleasant minutes in strangling him.'"[53]

Clarence Darrow had sneered at the state for its claim that ransom was the motive for the murder. But, Crowe continued, the Bowman-Hulbert report itself, a report commissioned by the defense, demonstrated that money provided the rationale for the kidnapping. Had not Nathan and Richard first fixed on kidnapping a boy whom Nathan disliked, a boy who had insulted Nathan? At that moment, they had not yet thought of a secure way to obtain the money, and so they had abandoned the plan. But if they had been seeking a thrill, why would they not go ahead with the plan? If the ransom was insignificant, as Clarence

Darrow had claimed, why would they abandon their plan on account of the difficulty in obtaining the ransom? And why had Nathan and Richard asked that the ransom be paid in old, unmarked bills? If they had desired only excitement, a thrill, what difference would it have made if the ransom money was marked or unmarked? If they had had no need of the money, why would they have asked for old bills?

"Money is the motive in this case," shouted Crowe, taking up the report once again, "and I will prove it repeatedly by their own evidence. . . . 'Neither of them, however, could think of any simple or certain way of securing the money. They continued to discuss the matter, weighing the pros and con, suggesting methods only to pick flaws in them. In March 1924 the patient conceived the idea of securing'—What? The thrill? The excitement? No. '— conceived the idea of securing the money by having it thrown off of a moving train. This idea was discussed in great detail, and gradually developed into a carefully systematized plan.'"[54]

They had kidnapped Bobby Franks for the ransom, but because Bobby could identify Richard to the police, they had killed him as soon as he had stepped into the car. The murder was ancillary to the kidnapping. If they could have kidnapped the boy without killing him, they would have done so, but since they would have put themselves at risk of capture, they had to commit murder.

"Then the motive for the murder was their own self preservation. You do not have to take my word for it. Take the word of . . . the alienists, who say the boys told them that themselves. 'It was necessary to kill him at once, to avoid any possible identification by the victim should he escape, or their plans go awry.' Was this killing done as we have been led to believe by the defense, merely for the thrill, your honor, or the excitement? What does the doctor further say on that? 'The patient'—Loeb—'did not anticipate the actual killing with any pleasure.' It was not for the thrill or the excitement. The original crime was the kidnaping for money. The killing was an afterthought, to prevent their identification, and their subsequent apprehension and punishment. He said he did not anticipate the killing with any pleasure. It was merely necessary in order to get the money. Motive? 'The killing apparently has no other significance'—now, this is not my argument, your honor, but on page 103 of their own report, their own evidence—'The killing apparently has no other significance than being an inevitable part of a perfect crime in covering one possible trace of identification.' Drs. Hulbert and Bowman were told by these defendants, as I told your honor, that the killing had no significance here except to prevent their being apprehended and convicted if the victim escaped."[55]

Crowe had now finished reading from the Bowman-Hulbert report. As he replaced it on the table, he took up a sheaf of letters held together by a large black metal clip. Several were from Richard's elder brother Allan; others were from Richard's classmates at the University of Michigan; and, as Crowe read each one to the courtroom, his audience heard the evidence of Richard's gambling. Here was a letter from Allan Loeb, dated 19 May 1924, just two days before the murder, warning Richard not to wager so high. Allan was glad to hear that Richard had won so much money from Sammy Schmaltz in a recent card game, but suppose, he warned Richard, instead of winning such a large amount, he had lost. And here was a letter from one of Richard's friends at the University of Michigan, regretting that he had not seen Richard on a recent visit to Chicago—"but I always feel as though I am intruding when you guys are gambling, because I don't gamble that high"—but hoping, nevertheless, to see him soon.[56]

Crowe had more documents on the table, bank statements for Richard's accounts. He picked them up, then spread them fanwise before him on the table. What, Crowe asked, could explain the large amounts of money that flowed into and out of Richard's accounts each month? Richard received a monthly allowance of $250 from his father; yet each month, large sums of money, considerably larger than his allowance, entered and left his bank accounts. In May 1923, he had deposited $645 into his account at the Bank of Charlevoix; in June, he had deposited $683; in July, $588; and in September, $602. In October, Richard had deposited $535 in his account at the Hyde Park State Bank; in November, $1,549; and in December, $420. In 1924, he had continued to deposit approximately $500 into his account each month.

On Thursday, 15 May, just one week before the murder, he had deposited $536.[57]

What was the source of this money? Had he won it at cards? Or was it the proceeds of his crimes? "Would A, B, C and D explain it," Crowe asked, "or explain part of them, or are these moneys that he won in gambling? . . . All the way through, if your honor please, all the way through this most unusual crime runs money, money, money."[58]

It was now almost over. Crowe spoke again on Thursday, 28 August, excoriating Darrow for his philosophy—"his peculiar philosophy of life"—and warning Caverly that any sentence less than hanging would be tantamount to the court's approval of Darrow's beliefs. It was not an end to capital punishment that Darrow sought, Crowe cautioned, but an end to all punishment. For if Leopold and Loeb were not accountable for their actions, could anyone be held to account for any action? Environment and heredity had determined the boys' actions, Darrow had argued, and as a consequence, any punishment for the murder was inappropriate and futile. Darrow, in his closing speech, had absolved Leopold and Loeb of blame for the murder—his success would surely undermine the system of criminal justice.[59]

To sentence them to the penitentiary would be to accept Darrow's argument. Without fixing responsibility, how could one inflict punishment? And without punishment, what would deter crime? It was a recipe for chaos, Crowe warned, and Caverly, if he failed to sentence Leopold and Loeb to death, would condemn himself to obloquy. "I want to tell you the real defense in this case, your honor." Crowe's nasal voice, raspy after speaking for three days, rose above the courtroom like a buzz saw. Crowe's anger was visible in his face as he pointed an accusatory finger at Clarence Darrow. "It is Clarence Darrow's dangerous philosophy of life. He said to your honor that he was not pleading alone for these two young men. He said he was looking to the future, that he was thinking of the ten thousand young boys that in the future would fill the chairs his clients filled and he wants to soften the law. . . . I want to tell your honor that it would be much better if God had not caused this crime to be disclosed. It would have been much better if it went unsolved and these men went unwhipped of justice. It would not have done near the harm to this community as will be done if your honor, as chief justice of this great court, puts your official seal of approval upon the doctrines of anarchy preached by Clarence Darrow as a defense in this case. Society can endure, the law can endure and criminals escape, but if a court such as this court should say that he believes in the doctrine of Darrow, that you ought not to hang when the law says you should, a greater blow has been struck to our institutions than by a hundred, yes, a thousand murders."[60]

It had been Robert Crowe's most eloquent speech in the Criminal Court. He had countered the defense point by point, blow by blow; he had exposed Darrow as a dangerous charlatan; he had even established a motive for the crime. Crowe resumed his seat with quiet confidence and, around him, his colleagues and associates pressed forward to touch his arm and to whisper their congratulations.

John Caverly had already started speaking, addressing himself to the many critics who had faulted his conduct of the hearing. There had been no delay in the administration of justice, Caverly explained. The police had arrested Leopold and Loeb just ten days after the murder; the state's attorney had indicted the suspects within a few days; and the trial had begun six weeks after the grand jury had voted the indictments. The Criminal Court had brought the indictments to trial ahead of thirty-four other indictments for murder in Cook County that year. The wealth and reputation of the families had had no bearing on the case and had never caused any delay in the proceedings.[61]

Some critics wondered why—because Leopold and Loeb had readily confessed—it had been necessary for the Criminal Court to hear any evidence on the murder. But, according to the criminal code of Illinois, Caverly explained, it was the obligation of the court to listen to testimony both in mitigation and in aggravation if either the defense or the prosecution so requested. Commentators in the daily newspapers had frequently made comparisons with the speedy administration of criminal justice in Britain, but such comparisons were beside the point. Since a defendant could not be legally executed in Illinois before the tenth day of the term of the state supreme court after judgment, there could have been no executions in Illinois, whatever the circumstances of the case, before October.[62]

John Caverly had finished. It remained only that he set a date for sentencing, and then the hearing would end. "I am going to take this case under advisement, gentlemen." Caverly leaned forward slightly, speaking to the attorneys gathered before him. "I think I ought to have ten days or so. . . . I will fix the day at September 10th, at 9.30 o'clock, and I will say to those people who are here now that there will be nobody admitted in this room on that day, except members of the press and members of the family and sheriffs and the State's Attorney's staff."[63]

The bailiffs started moving around the room, quietly persuading the crowd to disperse. The photographers abandoned their vantage points, relinquishing their positions at the front of the court; the reporters gathered together their notebooks and pens, pausing only to gossip briefly among themselves; and the stenographers boxed up their machines for the final time. Robert Crowe, ebullient, smiling broadly, and confident of victory, had lit a large cigar and, surrounded by friends and colleagues, was striding toward the exit. Clarence Darrow spoke briefly with Caverly and, looking somber and subdued, stepped ponderously toward the elevator that would take him down to Austin Avenue. The courtroom was soon silent, empty, abandoned—nothing moved except the hands of the clock on the wall as they counted down the hours that remained before John Caverly would pronounce sentence.[64]

16 | SENTENCING

The testimony in this case reveals a crime of singular atrocity. It is, in a sense, inexplicable; but it is not thereby rendered less inhuman or repulsive. It was deliberately planned and prepared for during a considerable period of time. It was executed with every feature of callousness and cruelty. . . . The court is satisfied that neither in the act itself, nor in its motive or lack of motive, nor in the antecedents of the offenders, can he find any mitigating circumstances.[1]

John Caverly, Chief Justice of the
Criminal Court, 10 September 1924

BRIGHT SUNLIGHT FLOODED THE LIVING room. The maid had recently cleaned the apartment, and swirls of dust, launched into the air by her exertions, were caught in the rays of light that filtered through the large windows that faced onto Lake Michigan.

The ringing of the telephone broke the stillness of the afternoon. John Caverly was not there to answer it—he was spending the day at a funeral service for a college friend—but his wife, Charlotte, was in their apartment at the Edgewater Beach Hotel, and now she stepped across the living room to the hallway to pick up the receiver.

Even though the hearing on Nathan Leopold and Richard Loeb had almost ended, she was still finding it difficult to relax. So many cranks had bombarded John with their demands and threats—hundreds and hundreds, it seemed, all wanting the judge to send Leopold and Loeb to the gallows and threatening to kill John if he saved them from execution and sent them to the penitentiary.

She answered the phone and heard the click as the operator made the connection. The man's voice on the other end was deep and authoritative; it boomed the news down the wire with sudden, shocking clarity,

"This is Captain Roberts of the police department." The speaker paused slightly as if he were gathering breath. "Your husband, the judge, was shot to death as he was entering the gate of Calvary cemetery. He is there now! Come quick!"

Charlotte Caverly gave a short, sharp scream. The receiver fell to the floor. It was only a few steps to the door, where, outside the apartment, a police guard was standing watch.

"Quick! Get an automobile," she shouted at the young constable. "My husband has been shot."[2]

It was a cruel hoax. John Caverly stood by the cemetery entrance, chatting in a small group of college friends, as the police car screeched to a halt and his wife ran to his side, crying that she had thought he was killed.

IT WAS A MALICIOUS TRICK THAT RATCHETED the tension tighter, now only nine days before Wednesday, 10 September, when Caverly would pronounce his decision. Caverly was, for the moment at least, the focus of the cranks; he was receiving hundreds of letters every day urging the death penalty for Leopold and Loeb. Occasionally the threat to his personal safety was more visceral: on 5 September, Harry Rabinowitz, a former patient at the Illinois Northern Hospital for the Insane, was found roaming the corridors of the Criminal Court Building with a razor in his pocket, demanding to speak to Caverly.[3]

Caverly's term as chief justice of the Criminal Court concluded on 31 August, only three days after Robert Crowe's closing statement had marked the end of the hearing. Caverly would have preferred his valediction to be less controversial, less contentious. As he moved through his rooms in the Criminal Court Building on Friday, 30 August, packing up his law books, he reflected that whatever his decision on 10 September, he was certain to disappoint someone; his career as a judge would end in the most explosive possible manner.[4]

He had not yet, Caverly admitted to a reporter from the *Chicago American*, decided on the punishment; he would think it over that week and write his verdict on the following weekend. He regretted only that the decision was his alone—it was a heavy burden for one man to carry. "I wish this case had gone to a jury. If it had gone to a jury I would be the thirteenth man and not the one and only one to render the decision. I think at least three judges should sit in all such cases." Perhaps, as part of his closing statement, he would suggest "a new law to cover cases of this kind . . . that hereafter when a plea of guilty is entered or a jury trial waived in a capital case, three judges be required to hear the case and render a decision."[5]

WHILE JOHN CAVERLY MARKED the conclusion of the hearing with arrangements for his retirement, Jacob Franks was preparing to sell the family home on Ellis Avenue. The situation had become insufferable: every day, crowds of spectators gathered outside the house, gawking, pointing, staring, waiting expectantly for a member of the family to appear, and ignoring requests from the police guard to move on. Cars passed slowly up and down the street, circling the block, their occupants hoping to glimpse something that would make the journey to Kenwood worthwhile. And each morning, the mailman would deliver hundreds of letters, some in sympathy, but the majority in hatred and anger and avarice, threatening the Franks children; demanding money;

scolding the parents for some imaginary reason; or proposing fantastical theories about Bobby's death.[6]

It was a bitter daily reminder of their son's death that Jacob and Flora Franks could see the Loeb family home on the other side of the street; it was an unpleasant coincidence that fifteen years previously, Jacob Franks had purchased from Albert Loeb the lot on which his house stood. And so, on 30 August, Joseph Trinz, owner of the movie theater chain Lubiner & Trinz, bought the house for $60,000. The Franks family then moved to a suite of rooms in the Drake Hotel, far from the street that had given them so much pain.[7]

Throughout the hearing, Albert and Anna Loeb had stayed at their country estate, Charlevoix. Now it seemed unlikely that they would ever return to their house at 5017 Ellis Avenue; it was more probable that they would sell it as quickly as possible.

Only Nathan Leopold Sr. had any desire to remain in Kenwood; a widower since the death of his wife three years previously, he was reluctant to move away from his many friends in the neighborhood. "I have known happiness here," he told his sons, "I have found peace in the past in this home, and no matter where I go, I can find no greater peace."[8]

WHILE THE FAMILIES AGONIZED OVER such decisions, Nathan Leopold and Richard Loeb spent their days in the Cook County jail greeting visitors, playing baseball in the prison yard, and talking with reporters.

Some of their observations to the journalists seemed calculated to provoke, to provide images of pampered youths now confined to a prison regimen that was, nevertheless, not unduly onerous. The warden, Wesley Westbrook, had arranged for Sunday concerts in the prison; Nathan and Richard attended with the other prisoners and seemed to enjoy themselves, even if there was an occasional reminder of happier days. Richard recalled to a journalist that he had first heard the tune "Hot Lips" at a "dancing party on a yacht on Lake Michigan three years ago. I was dancing with my partner along the deck, close to the rail, the waves rolling, the boat pitching and tossing, to that tune." And now he was hearing it again, but this time in the prison canteen inside the county jail.

But, Richard said, things could be worse, and he was not at all despondent. Prison life was good for him; he now had "regular meals, regular exercise and regular sleep. . . . I am feeling fine. Instead of getting in at 3 a.m. and getting up at 7 to play golf or tennis, I now get at least eight hours regular sleep."[9]

Richard and Nathan were never bored. There were always visitors: former girlfriends, relatives, and classmates—and many casual visitors, unknown to either of them, who simply dropped by for a chat and a gossip. The murderers had become celebrities; and in the relaxed atmosphere of the county jail, Wesley Westbrook permitted them to see anyone they wished. On one memorable occasion, six players from the Chicago Cubs appeared at the warden's office with a request "to tour the jail and see the young murderers." Charles (Gabby) Hartnett, one of the team's leading sluggers, spent time with Nathan in the prison yard, coaching him on his batting style, advising him on his swinging movements and his stance at the plate.[10]

Their celebrity was exhilarating. Their every remark found its way into the newspapers: only Edward, Prince of Wales, then on a weeklong visit to the United States, received more attention in the media. Nathan announced plans to write his biography, which, he promised, he would offer to the newspapers for serialization before publishing it as a book. "I want to write my memoirs," he told the reporters, "including an absolutely frank and clear record of my life in jail and of the reactions experienced by a prisoner. . . . Perhaps I will sell it to the highest bidder; perhaps the reporter who has given me the best breaks will get it. I don't know just yet."[11]

And if he were to be executed? Nathan had already drawn up his will; he would leave his bird collection to the Field Museum of Natural History, and no doubt his specimens would take pride of place among the museum's collections.[12]

Nathan had read in the newspapers that bookies were offering odds as high as three to one against a death sentence. Thousands of dollars had been wagered on the result in Chicago's betting shops. Perhaps,

Nathan suggested to the reporters, they should have a wager among themselves. "You fellows ought to get up a parlay on it," he joked. He would like to bet on the result himself, he added, but the regulations in the county jail forbade the prisoners from gambling.[13]

Nathan was an intellectual, of course—they had not forgotten, had they?—and, if he was hanged, he informed the journalists, he would communicate with them from beyond the grave, answering their questions on such topics as the nature of happiness, the relationship between spiritual and physical existence, the rewards and penalties of the afterlife, and the ability to experience sensations after death.

Perhaps, Nathan continued, he would make a speech from the gallows, a speech that would command everyone's attention! "I will say something," he predicted to the reporter from the New York Sun, "that will make the world listen."[14]

His brother Michael visited Nathan in jail to warn him of the distress his comments were causing his father, but Nathan was reluctant to leave the stage—it was impossible to force him away from the spotlight, no matter how much grief he caused his relatives.

CLARENCE DARROW HAD LONG AGO abandoned all hope of getting Nathan to desist from making foolish statements to the press. In any case, the defense attorneys were preoccupied with possible appeals if Caverly imposed the death penalty.

For example, could the defense appeal to the Illinois supreme court for a second trial on a writ of error? Because of the guilty plea, Darrow believed, that possibility would be the least likely option available to the defense. "I'm of the opinion that the court has final jurisdiction because of the plea," Darrow told a reporter from the Chicago American; "I doubt if a writ of error could be prayed for."[15]

On the other hand, the trial of Gene Geary in 1921 had provided a precedent for an appeal based on the claim that Nathan and Richard had become insane since sentencing. It had worked for Gene Geary; why would it not work for them? True, a jury must decide the sanity of Nathan and Richard, but perhaps, Darrow believed, enough time would have elapsed between the murder and a second trial for some of the public indignation to fade away.

That was their best chance, and so, even before Caverly had given his verdict, statements began to appear in the newspapers—planted by the defense attorneys, of course—that both Nathan and Richard were rapidly deteriorating. Nathan Leopold's mental condition was already cause for concern, one anonymous source claimed; despite his apparent buoyancy in prison, Nathan showed "very definite traces of dementia praecox."[16]

If the Illinois supreme court allowed an appeal on the claim that Nathan and Richard had become insane since sentencing, the jury in a second trial would decide on the sanity of the defendants. If they were sane, they would be immediately executed; if, however, they had become insane, then the court would send them to the Illinois Asylum for Insane Criminals at Chester and the death sentences would be carried out only if they regained their sanity.[17]

Other possibilities existed but seemed remote. The judge might, on his own initiative, decide that the defendants' sanity was in question; if so, he would, instead of passing sentence, convene a jury to decide the question of their sanity.

Alternatively, Clarence Darrow could present a motion to the judge asking permission to withdraw the guilty plea and change the plea to not guilty. The recent trial of Russell Scott, a street hoodlum who had killed a store clerk during a robbery at the City Hall pharmacy, gave Darrow a legal precedent. Scott's lawyer, Walter Stanton, had insisted that the court had not formally notified his client that the judge could send him to the gallows. But this too seemed an improbable course of action for Darrow. John Caverly had been punctilious in advising Nathan and Richard that he had the power to sentence them to death if they pleaded guilty.[18]

Such speculation might continue endlessly—or at least until the judge pronounced his verdict on 10 September.

IN THE CRIMINAL COURT BUILDING on the eve of sentencing, the sheriff, Peter Hoffman, was meeting with the chief bailiff, Thomas

Brockmeyer. Hoffman was worried. He had received many threats—threats to kill the judge, threats to blow up the Criminal Court Building, threats to lynch Leopold and Loeb. And as many as 5,000 people might gather outside the Criminal Court, all hoping to enter the courtroom; Hoffman had to ensure that the crowd did not overwhelm his police force.[19]

So, on Tuesday evening, just fourteen hours before Caverly was to pronounce sentence, Hoffman rehearsed with Brockmeyer the security details for tomorrow's court hearing. There would be seventy highway policemen, all on motorcycles, to guard the streets around the Criminal Court Building; fifty mounted policemen would patrol Austin Avenue to protect the entrance; and over 100 patrolmen would establish a cordon around the building. Five squads of detectives would gather immediately in front of the entrance, both to deter illegitimate intruders and to provide protection to the judge and the attorneys as they arrived. Plainclothes policemen would mingle with the crowd beyond the line of uniformed patrolmen; they were there to spot potential assassins and gunmen. Thomas Brockmeyer would assign dozens of sheriffs and bailiffs to the corridors and elevators inside the Criminal Court Building. All other court sessions had been canceled, and no one would be allowed into the building except to attend Caverly's court on the sixth floor.[20]

Clarence Darrow, Walter and Benjamin Bachrach, members of the Leopold and Loeb families—all had received death threats through the mail. Even the psychiatrists were in fear of their lives—Harold Hulbert had requested an armed bodyguard after death threats had arrived at his home. But clearly Caverly was in the greatest danger; he told a reporter from the *New York Times* that he had "received threats which appear to have been sent in good faith, telling me that I will be killed in every manner, from crucifixion to being blown to pieces."[21]

Could anything go wrong? Hoffman could not imagine tighter security; he had checked and rechecked all the possibilities. Could someone, nevertheless—a lone gunman, perhaps—get access to the building and kill Nathan Leopold and Richard Loeb? Was Caverly safe from an assassin? Had all possible precautions been taken?

At eight-thirty on the morning of Wednesday, 10 September, Caverly, wearing a black suit and a gray fedora, emerged from the Edgewater Beach Hotel. Michael Hughes, the chief of detectives, escorted the judge to the limousine waiting by the curb and sat next to him on the rear seat. Two detectives, both dressed in street clothes, sat on a seat directly opposite, facing the rear of the car; each carried a machine gun, and Caverly noticed that each had a large black revolver tucked inside his belt. At the front, a police marksman sat next to the driver, his pump-action shotgun resting at a slight angle to his arm.

The limousine purred its way south on Sheridan Road. Two squad cars provided an escort; each contained armed deputies, their guns hidden unobtrusively below the line of sight from street level.

At Dearborn and Illinois streets, the lead driver showed his star to the police captain and the cavalcade made its way through the first police line. At Austin Avenue, the mounted police moved aside to let the cars pass, and as Caverly's car drew up to the entrance of the Criminal Court Building, Peter Hoffman detached himself from the small group of detectives to usher the judge into the building.[22]

It was now five minutes past nine and already the courtroom was full. No casual spectators were present—Hoffman had restricted entry to those with an immediate interest in the case: relatives and family members, attorneys and expert witnesses, journalists, photographers, court officials, and bailiffs. The crowd waited expectantly. Almost 200 people now filled the courtroom. Albert and Anna Loeb were not present to support their son—Albert Loeb had had a heart attack four days earlier, and he was recovering at Charlevoix. But Richard's brother Allan and his uncle Jacob Loeb were both in the courtroom, as were Nathan's father and his elder brother, Michael. Jacob Franks had been a daily presence in the courtroom throughout the hearing, but now he was absent. Only one member of the Franks family was in court that morning: Edwin Greshan, Bobby's uncle, sat immediately behind the state's attorney, waiting expectantly for the judge to appear.[23]

It was now nine-thirty. Caverly had given his permission to the radio station WGN to transmit from the courtroom that day, and now the broadcast was going out live across Chicago. Throughout the city, groups of Chicagoans clustered around radio sets to listen: the metropolis had paused in its morning bustle to hear the verdict. Housewives, shopkeepers, clerks, stenographers, construction workers, bankers and businessmen in the Loop, salesmen, transit workers—the city had come to a halt.[24]

Caverly had already entered the courtroom and was now mounting the steps to the bench. He carried a sheaf of documents in his right hand, and as he took his position he began to open a brown manila envelope and remove the three sheets of lined paper on which he had written his verdict.

"Hear ye, hear ye," the bailiff's voice suddenly rang out through the court, bringing the spectators to order, "this honorable branch of the Circuit Court of Cook County is now in session." On the other side of the room, the clerk sang out the signal for the appearance of the defendants: "Richard Loeb and Nathan Leopold Jr." From a side entrance in the middle of the courtroom, both boys appeared, surrounded by guards, to make their way to chairs at the front of the room, slightly behind Clarence Darrow.

Before delivering his decision, Caverly addressed the defense attorneys, "Have the two defendants anything to say in either case?"

Benjamin Bachrach replied in a firm, clear voice, "No, your honor."

Caverly began reading. First he took up the appeal for mitigation of punishment; the defense had suggested the guilty plea, the age of the defendants, and their mental condition as grounds for mitigation.

But the judge replied that the guilty plea in this case did not conform to the customary pattern. It had been pleaded without the knowledge or consent of the state's attorney and had not lessened the work either of the court or of the state's attorney: "the plea of guilty did not in this particular case, as it usually does, render the task of the prosecution easier by substituting admission of guilt for a possibly difficult and uncertain chain of proof. . . . The plea of guilty, therefore, does not make a special case in favor of the defendants."[25]

So there was nothing in mitigation on account of the guilty plea!

Caverly's voice had become a monotone; it droned on into the still air of the courtroom, flat and unemotional, but still the audience sat entranced, listening to every word.

"By pleading guilty," Caverly continued, "the defendants have admitted legal responsibility for their acts; the testimony has satisfied the court that the case is not one in which it could have been possible to set up successfully the defense of insanity." So Caverly would not, after all, convene a jury to decide the sanity of the defendants—perhaps Darrow would consider that route on appeal, but Caverly had concluded that the defendants could distinguish right from wrong and were thus legally sane.

Did the psychiatric evidence mean anything? Was Caverly willing to accept the psychiatrists' testimony as evidence of mental disease and consider it in mitigation?

"The court . . . feels impelled to dwell briefly on the mass of data produced as to the physical, mental and moral condition of the two defendants. They have been shown in essential respects to be abnormal. . . . The careful analysis made of the life history of the defendants and of their present mental, emotional, and ethical condition has been of extreme interest. . . . And yet the court feels strongly that similar analyses made of other persons accused of crime would probably reveal similar or different abnormalities. . . . For this reason the court is satisfied that his judgment in the present case cannot be affected thereby."

Elliptical language, but clear enough—now it seemed that Caverly was also to deny mental disease as a mitigating factor.

"The testimony in this case reveals a crime of singular atrocity. It is, in a sense, inexplicable; but it is not thereby rendered less inhuman or repulsive. It was deliberately planned and prepared for during a considerable period of time. It was executed with every feature of callousness and cruelty. . . . The court is satisfied that neither in the act itself, nor in its motive or lack of motive, nor in the antecedents of the offenders, can he find any mitigating circumstances."

Nathan Leopold Sr. sat directly behind his son, his arms gripping the back of his son's chair, his head inclined down, his eyes fixed on the floor. He raised his head to look at the judge; there were tears forming in his eyes as he heard that there was to be no mitigation. Jacob Loeb stared fixedly ahead, not directly at the judge but at the dais—he too looked forlorn as he heard the words that would kill his nephew. Toward the back of the court, there was now a slight stirring; the reporters were preparing to race to the telephones to read the death sentence to their editors; the messengers were already moving toward the door, ready to tell the wire services that Leopold and Loeb were to be hanged.[26]

Caverly had promised himself to include in his sentencing an appeal that in the future, such decisions not be devolved upon a single judge; now he made good on his promise. "In reaching his decision the court would have welcomed the counsel and support of others. In some states the legislature in its wisdom has provided for a bench of three judges to determine the penalty in cases such as this. Nevertheless the court is willing to meet his responsibilities."

But now, when everyone had already decided that Nathan and Richard were to be executed, Caverly began reading the words that would offer them hope.

"It would have been the path of least resistance to impose the extreme penalty of the law."

Nathan and Richard exchanged glances; could this be their salvation from the scaffold?

The words came slowly, almost ponderously, as though Caverly were teasing the courtroom with his verdict. "In choosing imprisonment instead of death the court is moved chiefly by the consideration of the age of the defendants, boys of 18 and 19 years. . . . The court believes that it is within his province to decline to impose the sentence of death on persons who are not of full age.

"This determination appears to be in accordance with the progress of criminal law all over the world and with the dictates of enlightened humanity. More than that, it seems to be in accordance with the precedents hitherto observed in this state. The records of Illinois show only two cases of minors who were put to death by legal process—to which number the court does not feel inclined to make an addition.

"Life imprisonment may not, at the moment, strike the public imagination as forcibly as would death by hanging but to the offenders, particularly of the type they are, the prolonged suffering of years of confinement may well be the severer form of retribution and expiation.

"The court feels it proper to add a final word concerning the effect of the parole law upon the punishment of these defendants. In the case of such atrocious crimes it is entirely within the discretion of the department of public welfare never to admit these defendants to parole. To such a policy the court urges them strictly to adhere. If this course is persevered in the punishment of these defendants will both satisfy the ends of justice and safeguard the interests of society.

"In number 33623, indictment for murder, the sentence of the Court is that you, Nathan F. Leopold, Jr., be confined in the penitentiary at Joliet for the term of your natural life. . . .

"In 33623, indictment for murder, the sentence of the Court is that you, Richard Loeb, be confined in the penitentiary at Joliet for the term of your natural life. . . .

"In 33624, kidnaping for ransom, it is the sentence of the Court that you, Nathan F. Leopold, Jr., be confined in the penitentiary at Joliet for the term of ninety-nine years.

"In 33624, kidnaping for ransom, the sentence of the Court is that you, Richard Loeb, be confined in the penitentiary at Joliet for the term of ninety-nine years.

"The Sheriff may retire with the prisoners."[27]

THE VERDICT—NINETY-NINE YEARS for kidnapping, life for the murder—was a victory for the defense, a defeat for the state. The guards allowed Nathan and Richard to shake Darrow's hand before escorting the prisoners back to the cells. Two dozen reporters crowded around the defense table to hear Darrow's response to the verdict, but even in his moment of victory, Darrow was careful not to seem too triumphal. "Well, it's just what we asked for but . . . it's pretty tough." He pushed back a lock of hair that had fallen over his forehead. "It was more of a punishment than death would have been."[28]

He gave a characteristic shrug of his shoulders, a shrug of relief that he could now focus on the cause for which he had argued so long. "I have always hated capital punishment. This decision . . . caps my career as a criminal lawyer and starts my path in another direction. . . . I shall begin now to plan a definite campaign against capital punishment in Illinois. Perhaps I may be able to take up the matter with the legislature immediately."[29]

Nathan Leopold Sr. had already left the courtroom—he was too overcome to talk to the journalists—but Jacob Loeb remained behind to say a few words. "We have been spared the death penalty; but what have these families to look forward to? . . . Here are two families whose names here stood for everything that was good and reputable in the community. Now what have they to look forward to? Their unfortunate boys, aged 19 years, must spend the rest of their lives in prison. What is there in the future but grief and sorrow, darkness and despair?"

Robert Crowe was furious at the judge's decision; how could the death penalty ever again be imposed if these two malicious killers had escaped with a prison term? True, Caverly had asked that Leopold and Loeb never win parole, but it was at least possible that they would eventually be released. It was a bitterly disappointing verdict, and in his statement to the press, Crowe made sure everyone knew whom to blame. "When the state's attorney arrested the defendants he solved what was then a mystery. And by the thoroughness of his preparation of the case, the state's attorney forced the defendants to plead guilty, presented a mountain of evidence to the court and made his arguments.

"The state's attorney's duty was fully performed. He is in no measure responsible for the decision of the court. The responsibility for that decision rests with the judge alone."[30]

Later that day, Jacob Franks also spoke to the reporters. He was pleased that it was finally over. There was now no possibility that the defense would appeal the sentence. "There can be no hearing in regard to their sanity," Franks said; "there can be no appeal, there can be no more torture by seeing this thing spread over the front pages of the newspapers. It will be easier for Mrs. Franks and for me to be relieved of the terrible strain of all this publicity."[31]

NEITHER NATHAN NOR RICHARD HAD ever expressed remorse for the killing, and neither thought now to use their final interview with the press to admit contrition. Nathan, back in his cell in the county jail, was his customary imperious self; he called to the sheriff, Peter Hoffman, with one final request.

"Go out," he commanded, "and order us a big meal. Get us two steaks"— he held out his thumb and forefinger—"that thick!"

"Yes, and be sure," Richard chimed in, "they are smothered in onions. And bring every side dish you can find. This may be our last good meal."

"And," Nathan added, "bring chocolate éclairs for dessert."

At eight o'clock that evening, Nathan was fast asleep on his bunk. Richard sat smoking a cigarette, sitting on the edge of his bed, an unfinished novel lying beside him, watching through the bars of his cell as the guards patrolled the corridor. Detectives from police headquarters stood in the main lobby of the Cook County jail while uniformed police, in addition to the jailers, kept watch on the hallways and corridors.

Tomorrow they would leave on a dangerous journey to the Joliet penitentiary.

Feelings about the verdict ran deep in Chicago. It was a provocation that two pampered rich boys had gotten away with murder—every Chicagoan had hoped to see Leopold and Loeb swinging from the end of a rope. It seemed a travesty, an affront, that Bobby Franks was in his grave yet Leopold and Loeb were very much alive, eating chocolate éclairs and bantering with the journalists.

That evening Robert Crowe issued another statement. It was a provocative, inflammatory statement that said more about the boys' relationship than anyone had ever before publicly revealed; Crowe now gave substance to the rumor that Leopold and Loeb were homosexuals.

"In malice, premeditation, and deliberation the crime of these defendants is unequaled in the criminal history of the state. It is an

atrocious and cold blooded murder . . . executed after months of planning and careful deliberation. . . . The evidence indicated acts of perversion between Leopold and Loeb extending over a long period of
time. The evidence indicated that Loeb had committed other crimes . . .
major crimes of a serious nature. Both defendants were known to have
associates of a loose and immoral character, and Loeb had a venereal
disease at 15.

"Both had the reputation of being immoral . . . degenerates of the
worst type. . . . The evidence shows that both defendants are atheists
and followers of the Nietzschean doctrines . . . that they are above the
law, both the law of God and the law of man. . . . The murder and kidnaping for ransom of 14 year old Robert Franks struck terror to the
heart of every father and mother throughout the community. . . . It is
unfortunate for the welfare of the community that they were not sentenced to death."[32]

Crowe might have waited until Leopold and Loeb were safely locked
up in Joliet Prison before releasing his statement. Now he had magnified the prisoners' villainy and greatly increased the danger to their
lives on the car journey from Chicago to the penitentiary. Would someone take Crowe's words as a license to kill? Would there be an ambush
on the road to Joliet?

FEARS OF AN ATTACK PROVED exaggerated; no one ambushed the
motorcade. But there was almost a nasty accident on the road; as the
three-car convoy proceeded along the highway, the brakes on the lead
car, a black Cadillac sedan, suddenly locked. Leopold and Loeb,
traveling in the second car, a Packard limousine, at fifty miles an hour,
received an unpleasant jolting—their driver swerved to avoid the Cadillac, veered off the roadway, and ended up on the adjacent tracks of
the Chicago, Joliet and Elgin Railroad. They suffered only minor
bruises, and after the sheriffs had pushed the Packard back onto the
road, the motorcade proceeded once again to the penitentiary.[33]

As they approached the prison, they could see the high sandstone

35. LEOPOLD AND LOEB ENTER JOLIET PRISON.

walls of the penitentiary illuminated in the headlights of the cars. A huge crowd waited by the large gates to greet the two celebrities; as the cars approached, a roar of recognition rose up from the mob. Sheriffs and prison guards battled to clear a path through the prison gates, and within seconds Nathan Leopold and Richard Loeb were inside Joliet Prison.

The lock in the center door clanked as the key was turned to shut out the world. The prison, first opened in 1858, was a forbidding place at the best of times; now, in the twilight, the massive stone walls behind them and the steel-barred gates in front conspired to give the penitentiary a menacing, threatening atmosphere. Richard stumbled on a paving stone, but caught himself, as he stepped toward the first steel gate; Nathan looked around and noticed the prison guards staring silently down at them from a second-floor gallery, their rifles, cradled in their arms, pointing skyward.[34]

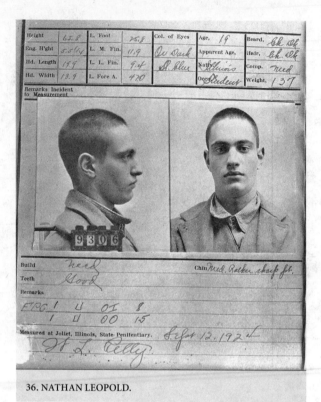

Height	65.8	L. Foot	75.8	Col. of Eyes		Age,	19	Beard,	Bk Bk
Eng. H'ght	5.5½	L. M. Fin.	11.9	Gr Dark		Apparent Age,		Hair,	Bk Bk
Hd. Length	18.9	L. L. Fin.	9.4	Sl. Blue		Nat Illinois		Comp.	med
Hd. Width	13.9	L. Fore A.	47.0			Occ Student		Weight,	137

Remarks Incident
to Measurement

Build — med
Teeth — Good
Remarks
ETPG 1 U OI 8
       1 U OO 15

Measured at Joliet, Illinois, State Penitentiary. Sept 12, 1924

36. NATHAN LEOPOLD.

The warden, John L. Whitman, received the confinement papers from the Cook County sheriff, who turned to leave for the ride back to Chicago. It was already eight-thirty in the evening; there was no time tonight to go through the customary procedures—photographs, medical history, paperwork; those could wait for the morning. Three guards escorted the prisoners across the jail yard, past the shadowy form of the bakery on the left, and down a gravel path to the isolation block for new arrivals. The prisoners had ten minutes for a shower in the bathhouse and then a new set of clothes: Richard had discarded his golf sweater and gray flannel trousers and Nathan had removed his suit jacket and trousers; now the guards provided both prisoners with the standard prison uniform of blue denim jacket and pants.[35]

Both boys lay on straw mattresses in their cells—Nathan at the east

Height	74.7	L. Foot	27.0	Col. of Eyes	19	Age,	19	Beard.	Ch Dk
Eng. H'ght	5.8¾	L. M. Fin.	11.6			Apparent Age,		Hair.	Ch Dk
Hd. Length	19.6+	L. L. Fin.	9.9			Illinois		Comp.	med
Hd. Width	15.2	L. Fore A.	47.8+					Weight,	160

Remarks Incident to Measurement

Build _med._

Teeth _Good_

Remarks

EPC 5   R   17
_17   Uw   15_

Measured at Joliet, Illinois, State Penitentiary. _Sept 12, 1924_

By _Fi L Pitty_

37. RICHARD LOEB.

end of the block; Richard, as far distant as possible, in a cell at the other end of the corridor. In the darkness, staring at the ceiling, not thinking to go asleep, but just running over the day's events, they could hear the murmur of the guards' voices in the corridor, beyond the cell bars.

Very soon both Nathan and Richard were fast asleep; they spent their first night in Joliet peacefully.

17 | THE AFTERMATH

I was asked in Pottsville whether L & L would ever get out. I replied that the law of Ill. permitted a pardon or parole after twenty years:—Whether they would ever get out no one could say.[1]

Clarence Darrow, December 1924

C— sort of hates to admit that he is *NOT* rather well-off, after all the world supposing that he reaped *such* a reward from the L-&-L case ooo, ooo, lalala-lalala-LA! while, in truth, for that he received LESS than for anything that took so much time and tissue out of him and his life.[2]

Ruby Darrow, n.d. (1925)

LIFE IN PRISON! CAVERLY'S DECISION, according to the editor of the *Newark Evening News*, was a travesty of justice. It would surely confirm the popular prejudice that even in a court of law, the rich could purchase the result they desired. "There is one law for those who can command unlimited resources and the highest legal talent, another for the poor devil who must take his chance with the best he can afford. . . . The machinery of justice in Illinois has once more operated to an end that comes close to accounting for the murder-ridden criminal record of Chicago."[3]

It was a theme endlessly repeated in newspaper editorials: money had subverted justice; wealth had done away with the principle that all were equal before the law. The crime had been atrocious, one that conspicuously deserved the death penalty, yet the defendants had escaped the scaffold solely because they had had the wherewithal to purchase the guile and ingenuity of Clarence Darrow. "In the criminal history of the country there is nowhere recorded a more cold-blooded, a more sinister and cruel murder than that of young Franks," the San Francisco *Bulletin* declared. "It was done with extreme cunning by youths—one 19 years of age, the other 18—of exceptional education, intelligence and careful breeding. In the face of these facts Judge Caverly has given to Leopold and Loeb an 'easy sentence.' . . . Judge Caverly's verdict . . . will tend to a lowered confidence in our machinery of justice. . . . It is to be feared that it will augment a growing sense that there is one law for the obscure and another for the socially powerful." The editor of the *Kansas City Post* warned that anarchists and other malcontents would point to the judge's decision as evidence of a divided society: "The theory that there is one set of laws for the rich and another for the friendless poor has received substantial support as a civil propaganda gnawing at the very vitals of national confidence and pride."[4]

But did the wealth of the defendants in fact have any influence on the decision? Caverly had based the sentence on only one criterion—the youth of Leopold and Loeb—and in his conclusion he had explicitly disregarded the psychiatric evidence. In this light, therefore, the efforts of Clarence Darrow and the testimony of the medical experts had been of no account and had no effect on Caverly's determinations. "What the lawyers did or said for the defense went for nothing," wrote the editor of the *New York Times*. "Judge Caverly simply ignored it. Had the youthful murderers been poor and friendless they would have escaped capital punishment precisely as Leopold and Loeb have escaped it. The Judge has effectually stopped the mouths of those who might have been inclined to complain that in Illinois there is one law for the poor and another for the rich."[5]

But was this not, nevertheless, an arbitrary decision? What was it about the youth of Leopold and Loeb that entitled them to escape hanging? There was no clause in the Illinois statutes that excused murderers younger than twenty-one from the death penalty. On what grounds did Caverly use their age as a reason to save Leopold and Loeb from the scaffold? Did Caverly believe that because they were nineteen and eighteen years old, respectively, their judgment was therefore necessarily inchoate and immature? Was their sense of responsibility necessarily diminished because they were still teenagers? Neither Leopold nor Loeb had shown any signs of immaturity in his academic career; moreover, the planning of the murder had demonstrated calculation and determination, qualities difficult to reconcile with immaturity. "It is narrow legalism to excuse Loeb and Leopold on the score of their youth," the *St. Paul Dispatch* argued. "In a formal sense they certainly do comply with the definition. They are, in years, youths and they did enter a plea of guilty. Yet, in any real sense they are not youths, their crime was not an outburst of youthful irresponsibility, and if they had not committed this crime no one would have judged them intellectually 'immature.'"[6]

At what point had Caverly arrived at his decision? He had known the age of each defendant at the beginning of the hearing. Had he determined, at that moment, that they were too young to hang? Surely not! "It is repugnant to all our concepts of law and justice," wrote the editor of the New York *Sun*, "to suppose that a Judge, knowing that the law provided for capital punishment in certain cases, would take his seat to try these cases, predetermined not to inflict capital punishment." Yet it seemed equally unlikely that Caverly would suddenly decide, during the hearing, that the youth of Leopold and Loeb precluded the death penalty. It was a puzzle made even more inscrutable by the defendants' behavior in the courtroom, continued the *Sun*. "During the trial Loeb and Leopold did not conduct themselves in a manner suggestive of youth. Neither indicated the least repentance for the shocking crime to which they had pleaded guilty. . . . Not once, we are sure, did either of the murderers impress anybody—except perhaps Judge Caverly—with his youth. . . . And yet it must have been during that period that the Judge, who had begun the trial knowing the ages of the defendants and knowing that capital punishment still existed in Illinois, decided within himself that . . . these murderers were too young to be hanged."[7]

And if murderers below the age of twenty-one should not be executed, should not all such murderers be spared? Why some and not others? Many youths had received the death sentence in Cook County for lesser crimes; many were now sitting in the Cook County jail awaiting execution. Should not those cases now be reviewed?

In the excitement attendant on the sentencing, everyone had forgotten about Bernard Grant, the nineteen-year-old convicted of the murder of Ralph Souders, the policeman guarding the A&P store on Morgan Street. But now the newspapers took up Grant's cause. Leopold and Loeb had escaped death, but Grant sat in Cook County jail awaiting his imminent execution. "Bernard Grant, of Chicago, is puzzled," the *Detroit Free Press* explained, "and what's bewildering him is this: Bernard is nineteen years old, just the age of Nathan Leopold. But while Leopold escaped the gallows on account of his 'youth,' Bernard is to be hanged by the neck until he is dead. . . . Bernard thinks this isn't fair. Yet it is all plain enough if only you get the right angle. Bernard Grant is a poor boy. He was obliged to quit school at fourteen in order to help support his family. Consequently, he never was able to save enough money to hire a high-priced, emotional lawyer who makes a specialty of cheating the gallows. When he got into trouble, he had to take what counsel he could get. . . . The very fact that Grant thinks an injustice is being done to him shows how inexperienced and unsophisticated he is. Without money, without influence, without ability to entertain the crowd, without opportunity to get the alienists to talking, and writing yards and yards of deduction largely buncombe, it was silly of him to think he ever had a chance." According to the *Cleveland Plain Dealer*, a movement was afoot in Chicago to petition the governor of Illinois to commute Grant's death sentence to life in prison. "There are murmurs in Chicago. . . . Grant is without education, son of a day laborer. . . . There is a feeling that the execution of the capital sentence will be a proof of the double standard of law—one law for the poor and another law for the rich."[8]

Would Clarence Darrow exert himself on behalf of Bernard Grant? Grant was as deserving as Nathan Leopold and Richard Loeb—perhaps more so. Mary Grant, his mother, claimed that he had been wrongly identified and bitterly compared his fate with that of Leopold and Loeb: "My boy is innocent. He was home asleep when they say he killed the policeman. . . . They convicted my boy just the same. . . . What can we do? We were not able to hire alienists at $250 a day to say he is insane." Even the *Chicago Daily Tribune*, the scourge of the criminal class, now urged clemency for Grant—"if he hangs while Loeb and Leopold live, the inequality of our process of justice will be gross"—while simultaneously admitting that life in prison for the murderer of a policeman would, as a general rule, be a regrettable outcome.[9]

Grant did eventually win a reprieve—the governor of Illinois, Len Small, postponed the execution until he could decide whether to commute the death sentence. Yet criticism of Caverly continued unabated. The more one examined the judge's rationale, the more illogical it seemed. Caverly had claimed, in his summation, that life in prison for Leopold and Loeb would be more of a punishment than death. That assertion was debatable, to say the least, but more to the point, was it certain that Leopold and Loeb would spend the remainder of their days in the penitentiary, or was it more probable that sooner or later their lawyers would petition the parole board for their release?[10]

The general condemnation of Caverly stemmed in great part from a widespread apprehension that somehow, by one means or another, the two killers would obtain an early release. Caverly himself had fueled such speculation by foolishly omitting to say whether the two sentences— life plus ninety-nine years—should run consecutively or concurrently. According to the Illinois criminal code, when a judge failed to state that two sentences were to be served consecutively, they would run concurrently, with the prisoner serving the longer of the two. "The law holds," declared Hinton Clabaugh, supervisor of pardons and paroles for Illinois, "that in case one sentence is longer than the other the longer one takes precedence. . . . Therefore it must be decided which is longer in the case of Leopold and Loeb—ninety-nine years or life. What can be longer than life?"

But if Nathan and Richard were serving life sentences, then, according to the statutes, they would both be eligible for parole after twenty years. They could, in addition, earn early release, at the discretion of the parole board, for good behavior. Either boy might be released from the penitentiary after just eleven years and three months! "I don't mean to say," Clabaugh concluded hastily, "that Leopold and Loeb will necessarily be out at the end of eleven years. . . . But I do say it is hard to see how their legal privileges can be denied them any more than to other convicts."[11]

Eleven years! That would make a mockery of the law! Could they really win their freedom as early as 1935? They would then be just thirty years old; neither would yet have even reached middle age.

Would the parole board, at some point in the future, remit the sentences? No one, in 1924, could predict the decisions of the parole board. But even if the board held firm and resolved that both Leopold and Loeb should remain behind bars, there was always the possibility that executive action by the governor of Illinois might result in their early release. The governor had the power either to grant a pardon or to commute the sentences. In response to inquiries from several journalists, a spokesman for the governor's office stated the constitutional right of the executive to pardon the prisoners—"the governor . . . would be legally permitted to pardon Leopold and Loeb"—but hastened to add that Len Small had no thought of committing political suicide by releasing the two convicts.[12]

Despite such reassurances the editorials continued their drumbeat against early release. The example of Harry Thaw was proof that even the most cynical and callous killer could eventually win his freedom. Thaw had spent several years in an asylum after his murder of Stanford White, but through the persistence of his lawyers he had won his release. Might not Leopold and Loeb do the same? The public demanded capital punishment for such crimes, the *St. Louis Globe-Democrat* explained, precisely because a life sentence rarely meant permanent confinement. "There would be much more public satisfaction with the verdict if 'life imprisonment' meant imprisonment for life. . . . But in American practice it is rare that criminals under such a sentence of imprisonment are confined until the grave releases them. . . . We believe it is seldom, indeed, that 'life imprisonment' involves confinement for more than twenty years, and it is highly improbable that these men will be compelled to serve longer than that."[13]

Nathan Leopold and Richard Loeb would be able to buy favorable treatment in the penitentiary, and their lawyers would doubtless appeal their imprisonment and win their freedom. "In prison," the *Atlanta Journal* predicted, "the money behind Loeb and Leopold will lead to special favors for them. They will receive visitors, will publish their distorted views to the world, and will in every way attempt to feed fat the notoriety and public attention they have received these last few months." The judge had recommended life without the possibility of parole for the two defendants, but who could guarantee their perpetual punishment? The public memory of the killing would gradually fade away, and the defense attorneys would work diligently behind the scenes in favor of an early release. "Time alone will fix the merit of the life sentence passed upon Loeb and Leopold," the Memphis *Commercial Appeal* concluded warily. "If these boys are confined in the penitentiary the rest of their natural lives the ends of justice may be served, but if they are later pardoned those who do it will assault justice and disgrace their office."[14]

A handful of editorials pointed out that Caverly, by relying on precedent in reaching his decision, had exercised judicial restraint and resisted popular pressure. "A careful reading of the judge's opinion," the *Birmingham Age-Herald* said, "shows that he kept entirely within the law of Illinois in his decision." It was an admirable demonstration of judicial fortitude, said the *Charleston Gazette*: "The verdict is in, and we hope that the recommendations of the man who was called upon to reach a momentous decision will be accepted with equanimity. . . . Justice Caverly acted with an eye to justice to all concerned and . . . his verdict was the result of the evidence submitted to him and the facts as he conceived them."[15]

But such opinions, praising Caverly for his independence from public opinion, counted for little when set against the tsunami of criticism that otherwise crashed down on him. The decision had been wrong on many counts, the editorials claimed, and it had been most pernicious in its effect on the public's perception of the legal system.

Caverly's inattention to detail—why had he not ordered the sentences to run consecutively?—had allowed the awful possibility that two notorious murderers might yet walk the streets of Chicago. Such a result would strip the law of its dignity and reveal justice as a pretense. According to the Louisville *Courier-Journal*, "The Judge's refusal to subject these two fiends to the just penalty of the law will intensify general contempt for those whose duty it is to enforce the law and whose weakness in refusing to do their duty has done so much to bring the law itself into contempt. As long as our judges and juries as a rule are actuated by such tenderness to murderers as that of Judge Caverly . . . murders will multiply."[16]

And if the penalty was no more than a few years in the penitentiary, then there would surely no longer be any deterrent to murder. The murder rate in Cook County was already alarmingly high, warned the *Chicago Daily Tribune*, and Caverly's decision would accelerate the trend upward. "The Franks case decision already has resulted in the commutation of penalties which, without it, would have been exacted without criticism and which accord fully with the law. . . . Murder has been made a less hazardous crime than ever and it was already one of the least hazardous. . . . The taking of life has become almost a commonplace. This represents a state of morals alarming to any one who considers the elements of civilized society. It is a condition which cannot be ignored safely and most certainly calls for a restoration rather than a further weakening of the safeguards civilization has had to create and maintain for the security of human life."[17]

Robert Crowe, in his closing speech in court, had cautioned Caverly that any sentence less than hanging would be an inducement to others to imitate Nathan Leopold and Richard Loeb; and already, it seemed, Crowe's prediction had found confirmation in the vicious murder of Bessie Gaensslen, an elderly woman living alone in an apartment on the

West Side of Chicago. Anna Valanis, eighteen years old, had confessed to the crime: she, along with three other teenagers, had broken into the woman's apartment looking for money. Bessie Gaennslen had fought back courageously but, predictably, her attackers had overwhelmed her. One of the four had knocked her to the ground; a second had jumped on top of her, holding down her arms to prevent her from struggling. Anna's brother, Anthony, nineteen years old, had strangled the victim with the telephone wire as his confederates looked on.[18]

The four teenagers were now in police custody, but they had no fear of the scaffold—they would ask the judge to appoint Clarence Darrow as their attorney; and Darrow would surely save them from execution. "We'll have the court appoint Mr. Darrow to defend us," Anna Valanis confided to the reporters. "We know our stuff; if we cannot hire a lawyer the judge must furnish us one and we want Darrow."[19]

Why, indeed, should anyone now fear capital punishment? It remained on the books, of course, but in practice it was ineffectual. The sentencing of Leopold and Loeb had created a precedent that would be impossible to overcome, and no prosecutor could any longer have confidence that he would win the death penalty in Illinois. Caverly's decision had lessened the deterrent to murder.

Yet not everyone was sure that Caverly had been wrong. Lawyers and jurists, reluctant to criticize publicly one of the most prominent judges in Illinois, were more cautious in their opinions. Louis Marshall, a leading member of the Chicago bar and a senior partner in Guggenheimer, Untermyer, & Marshall, believed that Caverly had presided over the courtroom with decorum and had reached a creditable result. "The proceeding adopted by Judge Caverly was proper," Marshall commented to a reporter from the *Boston Daily Globe*. "The policy of our laws is not vengeance but protection of society from similar offences." John McIntyre, a judge on the Court of General Sessions, believed that "the judgment is a wise disposition on the part of the court." One of his colleagues on the Court of General Sessions, Cornelius Collins, stated that "Judge Caverly was in a better position to judge than any other person and that to him the judgment imposed was a solemn duty."[20]

Religious sentiment was divided equally between praise and condemnation. Caverly's decision, predicted Simon Long, the pastor of Wicker Park Lutheran Church, "will do more to make Bolshevists than anything that has happened in a long time. I fear its results upon society. It emphasizes the fact that only the poor may be hanged." Martin Luther Thomas, a representative of Deerfield Presbyterian Church, agreed that Caverly had fomented resentment against the wealthy in permitting "these men [to] escape the sword of justice because of their money and influence." But John Thompson, a minister of First Methodist Episcopal Church, disagreed, saying that the life sentence was the consequence of "a well-balanced, finely judicial decision." Johnston Myers, a spokesman for Immanuel Baptist Church, expressed satisfaction with the result if, of course, "there is to be no pardon and the boys will be treated like ordinary prisoners."[21]

Jewish opinion had been conspicuously absent throughout the hearing. No representative of the city's Jewish cultural institutions had yet allowed himself to be quoted in the newspapers; no rabbi had made any comment on the murder or its aftermath. The killers were scions of two of Chicago's most prominent Jewish families—it was, no doubt, better to remain silent than to blunder inadvertently into a controversy that might harm the Jewish community still further. Only now, after sentence had been pronounced, did the *Jewish Daily News* express its circumspect belief that the crime was a consequence of the materialistic age. "The fault lies in our entire aspect of life. . . . The insistence that all that counts is money, the piling up of wealth, the production of things that can be sold in the open market, the self-sufficiency of man that he owes no responsibility but to himself, the virtual dethronement of God—all these are responsible for what is transpiring. . . . Judge Caverly has not just pronounced sentence upon the ill-starred youths. He has rendered a verdict against our present age. The truth is—and it must be faced—that our civilization is bankrupt."[22]

Psychiatrists and child guidance experts were unanimous in praising the judge. Caverly had ignored the psychiatric testimony in reaching his decision, yet prominent members of the medical community viewed the verdict as a victory for science and as an advance for the treatment of the mentally ill. Edward S. Cowles, a neurologist and director of the National Association for the Advancement of Scientific Healing, said, "Judge Caverly has made a great forward step, and this affair should call attention to the need of more careful study of the child's mind and personality." A. A. Brill, the author of *Fundamental Conceptions of Psychoanalysis*, believed, from reading the newspaper accounts, that "there is no possibility of curing these youths. . . . I approve of Judge Caverly's effort to make sure they will never go free. But they are sick and the whole basis of our civilization is to take care of the sick, not to kill them." Max Schlapp, a professor of neuropathology at the New York Postgraduate Medical School, contradicted Brill—"it is probable that they could be cured"—yet agreed that Caverly's decision had been correct.[23]

The medical experts who had participated in the courtroom hearing—White, Glueck, Healy, Krohn, Church, and the rest—all refrained from commenting on the judge's decision. The psychiatrists for the defense had expected that their participation in the case would lead to reform of the legal process, but their advocacy for change found few echoes outside the medical journals. A writer for the *San Francisco Chronicle* took up White's suggestion that psychiatric testimony be given in an impartial manner, and the editor of the Washington *Evening Star* deplored the tainted psychiatric evidence—"neither the defense nor the prosecution should be permitted to becloud the issue and confine the minds of jurymen by offering expert opinions which are shaped by the source of the fees"—but such comments were few and far between.[24]

WILLIAM ALANSON WHITE, THE MOST prominent expert witness for the defense, was also the most vulnerable. White had built his public persona through his ability to take the middle ground between the psychiatric community, represented by the membership of such organizations as the American Psychiatric Association, and a general readership curious to learn about the new science of Freudian psychiatry. During the 1920s, White, more than any other American psychiatrist, was responsible for bringing psychiatry before a popular audience.

But his public career rested on his professional accomplishments, which depended in turn on his stewardship of St. Elizabeths Hospital. The Department of the Interior had formal jurisdiction over St. Elizabeths, and both the United States Senate and the House of Representatives had the authority to investigate conditions there. For some members of the House, White made an inviting target. He had been closely identified with Clarence Darrow's defense of Nathan Leopold and Richard Loeb, and, in the public mind at least, he was at least partially responsible for enabling the prisoners to evade justice. Rumors of an investigation into White's management of St. Elizabeths circulated through Washington during 1925. Not until April 1926, however, when Thomas Lindsay Blanton, a representative from Texas, charged that army veterans suffered from intolerable living conditions at St. Elizabeths, did Congress resolve to empower the comptroller general to investigate the administration of the hospital.[25]

His report appeared in December 1926. It was harshly critical of White's administration. There was a lack of recreational facilities for the patients, there was serious overcrowding on the wards, and there were inadequate safety measures in case of fire. White had transformed the hospital into a center of psychiatric research, yet the stated purpose of St. Elizabeths, the report noted, was to treat the mentally ill. Strictly speaking, White had exceeded his mandate as hospital superintendent by enlarging the role of the hospital; Congress had never intended it as a site for medical research. Finally, and most seriously, there was scant regard for the constitutional rights of the patients—they had no access to disinterested legal or financial assistance.[26]

Despite the severity of the report, White survived. He had as many supporters in Congress as he had enemies, and his allies viewed the criticisms as politically motivated. White continued to win honors and acclaim in the psychiatric profession. In 1926 he was president of the American Psychoanalytic Association, and in 1930 he presided over the First International Congress on Mental Hygiene in Washington, D.C. He remained at St. Elizabeths Hospital until his death in 1937.[27]

.   .   .

PREDICTABLY, CLARENCE DARROW ALSO RECEIVED public criticism for his role in saving Leopold and Loeb from the scaffold. Darrow
was the villain of the piece—he had organized the defense and by
means of the guilty plea had tricked the court into acquiescence. But
Darrow, unlike White, could shrug off his enemies with practiced
ease—he had become accustomed to such hostility and typically paid
no attention to his detractors.

In any case he was too busy to respond. He had begun his campaign against capital punishment in October 1924, just weeks after
the end of the hearing, and that fall he had already committed himself to a series of lectures and talks. Thousands turned out to hear
him speak, and wherever he went, the crowds followed. In the wake of
the Leopold-Loeb hearing, Darrow had regained his stature as a national celebrity. He always preferred to debate with a well-known public official; his opponent served as the foil for his jokes and gave him an
opportunity to ridicule those who advocated the death penalty. His appearance at the Manhattan Opera House in New York that October was
the highlight of his fall speaking tour. Alfred Talley, a judge on the
Court of General Sessions, spoke in favor of a motion in support of
capital punishment; Lewis Lawes, the warden of Sing Sing prison and
an opponent of the death penalty, chaired the debate; Darrow spoke in
opposition. The hall was packed to overflowing with an audience of
3,000 New Yorkers; hundreds more stood outside on 34th Street, hoping to catch a glimpse of Darrow as he left the building, and dozens of
journalists were in attendance, ready to write up their reports for the
morning newspapers. There was nothing new in Darrow's talk that
evening—he repeated his criticisms of the electric chair and the scaffold, scolded those who believed in free will and moral responsibility,
and ended his contribution to the debate with a ringing admonition
that the barbarism of capital punishment be no longer a part of the
penal code. "There isn't," Darrow concluded, "a single admissible argument in favor of capital punishment. . . . We believe that life should be
protected and preserved. The thing that keeps one from killing is the

emotion they have against it; and the greater the feeling of sanctity that the State pays to life, the greater the feeling of sanctity the individual has for life."[28]

Darrow's triumph in the Leopold-Loeb hearing now endowed his opinions with authority and gravitas. Darrow had no education or training in criminology other than that provided by his courtroom experience, yet the popular press accorded him the status of an expert on all questions connected with crime and the criminal justice system. Also, Darrow had no knowledge of science apart from that gleaned by reading popular texts, yet his pronouncements on science, medicine, and psychiatry now found their way into the newspapers. New York politicians and business leaders had recently announced the construction of a neuropathic hospital—the first in the country—at a cost of more than $2 million for the treatment of the mentally ill. The founders of the new hospital sought, and received, Darrow's endorsement of the plan as the most essential component of the campaign against crime. If mental defectives, Darrow stated, could be identified at an early stage and if treatment facilities were readily available, then the crime rate would rapidly fall. "This movement should be countrywide," Darrow asserted. "The case of Loeb and Leopold is, after all, merely an isolated instance. . . . Modern science says that young mental defectives can be adjusted to meet the problems of life in a normal manner. . . . Correct diagnosis, proper treatment, and healthful environment and influences can bring about cures that, in their wider application, spell crime prevention."[29]

Darrow had launched his campaign against the death penalty in October 1924. Eight months later, on 25 May 1925, a special grand jury, meeting in Dayton, Tennessee, indicted John T. Scopes, a twenty-four-year-old science instructor, for teaching the theory of evolution to a high school biology class. The trial of Scopes, Darrow believed, would pit science against ignorance, knowledge against superstition, secular thought against religious fundamentalism. It was a chance for Darrow to grab the national spotlight yet again, and so on 10 July, he found himself in the sweltering heat of a Tennessee courtroom leading the defense of Scopes against the forces of reaction.

Darrow lost the case—the jury found Scopes guilty. The defense had hoped to appeal the conviction to the United States Supreme Court and then, in front of a national audience, demonstrate that the Tennessee statute was unconstitutional. But the Tennessee supreme court overturned the original conviction on a technicality; there was to be no appeal before a higher court. To the leaders of the American Civil Liberties Union (ACLU) it seemed that their financial support of the defense attorneys had gone for naught—the statute remained on Tennessee's books, and the antievolution movement spread outward from Tennessee to other southern states. Mississippi (in 1926) and Arkansas (in 1928) both outlawed the teaching of evolution in public high schools.

The trial had been a disappointment for the ACLU, but for Darrow it had been a personal triumph. He had shifted the focus away from a defense of the constitutional rights of the defendant—had it been legitimate for Scopes to teach evolution to his class?—and toward a debate on the literal truth of the biblical account of creation. He had lured the prosecuting attorney, William Jennings Bryan, onto the witness stand. Bryan, like Darrow, was a larger-than-life character; he had been a presidential candidate in 1896 at only age thirty-six, had been a member of Woodrow Wilson's cabinet until his resignation in 1915, and was now a national spokesman for the fundamentalist movement. The confrontation between Darrow and Bryan was the centerpiece of the Scopes trial. Bryan, responding to Darrow's questions, was obdurate in his defense of the literal truth of the Bible; and Darrow, as a consequence, could compel Bryan to reveal to the world both his ignorance of modern science and his imprecise understanding of the Bible. Darrow emerged from the Scopes trial with his reputation intact and enlarged—he was now the darling of the intellectuals, the hero of the age, the voice of reason, and a spokesman for modern science and progressivism.[30]

WHILE CLARENCE DARROW'S FAME REACHED the stratosphere, Robert Crowe's reputation as state's attorney dwindled and diminished in the years following the Leopold-Loeb hearing. The murder rate in Chicago had doubled during Crowe's tenure as state's attorney yet the number of convictions in the courts had declined precipitously. Gangland killings were a daily event, and no one seemed able to stop the violence. Crowe now had seventy deputies on his staff, and his annual budget had increased by more than $100,000, yet the gunmen always seemed able to escape justice.

A rumor began to be whispered in Chicago: was Robert Crowe or someone in Crowe's office secretly working with the gangsters? Had the mob corrupted the state's attorney or members of his staff?

On 27 April 1926, at eight o'clock in the evening, William McSwiggin, an assistant state's attorney who was one of Crowe's closest aides, emerged from the Pony Inn, a saloon on West Roosevelt Road in the town of Cicero, a few miles west of Chicago. As McSwiggin and his drinking companions walked toward their Lincoln automobile, a motorcade—five cars, one following closely behind another—moved slowly down the street toward them. As the fourth car passed McSwiggin and his friends, there was a hail of bullets, fired from a machine gun. McSwiggin and two others died later that night; the remaining two escaped unhurt.

It soon emerged that McSwiggin had spent his final hours drinking with the leaders of the O'Donnell gang. Myles O'Donnell and his brother, Klondike, along with Tom (Red) Duffy and Jim Doherty, had been feuding with the Italian gangs over the control of the beer trade. Duffy and Doherty had died alongside McSwiggin that evening; the O'Donnell brothers had ducked behind a car and lived.

Why had McSwiggin been drinking with gangland leaders? Had he been working with the O'Donnells? Had the mobsters corrupted him? Could corruption have spread further within Crowe's department?

Robert Crowe pointed the finger of blame at Al Capone. The O'Donnells had been competing with Capone over control of the saloons and speakeasies in Cook County and Capone's men had struck back. The gunmen had intended to kill the O'Donnells, and McSwiggin had been in the wrong place at the wrong time. But Capone was responsible for the death of McSwiggin, Crowe asserted, and most probably it had been Capone himself who had fired the machine gun.

But Crowe was never able to explain why a member of his staff had been drinking with prominent members of the Chicago underworld. Crowe seemed to have something to hide or, at the very least, seemed reluctant to reveal the truth. He petitioned the Cook County Criminal Court to impanel a grand jury investigation into McSwiggin's death but simultaneously ensured that his political allies controlled the grand jury. The findings of the grand jury were inconclusive. No one was ever indicted for the killing of McSwiggin.[31]

There never was any proof of collusion between Crowe's office and the criminal underworld, yet suspicion lingered. And by 1928, public sentiment against Crowe had hardened. He had been in office for eight years, and criminal violence in Cook County continued unabated. Crowe had hoped to be the Republican candidate for state's attorney a third time, in the elections in 1928, but his star, even within the Republican ranks, had dimmed and he failed to win the primary election. His opponent, John Swanson, a judge on the Circuit Court, defeated him handily. It was a welcome sign, according to the *Chicago Daily Tribune*, that the public had finally given up on the political machine that Crowe had so carefully constructed. Everyone was tired of the bombings, shootings, kidnappings, and murders that had given Chicago the national reputation of a city of crime. "A machine which embraced all the jobs at the city hall . . . which had an army of workers in nearly every precinct, the most extensive machine organization in Chicago's history, was pushed into the ditch by a . . . group which had behind it nothing but public sentiment." Robert Crowe's political career was over. He had been forced out of office just four years after his prosecution of Nathan Leopold and Richard Loeb.[32]

WHILE ROBERT CROWE FOUGHT HIS political corner against enemies inside and outside the Cook County Republican Party, Nathan Leopold and Richard Loeb grew accustomed to the daily monotony of prison routine. The guards had put Nathan in a cell in the East Wing of Joliet Prison and, mindful that the two murderers be kept as far apart

38. JOLIET PRISON. The state prison at Joliet opened in 1858. This photograph shows the main entrance to the prison.

as possible, had sent Richard to the other side of the penitentiary, where he occupied a cell in the West Wing.

The prison, now almost seventy years old, was a crumbling wreck. The prison complex was a grim gray edifice with massive stone walls, enclosing a series of starkly cheerless buildings. An unhealthy, unpleasant odor permeated the cell blocks, and each individual cell—small, dark, claustrophobic, and slightly damp—was as repulsive a space as one could imagine. There were no flush toilets, of course—in the mornings, before breakfast, each prisoner carried his waste in a bucket to a large trough in the prison yard. The architect had provided the cell blocks with windows so narrow that there was little natural light. It was unbearably hot in the summer and freezing cold in the winter.[33]

Nathan remained at Joliet Prison only until May 1925, when he obtained a transfer to the new prison at Stateville, three miles north of the town of Joliet. The Stateville prison, built in anticipation of the closure of Joliet Prison, consisted of four roundhouse buildings, each of which had an open tower in the center of a large space surrounded by a circular arrangement of prison cells. The guards standing in the central tower could thus observe all the prisoners in their cells.[34]

Stateville was one of the most modern penitentiaries in the United States—its circular panopticon design was unusual and innovative—but discipline within the prison was almost nonexistent. The Illinois state legislature had provided the funds for prison construction but had omitted to ensure a decent wage for the prison guards—the monthly salary was only $100, and there was no pension plan—and, as a consequence, corruption was endemic among the staff. Any convict with money could buy any privilege he desired, and by the early 1930s, internal discipline at Stateville had passed out of the hands of the prison administration. A dozen rival gangs competed for control of the prison. Each gang had constructed a motley collection of tar-paper shacks in the prison yard as its headquarters, and within these shacks the gangs operated whiskey stills, cultivated marijuana plants, and hired out the younger and more vulnerable prisoners as prostitutes.[35]

Not until March 1931, after Richard Loeb had been transferred from Joliet Prison to Stateville, did Nathan and Richard live in the same prison. Neither joined one of the many gangs operating behind the prison walls, but both soon gained influence over their fellow prisoners and, at the same time, were able to curry favor with the prison administration.

Both had an education far in advance of the majority of the prisoners at Stateville. Nathan, in particular, showed an eagerness to use his education in the service of the prison management, willingly performing various clerical jobs. Under other circumstances his contributions might have seemed nugatory, but Stateville in the late 1920s and early 1930s had a woeful lack of paid clerical staff, employing just six people in administrative positions inside a prison that held almost 4,000 inmates. Nathan was not a model prisoner; he had an uneven disciplinary record at Stateville and was punished several times with solitary confinement. Yet successive wardens recognized his clerical talents as a

39. STATEVILLE PRISON. The prison at Stateville opened in 1925. In its original form, the prison complex consisted of four cell blocks. A guard tower, surrounded by a circular arrangement of four tiers of cells, stood in the center of each cell block. This photograph was taken in 1931.

valuable resource that helped the prison function more efficiently, and over time he won the confidence of the senior officers.[36]

Frank Whipp, the warden at Stateville in the early 1930s, emphasized reform and rehabilitation in his management of the prison. A major purpose of the penitentiary, according to Whipp, was an end to recidivism. The sooner a prisoner demonstrated eligibility for parole, the better. Nathan Leopold quickly won his way into Whipp's good books. There was little possibility that Whipp would recommend Nathan's parole, but Nathan adopted Whipp's reform ideology and made sure that Whipp realized it. Nathan assisted the prison sociologist, Ferris Laune, in his attempts to determine the suitability of various categories of prisoners for early release and even published an article (under a pseudonym) on the subject in the *Journal of Criminal Law and Criminology*. Nathan received an appropriate reward for these efforts. By his own account, he soon had the run of the prison—he could go anywhere, and after 1933, he was infrequently subject to the disciplinary regimen imposed on other prisoners.[37]

RICHARD LOEB WAS LESS EAGER to work in tandem with the prison administration. Yet he, too, quickly won a position of privilege within Stateville, in large part because of the money at his disposal. Richard kept a permanent deposit of $500 in the prison office. This sum, always made good by his brothers, was available for his personal use at any time. His parents, unaware that Richard had a private banking arrangement within the prison, sent him an additional fifty dollars each month.[38]

Loeb used his money wisely, carefully bribing the prison guards to grant him privileges. He had keys to parts of the prison normally accessible to other inmates only at specific times of the day and on a restricted basis. Loeb was one of a small number of prisoners (Nathan Leopold was another) allowed to buy whatever he wished from the commissary; and he could, if he desired, eat his meals in the privacy of his cell. It was not even necessary, according to one account, for Richard to wear the prison uniform—he customarily wore a white shirt and flannel trousers.[39]

Richard's influence over the guards could be used in the pursuit of sexual favors from other inmates. Convicts who were willing to have sex with Richard might be rewarded with cigarettes, alcohol, a larger cell, and an easy job within the prison; but a prisoner who fell out of favor with Richard might find himself shoveling coal in the yard or laboriously weaving rattan chairs in the furniture shop.[40]

James Day, twenty-one years old, was serving a one- to ten-year sentence in Stateville for armed robbery when he first met Richard Loeb in 1935. Day was short, just five feet, six inches tall; weighed 135

pounds; and had a mottled, blotchy complexion. His life had been un-
settled. He had never known his father, and his mother had died in
1921, when Day was just eight years old. He moved to Chicago to live
with his uncle and aunt, but he proved to be a difficult child, constantly getting into trouble for fighting, thieving, and petty crime. He
first attracted the attention of the police in 1928, at the age of fifteen;
in that year the Juvenile Court ordered that he be held in St. Charles
School for Boys, a reform school. He served a second sentence in the
Boys' Reformatory at Pontiac. In 1935, not long after he reached his
majority, Day graduated to a cell in Stateville Prison.

Richard took an immediate interest in Day's welfare. He arranged
for the guards to transfer Day to C House, to a cell in the same gallery
as his own, and he began sending Day presents—cigarettes and small
gifts of money. The older man—Richard was now thirty—used his influence to get Day a job in the prison office building and hinted that he
might even be able to get Day a parole hearing. It would not be difficult,
Richard suggested, for a clever lawyer to make an effective appeal before the parole board on Day's behalf.

It was a calculated scheme, on Richard's part, to put Day in a
dependent position so that he would agree to have sex with Richard.
Day resisted but Richard was persistent. He reminded Day that he might
lose all his privileges; yet all he had to do was comply with Richard's
request—would it not be better for Day to submit to his demands?

On the morning of 28 January 1936, George Bliss, a convict in C
House, surreptitiously passed a straight razor to James Day. Bliss had
stolen the razor that week from the barbershop and had successfully
concealed it from the prison guards. Just after noon, a work detail began its march from the dining hall, the prisoners walking in double file
under the supervision of a single guard. James Day was the last in line,
and as his column moved through the prison, he slipped away. Earlier
that day, Richard Loeb had mentioned that he would take a shower at
noon, suggesting casually that Day might meet him at the shower room.
Richard had a key and could lock the room from the inside, thus allowing them to meet in private.

Day was in an angry, violent mood. Richard had been pestering him for weeks, demanding that they have sex, and threatening to withdraw all his privileges. He entered the shower room and saw Richard, naked, advancing toward him. Day struck at his tormentor with the razor, cutting him on the neck and abdomen, slashing furiously, inflicting fifty-six wounds before turning away and leaving the room, his victim collapsed on the floor in a sea of blood.

Richard died later that day. The prison doctors worked furiously to save him, suturing the cuts, but Richard had lost too much blood. Nathan rushed from his cell to the prison hospital and watched helplessly as his friend, his companion, his lover, lay dying on the operating table. And when it was over, after the surgeons and doctors and prison guards had all left the room, Nathan remained behind, to wash the body, to gently cradle Richard's head in his arms, and to grieve silently over the loss of his companion.[41]

At the trial of James Day later that year, no one, not even Nathan, contradicted Day's account. The state's attorney had demanded the death penalty for the murder of Richard Loeb. Any convict who testified on the witness stand against Day would be responsible for sending him to the electric chair.[42] Who among those prisoners who knew the truth would want to return to Stateville to face retribution for sending a fellow prisoner to his death? Richard Loeb had died; he could not be brought back to life. Better to allow Day to claim that Richard had demanded a homosexual encounter than to risk one's own life. The jury found Day not guilty on all charges.

Few of the guards at Stateville believed Day's claim that he had acted in self-defense. Why, for example, had it been necessary for Day to stab Richard fifty-six times? And how had Day managed to emerge from their encounter in the shower room without a scratch or even so much as a bruise?

Richard's death had created an uproar outside the prison walls, and the revelation that Richard had corrupted the guards to obtain special privileges had deeply embarrassed the new warden, Joseph Ragen. Nothing, Ragen now realized, would be more humiliating for the institution than to have scandal touch Nathan Leopold also. As a consequence, Nathan found himself under severe scrutiny in case he, too, should step out of line. Ragen now decreed that Nathan should no longer have a cell mate; nor was he to walk around the prison without a guard to accompany him; and all his privileges were to be revoked.

The years following Richard's death were lonely, bitter years for Nathan. He was surrounded by hundreds of men, yet he keenly felt his social isolation within the prison. "These years after Dick's death," Nathan wrote in his autobiography, "were not altogether pleasant. Officially there were a number of restrictions on me, and these galled me a lot. It is never easy to get along in a situation where you stick out like a sore thumb. . . . The fact that I had to cell alone, that I had to be accompanied by a keeper—these were widely misinterpreted. They made it much harder for me to get along. And the fact that I brought 'heat' wherever I went didn't make it any easier."[43]

Yet Nathan survived and even began to contemplate the possibility of parole. To dream that he might win his release from Stateville had always seemed an impossible flight of fancy. Yet memories would eventually dim; his antagonists—Crowe's successors in the state's attorney's office—would eventually relax their grip, and perhaps Nathan could convince the parole board of his contrition for that terrible crime so long ago.

At the time of Richard's death in 1936, Nathan had already served twelve years—he would be eligible for parole on the life sentence in 1944, after serving a total of twenty years. The parole board would require him to proclaim his regret for the killing of Bobby Franks, of course, but that would not be difficult. He needed also to demonstrate, by good works if possible, that he had undergone rehabilitation: that he had atoned for his deed and that there was no likelihood that he would commit some comparable act on his release.

In the early 1930s, several inmates had established a prison school at Stateville to teach the other prisoners. It had been an ambitious undertaking—in the first year, seventy convicts had enrolled in classes in English composition, algebra, geometry, bookkeeping, and history. The warden had endorsed their initiative and had provided money from the Inmates' Amusement Fund for paper, pencils, textbooks, and mimeograph supplies. Both Nathan and Richard had been involved with the school from its inception, and in the years following Richard's death, Nathan attempted to ease his pain and his loneliness by immersing himself in the management of the school. It was, by his account at least, a grand success—soon some 400 prisoners were taking classes. Nathan had intended the school as a memorial to Richard, but its rapid expansion proved its eventual downfall. The warden, Joseph Ragen, taking note of the popularity of the classes among the inmates, directed that each student's academic record be reported to the central administration. Ragen intended that each prisoner's academic accomplishments be presented to the parole board as tangible evidence of rehabilitation. But he had not foreseen the predictable outcome: prisoners with no previous interest in study and with no desire to learn now enrolled with the intention of forcing their teachers, by threats if necessary, to award superlative grades to present to the parole board in order to win early release.[44]

In 1941 the warden transferred Nathan to a position as an X-ray technician in the prison hospital. Later that year Nathan wheedled his way into a position as a nurse in the hospital's psychiatric ward. He now had more responsibility—and less supervision—than before. The prison doctors relied on the nurses to look after the psychiatric patients, even occasionally allowing them to medicate those in their care. "The bug cells," Nathan recalled in his autobiography, "were a new world, entirely different from the rest of the prison. . . . No more marching into the cell house every evening and out again next morning. Here we each had a nice clean cell, larger than the ones in the cell house. And we were on twenty-four-hour detail; that is, our cells were never locked. . . . There was very little routine or discipline as regards the nurses on the new assignment. There were no rules, and we were permitted to do pretty much as we pleased."

In September 1944 scientists working for the federal government arrived at Stateville in connection with a project to test antimalarial drugs. In Europe the war was in its final stages, but troops fighting in the Pacific theater still faced an arduous challenge from the Japanese. Might the American troops be decimated by disease? Could the United

States quickly produce drugs to combat malaria? Would the prisoners at Stateville be willing to volunteer as guinea pigs and allow the federal scientists to test the effectiveness of antimalarial drugs? The doctors would infect the volunteers with malaria and observe the course of the disease under treatment—it would necessarily be an unpleasant and even dangerous experience for those prisoners who volunteered. The scientists had already begun to test their drugs on patients at Manteno State Hospital for the Insane but they needed many more volunteers if the tests were to be reliable.[45]

Almost 500 prisoners volunteered. Nathan, one of the first to volunteer, caught malaria on 19 June 1945. Two weeks later, on Monday, 2 July, he experienced the first symptoms. His body began shaking uncontrollably, his teeth started chattering, his head felt as if it were about to split in two, and his temperature shot up to 104. Nathan had caught the Chesson strain of malaria. The first attack would last five days and would normally recur every two weeks. The doctors administered thirty milligrams of plasmochin and 0.6 gram of chloroquine to each volunteer with malaria, and at the first signs of relapse, they used sixty milligrams of pentaquine and two grams of quinine.

The combination of drugs was effective in preventing the appearance of symptoms, but it was too toxic as a cure for malaria. Nathan, at age forty, had previously been healthy, with no signs of illness or disease, yet, now, in the aftermath of the antimalarial experiments, he had symptoms of kidney disease and diabetes. But perhaps his participation as a volunteer would have at least one positive outcome—in 1946 a rumor started within the prison that the governor of Illinois would shorten the sentences of those prisoners who had volunteered. Would Nathan be a beneficiary of the governor's consideration? Nathan had become eligible for parole on his life sentence in 1944, twenty years after he had been first imprisoned. But he would not become eligible for parole on the other sentence—ninety-nine years for the kidnapping—until 1957, after having served one-third of the sentence. If the governor were to reduce his term, Nathan might soon be eligible for parole on both sentences.

But was not Nathan in a class by himself? The murder of Bobby

Franks had been sui generis in its wantonness and cruelty. Should not Nathan serve out the rest of his days in prison as the judge, John Caverly, had intended?

The notoriety of the crime had embedded the killing in the city's collective memory. It had become woven into the tapestry of the history of Chicago. And for those few Chicagoans who might have forgotten the details of the murder, there was a grisly reminder in July 1946 in the arrest of William Heirens for the killing of six-year-old Suzanne Degnan. The police had claimed that Heirens, a good-looking, dark-haired seventeen-year-old sophomore at the University of Chicago, had abducted the little girl from her bedroom in the middle of the night, leaving behind a ransom note for the parents. He had allegedly strangled Suzanne with his hands, carried the body to the basement of a nearby apartment building, dismembered it with a butcher knife, and disposed of the body parts in the city sewers.[46]

Neither his professors nor his classmates at the University of Chicago could reconcile Heirens's confession with their knowledge of him as a studious, mild-mannered, good-natured young man. Heirens, like Leopold and Loeb, was an intellectual prodigy who had skipped his senior year at high school to enroll at the university. He had belonged to the Calvert Club, a Catholic student group, and had been a member of the university wrestling team. He was, his shocked friends proclaimed, just about as normal an individual as one might expect to find on the campus.[47]

The Chicago newspapers, in recounting the murder of Suzanne Degnan, ceaselessly compared it with the murder of Bobby Franks twenty-two years earlier, dwelling on the uncanny similarities between the two killings. Yet when the governor of Illinois, Adlai Stevenson, did eventually consider Nathan's petition for clemency, he ignored the sensationalism of the newspaper reports and acted on a recommendation from the parole board to reduce Nathan's sentence to eighty-five years. "The commutation in this case," Stevenson announced, "was recommended and is being made pursuant to a program to reward prisoners who voluntarily risked their lives in malaria experiments for the armed services. . . . The parole board has given special consideration to prisoners who voluntarily participated in the malaria research program. It is the conclusion of the board, and I concur, that Nathan Leopold is also entitled to this consideration."[48]

The difference might have seemed trivial. Eighty-five years or ninety-nine years—under either sentence, Nathan would spend the remainder of his days at Stateville. But in terms of his early release, there was a significant distinction. Nathan could not previously have hoped for parole until 1957; now he would be eligible for parole as soon as January 1953.

By 1952 Nathan had begun to believe that he might soon win his freedom. It might happen; it could happen . . . but Nathan, in an interview with the *Chicago Daily Tribune*, seemed intimidated, almost cowed, by the prospect. He had thought often of his release from Stateville but had given no consideration to the practical problems of emerging as a free man. Where would he go? What would he do? "I have no plans," he confessed to the reporter. "I don't know where I'll go, except it won't be Chicago."

His two brothers, Mike and Sam, had changed their names not long after the murder of Bobby Franks. Would he also, the journalist asked, take on a new identity?

"I don't know," Leopold slowly replied, as though the question had never occurred to him.

Could he tell the readers of the *Tribune* about his years in prison? the reporter asked. How had he spent his days?

"I have studied. I have learned a lot," Nathan boasted, suddenly eager to tell the world, once again, of his intellectual ability. "I read some 26 or 27 languages—Polish, Sanskrit, Hebrew, Russian, Egyptian—as well as the more common ones. I've studied mathematics, too. I went about as far in math as it was possible to go in prison."[49]

THE FOLLOWING YEAR NATHAN APPEARED before members of the parole board. There was a sadness about him as he sat across a wooden table from the three members of the board. His cockiness was gone, worn down by the long years of incarceration, and in its place there was an air of quiet resignation. His paunch pressed against the belt of his trousers; his large, bulbous, heavy-lidded eyes looked out from a fleshy, pallid face; his hair, still black, was now receding away from the temples; and his nicotine-stained fingers revealed that he still smoked as compulsively as ever. Nathan Leopold, dressed in a denim shirt and blue jeans, his prison number—9306D—stenciled on the back of his shirt, now bore little resemblance to the teenager who had first entered Joliet Prison in 1924.[50]

"I would like to say," Nathan began, "that I was only 19 when I committed the crime. Today I'm a man of 48. Over 60 per cent of my life has been spent in prison. My life has changed completely. My personality has changed. My outlook has changed. I assure you I never would be in trouble again if paroled."

Why had he murdered Bobby Franks? one member of the board asked. How did he now explain the killing?

"I couldn't give a motive which makes sense to me," Nathan answered. "It was the act of a child—a simpleton kid. A very bizarre act. I don't know why I did it. I'm a different man now. I was a smart aleck kid. I am not anymore. . . . I can only tell you that what happened in 1924 can't happen again." It had been, and it remained, an inexplicable act by two foolish boys, Nathan repeated. He was unable to account for the murder. "It seems absurd to me today, as it must to you and all other people. I am in no better position to give you a motive than I was then."[51]

Nathan had known that the parole board would ask about his plans if he were to win his freedom, yet in that regard he had come unprepared. In response to a question from a member of the board, he replied that he had not given the matter much thought. Perhaps, he answered with a slight smile, in a misguided attempt to strike a humorous note, he would sell neckties or work behind a soda fountain. Anything would do, he concluded; he certainly had no grand ambition to make a career for himself.[52]

Nathan had intended to make a good impression, but to his listeners sitting across the table, his answers seemed too trite and too quick. There was still something about Nathan's manner reminiscent of the arrogance of youth. His remarks seemed almost offhand. He was not sufficiently contrite.[53]

Robert Crowe, emerging from retirement to write a note of protest to the parole board, forcefully urged the members not to grant parole. Crowe pointed out that at the original hearing in 1924, the judge had extended mercy to Leopold by giving him a life sentence. There was no reason for the parole board to grant mercy to Leopold a second time. "I thought at the time," Crowe explained, referring to both Leopold and Loeb, "they ought to hang. There were no extenuating circumstances; it was a brutal murder."[54]

Victor Knowles, the chairman of the parole board, had no hesitation in denying parole. Leopold, Knowles explained to the press, was a liar and a fraud who had exaggerated his contributions to the malaria project and who continued to embellish his supposed achievements during his years in prison. Leopold's absurd claim to be able to read twenty-seven languages was a case in point. Who could be so gullible as to believe something so preposterous? Leopold had not expressed sufficient contrition for the murder, Knowles continued, and his attempt to pass it off as merely an irresponsible act by two adolescents was tantamount to denying his culpability.[55]

Five years would pass before the parole board would again consider Nathan Leopold's petition. Those years had given Nathan time to prepare and to consider the lessons he learned from his failure in 1953. He had hired a competent lawyer, Elmer Gertz, to present his case before the board, and he had reached out beyond the prison walls to enlist the support of prominent sympathizers. Former classmates at the University of Chicago—Abel Brown, Arnold Maremont, and others—had secured job offers for Nathan. Everyone agreed that it would be impossible for Nathan to return to Chicago: it was important for him to avoid the glare of newspaper publicity if he was to serve out his parole successfully. One job offer had come from Florida, a second from California, and a third from Hawaii—all at a sufficient distance from Chicago. Might Nathan be willing to work in Puerto Rico? The Church of the Brethren, a small Protestant group with its headquarters in Elgin, Illinois, had built a mission hospital in the village of Castaner, sixty-five miles southwest of the capital, San Juan. A representative of the church, Harold Row, had met Nathan's younger brother, Sam, several years earlier and now offered to sponsor Nathan's employment as a medical technician at the Castaner hospital.[56]

Elmer Gertz, speaking before the parole board on 5 February 1958, reminded his audience that Nathan presented no risk of violating parole. He had four job offers, and more to the point, he had proved himself rehabilitated by his good works in prison. Nathan had helped organize a school for inmates within Stateville; he had been a volunteer for the malaria project in the 1940s; and he had worked steadily and conscientiously as an X-ray technician and as a psychiatric nurse in the prison hospital. What more could the parole board require of Nathan Leopold? Should he remain in Stateville solely on account of his notoriety while other inmates obtained their freedom? In the years since 1950, Gertz continued, the board had paroled almost 200 murderers, yet it had continued to deny Nathan Leopold his freedom. Art Newman, a notorious gangland killer, had murdered seven people; the state's attorney had demanded that he remain behind bars for the remainder of his life; and yet the parole board had released Newman after he had served twenty-six years. Nathan Leopold had now lived in prison for his entire adult life, a total of thirty-three years. Was it just that Nathan be denied his liberty? At Stateville, only one other inmate— Russell Pethick, the murderer of a young woman and her infant son—had been imprisoned longer than Nathan Leopold! "Few convicts have ever served as long as Nathan Leopold," Gertz stated, "and some have been convicted of murders more brutal even than his. Some of them, unlike him, have previously been convicted of other heinous offenses or have violated probation or parole. Very few have had as fine prison records as Leopold."[57]

Unpleasant, ugly rumors had circulated that Nathan was a homosexual, Gertz continued, and that he had sex with other inmates in Stateville. But that was false. Nathan had a brief infatuation with Richard Loeb many years previously, but that relationship had been a juvenile affair. Nothing had occurred within Stateville. Nathan's disciplinary record in the prison contained no mention of homosexuality. "Gentlemen, let me say this openly and without equivocation. Nathan Leopold is not now, and has not been since his imprisonment, a sexual deviate, or, indeed, a sexual problem in any respect. The prison records will bear out, and the public should know it, that there is not the slightest evidence of any sexual impropriety on his part. . . . I hope I have made my meaning clear."[58]

The gossip about Nathan's sexuality was symptomatic of the myths that now overlay the true story. Even now, thirty years after the murder, the public remained fascinated by the case. The tabloid newspapers eagerly fueled the public's appetite by retailing half-truths and outright lies. The facts had been lost in the making of a legend that now bore little relationship to reality.

It was important, Gertz reminded the parole board, to go back to the original court documents and, in determining whether to grant Leopold parole, to consider which of the two boys had been principally responsible for the murder of Bobby Franks. The transcript of the 1924 courtroom hearing showed that Richard Loeb had initiated the scheme to kidnap and kill a young child, that Loeb had planned the details of the ransom demand, that Loeb had imagined himself the master criminal, and that Loeb had struck the deathblow with the chisel in the back of the automobile. Nathan Leopold had participated in the killing, but only as an accomplice, content to follow the other boy's lead. "We have no desire," Gertz explained, "to labor the point that Loeb's share in the crime was greater than Leopold's, because in a legal and moral sense both were guilty. But it is necessary once and for all to let the truth be known." It was not that Nathan bore no responsibility for the murder—such a suggestion would be a step too far—but that Nathan had been too infatuated with Richard to resist the other boy's criminal intent.[59]

A succession of character witnesses now appeared to speak on Nathan's behalf. John Bartlow Martin, a writer for the *Saturday Evening Post* who had interviewed Nathan in prison; Martin Sukov, a prison psychiatrist; Eligius Weir, the prison chaplain at Stateville; and the poet Carl Sandburg, then Chicago's most celebrated literary figure—all testified that Nathan had earned parole through his outstanding rehabilitation.

Finally it was Nathan's turn to speak. He had learned from his previous experience five years earlier; now he was ready to proclaim his remorse. "Gentlemen," he began, "it is not easy to live with murder on your conscience. The fact that you know you did not do the actual killing does not help. My punishment has not been light. I have spent over one-third of a century in prison. During that time I have lost most of those who were near or dear to me. I never had an opportunity to say a prayer on their graves; I forfeited all home and family; forfeited all the chances of an honorable career. But the worst punishment comes from inside me. It is the torment of my own conscience. I can say that will be true the rest of my days. . . . All I want in this life is a chance to prove to you and the people of Illinois, what I know in my own heart to be true, that I can and will become a decent, self-respecting and law-abiding citizen, to have a chance to find redemption for myself by service to others. It is for that chance that I humbly beg."[60]

The members of the parole board listened politely as Nathan continued to talk. Soon he had finished. John Bookwalter asked Nathan about his attorney's assertion that Richard Loeb had conceived and planned the murder of Bobby Franks. Was it, Bookwalter inquired, also Nathan's belief "that Loeb had a stronger personality . . . and [that] you were more or less a follower?"

"Yes, sir," Nathan replied.

"Through your adoration for him?"

"That is correct."

"As you sit there today, don't you take a equal share of blame for this?"

"Definitely."

"You are not trying to place it on him?"

"Believe me," Nathan explained, "it is not easy to try to push blame on a man that is dead. . . . I did not want to throw blame on another. It is not an attractive thing to do, but I must answer the question honestly."

Bookwalter was still not satisfied. Leopold seemed to want to have it both ways: to express his remorse and yet to deny that he had any meaningful role in the murder. Bookwalter knew the details of the case; he had read the transcripts of the courtroom hearing; and now he probed again.

"You are taking an equal share of responsibility?"

"Very definitely. . . ."

"I understand there were articles used in this crime purchased by you and stored in your house?"

"My share was equal," Nathan replied cautiously. Bookwalter's manner was skeptical. Was Nathan to be denied parole a second time?[61]

If the board did grant him parole, Bookwalter added, suddenly changing the subject, did Nathan realize that he was to avoid television and radio appearances? Did he understand that he was not to give out statements to the newspapers? Every media outlet in the country would want an interview with him. Already there was a rumor that Ed Murrow, the CBS correspondent, wanted Nathan to appear on his television show *See It Now*. "I don't want," Nathan replied hastily, "any part of lecturing, television or radio, or trading on the notoriety. That is the last thing. . . . All I want, if I am so lucky as to ever see freedom again, is to try to become a humble little person."[62]

On 20 February 1958 the news reached Stateville that the board had agreed to parole Nathan Leopold. Three weeks later, on 13 March, on a clear crisp winter morning, Nathan emerged from the prison to confront an immense scrum of newspaper reporters, television cameramen, and photographers. He had left his prison uniform behind; he now wore an ill-fitting blue suit that seemed slightly too large for his diminutive frame. He blinked nervously at the crowd as the reporters shouted questions at him, and suddenly the mob pressed forward, ready to record his first words back in the free world.[63]

"I appeal as solemnly as I know how," Nathan said in a tremulous voice, speaking into a microphone, "to you and to your editors . . . to agree that the only piece of news about me is that I have ceased to be news. I beg, I beseech you and your editors and publishers to grant me a gift almost as precious as freedom itself—a gift without which freedom ceases to have much value—the gift of privacy. Give me a chance— a fair chance—to start life anew."[64]

It was a futile appeal. The crowd pushed forward again. Elmer Gertz gently pulled Nathan away from the microphone and nudged him in the direction of a waiting limousine, its engine running, the driver ready to make a quick exit. The reporters also, suddenly realizing that Nathan was about to leave, began to scramble, pushing and shoving each other as they ran toward their cars, desperate not to be left behind, desperate not to miss the scoop that each imagined was within his grasp.

Back to Chicago! The caravan of automobiles roared away with Leopold's car in front. They raced pell-mell along the Chicago road at ninety miles an hour, horns blaring, until they reached Oak Park, west of the city. Ralph Newman, one of Nathan's closest friends, had offered his home as a temporary refuge. But, already, as Nathan watched from a downstairs window, he could see dozens of reporters running from their cars toward the house as though to set up a siege. At two o'clock that afternoon the police arrived to escort Nathan to Chicago, where he planned to stay at an apartment on Lake Shore Drive with his college friend Abel Brown.[65]

It had become impossible for Nathan to stay even a few days in Chicago. He had hoped to visit the graves of his parents. But the journalists had discovered his hiding place and were camped outside, waiting for him to leave the apartment building. They obviously had no intention of respecting his plea for privacy. There was no alternative: he would leave Chicago for Puerto Rico as soon as possible. Only when he had left the United States would he find peace. The next day Nathan boarded a plane at O'Hare Airport for New York for a connecting flight to San Juan. Finally he was a free man.[66]

THE TRANQUILLITY OF CASTANER was a welcome change from the bustle of Chicago. High in the mountains, at an altitude of 4,000 feet, with a temperate climate, and surrounded by banana and coffee plantations, the village was an oasis of quiet. Nathan Leopold spent his days peacefully, working as a medical assistant at the village hospital, enrolling as a graduate student in social work at the University of Puerto Rico, and finding friends among the small community of North Americans on the island.[67]

It might have been idyllic—except for one nagging irritation. Meyer Levin, a contemporary of Leopold and Loeb at the University of Chicago, had written a novel, *Compulsion*, based on the murder. Levin's writing style was overwrought, exaggerated, and fanciful, and his description of the character based on Nathan Leopold was far from flattering. Now Nathan learned that Twentieth Century Fox was to make a movie of the novel starring Orson Welles. It was yet one more invasion of his privacy, Nathan decided, and in October 1959 he instructed Elmer Gertz to file suit against Levin and the film production company, Darryl F. Zanuck Productions, for the "appropriation of the name, likeness, and personality of Leopold and conversion of same for their profit and gain."[68]

To most observers, Leopold's lawsuit seemed risible. One of the most notorious murderers in American history, the brutal killer of a fourteen-year-old boy, was now complaining that a fictionalized account of the crime was an appropriation of his name! Leopold had filed suit for $1.4 million; if he were to collect in the courts, would he not, in fact, profit from his crime? Meyer Levin, who had publicly supported Leopold's parole the previous year, was indignant that his generosity had been rewarded with such base ingratitude. "Leopold was now a victim, a man who had suffered thirty years of imprisonment as if in a death camp," Levin sputtered angrily in an autobiographical account. "He was a kind of culture hero. . . . There had been an astute image-creation campaign, picturing him as a master of fourteen languages, a savant, and now a hospital volunteer in a remote monastery, a kind of Dr. Schweitzer! . . . In his lawsuit Nathan Leopold was daring the highest feat of all—he would at last collect the kidnap-murder ransom, and many times over! It would be handed to him by a court! What a justification for himself, and his dead friend Dickie Loeb! He and Dickie had done the killing, they were the authors of the action, a sort of natural copyright was claimed, all accounts of the crime must pay royalties to them—or at least to Leopold for his half!"[69]

Levin was right to be indignant. The case wound its way endlessly through the courts, eventually reaching the Illinois supreme court in 1970; there, it was finally dismissed. Levin spent tens of thousands of

40. THE HAPPY COUPLE. This photograph, taken on 26 June 1964, shows Nathan Leopold and his wife, Trudi Feldman, at a press conference in Chicago. Leopold was in Chicago to attend the World Conference of the Church of the Brethren.

dollars in his defense. In the decade of legal wrangling over the case, no publisher would reissue *Compulsion* after its initial print run for fear of incurring potential damages if the courts did decide in favor of Leopold.[70]

While his lawsuit kept the attorneys busy in Chicago, Nathan continued to live peacefully in Puerto Rico. Not long after his arrival in the island, he had met a fifty-three-year-old woman from Baltimore, Trudi Feldman, the widow of a physician; and in October 1961, after obtaining the permission of his parole board, they exchanged vows at a wedding ceremony in Castaner. They lived comfortably—Nathan had inherited $50,000 on his father's death in 1929, and it had been accumulating interest throughout his imprisonment. Trudi, for her part, had an independent income as the owner of a flower shop in San Juan.[71]

In 1963 Nathan won his release from parole. Finally he could drink alcohol, drive an automobile, and stay out at night; best of all, he could now travel outside Puerto Rico. Neither Trudi nor Nathan had seen much of the world, and during the 1960s they made up for lost time, traveling throughout Europe, South America, Asia, and the Middle East. Nathan returned to Chicago often, to see old friends, to tour the South Side neighborhood near the university, and to place flowers on the graves of his mother and father and two brothers.[72]

It had been so long ago—that summer of 1924, in the stuffy courtroom on the sixth floor of the Cook County Criminal Court—and now he was the sole survivor. William Alanson White had died in 1937, honored as the leader of the American psychiatric profession. Clarence Darrow had died in 1938, exalted as the greatest lawyer of his generation. John Caverly had suffered a fatal stroke while on vacation in Bermuda in 1939. Benjamin Bachrach and his younger brother, Walter, had died within a few months of each other, in December 1950 and March 1951, respectively. Robert Crowe had lived until 1958, spending his final years in a retirement home. Richard Loeb, of course, had expired on the operating table in the Stateville prison.

He had atoned for his crime, Nathan believed. In any case, the murder had passed into legend. It had become a catchphrase—the Leopold and Loeb case—and in the absence of any authoritative account of the murder, newspaper writers had been free to embellish it as they pleased. They recounted the story in detail one more time, on 29 August 1971, when Nathan Leopold died of a heart attack. His body was donated to the University of Puerto Rico for medical research. There was no funeral service.[73]

LEOPOLD AND LOEB IN FICTION

In April 1927, F. Scott Fitzgerald sat down with a reporter for the New York *World* over drinks at the Plaza Hotel in New York to reveal that he had been writing a novel based on the Leopold-Loeb case. His new book, Fitzgerald confided, would be darker and more pessimistic than his previous accounts of American youth—it would reflect his conviction that American culture and society were set inexorably on a path to self-immolation and destruction. What episode in the Jazz Age could better express Fitzgerald's pessimism and despair than the random murder of a fourteen-year-old child by two wealthy hedonistic teenage lovers?[1]

Fitzgerald never did write his novel, but in 1929, the first fictional account of the murder appeared—not in the United States, but on the London stage. The success of the play *Rope* abruptly lifted its author, Patrick Hamilton, from abject poverty to financial independence. "How can I begin to describe to you the *uncanniness* of my success?" Hamilton wrote to his brother. "For it is not only the money—it is fame. . . . And all through *Rope*. It is all too funny." In his play Hamilton moved the action from Chicago to a Mayfair apartment in London. His two killers, Wyndham Brandon and Charles Granillo, collaborate in the murder of a close friend by each pulling on one end of a rope. They then stuff the corpse into a large chest. They invite other acquaintances, including the father of the victim, to a dinner party with the buffet laid out on the top of the chest. One guest, Rupert Cadell, shares the Nietzschean philosophy of the two murderers but, on opening the chest and discovering the corpse, denounces the murder and calls the police. The first stage production of *Rope* was at the Strand Theatre in March 1929. Critics alternately praised and condemned the play for its macabre and violent theme, but it continued to earn Hamilton substantial royalties until his death in 1974.[2]

In 1948 Alfred Hitchcock produced the screen adaptation of Hamilton's play. Hitchcock had conceived of *Rope* as an inexpensive movie—the action occurs in a single room, and there are fewer than a dozen characters—but his decision to film it in a series of long takes cost him more time and money than he had anticipated. *Rope* begins with the murder as a sexual act. The two killers, Brandon Shaw and Philip Morgan, then hide the corpse in a chest and host a dinner party in their New York apartment. Some critics regarded the film as one of Hitchcock's least successful, overburdened with suggestive theories and clumsily concluded with a monologue by Rupert Cadell (played by James Stewart). Others have praised its complex portrayal of Brandon as both aggressively self-assured and painfully vulnerable; Brandon has an overwhelming lust for power and control and yet is desperately fearful of his own impotence. The film did poorly at the box office. The production company, Warner Bros., belatedly realized that a homosexual relationship framed the murder and its aftermath; the Anti-Defamation League protested against the movie's depiction of two Jews as homosexual murderers; and the National Review Board decreed that only mature audiences could see the film. *Rope* was a commercial success in New York but flopped everywhere else.[3]

In 1953, Nathan Leopold's initial request for parole reawakened public interest in the murder and ignited a national debate about crime and punishment and the wisdom of releasing prisoners convicted of heinous crimes. The furor over Leopold's parole application prompted three novelists to write fictional accounts. The playwright James Yaffe set his novel *Nothing but the Night* in New York City. Mary-Carter Roberts, the book editor of the Washington *Evening Star*, intertwined two other stories around her version of the murder in *Little Brother Fate*. Meyer Levin, in *Compulsion*, claimed historical accuracy in his interpretation of the killing. All three novels appeared within a few months of one another.[4]

Compulsion is best remembered today not because of its literary merits but because it was adapted as a movie, starring Orson Welles as Clarence Darrow and E. G. Marshall as Robert Crowe. Welles stipulated in his contract that he was to spend just ten days filming his role. Yet he turned in a remarkable performance as the defense attorney. Welles is a charismatic presence throughout the film and his dramatic closing speech is one of the best performances of his career.[5]

Fictional accounts of the murder continue to appear. The movie *Swoon*, an avant-garde production that depicts the relationship between Leopold and Loeb in explicitly sexual terms, appeared in 1992. Shot in black-and-white, *Swoon* alternates between, on the one hand, precisely realistic scenes that convey a sense of documentary verisimilitude and, on the other, scenes that are bizarrely anachronistic. Another film, *Murder by Numbers*, directed by Barbet Schroeder, appeared in 2002 and takes San Benito, California, as its mise-en-scène. Its resemblance to the actual murder is comparatively slight. Two teenagers, Richard Haywood and Justin Pendleton, plot the perfect crime. Their random murder of a woman is less significant than the developing relationship between the two killers. A second relationship, between a homicide detective and her junior partner in the police department, shadows the first. Both relationships are pathological and assume a degree of control by one person over the other.

The screenwriter John Logan wrote *Never the Sinner*, a play based on the case, after reading *Compulsion* in high school. As an undergraduate at Northwestern, Logan read the courtroom transcripts in the archives at the university and wrote the first version of his play in a drama class. *Never the Sinner* premiered in 1985 in Chicago, and after its production in New York, it won the Outer Critics Circle Award.[6]

Most improbably, the murder has inspired a musical drama, *Thrill Me: The Leopold and Loeb Story*. A production of the York Theatre Company, *Thrill Me* premiered in 2003 at the Fourth Annual Midtown International Theatre Festival in New York City. The composer, Stephen Dolginoff, used Leopold's 1958 parole hearing to frame the events of 1924 and the pathological relationship between Nathan Leopold and Richard Loeb.

AUTHOR'S NOTE

Several years ago, on a wintry afternoon just a few weeks before Christmas, I found myself in London, in the part of the city known as King's Cross, close by the railroad station of the same name. I had to return to Brighton, a town on the south coast, that evening. I had an afternoon to kill before my departure from London, but I had no thoughts of spending the remainder of my time in King's Cross, then a notoriously seedy and dilapidated neighborhood. But, in the near distance, just ahead, I could see a large, ornate building, with rococo decoration, painted in red and green with touches of gold. The legendary Scala cinema! It was one of London's few remaining repertory cinemas, first opened in 1920, a glorious behemoth of a building with more than 1,000 seats in its auditorium. The film that afternoon was *Rope*, one of Alfred Hitchcock's classics, and on a whim I bought a ticket and entered. Two hours later I came away intrigued by Hitchcock's portrayal of two young men who murder a friend for the thrill of the experience.

I had never previously heard of the Leopold-Loeb case; but as I began to learn more about the events in Chicago in 1924, I realized that no one had yet written a book that considered the episode in its complexity and intricacy. No one, moreover, had written about the science that was so prominent a part of the courtroom battle between Clarence Darrow and Robert Crowe. What did the defense hope to show through its scientific analysis of the defendants? How would the state's attorney counter the scientific evidence? Would the scientific testimony of the psychiatrists and the endocrinologists convince its intended audience, the judge?

Much of this book reflects my education and training as a historian. It has been my great fortune to have studied and taught at many magnificent universities. My greatest intellectual debt has been to my teachers in the history of science at the University of Pennsylvania. As a student at Penn, I learned a proposition that now seems commonplace—that science is as much a cultural construct as it is a body of knowledge—but that then, in the 1980s, seemed radical and innovative. Penn possesses those resources for learning that one would expect of a member of the Ivy League—great teachers, outstanding libraries, and a supportive environment—and my studies at the university were both pleasant and productive.

I began this project during a three-year fellowship in the history of medicine at the National Institutes of Health (NIH) in Bethesda, Maryland. The research and writing continued during an appointment from 2004 to 2006 as a visiting associate professor of history at George Mason University, and the book has now come to its conclusion during my first year as an associate professor at John Jay College, City University of New York. At all three institutions—NIH, Mason, and John Jay—I have been blessed with stimulating colleagues, a welcoming environment, and access to great libraries, all of which have contributed greatly to the completion of this book.

My approach to writing this book reflects a contemporary concern of professional historians that their work should reach a wider audience. The history profession has never been in better shape. Undergraduate enrollment in history at the major colleges rises year by year; hundreds of excellent books on a dazzling variety of subjects pour from the presses; and employment opportunities for historians now exceed the number of doctorates in history awarded annually. Yet not infrequently, at meetings of such groups as the American Historical Association and the Organization of American Historians, one hears the jeremiad that historians, by writing too exclusively on narrowly focused topics, are isolating themselves from an American public that is, nevertheless, eager to read about its past.

I have attempted, therefore, to tell this story in a literary style. It is a narrative history that aims to recapture the drama of the events that it describes. Yet, at the same time, I have not avoided those complex issues that give the story its significance.

The courtroom provided the stage for two competing ideologies of crime and punishment. Do impersonal forces—economic, psychological, biological—compel individuals to act in certain ways? If so, then crime is a consequence of factors beyond conscious control and punishment is both futile and counterproductive. Or is criminal behavior a consequence of deliberate choice? Does the criminal freely decide to break the law? Is so, then punishment is both relevant and necessary. Clarence Darrow aimed to demonstrate a philosophy of behavior that left no space for free will; Robert Crowe set out to show that Nathan Leopold and Richard Loeb acted deliberately and knowingly.

Each actor in the courtroom drama sought to use the hearing as an opportunity to display his agenda. Clarence Darrow wished to demonstrate the viciousness of capital punishment and to argue for its abolition. Robert Crowe hoped that his success in the courtroom would translate into political approval at the polls and his election as Chicago's next mayor. The defense psychiatrists expected that their participation in the hearing would elevate and expand the role of psychiatry in the American legal process.

To write a book is no simple matter. One begins without any guarantee of success, without any assurance that it will find a publisher, and without knowing if the story has sufficient importance to command an audience. It demands patience and endurance, and perhaps most important of all, it requires the advice and support of colleagues and friends. I have been fortunate to have had invaluable help in writing this book. Nancy Unger took time from her own research and teaching to read successive drafts of each chapter and to provide corrections and suggestions—her generosity has made this a better book. Joe Berman also read the manuscript with an infectious enthusiasm that reassured me that I was indeed on the right track. Nancy Gist provided wonderful support from the beginning and carefully read each chapter as I wrote it. Three members of the George Mason faculty—Jack Censer, Marion Deshmukh, and Mack Holt—extended crucial help at an opportune time. Over the past six years, Scott Bradwell, Julie Brown, John Burnham, Roger Cooter, Hamilton Cravens, Walter Hickel, Jennifer Karsen, Olaf Kula, Carol Ann Langwith, Russell Maylone, Laura McGough, John Russick, Rosa Salguero, Yumiko Yamamori, and Joelle Ziemian each helped in one way or another to make my task less arduous. Emily Forland, my agent at the Wendy Weil Agency, secured the acceptance of the book proposal at HarperCollins, and both Emily and my editor at HarperCollins, Hugh Van Dusen, provided helpful feedback at every stage. I presented versions of this book to audiences at the History of Science Society, the Society for the History of Children and

Youth, the American Association for the History of Medicine, the Institute for the History of Psychiatry at Weill Medical College of Cornell University, and the National Museum of American History, Smithsonian Institution. Each forum was the occasion of spirited discussion and debate and helped shape the book in different ways.

SOURCES

Although the Leopold-Loeb case was one of the most infamous murders of the twentieth century, historians have largely ignored it. This seems counterintuitive. Everyone knows about the two brilliant college boys who killed a child for the thrill of the experience—and so, because the murder is so familiar, the reasoning goes, there must be several books, at least, about the killing of Bobby Franks. Crime and punishment, the random selection of the victim, the absence of remorse, the wealth and intelligence of the two killers, Clarence Darrow as the defense attorney, Chicago in the 1920s as a backdrop—how could there not be a barrel of books about the case? The abundance of source material should have attracted historians like bees to honey, yet until now only a single book, written more than thirty years ago, and a handful of articles in scholarly journals have been published.[1] The wealth of the source material—courtroom transcripts, records of the state's attorney's office, psychiatric reports—has allowed me to give this story immediacy and vividness and has enabled me to reconstruct it in detail. Here, I have listed the principal sources used in writing this book. I have indicated in **boldface** the abbreviated form used in the endnotes.

MANUSCRIPT SOURCES

I.

People of the State of Illinois vs. Nathan Leopold and Richard Loeb, Stenographic Transcript, Boxes 19–22, Leopold-Loeb Collection, Series LXXXV, Special Collections, Northwestern University Library, Northwestern University (abbreviated as **Trial Transcript**).

Original stenographic transcriptions of courtroom proceedings do not normally survive. Verbatim transcriptions are usually destroyed immediately after the disposition of a case. Fortunately, the stenographic transcript of the Leopold-Loeb hearing still exists. Elmer Gertz, who represented Nathan Leopold in his parole application, donated his copy, along with much other material on Leopold, to Northwestern University.

Because Robert Crowe insisted on presenting almost 100 witnesses in order to persuade the judge to hand down the death penalty and because those witnesses provided abundant detail from different perspectives, the transcript of the courtroom hearing is an invaluable source in reconstructing the murder. The to-and-fro between the defense and prosecution, the arguments between the state's attorney and the judge on the admissibility of evidence, and the testimony of both sets of psychiatric experts—all this is contained in great detail in the courtroom transcript.

One section of the transcript is missing. At the conclusion of the hearing, Darrow borrowed the section that contains his closing speech. He rewrote his speech, cutting out long passages, correcting his syntax, and streamlining his argument, and then published the amended version as a pamphlet. Darrow's speech in the courtroom was ponderous, disorganized, prolix, and often tedious; but subsequent commentators, unaware that the published version is not the speech that Darrow gave in court, have praised Darrow's summation as a masterpiece. Fortunately several newspapers transcribed Darrow's original speech and, in writing this book, I have used the transcription provided by the *Chicago Herald and Examiner*. (Darrow never did return the borrowed section of the transcript, and it remains missing.)[2]

II.

Statements of Nathan F. Leopold and Richard Albert Loeb, Made in the Office of the State's Attorney of Cook County, Folder 3, Box 2, Harold S. Hulbert Papers, Series 55/23, University Archives, Northwestern University.

The state's attorney questioned Nathan Leopold and Richard Loeb from Thursday 29 May until Monday 2 June. That weekend Leopold and Loeb talked and talked and talked . . . and then talked some more. Stenographers took it all down. The transcripts of the prisoners' confessions are preserved at Northwestern University and, as one might expect, they reveal a stunningly candid picture of the crime. In a series of statements, both Leopold and Loeb discussed the murder in detail, described its planning and execution, and talked also of their thoughts, expectations, fears, desires, and motivation.

Friday, 30 May 1924

Statement of Nathan F. Leopold Jr., Made in the Office of the State's Attorney of Cook County . . . on Friday, May 30, 1924, at 1:35 a.m. (abbreviated as **Leopold Statement**).

Statement of Nathan F. Leopold Jr., Made in the Office of the State's Attorney of Cook County . . . on Friday, May 30, 1924, at 6:30 p.m. (abbreviated as **Leopold Statement**).

Statement of Nathan F. Leopold Jr., Made in the Office of the State's Attorney of Cook County . . . on Friday, May 30, 1924, at 9:15 p.m.

Statement of Nathan F. Leopold Jr., Made in the Office of the State's Attorney of Cook County . . . on Friday, May 30, 1924, at 10:30 p.m. (abbreviated as **Leopold Statement**).

Additional Statement of Nathan F. Leopold Jr., Made in the Office of the State's Attorney . . . Friday, May 30, 1924, at 11:45 p.m. (abbreviated as **Additional Leopold Statement**).

Saturday, 31 May 1924

Additional Statement of Richard A. Loeb, Made in the Office of the State's Attorney . . . on Saturday, May 31, 1924, at 1:00 a.m. (abbreviated as **Additional Loeb Statement**).

Statement of Richard Albert Loeb, Made in the Office of the State's Attorney of Cook County . . . on Saturday, May 31, 1924, at 4:00 a.m. (abbreviated as **Loeb Statement**).

Statement of Nathan F. Leopold Jr., Made in the Office of the State's Attorney of Cook County . . . on Saturday, May 31, 1924, at 4:20 a.m. (abbreviated as **Leopold Statement**).

Sunday, 1 June 1924

Statement of Nathan F. Leopold Jr. and Richard Albert Loeb, Made in the Office of the State's Attorney of Cook County, Criminal Court Building, Chicago, Illinois, June 1, 1924, at 2:50 p.m. (abbreviated as **Leopold Loeb Statement**).

Statement of Nathan Leopold and Richard Loeb . . . on Sunday, June 1, 1924, at 6:30 p.m. in the Courtyard of the Cook County Jail, While Viewing Willys-Knight Automobile, Property of Rent-A-Car Company.

Statement of Nathan Leopold and Richard Loeb . . . on Sunday, June 1, 1924, at 8:20 p.m. in the Office of the State's Attorney of Cook County (abbreviated as **Leopold Loeb Statement**).

Statement of Nathan Leopold and Richard Loeb and Others Taken on Trip to South Side, June 1, 1924, . . . in Custody of Three Police Officers, with Assistant State's Attorney John Sbarbaro and F. A. Sheeder, Shorthand Reporter (abbreviated as **Leopold Loeb Statement on Trip to South Side**).

Statement of Nathan Leopold and Richard Loeb and Others, Made in the Office of the State's Attorney . . . on Sunday, June 1, 1924, at 11:30 p.m.

Monday, 2 June 1924

Statement of Nathan F. Leopold Jr., Made in the Office of the State's Attorney of Cook County . . . on Monday, June 2, 1924, at 12:01 a.m. (abbreviated as **Leopold Statement**).

Statement of Aaron B. Adler, Made in the Office of the State's Attorney of Cook County, Criminal Court Building, Chicago, Illinois, on Monday, 2 June 1924, at 12:40 a.m. (abbreviated as **Adler Statement**).

III.

Karl M. Bowman and Harold S. Hulbert, *Report of Preliminary Neuro-Psychiatric Examination (Richard Loeb)*, Box 2, Folder 1, Harold S. Hulbert Papers, Series

55/23, University Archives, Northwestern University [abbreviated as **Bowman-Hulbert Report (Loeb)**].

Karl M. Bowman and Harold S. Hulbert, *Report of Preliminary Neuro-Psychiatric Examination (Nathan Leopold Jr.)*, Box 2, Folder 2, Harold S. Hulbert Papers, Series 55/23, University Archives, Northwestern University [abbreviated as **Bowman-Hulbert Report (Leopold)**].

Several psychiatrists examined Nathan Leopold and Richard Loeb. Karl Bowman and Harold Hulbert submitted their report at the end of June 1924. The Bowman-Hulbert report contains detailed accounts of each defendant's childhood, education, upbringing, and adolescence; it also includes Loeb's fantasy life as a master criminal and Leopold's desire to be a powerful slave. Each defendant also recounted his version of the murder and its immediate aftermath. Archivists at Northwestern University uncovered the reports (along with the statements of Leopold and Loeb) in a vault in the basement of the university's law school. Harold Hulbert had collected materials connected with the case and these materials had been stored—forgotten and unnoticed—until their discovery in 1987.

IV.

Notes Relating to the Leopold-Loeb Court Case [1924], (Richard Loeb), Folder E37, Box 1, Records of Superintendent William Alanson White, Records of St. Elizabeths Hospital (Record Group 418.3.3), National Archives [abbreviated as **William Alanson White Notes (Loeb)**].

Notes Relating to the Leopold-Loeb Court Case [1924], (Nathan Leopold), Folder E37, Box 1, Records of Superintendent William Alanson White, Records of St. Elizabeths Hospital (Record Group 418.3.3), National Archives [abbreviated as **William Alanson White Notes (Leopold)**].

William White interviewed Nathan Leopold and Richard Loeb during the first week in July. White kept his handwritten notes from his interviews; these notes are preserved in a collection of White's papers at the National Archives in Washington, D.C.

V.

Psychiatric Reports re: Leopold and Loeb "Trial," Adolf Meyer Papers, Alan Mason Chesney Medical Archives, Johns Hopkins Medical Institutions (abbreviated as **Psychiatric Reports**).

The expert witnesses for the defense each prepared summaries of their reports on Nathan Leopold and Richard Loeb. These summaries, often only a few pages in length, provide succinct analytical statements on the medical and psychiatric condition of the defendants.

NEWSPAPERS

The fierce competition between Chicago's six daily newspapers and the public's insatiable fascination with Nathan Leopold and Richard Loeb produced an avalanche of newspaper coverage. The Chicago newspapers alone printed hundreds of articles on the case during 1924, and if one were to include the coverage by out-of-town newspapers, the total might easily exceed several thousand. Each Chicago newspaper employed several journalists to cover the case. As a consequence, Chicagoans in 1924 could learn all they wanted to know—and a great deal that they did not care to know—about the murder. The attorneys for each side cultivated the reporters, assiduously feeding them information that would tilt public opinion one way or the other. The reporters had unlimited access to the defendants, often spending hours chatting with them outside their cells in the Cook County jail.

I had imagined, in the early stages of my research, that reading the articles in a single newspaper would provide a comprehensive account of the case, but just as soon as I looked at a second newspaper, I realized my error. I discovered that there were details in the *Chicago Daily Journal*, for example, that had gone unmentioned in the reports of the *Chicago Daily Tribune* (and vice versa). Clearly, it would be foolish to base my account on only one or two newspapers; and so, in the early stages of my research, I resolved to read through all six of the city's daily newspapers. Because these newspapers have frequently altered their titles, usually on account of a merger with some other paper, or, alternatively, in an effort to abbreviate, I have been careful to cite the exact title of a newspaper as it appeared at the time.

The *Chicago Daily Tribune* and its sister paper, the *Chicago Sunday Tri-*

bune, first appeared in 1847. In the 1920s the *Tribune*, a morning newspaper, saw itself as the mouthpiece of Chicago's leading businessmen and, in this capacity, was fiercely opposed to the gangsterism that was harming the city's general prosperity. The *Tribune*, while generally supporting the Republican cause, consistently opposed the Republican mayor, William Hale Thompson, who, according to the *Tribune* at least, was responsible for the corruption of politics in Chicago. The *Tribune* was the mouthpiece of the reform movement and briefly supported Robert Crowe in the early 1920s in his opposition to the City Hall machine.[3]

William Randolph Hearst owned both the *Chicago Herald and Examiner*, a morning newspaper that first appeared in 1918; and the *Chicago American*, an afternoon newspaper founded in 1900. Hearst's reputation for sensationalism and yellow journalism derives from his ownership of the *New York Evening Journal*, which advocated overseas expansionism and militarism during the Spanish-American War. Neither the *Chicago Herald and Examiner* nor the *Chicago American*, however, was especially sensationalist. The *Chicago American* had a tabloid style in the 1920s, but its coverage of the Leopold-Loeb hearing was generally reliable and responsible. The *Chicago Herald and Examiner* was the superior of the two Hearst newspapers in the extent of its coverage of the case. Hearst consolidated the two newspapers in 1939 as the *Chicago Herald-American*. In 1953 it became again the *Chicago American*. After a change of ownership and several other name changes, the newspaper finally expired in September 1974.[4]

The *Chicago Daily News*, an afternoon paper that first appeared in 1875, never let its rivals forget that it had scooped them in the early stages of the police investigation. James Mulroy and Alvin Goldstein, two recent graduates of the University of Chicago, were cub reporters for the *Chicago Daily News* in 1924. Mulroy and Goldstein won the Pulitzer Prize in 1925 for their inspired guess that the typewriter used by Nathan Leopold to type his law notes might also have been used for the ransom letter. The *Chicago Daily News* was distinctive among Chicago newspapers for the clarity of its writing, but its coverage of important events was never as comprehensive or as detailed as the coverage provided, say, by the *Chicago Daily Journal*. The publisher of the *News*, Victor Lawson, disliked Robert Crowe and consistently denounced the state's attorney as a demagogue who used the resources of his office to crush opposition to his electoral machine. Lawson's animus toward Crowe never became an issue, however, in his paper's coverage of the Leopold-Loeb hearing.

The *Chicago Evening Post* first appeared in 1890 and was the least distinguished of the city's newspapers. Its coverage of the murder was competent yet largely routine. The *Post*'s journalists rarely reported any aspect of the case that had gone unnoticed by its rivals. The *Chicago Evening Post* could not survive the Great Depression and disappeared in 1930.

The *Chicago Daily Journal*, an evening paper that first appeared in 1844, was distinctive in its appearance (it was printed on pale green paper) and in its support for the Democratic Party. Its coverage of the Leopold-Loeb case was unrivaled. It devoted more column inches to the murder than any other paper, including the *Chicago Daily Tribune*, and its reporters seemed to be everywhere, uncovering new facts, pursuing fresh leads, and interviewing anyone with even the slightest connection to the case. The *Chicago Daily Journal*, despite the breadth and extent of its coverage, failed to survive, and merged in 1929 with the *Chicago Daily News*.[5]

AUTOBIOGRAPHIES

An autobiography—one might imagine—would provide an insider's perspective. The author's account would be direct, objective, and truthful; it would provide an immediately accessible description of events. If only that might be so! In reality few individuals can resist exaggerating their accomplishments. One of Robert Crowe's assistants, Joseph Savage, wrote his autobiography in 1975, fifty years after the murder; and as one might expect for an account written so long after the event, it is full of errors. Less forgivably, Savage assigns himself the leading role in the investigation of the murder and appropriates Crowe's triumphs for himself.[6]

Clarence Darrow was seventy-three when he wrote his autobiography. Darrow was a protagonist in some of the most sensational trials of his day, and he devotes just two brief chapters to the Leopold-Loeb case. In the first, Darrow outlines the facts of the murder, and in the second he provides an analysis of his defense. His animosity toward Robert Crowe had softened in the years since the hearing and little remains of the hostility and contempt for the state's attorney that Darrow expressed so frequently during the courtroom battles. Darrow always believed the best of his clients and, notwithstanding all the evidence to the contrary, he describes Richard Loeb as "a kindly boy" and Nathan Leopold as "genial, kindly, and likable." Otherwise Darrow's account is generally accurate.[7]

Whereas Joseph Savage was careless with the facts, Nathan Leopold, who completed his autobiography in 1958, was careless with the truth. The first five chapters of *Life Plus 99 Years* deal with the events surrounding the murder; the remainder of the book is an account of Leopold's experiences in Joliet and Stateville. Leopold wrote his autobiography as part of his campaign to win parole, and it should be read in that light. It is an immensely clever book, written in a clear and engaging style that portrays the author as a lovable rogue who constantly struggles, despite adverse circumstances, to improve the lives of his fellow prisoners. The establishment of the prison school, his work as an X-ray technician, his stint as a nurse in the psychiatric ward, his participation in the malaria experiments—everything, in Leopold's account, is undertaken self-lessly for the betterment of mankind. The publication of his autobiography came too late to be considered by the parole board, but it succeeded in creating a picture of Nathan Leopold that persists to the present. There is no evidence, for example, that Leopold could speak several languages or that he had an exceptional IQ, yet such myths have been repeated so often that they have now come to be accepted as true.[8]

NOTES

CHAPTER 1: THE KIDNAPPING

1. Trial Transcript, fols. 30, 38, 50, 69.
2. Ibid., fol. 67.
3. "Moron Theory Gains Favor in Franks Murder Inquiry," *Chicago Daily Journal*, 23 May 1924.
4. John Herrick, "Jail Policeman in Franks Quiz; Tutors Freed," *Chicago Daily Tribune*, 29 May 1924; "Harvard School Head Calls Robert Franks Bright Youth," *Chicago Daily Tribune*, 23 May 1924; "Moron Theory"; "Franks, as Debater, Won on Plea to Save Necks of Murderers," *Chicago Daily Journal*, 4 June 1924.
5. John Kelley, "Jacob Franks, Father of Slain Boy, Started as Pawnbroker; Made Fortune in Realty," *Chicago Daily Tribune*, 23 May 1924.
6. Ibid.; "Franks without Enemies, Says Old Time 'Pal,'" *Chicago Sunday Tribune*, 25 May 1924.
7. "Ettelson Sets Mark for Longest Term as City Law Chief," *Chicago Daily Tribune*, 9 November 1920.
8. "Ettelson Tells of Vain Effort to Spring Trap," *Chicago Daily Tribune*, 23 May 1924.
9. Ibid.
10. Trial Transcript, fol. 107.
11. "Moron Theory."

12. "Kidnap Rich Boy; Kill Him," *Chicago Daily Tribune*, 23 May 1924.

13. Ibid.

14. Trial Transcript, fols. 82–84.

15. "Kidnapers Slay Millionaire's Son as $10,000 Ransom Waits," *Chicago Herald and Examiner*, 23 May 1924; "Tony Minke, Finder of Boy's Body, Gives Details of Discovery," *Chicago American*, 23 May 1924.

16. Trial Transcript, fols. 300, 323.

17. Ibid., fols. 88–89, 91–92, 94, 309.

18. Ibid., fol. 306.

19. Ibid., fols. 316, 319–320.

20. "Kidnap Rich Boy."

21. Ibid.

22. Ibid.; "Cub Reporters Win Franks Case Glory," *Chicago Daily News*, 31 May 1924.

23. Leopold Statement, 2 June 1924, 12:01 a.m., fol. 329.

24. Ibid., fols. 327–328.

25. Trial Transcript, fol. 634.

26. "Moron Theory"; "Collins Orders All Policemen to Look for Franks' Slayer," *Chicago American*, 23 May 1924.

27. "Kidnap Rich Boy"; James Doherty, "Kidnaped Boy Died Fighting," *Chicago Daily Tribune*, 24 May 1924; "Question Woman in Franks Murder," *Chicago Daily Journal*, 26 May 1924.

28. "Expert Fixes on Kind of Machine Kidnaper Used," *Chicago Daily Tribune*, 24 May 1924; "Kidnapers' Ransom Letter Shows Hand of Expert Letterer," *Chicago Daily Tribune*, 24 May 1924; Charles V. Slattery, "Franks Boy Gagged, Died Fighting," *Chicago Herald and Examiner*, 24 May 1924.

29. "Police Delve into Past of Boy's Teachers," *Chicago Sunday Tribune*, 25 May 1924.

30. "Kidnap Rich Boy"; Doherty, "Kidnaped Boy."

31. "Moron Theory."

32. "Raid Dope Rings for Franks Slayers," *Chicago Daily Tribune*, 28 May 1924; "Harvard School Not Hurt by Franks Case, Principal Says," *Chicago Daily Tribune*, 28 May 1924; "Aided Franks' Murder Car," *Chicago Daily Journal*, 27 May 1924.

33. "Moron Theory"; James Doherty, "Girl Vanishes as Franks Did," *Chicago Daily Tribune*, 26 May 1924; "Pence Vouches for His 3 Instructors," *Chicago American*, 23 May 1924.

34. "Frees Franks Teachers," *Chicago Daily Journal*, 28 May 1924; "New Franks Clues," *Chicago Evening Post*, 29 May 1924.

35. "Eyewitness Tells of Boy's Midnight Burial," *Chicago American*, 27 May 1924.

36. Doherty, "Kidnaped Boy"; Doherty, "Girl Vanishes."

37. James Doherty, "All City Hunts Kidnapers," *Chicago Sunday Tribune*, 25 May 1924.

38. Doherty, "Girl Vanishes"; "Coroner Renews Hunt for Clues at Death Scene," *Chicago American*, 27 May 1924.

39. Doherty, "Girl Vanishes."

40. "Aided Franks' Murder Car."

41. "Even Dogs Bark at Gray Cars," *Chicago Daily Tribune*, 28 May 1924.

42. "Slayer of Franks Boy May Be Suicide," *Chicago Daily News*, 24 May 1924; Doherty, "All City."

43. Doherty, "Kidnaped Boy"; Trial Transcript, fol. 95.

44. Doherty, "Kidnaped Boy"; "Dig For Franks Boy Clews," *Chicago Daily Tribune*, 27 May 1924; "Question Woman."

45. "Raid Dope," *Chicago Daily Tribune*, 28 May 1924.

46. Ibid.

47. "Slain Boy's Father Gets Death Note; Hunt Drug Addict," *Chicago Evening Post*, 24 May 1924.

48. Doherty, "Girl Vanishes"; "Girl, 17, Missing; Fear Her Victim of Franks Plot," *Chicago Daily Tribune*, 26 May 1924.

49. "Find Gertrude Barker: Male Companion Held," *Chicago Daily Journal*, 27 May 1924.

50. Maurine Watkins, "Simple Funeral Service Is Held for Franks Boy," *Chicago Daily Tribune*, 26 May 1924.

51. Ibid.; "Classmates Lay Franks to Rest," *Chicago Daily Journal*, 26 May 1924.

52. "Try to See Franks Slayer through His Spectacles," *Chicago Daily Tribune*, 29 May 1924.

53. Doherty, "Girl Vanishes."

54. Ibid.; "Talks of Franks Case, Found Dying of Drug," *Chicago American*, 29 May 1924.

55. "Glasses, Note Franks Clews," *Chicago Daily Journal*, 31 May 1924.

CHAPTER 2: THE RELATIONSHIP

1. "Psychiatrists' Report for the Defense (Joint Summary)," *Journal of the American Institute of Criminal Law and Criminology* 15 (November 1924): 360.

2. Trial Transcript, fols. 1870, 1873.

3. Ibid., fols. 1916–1917.

4. Bowman-Hulbert Report (Leopold), fol. 27.

5. Jean F. Block, *The Uses of Gothic: Planning and Building the Campus of the University of Chicago, 1892–1932* (Chicago: University of Chicago Press, 1983).

6. "Samuel F. Leopold," in Paul Gilbert and Charles Lee Bryson, *Chicago and Its Makers* (Chicago: F. Mendelsohn, 1929), 665.

7. Ibid.; Bowman-Hulbert Report (Leopold), fol. 3.

8. Maureen McKernan, "Leopold Family a Big Factor in City Business," *Chicago Sunday Tribune*, 1 June 1924.

9. Bowman-Hulbert Report (Leopold), fols. 23, 24.

10. Ibid., fols. 17–18.

11. Ibid., fols. 18–20.

12. Ibid., fol. 18.

13. "Athletics," *Harvard School Review* (1920): 89–95.

14. Bowman-Hulbert Report (Leopold), fols. 24–25.

15. Ibid., fol. 24.

16. Maurine Watkins, "'Dick Innocent,' Loebs Protest; Plan Defense," *Chicago Sunday Tribune*, 1 June 1924; "Jacob M. Loeb," in Gilbert and Bryson, *Chicago and Its Makers*, 928.

17. Watkins, "'Dick Innocent.'"

18. Bowman-Hulbert Report (Loeb), fols. 13, 33; William Alanson White Notes (Loeb), fol. 4.

19. Bowman-Hulbert Report (Loeb), fols. 72–75.

20. William Harms and Ida DePencier, *Experiencing Education: 100 Years of Learning at the University of Chicago Laboratory Schools* (Chicago: University of Chicago Laboratory Schools, 1996), 4–10.

21. "Review of the Season," *Correlator* 16 (1918): 124–125.

22. "Molecules Hold Meeting," *University High School Daily*, 31 October 1917.

23. "Freshman Lit Club Officers Nominated," *University High School Daily*, 9 May 1918; "Election of Officers Closes Freshmen Lit," *University High School Daily*, 22 May 1918.

24. "Freshmen! Vote Today for Class Officers," *University High School Daily*, 11 January 1918; "Freshmen Elect Officers," *University High School Daily*, 15 January 1918; "Freshmen," *Correlator* 16 (1918): 25; "Freshmen to Wind Up Year with Large Party," *University High School Daily*, 6 June 1918.

25. Bowman-Hulbert Report (Loeb), fols. 14, 19.

26. Ibid., fol. 14.

27. Ibid., fol. 40.

28. Ibid., fol. 14; Trial Transcript, fols. 1285–1286.

29. Bowman-Hulbert Report (Loeb), fol. 12.

30. "Sophomore Literary Society Holds Initial Meeting," *University High School Daily*, 10 October 1918; "Soph Literary Society Holds Varied Meeting," *University High School Daily*, 5 December 1918.

31. Bowman-Hulbert Report (Loeb), fol. 24.

32. Ibid.; Official Transcript (Richard Albert Loeb), Office of the Registrar, University of Chicago.

33. Bowman-Hulbert Report (Loeb), fols. 14–15; Trial Transcript, fol. 1670.

34. "The Campus Club," *Cap and Gown* 26 (1921): 178–179.

35. Ibid., 179; Bowman-Hulbert Report (Leopold), fol. 28; Official Transcript (Nathan Freudenthal Leopold Jr.), Office of the Registrar, University of Chicago.

36. Bowman-Hulbert Report (Leopold), fol. 89; Bowman-Hulbert Report (Loeb), fol. 78.

37. Bowman-Hulbert Report (Leopold), fol. 92; Bowman-Hulbert Report (Loeb), fol. 85.

38. Bowman-Hulbert Report (Leopold), fols. 90–91; Bowman-Hulbert Report (Loeb), fols. 83–85.

39. Trial Transcript, fols. 1671, 1683–1684.

40. Bowman-Hulbert Report (Loeb), fols. 69–71.

41. Ibid., fol. 68; William Alanson White Notes (Loeb), fol. 6; Trial Transcript, fols. 1295–1296, 1534–1535.

42. Bowman-Hulbert Report (Leopold), fols. 92, 93–94; Bowman-Hulbert Report (Loeb), fols. 85–86, 92–93.

43. Bowman-Hulbert Report (Leopold), fol. 139; William Alanson White Notes (Leopold), fol. 17; Trial Transcript, fols. 1386–1387.

44. Bowman-Hulbert Report (Leopold), fols. 63–64; Trial Transcript, fols. 1329–1330, 1484–1485, 1703.

45. Trial Transcript, fol. 1485.

46. Bowman-Hulbert Report (Leopold), fols. 66–68; Trial Transcript, fols. 1486, 1704.

47. Bowman-Hulbert Report (Leopold), fols. 67, 133; Trial Transcript, fols. 1486–1487.

48. Trial Transcript, fols. 1337–1338, 1706.

49. Bowman-Hulbert Report (Loeb), fols. 26–27.

50. Bowman-Hulbert Report (Leopold), fols. 28–29, 46, 89–90; Nathan F. Leopold Jr., *Life Plus 99 Years* (Garden City, NY: Doubleday, 1958), 112; Minutes of Phi chapter, Zeta Beta Tau, Bentley Historical Library, University of Michigan.

51. "Differed in College Life," *New York Times*, 2 June 1924.

52. "Il Circolo Italiano," *Cap and Gown* 28 (1923): 186.

53. "The Undergraduate Classical Club," *Cap and Gown* 28 (1923): 167.

54. Official Transcript (Nathan Freudenthal Leopold Jr.), Office of the Registrar, University of Chicago.

55. "Honorary Order Elects Fifteen to Membership," *Daily Maroon* (Chicago), 16 March 1923.

56. Nathan F. Leopold Jr., "Reason and Instinct in Bird Migration," *The Auk* 40 (July 1923): 409–414; Nathan F. Leopold Jr., "The Kirtland's Warbler in Its Summer Home," *The Auk* 41 (January 1924): 44–58; Leopold, *Life Plus 99 Years*, 171.

57. Official Transcript (Richard A. Loeb), Office of the Registrar, University of Michigan; "Richard Loeb of Chicago Michigan's Youngest Grad," *Chicago Daily Tribune*, 1 June 1923.

58. Trial Transcript, fols. 1776–1777, 1795, 1833, 1835–1837, 1917, 1920, 1922–1923.

59. Bowman-Hulbert Report (Loeb), fol. 46.

60. Trial Transcript, fols. 1857–1858, 1927–1928, 1941–1942, 1945–1947, 1949–1954.

61. Ibid., fols. 1672–1673.

CHAPTER 3: PLANNING THE MURDER

1. Nathan Leopold Jr. to Richard Loeb, 10 October 1923, quoted in Trial Transcript, fol. 3815.

2. "2,000 Marines Go to Michigan with Team," *Chicago Daily Tribune*, 9 November 1923; "Wolverines, Marines in Grid War Today," *Chicago Daily Tribune*, 10 November 1923.

3. "2,000 Marines"; Sam Greene, "Michigan-Marine Corps Game Saturday Certain to Be Colorful Spectacle," *Detroit Free Press*, 10 November 1923.

4. "Denby Watches Michigan Trim Marines, 26 to 6," *Chicago Daily Tribune*, 11 November 1923; Lloyd Northard, "Amid Pomp and Ceremony Michigan Scores over Quantico Marines, 26 to 6," *Detroit Free Press*, 11 November 1923.

5. Bowman-Hulbert Report (Loeb), fols. 87–88.

6. Ibid., fol. 88.

7. Ibid., fol. 89.

8. Bowman-Hulbert Report (Leopold), fol. 96.

9. Bowman-Hulbert Report (Loeb), fol. 89.

10. Bowman-Hulbert Report (Leopold), fol. 97.

11. Ibid.; Bowman-Hulbert Report (Loeb), fol. 94.

12. Trial Transcript, fols. 1449–1450; Bowman-Hulbert Report (Loeb), fols. 94–95.

13. Bowman-Hulbert Report (Leopold), fols. 98–99; Bowman-Hulbert Report (Loeb), fol. 98.

14. William Alanson White Notes (Leopold), fols. 16–17; Bowman-Hulbert Report (Leopold), fols. 59, 100; Bowman-Hulbert Report (Loeb), fol. 101.

15. Bowman-Hulbert Report (Leopold), fol. 100; Bowman-Hulbert Report (Loeb), fol. 103.

16. Bowman-Hulbert Report (Loeb), fol. 105; Bowman-Hulbert Report (Leopold), fols. 100–101.

17. Leopold Loeb Statement, 1 June 1924, 8:20 p.m., fol. 297.

18. Trial Transcript, fol. 125.

19. Ibid., fol. 126.

20. Ibid., fols. 113–117, 121–122.

21. Loeb Statement, 31 May 1924, 4:00 a.m., fol. 47; Trial Transcript, fols. 155, 163.

22. Trial Transcript, fol. 163.

23. Ibid., fols. 144–146.

24. Ibid., fols. 148–151.

25. Leopold Loeb Statement, 1 June 1924, 2:50 p.m., fol. 204.

26. Ibid., fol. 205.

27. Leopold Statement, 30 May 1924, 1:35 a.m., fol. 363.

28. Ibid., fol. 363.

29. Ibid., fol. 366.

30. Leopold Loeb Statement on Trip to South Side, 1 June 1924, fols. 156–158.

31. "State Shows Every Step in Its Proof before Grand Jury," *Chicago Daily Journal*, 4 June 1924; Adler Statement, 2 June 1924, 12:40 a.m., fols. 333, 335–336, 337–338, 341, 344.

32. Loeb Statement, 31 May 1924, 4:00 a.m., fol. 51.

33. Christopher B. Booth, "The Kidnaping Syndicate," *Detective Story Magazine* 66 (3 May 1924): 1–47, on pp. 26, 36–37; "Franks Death Letter Like Current Story in Magazine," *Chicago Daily Tribune*, 24 May 1924.

CHAPTER 4: THE MURDER

1. Loeb Statement, 31 May 1924, 4:00 a.m., fol. 66.

2. Walter Scott Hastings, *Edwin Preston Dargan, 1879–1940: American Critic and Man of Letters* (Princeton, NJ: Princeton University Press, 1941).

3. George R. Havens, "E. Preston Dargan: A Career of Scholarship (1879–1940)," *Books Abroad* (Autumn 1941): 412–415.

4. Ibid., 414–415.

5. Leopold Statement, 30 May 1924, 10:30 p.m., fols. 447–449.

6. Ibid., fol. 406; Leopold Statement, 30 May 1924, 10:30 p.m., fols. 446–447, 491–492.

7. Leopold Loeb Statement, 1 June 1924, 2:50 p.m., fol. 211.

8. Ibid., fols. 212–214.

9. Ibid., fol. 213.

10. Loeb Statement, 31 May 1924, 4:00 a.m., fol. 55; Leopold Loeb Statement, 1 June 1924, 2:50 p.m., fol. 213–214; Leopold Statement, 31 May 1924, 4:20 a.m., fols. 10–12.

11. Trial Transcript, fols. 262–263.

12. Additional Loeb Statement, 31 May 1924, 1:00 a.m., fol. 513–514; Leopold Statement, 31 May 1924, 4:20 a.m., fol. 17.

13. Loeb Statement, 31 May 1924, 4:00 a.m., fol. 56.

14. "Four Boys on Kidnaping List," *Chicago Herald and Examiner*, 1 June 1924; "Young Millionaires Tell How They Killed Franks," *Chicago Daily Journal*, 31 May 1924.

15. Loeb Statement, 31 May 1924, 4:00 a.m., fol. 56.

16. Ibid., fols. 56–57; Leopold Statement, 31 May 1924, 4:20 a.m., fols. 16–17.

17. Leopold Loeb Statement, 1 June 1924, 2:50 p.m., fol. 215.

18. Trial Transcript, fols. 668–669.

19. Loeb Statement, 31 May 1924, 4:00 a.m., fols. 57–58.

20. Leopold Loeb Statement, 1 June 1924, 2:50 p.m., fols. 215–216.

21. Ibid., fol. 217.

22. Ibid., fols. 217–218.

23. Ibid., fol. 219.

24. "Have You Seen These Clothes Worn by Boy?" *Chicago American*, 23 May 1924.

25. Leopold Loeb Statement, 1 June 1924, 2:50 p.m., fol. 248.

26. Ibid., fols. 220, 248; Trial Transcript, fol. 35; Leopold Statement, 31 May 1924, 4:20 a.m., fols. 5, 20–21.

27. Leopold Loeb Statement, 1 June 1924, 2:50 p.m., fols. 221, 248.

28. Ibid., fol. 249; Loeb Statement, 31 May 1924, 4:00 a.m., fol. 68.

29. Leopold Loeb Statement, 1 June 1924, 2:50 p.m., fol. 224.

30. Loeb Statement, 31 May 1924, 4:00 a.m., fol. 63.

31. Ibid., fols. 64, 66.

32. Ibid., fols. 65, 66.

33. Ibid., fol. 67; Leopold Loeb Statement, 1 June 1924, 2:50 p.m., fols. 232–233.

34. Loeb Statement, 31 May 1924, 4:00 a.m., fol. 68.

35. Leopold Loeb Statement, 1 June 1924, 2:50 p.m., fols. 233–234.

36. Loeb Statement, 31 May 1924, 4:00 a.m., fol. 68; Leopold Statement, 31 May 1924, 4:20 a.m., fol. 25.

37. Loeb Statement, 31 May 1924, 4:00 a.m., fol. 68; Leopold Loeb Statement, 1 June 1924, 2:50 p.m., fol. 234.

38. Leopold Loeb Statement on Trip to South Side, 1 June 1924, fols. 157–158.

39. "Moron Theory Gains Favor in Franks Murder Inquiry," *Chicago Daily Journal*, 23 May 1924.

40. Loeb Statement, 31 May 1924, 4:00 a.m., fol. 69; Leopold Statement, 31 May 1924, 4:20 a.m., fol. 24.

41. Trial Transcript, fols. 234–237; Leopold Statement, 31 May 1924, 4:20 a.m., fols. 25–26; Leopold Loeb Statement, 1 June 1924, 2:50 p.m., fols. 235, 236.

CHAPTER 5: THE RANSOM

1. Leopold Loeb Statement, 1 June 1924, 2:50 p.m., fol. 278.
2. Trial Transcript, fols. 265–267; Loeb Statement, 31 May 1924, 4:00 a.m., fol. 70; Leopold Statement, 31 May 1924, 4:20 a.m., fols. 9, 27; "Clinch Youths' Confessions," *Chicago Sunday Tribune*, 1 June 1924.
3. Loeb Statement, 31 May 1924, 4:00 a.m., fol. 71.
4. Ibid., fol. 72; Trial Transcript, fols. 292–293; Leopold Statement, 31 May 1924, 4:20 a.m., fol. 7.
5. Leopold Statement, 2 June 1924, 12:01 a.m., fols. 327–328.
6. Loeb Statement, 31 May 1924, 4:00 a.m., fol. 73; Leopold Statement, 31 May 1924, 4:20 a.m., fol. 8; Nathan F. Leopold Jr., *Life Plus 99 Years* (Garden City, NY: Doubleday, 1958), 28.
7. Leopold Loeb Statement on Trip to South Side, 1 June 1924, fols. 164–165.
8. Trial Transcript, fols. 365–366
9. Leopold Statement, 31 May 1924, 4:20 a.m., fol. 28.
10. Loeb Statement, 31 May 1924, 4:00 a.m., fol. 74.
11. Leopold Statement, 30 May 1924, 1:35 a.m., fol. 406.
12. Ibid., fol. 407.
13. Ibid., fol. 354.
14. Trial Transcript, fols. 387–388.
15. Ibid., fols. 397, 402.
16. Ibid., fols. 388.
17. Ibid., fol. 388.
18. "Slain Boy's Teacher Hidden," *Chicago Daily News*, 23 May 1924; Trial Transcript, fol. 388.
19. Trial Transcript, fols. 389, 403.
20. Ibid., fols. 400, 404
21. Loeb Statement, 31 May 1924, 4:00 a.m., fol. 74.
22. Leopold, *Life Plus 99 Years*, 38–40.
23. Loeb Statement, 31 May 1924, 4:00 a.m., fols. 74–75.
24. Ibid., fol. 75.
25. Trial Transcript, fols. 376–377, 383–384.
26. Ibid., fols. 441–445.

CHAPTER 6: THE INTERROGATION

1. Leopold Loeb Statement, 1 June 1924, 2:50 p.m., fols. 284–285, 286.

2. Trial Transcript, fols. 467–468.

3. Leopold Statement, 30 May 1924, 1:35 a.m., fol. 369.

4. Ibid., fols. 381–382.

5. Ibid., fol. 377.

6. Ibid., fols. 429–432. See also Additional Loeb Statement, 31 May 1924, 1:00 a.m., fol. 516.

7. Leopold Statement, 30 May 1924, 1:35 a.m., fols. 366–367.

8. Ibid., fol. 363.

9. Ibid., fol. 366.

10. Ibid., fols. 371–373.

11. Ibid., fols. 397–399.

12. "Gin Party Leopold Alibi; Seek Death Typewriter," *Chicago Daily Journal*, 30 May 1924.

13. "Kin Aid Two in Franks Tangle," *Chicago Daily Journal*, 30 May 1924; "Both Fathers Stunned," *Chicago Daily News*, 31 May 1924.

14. "Gin Party."

15. "Youth Retain Friends' Faith during Their Long Ordeal," *Chicago Daily Tribune*, 31 May 1924.

16. "Kin Aid Two."

17. "Parents Disbelieve Confession; Battle of Millions Is Looming," *The World* (New York), 1 June 1924.

18. "Youth Retain."

19. Trial Transcript, fol. 397

20. "Cub Reporters Win Franks Glory," *Chicago Daily News*, 31 May 1924.

21. Trial Transcript, fols. 676–677.

22. Ibid., fol. 208.

23. Leopold Statement, 30 May 1924, 6:30 p.m., fol. 439–440.

24. Additional Leopold Statement, 30 May 1924, 11:45 p.m., fol. 499.

25. Leopold Statement, 30 May 1924, 10:30 p.m., fols. 450–452.

26. Ibid., fols. 484–485.

27. Leopold Statement, 30 May 1924, 1:35 a.m., fol. 391.

28. Additional Leopold Statement, 30 May 1924, 11:45 p.m., fols. 495–497.

29. Ibid., fols. 505, 505–506, 510.

30. Trial Transcript, fols. 262–264, 267.

31. Ibid., fols. 261–264.

32. "Shake Leopold-Loeb Alibi," *Chicago Daily Tribune*, 31 May 1924; "Confess as Auto Ride Alibi Is Swept Away," *Chicago Herald and Examiner*, 1 June 1924.

33. Leopold Loeb Statement, 1 June 1924, 2:50 p.m., fol. 193.

34. Ibid., fols. 193–194.

35. Additional Loeb Statement, 31 May 1924, 1:00 a.m., fols. 512–514.

36. Trial Transcript, fols. 2624–2625; Additional Loeb Statement, 31 May 1924, 1:00 a.m., fol. 514.

37. Leopold Loeb Statement, 1 June 1924, 2:50 p.m., fols. 194–196; "Confess," *Chicago Herald and Examiner*, 1 June 1924; Orville Dwyer, "Clinch Youths' Confessions," *Chicago Sunday Tribune*, 1 June 1924.

CHAPTER 7: THE CONFESSIONS

1. Trial Transcript, fols. 3037.

2. Ibid., fols. 1588–1589; "Young Millionaires Tell How They Killed Franks," *Chicago Daily Journal*, 31 May 1924.

3. Trial Transcript, fols. 1637–1638.

4. Loeb Statement, 31 May 1924, 4:00 a.m., fols. 44–45.

5. Ibid., fols. 61–62, 65.

6. Ibid., fol. 75.

7. Leopold Statement, 31 May 1924, 4:20 a.m., fols. 5, 42.

8. "How Franks Boy Was Killed Is Told," *Chicago Daily News*, 31 May 1924; Charles V. Slattery, "'Hang Leopold and Loeb,' Says Crowe; Killed Boy to Pay Blackmailer Theory," *Chicago Herald and Examiner*, 1 June 1924; "Killers Collapse," *Chicago American*, 31 May 1924; "Young Millionaires."

9. "Let Law Take Its Course, Says Franks, Father of Slain Boy," *Chicago Daily Journal*, 31 May 1924; "Father of Franks Boy Voices Deep Sympathy for Families of Culprits," *Chicago Herald and Examiner*, 1 June 1924.

10. Leola Allard, "Agony of Mothers of Slayers and Slain in Tragedy of Crime," *Chicago Herald and Examiner*, 1 June 1924; Maurine Watkins, "'Dick Innocent,' Loebs Protest; Plan Defense," *Chicago Sunday Tribune*, 1 June 1924.

11. Maureen McKernan, "Leopold Family a Big Factor in City's Business," *Chicago Sunday Tribune*, 1 June 1924.

12. "Re-Enact Franks Murder," *Chicago Evening Post*, 31 May 1924; "Four Boys on Kidnaping List," *Chicago Herald and Examiner*, 1 June 1924.

13. "'Experience' Seen as Motive," *Chicago Daily News*, 2 June 1924; "Modernistic Books Made Slayers of Students, Rosenwald Theory," *Chicago Daily Journal*, 2 June 1924.

14. Irving Cutler, *The Jews of Chicago: From Shtetl to Suburb* (Urbana: University of Illinois Press, 1996), 197–205; Lindsay Denison, "Leopold and Loeb Families Scored by Close Friend," *The World* (New York), 5 June 1924.

15. "Sad for Parents of Boys in Kidnaping," *Chicago Daily News*, 31 May 1924.

16. Slattery, "'Hang Leopold and Loeb.'"

17. Trial Transcript, fol. 158.

18. Ibid., fol. 688; Charles V. Slattery, "Untold Tales in Franks Case," *Chicago Herald and Examiner*, 31 August 1924.

19. Trial Transcript, fols. 476–477.

20. Ibid., fols. 256–257.

21. Ibid., fols. 258–259.

22. Ibid., fols. 690, 691, 694.

23. Orville Dwyer, "Clinch Youths' Confessions," *Chicago Sunday Tribune*, 1 June 1924.

24. Irving Stone, *Clarence Darrow for the Defense: A Biography* (Garden City, NY: Doubleday, Doran, 1941), 380–381.

25. "'I Wrote Note, Loeb Killed Him,' Says Leopold in First Interview," *Chicago Herald and Examiner*, 2 June 1924.

26. "3000 See Search for Typewriter," *Chicago Herald and Examiner*, 2 June 1924.

27. "'I Wrote Note.'"

28. Morrow Krum, "'This'll Be the Making of Me,' Says Loeb Boy," *Chicago Daily Tribune*, 2 June 1924.

29. "'I Wrote Note.'"

30. Leopold Loeb Statement, 1 June 1924, 2:50 p.m., fols. 166–168.

31. Trial Transcript, fols. 2645–2648; "Dr. Hugh T. Patrick," *New York Times*, 6 January 1939.

32. Leopold Loeb Statement, 1 June 1924, 2:50 p.m., fols. 170–180.

33. Trial Transcript, fol. 3288; Leopold Loeb Statement, 1 June 1924, 2:50 p.m., fol. 180.

34. Trial Transcript, fols. 3284–3286, 3337; "Deaths: William Otterbein Krohn," *Illinois Medical Journal* 52 (1927): 176; "Dr. W. O. Krohn, Noted Alienist, Taken by Death," *Chicago Daily Tribune*, 11 July 1927.

35. Leopold Loeb Statement, 1 June 1924, 2:50 p.m., fol. 185.

36. Lewis J. Pollock, "A Tribute to Archibald Church," *Quarterly Bulletin of Northwestern University Medical School* 26 (1952): 293–294.

37. Leopold Loeb Statement, 1 June 1924, 2:50 p.m., fols. 199–200.

38. Ibid., fols. 240–241.

39. Ibid., fols. 277–278.

40. Ibid., fols. 265–266.

41. Ibid., fols. 273–274.

42. Ibid., fols. 275–277.

CHAPTER 8: CLARENCE DARROW

1. Trial Transcript, fols. 4157–4158.

2. Clarence Darrow to Robert R. Gros, 4 November 1933, Folder 4, Box 1, Robert Gros Collection, Department of Special Collections, Stanford University Libraries.

3. "Is Held for Murder," *Chicago Daily Tribune*, 30 October 1893; "His Habits Strange," *Chicago Daily Tribune*, 15 December 1893; "Assassin Is on Trial," *Chicago Daily Tribune*, 14 December 1893; "Gives Himself Up," *Chicago Sunday Tribune*, 29 October 1893.

4. "Gives Himself Up."

5. "Harrison Is Killed," *Chicago Sunday Tribune*, 29 October 1893; "His Last Address," *Chicago Sunday Tribune*, 29 October 1893.

6. "Harrison Is Killed."

7. "Gives Himself Up."

8. "Assassin Is on Trial"; "Believe Him Insane," *Chicago Daily Tribune*, 16 December 1893; "Go Over to Defense," *Chicago Daily Tribune*, 19 December 1893; "Assassin Must Die," *Chicago Daily Tribune*, 30 December 1893.

9. "Fighting for a Life," *Chicago Sunday Tribune*, 31 December 1893.

10. M. L. Edgar, "Clarence S. Darrow," *The Mirror* 17 (16 May 1907): 13–14; Edward F. O'Day, "Clarence Darrow," *Town Talk* 20 (1 June 1912): 7, 23; "Who Is This Man Darrow?" *Current Literature* 43 (August 1907): 157–159.

11. Clarence Darrow, *The Story of My Life* (New York: Scribner, 1932), 41.

12. Paul Avrich, *The Haymarket Tragedy* (Princeton, NJ: Princeton University Press, 1984), 197–214.

13. Ibid., 279, 375–378, 391–394.

14. Ibid., 416–417, 419–421.

15. S. J. Duncan-Clark, "Clarence Darrow Opens His Fight against the Death Penalty," *Success* 8 (December 1924): 28–31, 123.

16. "To Cheat the Rope," *Chicago Daily Tribune*, 22 March 1894.

17. "Prendergast Shows No Emotion," *Chicago Daily Tribune*, 22 March 1894.

18. "Last Effort to Save His Life," *Chicago Daily Tribune*, 23 March 1894; "Not to Hang Today," *Chicago Daily Tribune*, 23 March 1894.

19. "Scene in the Court," *Chicago Daily Tribune*, 25 March 1894.

20. Darrow, *Story of My Life*, 361.

21. Ibid., 41, 96; John P. Altgeld, *Our Penal Machinery and Its Victims*, 2nd ed. (New York: A. C. McClurg, 1886), 21.

22. Ray Ginger, *The Bending Cross: A Biography of Eugene Victor Debs* (New Brunswick, NJ: Rutgers University Press, 1949), 92–93, 101–107; Nick Salvatore, *Eugene V. Debs: Citizen and Socialist* (Urbana: University of Illinois Press, 1982), 114–125.

23. Ginger, *Bending Cross*, 108–147; Salvatore, *Eugene V. Debs*, 126–135.

24. Ginger, *Bending Cross*, 164–167; Salvatore, *Eugene V. Debs*, 137–138.

25. Irving Stone, *Clarence Darrow for the Defense: A Biography* (Garden City, NY: Doubleday, Doran, 1941), 103–112.

26. J. Anthony Lukas, *Big Trouble: A Murder in a Small Western Town Sets Off a Struggle for the Soul of America* (New York: Simon and Schuster, 1997), 50–54, 108–109.

27. Ibid., 70–72, 197–200, 255–262.

28. Ibid., 707–711, 722–725.

29. Geoffrey Cowan, *The People v. Clarence Darrow: The Bribery Trial of America's Greatest Lawyer* (New York: Random House, 1993), 86–90, 101–109, 119–123, 137–138.

30. Ibid., 246–255.

31. Ibid., 279–283, 291–293, 429–433.

32. Kevin Tierney, *Darrow: A Biography* (New York: Thomas Y. Crowell, 1979), 281, 291, 306–310.

33. "Clarence Darrow to the Prisoners at Joliet," *Everyman* 11 (November 1915): 14–15.

34. "Finger Prints Move Slayer to Confess," *Chicago Daily Tribune*, 18 May 1915.

35. "Coroner Holds Pethrick [*sic*] after New Confession," *Chicago Daily Tribune*, 19 May 1915.

36. Ibid.; "Will Try to Hang Pethrick [*sic*]," *Chicago Daily Tribune*, 20 May 1915.

37. "Women Doctors Find Pethick's Mental Age 7," *Chicago Daily Tribune*, 9 September 1915.

38. Ibid.

39. "Woman Lawyer to Defend Pethick," *Chicago Daily Tribune*, 25 August 1915; "Three Medics to Examine Slayer," *Chicago Daily Tribune*, 24 September 1915.

40. "Finds Pethick's Mind below Par," *Chicago Daily Tribune*, 25 September 1915; "State Demands Sentence of Death for Pethick," *Chicago Daily Tribune*, 28 September 1915; "Women See Lesson of Protection in Case of Pethick," *Chicago Daily Tribune*, 29 September 1915.

41. Robert M. Lee, "Half Wit Boy Admits Killing Rich Widow," *Chicago Daily Tribune*, 29 April 1916; "Death Verdict for Hettinger; 'I'll Not Hang,'" *Chicago Daily Tribune*, 30 September 1916.

42. "Hettinger Boy Declines Pam's Offer of Life," *Chicago Daily Tribune*, 12 November 1916.

43. "Hettinger Will Plead Guilty to Avoid Death," *Chicago Daily Tribune*, 23 November 1916; "Mother's Wish Moves Youth to Admit Murder," *Chicago Sunday Tribune*, 26 November 1916.

44. In Illinois, the jury decides both the verdict and the sentence in capital cases.

45. "Taunted Wife Shoots Husband in Courtroom," *Chicago Daily Tribune*, 26 April 1919.

46. Ibid.

47. Maude Martin Evers, "Simpson Widow Quails before Pointing Hands," *Chicago Daily Tribune*, 19 September 1919.

48. "Cussin' Cards Cited to Help Mrs. Simpson," *Chicago Sunday Tribune*, 21 September 1919; "Mrs. Simpson Insane 2 Years, Says Witness," *Chicago Daily Tribune*, 20 September 1919.

49. Maude Martin Evers, "Experts Differ on Insanity of Mrs. Simpson," *Chicago Daily Tribune*, 24 September 1919.

50. Maude Martin Evers, "Mrs. Simpson to Learn Fate by Noon Today," *Chicago Daily Tribune*, 25 September 1919.

51. Maude Martin Evers, "Mrs. Simpson Found Insane; Faces Asylum," *Chicago Daily Tribune*, 26 September 1919; "Mrs. Simpson Goes to Begin Asylum Sentence," *Chicago Daily Tribune*, 3 October 1919; "Woman Slayer of Husband Found Guilty," *Chicago Daily Tribune*, 15 July 1921.

52. Darrow, *Story of My Life*, 250, 428; Abe C. Ravitz, *Clarence Darrow and the*

American Literary Tradition (Cleveland: Press of Western Reserve University, 1962), 6–12; John C. Livingston, *Clarence Darrow: The Mind of a Sentimental Rebel* (New York: Garland, 1988), 96–99.

53. Clarence Darrow, *Crime: Its Cause and Treatment* (New York: Thomas Y. Crowell Co., 1922), v.

54. Ibid., 31–32.

55. Ibid., 32–33.

56. Livingston, *Clarence Darrow*, xxix, 99–106.

57. Darrow, *Crime*, 34–35.

58. Percy F. Bicknell, *The Human Side of Fabre* (New York: Century, 1923); Augustin Fabre, *The Life of Jean Henri Fabre*, trans. Bernard Miall (New York: Dodd, Mead, 1923).

59. Clarence S. Darrow, *Insects and Men: Instinct and Reason* (Girard, KS: Haldeman-Julius, 1921)

60. Darrow, *Crime*, 46, 50.

61. Ibid., 36.

CHAPTER 9: ROBERT CROWE

1. "Is Death Penalty Crime Curb? Crowe and Gemmill Debate It," *Chicago Sunday Tribune*, 19 February 1928.

2. "If You See This Girl Telephone 'The Tribune,'" *Chicago Sunday Tribune*, 27 July 1919; "'Sure Janet's in Heaven,' Mother, Told News, Sobs," *Chicago Daily Tribune*, 28 July 1919; "New Evidence Tightens Net on Fitzgerald," *Chicago Sunday Tribune*, 27 July 1919.

3. "Girl Vanishes; Kidnaping Feared," *Chicago Evening Post*, 23 July 1919; "40 Hour Hunt Fails to Bare Clew to Child," *Chicago Daily Tribune*, 24 July 1919.

4. "Fitzgerald Is Kidnaper, Wife Says," *Chicago Evening Post*, 25 July 1919; "Arrest Wife of Fitzgerald in Lost Girl Case," *Chicago Daily Tribune*, 25 July 1919.

5. "Full Confession by Slayer of Janet," *Chicago Daily Tribune*, 28 July 1919.

6. "Janet's Slayer Must Hang, Say Prosecutors," *Chicago Evening Post*, 28 July 1919.

7. "Quick Trial of Janet's Slayer Blocked by Law," *Chicago Daily Tribune*, 29 July 1919; Editorial, "The Murder of Janet Wilkinson," *Chicago Daily Tribune*, 29 July 1919.

8. "Janet Buried; Playmates Are Pall-Bearers," *Chicago Evening Post*, 29 July

1919; "Slayer Laments—The Riots as Janet Is Buried," *Chicago Daily Tribune*, 30 July 1919.

9. "'Time Clock' of Scientific Grilling Which Brings Confession," *Chicago Daily Tribune*, 28 July 1919; "Fitzgerald in Daze as Murder Story Is Told," *Chicago Daily Tribune*, 23 September 1919.

10. "Fitzgerald in Daze."

11. "Judge Decrees Gallows Death for Fitzgerald," *Chicago Daily Tribune*, 24 September 1919.

12. Oscar E. Hewitt, "Crowe or Igoe? Both Are Young and Ambitious," *Chicago Daily Tribune*, 17 September 1920.

13. Ibid.

14. Douglas Bukowski, *Big Bill Thompson, Chicago, and the Politics of Image* (Urbana: University of Illinois Press, 1998), 26–27; Lloyd Wendt and Herman Kogan, *Big Bill of Chicago* (New York: Bobbs-Merrill, 1953), 113–114.

15. "City Job for R. E. Crowe," *Chicago Daily Tribune*, 25 June 1915.

16. E. O. Phillips, "Thompson Slate Sweeps 34 Wards," *Chicago Daily Tribune*, 14 April 1920.

17. Hewitt, "Crowe or Igoe?"

18. "Man Slain, 3 Kidnaped, Police Slugged at Polls," *Chicago Evening Post*, 15 September 1920; Joe D. Salkeld, "Count Votes; Worker Slain," *Chicago Daily Journal*, 15 September 1920.

19. "Man Slain"; Salkeld, "Count Votes."

20. Editorial, "Mud and Money," *Chicago Daily Journal*, 16 September 1920.

21. "Thompson Cleans Up City," *Chicago Daily Tribune*, 16 September 1920; "Mayor's Rule Unquestioned," *Chicago Daily Journal*, 16 September 1920; "Mayor's County Ticket Makes a Clean Sweep," *Chicago Evening Post*, 16 September 1920; "Party Leaders Face Big Task of Registration," *Chicago Daily Tribune*, 4 October 1920.

22. Hewitt, "Crowe or Igoe?"; "Chicago's Blanket Ballot: In 'Real Life' It Is about a Yard Square," *Chicago Daily Tribune*, 27 October 1920.

23. "Hoyne Raps Igoe, Igoe Raps Hoyne, in Democrat Row," *Chicago Daily Tribune*, 15 October 1920.

24. "Crowe to Rival: None Can Serve God and Mammon," *Chicago Daily Tribune*, 17 October 1920.

25. "Crowe Raps Igoe Backers; Igoe Bombards City Hall," *Chicago Daily Tribune*, 20 October 1920.

26. "Crowe Urges Moron Curb; Igoe Assails Judge Ruling," *Chicago Daily Tribune*, 24 October 1920; "Crowe Calls Igoe 'Servant of Profiteers,'" *Chicago Daily Tribune*, 19 October 1920; "Crowe Gets Strong Allies; Igoe Hears Good Reports," *Chicago Daily Tribune*, 23 October 1920; "Crowe Gets O.K. from Judges of Chicago Courts," *Chicago Daily Tribune*, 31 October 1920; "Crowe Gets New Support; Igoe Hits at City's Crime," *Chicago Daily Tribune*, 25 October 1920.

27. Arthur M. Evans, "County G.O.P. Slate Romps In 200,000 Victor," *Chicago Daily Tribune*, 3 November 1920; "'Great Victory,' Say Crowe and Fred Lundin," *Chicago Herald and Examiner*, 3 November 1920; "Winners in County Get Record Vote," *Chicago Herald and Examiner*, 4 November 1920.

28. "Staged Holdup; Slew Wife," *Chicago Daily Tribune*, 10 July 1920.

29. "Wanderer Jury Told How Gun Trapped Slayer," *Chicago Daily Tribune*, 15 October 1920.

30. "Duel in Dark: Ex-Army Man Avenges Death," *Chicago Daily Tribune*, 22 June 1920; "'Kiss for Julia, Bullets for Mrs. Wanderer,'" *Chicago Daily Tribune*, 26 October 1920.

31. "Mask Torn Off, Wanderer Is Crime Enigma," *Chicago Sunday Tribune*, 11 July 1920.

32. "Wanderer Jury."

33. "Puzzle Grows over Death of Soldier's Wife," *Chicago Daily Tribune*, 9 July 1920.

34. "Staged Holdup"; "Sister Tells of Wanderer's Love Affairs," *Chicago Daily Tribune*, 13 July 1920.

35. "Claims Torture Won Confession from Wanderer," *Chicago Daily Tribune*, 27 October 1920.

36. "25 Years for Wanderer," *Chicago Daily Tribune*, 30 October 1920.

37. Ibid.

38. Ibid.; "'Poor Boob' May Hang Wanderer at New Trial," *Chicago Daily Tribune*, 31 October 1920.

39. "25 Years"; "Sentence Makes Wanderer Grin, but Grin Fades," *Chicago Daily Tribune*, 4 November 1920.

40. "Election Brings Month Respite for Wanderer," *Chicago Herald and Examiner*, 2 November 1920.

41. "Carl Wanderer Again Must Face Gallows Noose," *Chicago Daily Tribune*, 8 January 1921.

42. "Wanderer Born Insane, Hickson Tells Jurors," *Chicago Daily Tribune*, 11 March 1921; "Alienist Holds Wanderer has Mind of Boy, 11," *Chicago Daily Tribune*, 12 March 1921; "Women Experts Hold Stage at Wanderer Trial," *Chicago Daily Tribune*, 15 March 1921.

43. "Decree Noose for Wanderer, 'Boob's' Killer," *Chicago Daily Tribune*, 19 March 1921.

44. George S. Buck, "The Crime Wave and Law Enforcement," *Outlook* 131 (3 May 1922): 16; Charles Frederick Carter, "The Carnival of Crime in the United States," *Current History* 15 (February 1922): 754; "Lawlessness: The Shame of America," *Current Opinion* 77 (July 1924): 16; Basil Thomson, "The Crime Wave and How to Deal with It," *Saturday Evening Post* 195 (24 February 1923): 9.

45. Theodore E. Burton, "Curbing Crime in the United States," *Current History* 23 (January 1926): 472–473; "Wanted: A New Crusade," *Current Opinion* 70 (February 1921): 150; Mark O. Prentiss, "War on the Growing Menace of Crime," *Current History* 23 (October 1925): 2–4; "Murder by Wholesale," *Literary Digest* 74 (22 July 1922): 34.

46. "Crowe to Quiz Those Who Lost in 'Monte Carlo,'" *Chicago Sunday Tribune*, 15 May 1921; "'Fixing' Charge Stirs Crowe; Raids Net 200," *Chicago Daily Tribune*, 19 June 1921; "Crowe's Raiders Sweep 2d Ward Clubs, Jail 200," *Chicago Daily Tribune*, 25 June 1921.

47. Richard C. Lindberg, *To Serve and Collect: Chicago Politics and Police Corruption from the Lager Beer Riot to the Summerdale Scandal* (New York: Praeger, 1991), 173–174; "Crowe Defies Fitzmorris in War on Gambling," *Chicago Daily Tribune*, 31 October 1921; "Cops Bootleggers!—Chief," *Chicago Sunday Tribune*, 25 September 1921.

48. Editorial, "The Coalition Victory," *Chicago Daily Journal*, 7 June 1924.

49. John R. Schmidt, *"The Mayor Who Cleaned Up Chicago": A Political Biography of William E. Dever* (DeKalb: Northern Illinois University Press, 1989), 66, 72.

50. "School Graft Trail Widens," *Chicago Sunday Tribune*, 7 May 1922; "New $1,000,000 School Quiz," *Chicago Daily Tribune*, 9 May 1922.

51. "Crowe Narrows School Quiz to Property Deals," *Chicago Daily Tribune*, 18 May 1922; "3 School Officials Indicted for Fraud," *Chicago Daily Tribune*, 24 August 1922; "13 Indicted in School Scandal: Order Arrests," *Chicago Sunday Tribune*, 3 September 1922.

52. "Grand Jury Seeking a Chat with Mr. Lundin," *Chicago Daily Tribune*, 15 September 1922.

53. "Jacob M. Loeb," in Paul Gilbert and Charles Lee Bryson, *Chicago and Its Makers* (Chicago: F. Mendelsohn, 1929), 928.

54. Philip Kinsley, "Board Danced to Lundin Whip, Hanson Swears," *Chicago Daily Tribune*, 9 June 1923; Philip Kinsley, "Lundin Partner in Rohm's Firm, Kin Tells Jury," *Chicago Daily Tribune*, 28 June 1923; Philip Kinsley, "Show Lundin's Companies Got Door Contracts," *Chicago Daily Tribune*, 29 June 1923.

55. Philip Kinsley, "Lundin Linked to 'Solid Six' in Graft Trial," *Chicago Daily Tribune*, 8 June 1923.

56. Philip Kinsley, "Lundin Didn't Boss Schools, Says 'Big Bill,'" *Chicago Daily Tribune*, 7 July 1923; "'Only Thompson's Office Boy'—Lundin," *Chicago Herald and Examiner*, 10 July 1923.

57. Philip Kinsley, "It's Friday, the 13th, and Lundin Case Goes to Jury," *Chicago Daily Tribune*, 13 July 1923; "Darrow Closes Lundin Plea in 3-Hour Speech," *Chicago Herald and Examiner*, 13 July 1923.

58. "Jury Frees Lundin and 15 Others," *Chicago Herald and Examiner*, 14 July 1923.

59. Editorial, "The Lundin Verdict," *Chicago Daily Tribune*, 16 July 1923.

CHAPTER 10: THE INDICTMENT

1. Richard Loeb to Anna Loeb and Albert Loeb, 28 July 1924, Folder 3, Irving Stone Papers, Bancroft Library, University of California, Berkeley.

2. Nathan F. Leopold, *Life Plus 99 Years* (Garden City, NY: Doubleday, 1958), 54–55.

3. Ibid., 54–55.

4. "Identifies Loeb in Moron Gland Attack on Midway," *Chicago Daily Journal*, 2 June 1924; "'Gland' Holdup a Puzzle; Police Quiz Students," *Chicago Daily Tribune*, 22 November 1923.

5. "Slain in Auto Near Midway," *Chicago Daily Tribune*, 26 November 1923; "Phone Tip Revives Tracy Murder Case," *Chicago Daily News*, 21 June 1924; "Two More Chicago Murders Linked with Student Killers; Grand Jury Inquiry Begins," *The World* (New York), 4 June 1924.

6. "Loeb, Leopold Sued by Woman," *Chicago Daily Journal*, 5 June 1924; "Woman Recites Attack by Franks Killers," *Chicago Daily Journal*, 17 July 1924; "Woman Sues Boy's Slayers," *Chicago Herald and Examiner*, 6 June 1924.

7. "Franks' Killers Gland Robbers?" *Chicago Daily Journal*, 2 June 1924; "Two More Chicago Murders," *The World* (New York), 4 June 1924.

8. "Files Suit against Loeb and Leopold," *Chicago Daily News*, 6 June 1924.

9. James Doherty, "Quick Trial for Boy Slayers," *Chicago Daily Tribune*, 3 June 1924; "Identifies Loeb," *Chicago Daily Journal*, 2 June 1924; "Writ Puts 2 Slayers in Sheriff's Hands," *Chicago Herald and Examiner*, 3 June 1924.

10. "Franks Story to Jury," *Chicago Daily Journal*, 3 June 1924; "Grand Jurors Who Will Hear Story of Robt. Franks Murder," *Chicago Daily Tribune*, 4 June 1924.

11. "Crowe Acts to Avert Franks Case 'Fixing,'" *Chicago Daily News*, 4 June 1924.

12. "Franks Story," *Chicago Daily Journal*, 3 June 1924.

13. "Boy Slayers Play Baseball in Jail; Victim's Father Weeps before Jury," *Chicago Herald and Examiner*, 4 June 1924.

14. "Killers Stalked Human Prey," *Chicago Daily Journal*, 4 June 1924.

15. "Passage for Leopold Booked on Liner," *Chicago Daily News*, 6 June 1924; "Ask Franks Trial in Month," *Chicago Daily Journal*, 6 June 1924; "Slayers in Court June 11," *Chicago Evening Post*, 6 June 1924.

16. "Ask Franks Trial"; "Slayers in Court."

17. "Ask Franks Trial."

18. "Ask Franks Trial"; "Killers Stalked."

19. "Leopold and Loeb Indicted as Kidnappers and Slayers; Sane, Says State's Alienist," *The World* (New York), 6 June 1924.

20. "Saw Loeb at Wheel before Kidnapping," *Chicago Daily News*, 9 June 1924; "Leopold and Loeb Will Plead Not Guilty to Killing," *Chicago Evening Post*, 9 June 1924.

21. "City Demands Franks Boy Slayers Be Brought to Trial Immediately," *Chicago Herald and Examiner*, 4 June 1924.

22. Ibid.

23. Editorial, "Justice Demands a Speedy Trial," *Chicago Herald and Examiner*, 3 June 1924.

24. C. L. Stevens, Letter, "For a Vigilantes' Committee," *Chicago Herald and Examiner*, 7 June 1924.

25. "Slayers' Parents' First Statement Bases All Hope on Insanity Plea," *Chicago Herald and Examiner*, 7 June 1924; "Won't Try to Buy Slayers' Freedom, Fathers Declare," *Chicago Evening Post*, 7 June 1924.

26. Editorial, "The Franks Case," *Chicago Daily Tribune*, 10 June 1924.

27. "Boy Killers Plead; Trial Set for Aug. 4," *Chicago Daily News*, 11 June 1924.

28. "Arraign Two Boy Killers Wednesday," *Chicago Daily Journal*, 10 June 1924.

29. "Caverly's Record Favors Life Terms," *Chicago Daily News*, 30 August 1924.

30. "Benjamin Charles Bachrach," in Paul Gilbert and Charles Lee Bryson, *Chicago and Its Makers* (Chicago: F. Mendelsohn, 1929), 776; "Benjamin Bachrach, Criminal Lawyer, 76," *New York Times*, 1 January 1951.

31. Geoffrey C. Ward, *Unforgivable Blackness: The Rise and Fall of Jack Johnson* (New York: Knopf, 2004), 296–349.

32. "Try Loeb Leopold on August 4," *Chicago Daily Journal*, 11 June 1924; "Boy Killers Plead"; "Franks Trial Aug. 4; Insanity Is Plea," *Chicago Herald and Examiner*, 12 June 1924; "Leopold, Loeb Trial Set for Monday, Aug. 4," *Chicago Daily Tribune*, 12 June 1924; "Loeb, Leopold Plead Not Guilty; Trial August 4," *Chicago Evening Post*, 11 June 1924.

CHAPTER 11: THE SCIENTISTS ARRIVE

1. Clarence Darrow, "Not a Milk and Water Theory," *Everyman* 11 (December 1915): 13.

2. "Expert Seeks Murder Gland," *Chicago Daily Journal*, 13 June 1924; "Work in Death Cell to Save Boy Slayers," *Chicago Daily News*, 13 June 1924.

3. Trial Transcript, fols. 1958–1960.

4. Bowman-Hulbert Report (Leopold), fol. 2; Bowman-Hulbert Report (Loeb), fol. 2.

5. Julia Ellen Rechter, "'The Glands of Destiny': A History of Popular, Medical and Scientific Views of the Sex Hormones in 1920s America" (PhD dissertation, University of California at Berkeley, 1997), xvii; John Chynoweth Burnham, "The New Psychology: From Narcissism to Social Control," in John Braeman, Robert H. Bremner, and David Brody, *Change and Continuity in Twentieth-Century America: The 1920s* (Columbus: Ohio State University Press, 1968), 351–398.

6. Benjamin Harrow, *Glands in Health and Disease* (New York: Dutton, 1922), 14–19, 23–25; André Tridon, *Psychoanalysis and Gland Personalities* (New York: Brentano's, 1923), 48, 51–60.

7. R. G. Hoskins, "The Functions of the Endocrine Glands," *Scientific Monthly* 18 (March 1924): 257–272.

8. Herman H. Rubin, *The Glands of Life* (New York: Bellaire, 1935), 26–30, 32–33; Tridon, *Psychoanalysis*, 18–21; Harrow, *Glands*, 93–97, 135–138, 140–144.

9. J. M. Murdock, "Endocrine Disturbances in Mental Defectives," *Pennsylvania Medical Journal* 25 (1921): 50; Nolan D. C. Lewis and Gertrude R. Davies, "A Correlative Study of Endocrine Imbalance and Mental Disease," *Journal of Nervous and Mental Disease* 54 (1921): 385–405, 493–512; 55 (1922): 13–32.

10. Karl M. Bowman, "Blood Chemistry in Mental Diseases," *American Journal of Psychiatry*, 2nd ser., 2 (1922–1923): 379–408.

11. Karl M. Bowman, Joseph P. Eidson, and Stanley P. Burladge, "Bio-chemical Studies in Ten Cases of Dementia Praecox," *Boston Medical and Surgical Journal* 187 (1922): 358–362, quotation on 362.

12. Karl M. Bowman and G. P. Grabfield, "Basal Metabolism in Mental Disease," *Archives of Neurology and Psychiatry* 9 (1923): 358–361, quotation on 360.

13. "Weird Apparatus in Slayers' Aid," *Chicago Herald and Examiner*, 15 June 1924; "More Doctors Test Leopold and Loeb," *Chicago Daily News*, 14 June 1924; "Test Slayers with Oxygen," *Chicago Daily Journal*, 14 June 1924.

14. "Work in Death Cell," *Chicago Daily News*, 13 June 1924; "Expert Seeks"; "Leopold-Loeb Defense Now Is Seen as Insanity," *Chicago Evening Post*, 13 June 1924; Trial Transcript, fols. 1989, 2093.

15. Trial Transcript, fol. 1989; Bowman-Hulbert Report (Loeb), fol. 52.

16. Bowman-Hulbert Report (Leopold), fol. 75; "Leopold, Jr., under Test of Mental Experts," *Chicago Daily Journal*, 16 June 1924.

17. "Needle Charts Leopold's Mind," *Chicago Daily Journal*, 17 June 1924; "Experts Use 'Flattery Machine' to Test Leopold's Vanity," *Chicago Herald and Examiner*, 17 June 1924; "Defense Alienists Find Leopold and Loeb Abnormal," *Chicago Evening Post*, 16 June 1924.

18. "X-Ray Now to Seek Flaws in Boy Slayers," *Chicago Daily Tribune*, 18 June 1924; "Needle Charts," *Chicago Daily Journal*, 17 June 1924; Trial Transcript, fols. 2096–2097.

19. Tal Golan, *Laws of Men and Laws of Nature: The History of Scientific Expert Testimony in England and America* (Cambridge, MA: Harvard University Press, 2004), 183–197.

20. Trial Transcript, fol. 1994; Bowman-Hulbert Report (Loeb), fol. 59; Bowman-Hulbert Report (Leopold), fol. 82.

21. Bowman-Hulbert Report (Loeb), fols. 60–62.

22. Bowman-Hulbert Report (Leopold), fols. 83–85; Trial Transcript, fols. 2061–2062.

23. "Leopold-Loeb Tests Fail, Hint," *Chicago Daily Journal*, 18 June 1924; Fred D. Pasley, "Are Glands or Boys to Blame in Franks Case?" *Chicago Herald and Examiner*, 18 June 1924.

24. "Leopold Angry over His Tests," *Chicago Herald and Examiner*, 18 June 1924; "Leopold Spurns Insanity Defense," *Chicago Herald and Examiner*, 18 June 1924.

25. "Concludes Test of Franks Killers," *Chicago Evening Post*, 17 June 1924.

26. "Leopold's Jail-Break Plot Foiled by Warden," *Chicago Herald and Examiner*, 28 June 1924.

27. "Another Expert Here to Test Slayers," *Chicago Daily Journal*, 2 July 1924; Leola Allard, "U.S. Expert to Test Slayers," *Chicago Herald and Examiner*, 1 July 1924.

28. Lawrence C. Moore, "William A. White—A Biography (1870–1937)," in Arcangelo R. T. D'Amore, ed., *William Alanson White: The Washington Years, 1903–1937* (Washington, DC: U.S. Department of Health, Education, and Welfare, 1976), 13–14.

29. William A. White, *Forty Years of Psychiatry* (New York, 1933), 28–32; Arcangelo R. T. D'Amore, "William Alanson White—Pioneer Psychoanalyst," in D'Amore, *William Alanson White*, 69–71.

30. William Alanson White Notes (Loeb), fols. 2, 3.

31. Ibid., fols. 6–7, 20–21.

32. William Alanson White Notes (Leopold), fol. 14.

33. Ibid., fols. 16, 17.

34. Psychiatric Reports, Unit I/4025 (William Alanson White), fols. 15–16, 18, 35–36.

35. "Other Holidays Recalled on 4th by Loeb, Leopold," *Chicago Daily Tribune*, 5 July 1924.

36. Trial Transcript, fols. 1433–1434; William Healy, *The Individual Delinquent: A Text-Book of Diagnosis and Prognosis for All Concerned in Understanding Offenders* (Boston, MA: Little, Brown, 1915).

37. James W. Trent Jr., *Inventing the Feeble Mind: A History of Mental Retardation in the United States* (Berkeley: University of California Press, 1994), 141–142, 155–166; Leila Zenderland, *Measuring Minds: Henry Herbert Goddard and the Origins of American Intelligence Testing* (Cambridge: Cambridge University Press, 1998), 235–250.

38. Trial Transcript, fols. 1455–1475.

39. Ibid., fols. 1516–1525.

40. "Franks Defense Expert Staff Still Growing," *Chicago Daily Tribune*, 9 July 1924; Trial Transcript, fols. 1660–1662; Bernard Glueck, "A Study of 608 Admissions to Sing Sing Prison," *Mental Hygiene* 2 (1918): 85–151; Bernard Glueck, "Concerning Prisoners," *Mental Hygiene* 2 (1918): 177–218; Bernard Glueck, "Psychiatric Aims in the Field of Criminology," *Mental Hygiene* 2 (1918): 546–556.

41. Trial Transcript, fols. 1674–1677; Psychiatric Reports, Unit I/1375 (Bernard Glueck), fols. 1–2.

42. Psychiatric Reports, Unit I/1375 (Bernard Glueck), fol. 18.

43. Ibid., fol. 27.

44. Edward Shorter, *A History of Psychiatry: From the Era of the Asylum to the Age of Prozac* (New York: Wiley, 1997), 156–164.

45. Nathan G. Hale Jr., *The Rise and Crisis of Psychoanalysis in the United States: Freud and the Americans, 1917–1985* (New York: Oxford University Press, 1995), 3–9, 23–24, 74–78; Catherine Lucille Covert, "Freud on the Front Page: Transmission of Freudian Ideas in the American Newspaper of the 1920s" (PhD dissertation, Syracuse University, 1975), 12–14, 26–34, 36–37; David Evans Tanner, "Symbols of Conduct: Psychiatry and American Culture, 1900–1935" (PhD dissertation, University of Texas at Austin, 1981), 173–180.

46. Gerald N. Grob, *Mental Illness and American Society, 1875–1940* (Princeton, NJ: Princeton University Press, 1983), 46–71.

47. Elizabeth Lunbeck, *The Psychiatric Persuasion: Gender and Power in Modern America, 1875–1940* (Princeton, NJ: Princeton University Press, 1994), 20–24, 46–49.

48. William A. White, *Insanity and the Criminal Law* (New York: Macmillan, 1923), 23–29, 224–230.

49. Janet Ann Tighe, "A Question of Responsibility: The Development of American Forensic Psychiatry, 1838–1930" (PhD dissertation, University of Pennsylvania, 1983), 320–323, 339–346.

50. White, *Insanity and the Criminal Law*, 102–106.

51. Tighe, "A Question of Responsibility," 321–322.

52. "Loeb Defense Hires Best of Mind Experts," *Chicago Sunday Tribune*, 6 July 1924.

53. Gerald Langford, *The Murder of Stanford White* (New York: Bobbs-Merrill, 1962), pp. 17–19, 233–234, 245–256.

54. "Darrow Lauds Kin of Killers," *Chicago Daily Journal*, 15 July 1924; "Leopold, Loeb Will Not Seek to Free Sons," *Chicago Daily Journal*, 10 July 1924.

55. "New Insanity Defense Seen," *Chicago Daily Journal*, 12 July 1924.

56. "Leopold and Loeb Are Superficially Both Sane," *Evening Telegram* (Toronto), 12 July 1924.

57. "Insanity School for Crowe Aids in Franks Case," *Chicago Sunday Tribune*, 13 July 1924; "Rival Counsel Get Primed for Franks Battle," *Chicago Daily Tribune*, 14 July 1924.

58. Philip Kinsley, "Lincoln Faces Death or Asylum," *Chicago Sunday Tribune*, 27 January 1924.

59. "'Not Guilty' Lincoln Plea in Court," *Aurora Daily Beacon-News*, 18 February 1924; "Lincoln Pivot of Franks Case," *Chicago Daily Journal*, 18 June 1924; "Lincoln Trial Test in Leopold Case," *Chicago Herald and Examiner*, 23 June 1924; "Delay Lincoln Sanity Quiz," *Chicago Daily News*, 23 June 1924.

60. "Crowe Attacks Franks' Killers' 'Insane' Defense," *Chicago Daily Tribune*, 18 July 1924.

61. "Radio Loeb-Leopold Trial?" *Chicago Daily Tribune*, 17 July 1924.

62. Roland Marchand, *Advertising the American Dream: Making Way for Modernity, 1920–1940* (Berkeley: University of California Press, 1985), 88–89.

63. Clayton R. Koppes, "The Social Destiny of the Radio: Hope and Disillusionment in the 1920s," *South Atlantic Quarterly* 68 (1969): 364–368.

64. "Public Gives Views on Loeb Trial by Radio," *Chicago Daily Tribune*, 18 July 1924.

65. "Opinions Vary on Proposal to Radio Trial," *Chicago Daily Tribune*, 18 July 1924; "Tribune Offer to Radio Trial Stirs Public," *Chicago Daily Tribune*, 18 July 1924; "City in Furore over Plan for Trial Broadcast," *Chicago Daily Tribune*, 19 July 1924.

66. "Leopold, Loeb, Won't Ask Change of Venue," *Chicago Daily News*, 19 July 1924.

67. "Radio of Trial Assailed," *Chicago Daily News*, 18 July 1924; "Judges of Two Courts Oppose 'Trial by Radio,'" *Chicago Herald and Examiner*, 19 July 1924.

68. "Franks Trial Delay Hinted," *Chicago Daily Journal*, 19 July 1924; "First Court Battle in Leopold-Loeb Case Tomorrow," *Chicago Herald and Examiner*, 20 July 1924; Genevieve Forbes, "Darrow Ready to Lay Franks Cards on Table," *Chicago Sunday Tribune*, 20 July 1924.

69. "Leopold-Loeb 'Jury Strategy' Mapped at War Council," *Chicago Herald and Examiner*, 18 July 1924.

CHAPTER 12: MITIGATION OF PUNISHMENT

1. Trial Transcript, fols. 1207, 1209.
2. "Killers Admit All; Fate Up to Judge," *Chicago Daily Journal*, 21 July 1924; "Leopold Dramatically Calm in Court; Loeb Fearful," *Chicago Herald and Examiner*, 22 July 1924.
3. "Breathless Crowds Jam Franks Hearing," *Chicago Daily News*, 21 July 1924; "Leopold Dramatically Calm," *Chicago Herald and Examiner*, 22 July 1924.
4. Genevieve Forbes, "Call 100 Franks Witnesses," *Chicago Daily Tribune*, 22 July 1924.
5. "Loeb, Leopold Plead Guilty; Begin Trial Next Wednesday," *Chicago Daily News*, 21 July 1924.
6. "Breathless Crowds."
7. Charles V. Slattery, "Leopold-Loeb Plead Guilty; Ask Mercy," *Chicago Herald and Examiner*, 22 July 1924; Forbes, "Call 100 Franks Witnesses"; Nathan F. Leopold, *Life Plus 99 Years* (Garden City, NY: Doubleday, 1958), 61.
8. "Killers Admit All," *Chicago Daily Journal*, 21 July 1924; Leopold, *Life Plus 99 Years*, 62.
9. "Leopold Dramatically Calm."
10. "Loeb, Leopold Plead Guilty."
11. Ibid.; "'Guilty,' Slayers' Plea," *Chicago Evening Post*, 21 July 1924.
12. "Loeb, Leopold Plead Guilty."
13. "Leopold Dramatically Calm."
14. "Crowe to Push Trial with All Possible Speed," *Chicago Daily Tribune*, 22 July 1924.
15. Slattery, "Leopold-Loeb Plead Guilty"; "Franks Waits Call to Stand," *Chicago Daily Journal*, 22 July 1924.
16. "Franks' Parents Testify; New Scandal Suppressed," *Chicago Daily Journal*, 22 July 1924.
17. "Crowds Sit Tense at Franks Hearing," *Chicago Daily News*, 23 July 1924.
18. "Mrs. Franks on Stand; Shown Son's Clothes," *Chicago Daily Journal*, 22 July

1924; "Parents of Franks Testify," *Chicago Daily News*, 23 July 1924; "Mrs. Franks, Grief Bowed, Is Center of Interest," *Chicago Daily News*, 23 July 1924.

19. "Mrs. Franks on Stand"; Trial Transcript, fols. 107–110.

20. "Jacob Franks Describes How Youths Worked," *Chicago Daily Journal*, 22 July 1924; Trial Transcript, fols. 78–84, 100–103.

21. Trial Transcript, fols. 71–72.

22. Genevieve Forbes, "State Closes Case Today," *Chicago Daily Tribune*, 29 July 1924.

23. Sam Putnam, "Court Fans, Alert for Thrills, Turn Eyes to Darrow," *Chicago Evening Post*, 30 July 1924.

24. "Boys Primp for Big Day," *Chicago Daily News*, 30 July 1924.

25. "Doctor, on Stand for Hours, Tells Name and Nothing More," *Chicago Daily Journal*, 31 July 1924; Genevieve Forbes, "Calm Alienist Storm Center of Franks Trial," *Chicago Daily Tribune*, 31 July 1924.

26. Trial Transcript, fols. 978–979.

27. Ibid., fols. 981–982.

28. Ibid., fols. 982, 999, 1000–1001.

29. *People v. Geary*, 297 Illinois 610–611 (1921); "T. J. Fell Tells Jury How Geary Killed Reckas," *Chicago Daily Tribune*, 24 July 1920; "5,000 Hunt Gene Geary, Mad Gunman," *Chicago Herald and Examiner*, 29 May 1920.

30. "Geary Warns Police He'll Fight to Last," *Chicago Herald and Examiner*, 30 May 1920; "Jurors Acquit Geary; Verdict Arouses Hoyne," *Chicago Sunday Tribune*, 7 March 1920.

31. *People v. Geary*, 297 Illinois 612–613 (1921).

32. Illinois Revised Statutes, Chapter 38 (Criminal Code), Section 285 (1917).

33. "Geary Violent in Cell; Doctor Starts Inquiry," *Chicago Daily Tribune*, 3 February 1921; "'Gene' Geary Tries Suicide; Nerve Fails," *Chicago Daily Tribune*, 25 April 1921.

34. "Geary Will Ask Jury to Save Him from Rope," *Chicago Daily Tribune*, 14 May 1921.

35. "Judge Will Name 3 Alienists to Fix Geary's Fate," *Chicago Daily Tribune*, 20 May 1921; "Gene Geary Held Sane; Expected to Hang June 17," *Chicago Daily Tribune*, 1 June 1921.

36. *People v. Geary*, 298 Illinois 242 (1921).

37. "Geary to Asylum," *Chicago Daily Tribune*, 24 September 1921.

38. Editorial, "Geary Beats the Rope," *Chicago Daily Tribune*, 26 September 1921.

39. Trial Transcript, fols. 981, 986–988, 1011, 1014.

40. *People v. Lowhone*, 292 Illinois, 34–36 (1920); "Innocent Man Is Killed Last Friday Morning When Frank Lowhone Shoots Max Nottingham," *Carmi Tribune-Times*, 10 April 1919.

41. *People v. Lowhone*, 296 Illinois, 400, 404 (1920); "Lowhone Is Executed," *Carmi Tribune-Times*, 15 April 1921.

42. Trial Transcript, fols. 1120–1121.

43. Ibid., fols. 1213–1214.

44. Charles V. Slattery, "Loeb and Leopold Win First Court Fight; Alienists Permitted to Go on Stand," *Chicago Herald and Examiner*, 31 July 1924.

CHAPTER 13: PSYCHIATRISTS FOR THE DEFENSE

1. Trial Transcript, fols. 1344–1345.

2. Ibid., fol. 1556.

3. Ibid., fols. 1691, 1708–1709.

4. "Killers' Dream Life Bared," *Chicago Daily News*, 1 August 1924; Trial Transcript, fol. 1245.

5. "Victory Stirs Defense," *Chicago Daily News*, 1 August 1924.

6. Ibid.

7. Trial Transcript, fols. 1279, 1283–1286.

8. Ibid., fols. 1284, 1293.

9. Ibid., fol. 1296.

10. Ibid., fols. 1317–1318.

11. Ibid., fols. 1318, 1329–1330, 1336, 1340.

12. William Alanson White Notes (Leopold), fol. 19.

13. Trial Transcript, fol. 1342.

14. Ibid., fols. 1342–1345.

15. Ibid., fol. 1349.

16. Ibid., fol. 1360.

17. Ibid., fols. 1391, 1407.

18. Ibid., fol. 1409, 1411.

19. Ibid., fols. 1412–1413.

20. Charles V. Slattery, "Crowe Accuses Alienist of Trickery," *Chicago Herald and Examiner*, 3 August 1924; John Ashenhurst, "Crowe Wages Fight on 'Dream' Defense," *Chicago American*, 2 August 1924; "Leopold Expects to Hang; Knew

Murder Wrong—Expert," *Chicago Daily Journal*, 2 August 1924; "Alienist's Tilt with Crowe as Shown by Q. & A.," *Chicago Sunday Tribune*, 3 August 1924.

21. "Boy Slayers Posed to Fool Alienists, Prosecutor Hints," *Chicago Daily News*, 2 August 1924; Genevieve Forbes, "Insanity Fixed, Crowe Hints," *Chicago Sunday Tribune*, 3 August 1924.

22. "Dejected? No, Just Thinking Out Next Move," *Chicago Herald and Examiner*, 3 August 1924.

23. "Concedes Even 'Superman' Might Make Mistakes," *Chicago American*, 4 August 1924.

24. Genevieve Forbes, "Expert Paints Crime-Twins," *Chicago Daily Tribune*, 5 August 1924.

25. "Slayers' Baseness Is Depicted," *Chicago Daily News*, 4 August 1924.

26. Trial Transcript, fols. 1467, 1524. On their emotional capacity, see Trial Transcript, fol. 1473.

27. "Hang the Slayers, Billy Sunday Says," *Chicago Herald and Examiner*, 5 June 1924.

28. "God Committed Death Penalty into Hands of State, Says Pastor," *Chicago Herald and Examiner*, 4 August 1924.

29. "Life of Child, Half Million Price of Thrill," *Chicago Daily Tribune*, 8 August 1924.

30. "Scores Boy Killers Case," *Chicago Daily News*, 5 August 1924; Thomas R. Marshall, "Imprison in Spite of Insanity," *Chicago Daily News*, 9 August 1924.

31. "Blames Parents of Dick and Babe for Criminality," *Chicago Daily Tribune*, 5 August 1924.

32. Lynn Dumenil, *The Modern Temper: American Culture and Society in the 1920s* (New York: Hill and Wang, 1995), 145–200; Michael E. Parrish, *Anxious Decades: America in Prosperity and Depression, 1920–1941* (New York: Norton, 1992), 71–93, 98–104, 147–149.

33. Kenneth T. Jackson, *The Ku Klux Klan in the City, 1915–1930* (New York: Oxford University Press, 1967), 95, 109; Sam Putnam, "Caverly Gets Threat Letters Signed 'K.K.K.'," *Chicago Evening Post*, 6 August 1924.

34. Putnam, "Caverly Gets Threat Letters"; "Guard Hartman Home Following Kidnap Threats," *Chicago Evening Post*, 19 June 1924; "Franks Home Offered for Sale," *Chicago American*, 19 August 1924; "Grewsome Symbol of Death Is Left Near Home of Loeb," *Chicago Daily Tribune*, 19 August 1924.

35. Putnam, "Caverly Gets Threat Letters"; Genevieve Forbes, "Darrow Calls Public Opinion Unfair to Boys," *Chicago Daily Tribune*, 4 August 1924.

36. Trial Transcript, fol. 1691.

37. Ibid., fol. 1692.

38. Ibid., fols. 1705–1706, 1711–1712.

39. "Loeb Killed Franks, He Tells Alienist," *Chicago Daily News*, 6 August 1924; Trial Transcript, fol. 1747.

40. Maurine Watkins, "Know Children, Expert's Word to All Parents," *Chicago Daily Tribune*, 7 August 1924.

41. Kathleen W. Jones, *Taming the Troublesome Child: American Families, Child Guidance, and the Limits of Psychiatric Innocence* (Cambridge, MA: Harvard University Press, 1999), 3–8, 44–50; David Spinoza Tanenhaus, "Policing the Child: Juvenile Justice in Chicago, 1870–1925" (PhD dissertation, University of Chicago, 1997), 332–353.

42. "Bares Loeb's Story of Strangling Plot," *Chicago Daily News*, 8 August 1924; "Nathan's Nature Kind, Dr. Hulbert Asserts," *Chicago Daily News*, 9 August 1924.

43. Trial Transcript, fols. 1988–1989.

44. Ibid., fols. 1989–1990.

45. Ibid., fols. 1991–1992.

46. Genevieve Forbes, "Slayers' Gland Systems Blamed for Diseased Minds," *Chicago Sunday Tribune*, 10 August 1924; Trial Transcript, fols. 1992, 1994, 1998, 2000.

47. Trial Transcript, fols. 2056–2058.

48. John Ashenhurst, "Tell Loeb's Glee as Mother Talks of Tar and Feather," *Chicago American*, 8 August 1924; Genevieve Forbes, "Loeb Hears Self 'Dissected,'" *Chicago Daily Tribune*, 9 August 1924.

49. Trial Transcript, fols. 2061–2062.

50. Forbes, "Slayers' Gland Systems."

51. Trial Transcript, fol. 2062.

52. Ibid., fols. 2067–2068.

53. Ibid., fol. 2068.

54. Ibid., fols. 2063, 2069.

55. Ibid., fol. 2069.

56. John Ashenhurst, "Ex-Sweethearts of Leopold Aid State in Gallows Fight," *Chicago American*, 9 August 1924; Charles V. Slattery, "Leopold

Like Man of 45, Says Expert," *Chicago Herald and Examiner*, 10 August 1924.

57. Trial Transcript, fols. 2069–2071.

58. Ibid., fols. 2073–2076.

59. Ibid., fols. 2092–2093.

60. Horry M. Jones, "A Simple Device for Measuring Basal Metabolism," *Journal of the American Medical Association* 75 (21 August 1920): 538–539; Robert C. Lewis, "The Jones 'Metabolimeter,'" in Frank B. Sanborn, ed., *Basal Metabolism: Its Determination and Application* (Boston, MA: Sanborn, 1922), 80–135.

61. Trial Transcript, fols. 2093–2094.

62. Ibid., fols. 2096–2097.

63. Ibid., fols. 2097–2098.

64. Ibid., fols. 2098–2100.

CHAPTER 14: PSYCHIATRISTS FOR THE STATE

1. Trial Transcript, fols. 2656–2657.

2. Ibid., fol. 2711.

3. Ibid., fol. 3042.

4. Ibid., fol. 3328.

5. "Double Guard over Loeb and Leopold," *Chicago Herald and Examiner*, 18 August 1924.

6. "Fools Folks on Piano," *Chicago Daily News*, 18 August 1924; Sam Putnam, "Leopold Explains Taste in Music as He Pounds Piano," *Chicago Evening Post*, 18 August 1924.

7. "Double Guard."

8. W. H. Carwardine, "Outlawing of War, Return of the 'Slipper Age,' Urged by Pastors," *Chicago Herald and Examiner*, 18 August 1924.

9. John Herrick, "Franks Trial Now Entering Final Phases," *Chicago Daily Tribune*, 18 August 1924.

10. Trial Transcript, fols. 3320–3323, 3325–3326.

11. Ibid., fol. 3327.

12. "Experts Exaggerate, State Doctor Avers," *Chicago Daily News*, 13 August 1924; Genevieve Forbes, "'Slayers Not Mentally Ill,'" *Chicago Daily Tribune*, 13 August 1924; John Herrick, "State's Alienists Ridicule 'Dream Defense,'"

Chicago Daily Tribune, 14 August 1924; Charles V. Slattery, "Attempt to Buy State's Alienist Is Crowe Hint," *Chicago Herald and Examiner*, 14 August 1924.

13. Trial Transcript, fol. 2731.
14. Ibid., fol. 2732.
15. Ibid., fols. 2736–2738, 2744–2750.
16. Ibid., fols. 2650–2657.
17. Ibid., fols. 2711, 2712–2713.
18. Ibid., fol. 2716.
19. Editorial, "They Only Confuse the Problem," *New York Times*, 15 August 1924.
20. Trial Transcript, fols. 2873–2875.
21. Ibid., fols. 2877–2878.
22. Russell N. DeJong, *A History of American Neurology* (New York: Raven, 1982), 75–77.
23. Trial Transcript, fols. 2902–2903.
24. Ibid., fols. 2906, 2907.
25. Ibid., fol. 2906.
26. Ibid., fols. 2822–2823
27. "Charges Crowe Had No Right to Quiz Youths," *Chicago Sunday Tribune*, 17 August 1924; "Calls Slayers as Normal as Average Youth," *Chicago Daily Tribune*, 16 August 1924; Adolf Meyer, "H. Douglas Singer, M.D., 1875–1940," *Archives of Neurology and Psychiatry* 45 (1941): 162–163; "H. D. Singer Dead; Noted Alienist, 65," *New York Times*, 30 August 1940.
28. Trial Transcript, fols. 3032–3041.
29. Ibid., fols. 3060, 3063, 3066, 3074.
30. Ibid., fols. 3189–3190.
31. Ibid., fol. 3193.

CHAPTER 15: CLOSING STATEMENTS

1. Trial Transcript, fols. 3463–3464.
2. Ibid., fols. 3766, 3768.
3. "State Demands Quick Death for Two Boy Killers," *Chicago Daily Tribune*, 21 December 1922; Genevieve Forbes, "Where Bullet Struck," *Chicago Daily Tribune*, 21 December 1922.
4. Trial Transcript, fols. 3582–3583.

5. "State Demands."

6. "Caverly Verdict Brings Hope to Condemned Boy," *Chicago Daily Tribune*, 12 September 1924; "Franks Decision Brings Hope to Condemned Boys," *Chicago Daily Tribune*, 13 September 1924.

7. Trial Transcript, fol. 3585.

8. Ibid., fols. 3585–3586.

9. Ibid., fols. 3591–3593.

10. "Turns on Cardinella at Trial for Murder," *Chicago Daily News*, 29 June 1920; "Gallows for Cardinella," *Chicago Daily News*, 30 June 1920; Trial Transcript, fols. 3603–3608.

11. Trial Transcript, fols. 3598–3602.

12. Ibid., fol. 3482.

13. Ibid., fols. 3465, 3467–3468.

14. Ibid., fols. 3663–3664, 3665–3666.

15. "Leopold Weeps under State's Attack," *Chicago Daily News*, 21 August 1924; Orville Dwyer, "Darrow Opens His Plea for Slayers Today," *Chicago Daily Tribune*, 22 August 1924.

16. Trial Transcript, fols. 3775–3776.

17. Ibid., fols. 3777–3780.

18. Ibid., fols. 3777–3780.

19. Ibid., fols. 3822, 3824, 3825, 3826.

20. Ibid., fol. 3830.

21. Ibid., fols. 3830–3831.

22. Ibid., fols. 3835, 3836, 3840, 3841.

23. Ibid., fol. 3869.

24. "Darrow, Master Pleader, Begs for Mercy; Women Faint as Crowds Mob Court," *Chicago Herald and Examiner*, 23 August 1924.

25. Ibid.

26. John Ashenhurst, "Darrow's Plea!" *Chicago American*, 22 August 1924; "Darrow Pleads for Mercy; Mobs Riot," *Chicago Daily News*, 22 August 1924; "4 Women to 1 Man Make Courtroom Like Sardine Can," *Chicago American*, 25 August 1924; "Relief from Heat Promised Chicago," *Chicago Herald and Examiner*, 23 August 1924.

27. "Darrow Pleads."

28. Trial Transcript, fol. 3887.

29. Ibid., fol. 3893; "Text of Darrow's Closing Appeal to Save Two Slayers," *Chicago Herald and Examiner*, 26 August 1924.

30. Trial Transcript, fol. 3893; "Offers 'Pact' of Slayers as Product of Diseased Minds," *Chicago American*, 25 August 1924.

31. Trial Transcript, fols. 3907–3908.

32. Ibid., fols. 3905–3907, 3910–3911.

33. "'Cry of the Dark Ages' Is Assailed by Darrow in Plea," *Chicago Herald and Examiner*, 24 August 1924.

34. "Text of Darrow's Closing Appeal."

35. "'Cry of the Dark Ages.'"

36. "Text of Darrow's Closing Appeal."

37. Ibid.

38. John Herrick, "Darrow Pleads for Parents," *Chicago Daily Tribune*, 26 August 1924; "Text of Darrow's Closing Appeal."

39. Charles V. Slattery, "Darrow Pleads for 'Boys of Future,'" *Chicago Herald and Examiner*, 26 August 1924; Herrick, "Darrow Pleads."

40. Trial Transcript, fols. 4157–4158, 4167–4168.

41. Ibid., fols. 4178–4180.

42. Ibid., fols. 4184–4185, 4201–4202, 4215.

43. "Row Stops Crowe's Attack on Slayers," *Chicago Daily News*, 26 August 1924.

44. Betty Walker, "Girl Reporter Causes Exodus," *Chicago Herald and Examiner*, 27 August 1924; "Women Insist on Listening to 'Unfit Matter,'" *Chicago Daily Tribune*, 27 August 1924.

45. "Women Insist"; Trial Transcript, fol. 4216.

46. Trial Transcript, fol. 4216.

47. Ibid., fol. 4219.

48. Ibid., fols. 4221–4222.

49. Ibid., fol. 4222.

50. Ibid., fols. 4259–4260, 4299.

51. Ibid., fols. 4299–4300, 4300–4301.

52. Ibid., fol. 4275.

53. Ibid., fols. 4244, 4274.

54. Ibid., fols. 4262–4263.

55. Ibid., fols. 4272–4273.

56. Ibid., fols. 4331–4332, 4334.

57. Ibid., fols. 4335–4336

58. Ibid., fols. 4337, 4341.

59. Ibid., fol. 4341.

60. Ibid., fol. 4364.
61. Ibid., fols. 4402–4404.
62. Ibid., fols. 4404–4405.
63. Ibid., fols. 4405–4406
64. "Caverly Decides Sept. 10; Jabs Crowe," *Chicago Daily News*, 28 August 1924; John Ashenhurst, "Trial Ends in Rebuke to Crowe; Sentence Sept. 10," *Chicago American*, 28 August 1924.

CHAPTER 16: SENTENCING

1. "Text of Judge Caverly's Decision of 1,000 Words," *Chicago Daily Tribune*, 11 September 1924.
2. "Crank Phoned Wife Caverly Was Shot," *Chicago American*, 2 September 1924; "Leopold Hopes, If Hanged, to Test Hereafter," *Chicago Daily Tribune*, 3 September 1924.
3. "Mumbler Looking for Caverly Held," *Chicago American*, 5 September 1924.
4. Charles V. Slattery, "Caverly Sifts Murder Evidence," *Chicago Herald and Examiner*, 30 August 1924; "Moving Day in Court Building Delays Caverly," *Chicago Daily Tribune*, 30 August 1924.
5. Edward L. Corey, "'Mind Not Made Up'—Caverly," *Chicago American*, 5 September 1924.
6. "Franks Sell Their Home of Cruel Memory," *Chicago Sunday Tribune*, 31 August 1924.
7. "Reminders of 'Bobby's' Fate Cause Sale of Franks House," *New York Times*, 1 September 1924; "Franks Sell."
8. "Loebs to Sell Home to Escape Haunting Memories, Is Report," *Chicago American*, 9 September 1924.
9. "Loeb Recalls Last Time He Danced to Tune He Hears Visitor Whistle," *Chicago American*, 4 September 1924.
10. Betty Walker, "Girl, Society Matron, See Two Slayers," *Chicago Herald and Examiner*, 30 August 1924.
11. "Memoirs Planned by Franks Slayer," *New York Times*, 4 September 1924.
12. "Leopold to Write Story of His Life," *Chicago American*, 3 September 1924.
13. "Leopold Wants to Bet That He Will Be Hanged," *The Sun* (New York), 9 September 1924; "Betting 3 to 1 Leopold, Loeb Will Not Hang," *Detroit Free Press*, 10 September 1924.

14. "Leopold Hopes," *Chicago Daily Tribune*, 3 September 1924; "Leopold Prepares for Death by Writing His Will in Prison," *The Sun* (New York), 3 September 1924.

15. "Gene Geary to Guide Loeb and Pal," *Chicago American*, 2 September 1924.

16. Corey, "'Mind Not Made Up'"; "Rope Penalty for Slayers Means Fight," *Chicago Daily Tribune*, 1 September 1924.

17. "Gene Geary," *Chicago American*, 2 September 1924; "4 Alienists Are Ready to Testify Leopold Jr. and Loeb Are Insane," *Chicago American*, 4 September 1924; "Darrow Plans New Moves to Aid Boys," *The Sun* (New York), 4 September 1924.

18. "Last Plea May Save Slayers from the Gallows," *Chicago Daily Tribune*, 4 September 1924; "Dooms Young Slayer to Gallows; Relents," *Chicago Daily News*, 14 June 1924; "Russell Scott, Loop Slayer, Gets Chance for Life," *Chicago Evening Post*, 11 July 1924.

19. "Call Riflemen as Escort for Caverly after Threats," *Chicago American*, 9 September 1924.

20. "Guards Arm for Loeb Sentence," *Chicago American*, 8 September 1924; "Call Riflemen."

21. "Killer's Alienist Afraid, Is Given Bluecoat Guard," *Chicago Daily Tribune*, 11 September 1924.

22. "Life or Death Ruling Today," *Chicago Daily Tribune*, 10 September 1924.

23. "Loeb's Father Stricken," *New York Times*, 7 September 1924; "Slayers of Franks Boy Get Life Terms," *The Sun* (New York), 10 September 1924.

24. "Today's Radio Programs," *Chicago Daily Tribune*, 10 September 1924.

25. "Text," *Chicago Daily Tribune*, 11 September 1924.

26. "Life for Slayers of Franks," *Chicago Daily News*, 10 September 1924.

27. "Text"; "Slayers of Franks, Too Young to Hang, Get Life Sentence," *New York Evening Post*, 10 September 1924.

28. Robert M. Lee, "Joliet Gets Slayers Today," *Chicago Daily Tribune*, 11 September 1924.

29. "Darrow Elated at Caverly's Decision," *Chicago Daily News*, 10 September 1924.

30. "Never Set Boys Free, Crowe Warns Board," *Chicago Daily Tribune*, 12 September 1924.

31. "Franks' Mother Glad It's Over," *San Francisco Chronicle*, 11 September 1924.

32. "Never Set Boys Free."

33. "Slayers' Trip from Jail to Prison," *Chicago Daily Tribune*, 12 September 1924.

34. Harry C. Read, "How Joliet Would Treat Boy Slayers," *Chicago American*, 2 September 1924.

35. "Chair Factory Benches Await Killers at Pen," *Chicago Daily Tribune*, 11 September 1924; Read, "How Joliet"; Tyrrell Krum, "Killers in 'Solitary' Cells," *Chicago Daily Tribune*, 12 September 1924.

CHAPTER 17: THE AFTERMATH

1. Clarence Darrow to Adolph Germer, December 1924, Folder 1, Box 4, Adolph Germer Papers, Wisconsin Historical Society.

2. Ruby Darrow to Lincoln Steffens, n.d. (1925), Series II, Lincoln Steffens Papers, Columbia University.

3. Editorial, "Franks Slayers' Sentence Helps to Explain Herrin," *Newark Evening News*, 10 September 1924.

4. Editorial, "Judge Caverly's Sentence," *The Bulletin* (San Francisco), 10 September 1924; Editorial, "The Franks Case Decision," *Kansas City Post*, 10 September 1924.

5. Editorial, "The Mercy of the Court," *New York Times*, 11 September 1924.

6. Editorial, "The Life Sentence," *St. Paul Dispatch*, 10 September 1924.

7. Editorial, "The Mind of the Judge," *The Sun* (New York), 16 September 1924.

8. Editorial, "Perfectly Comprehensible," *Detroit Free Press*, 15 September 1924; Editorial, "Consistency," *Cleveland Plain Dealer*, 14 September 1924.

9. "Pleads to Save Son from Gallows," *Chicago Sunday Tribune*, 14 September 1924; Editorial, "Grant's Sentence Should Now Be Commuted," *Chicago Daily Tribune*, 13 September 1924.

10. "Bernard Grant Wins Reprieve of Three Months," *Chicago Sunday Tribune*, 21 September 1924.

11. "Says Leopold and Loeb Can Be Paroled in 1935," *New York Times*, 1 September 1926.

12. "Power to Pardon Loeb and Leopold Held by Governor," *Evening Star* (Washington, D.C.), 11 September 1924.

13. Editorial, "Judge Caverly's Decision," *St. Louis Globe-Democrat*, 11 September 1924.

14. Robert T. Small, "Press of Nation Condemns Leopold-Loeb Sentence as Proof of Two-Law System," *Atlanta Journal*, 11 September 1924; Editorial, "The Loeb-Leopold Case," *Commercial Appeal* (Memphis), 11 September 1924.

15. Editorial, "The Chicago Verdict," *Birmingham Age-Herald*, 11 September 1924; Editorial, "Life Imprisonment," *Charleston Gazette*, 11 September 1924.

16. Editorial, "A Victory for Murder," *The Courier-Journal* (Louisville), 11 September 1924.

17. Editorial, "Disintegrating Society," *Chicago Daily Tribune*, 19 September 1924.

18. "Girl Confesses Murder," *Chicago Daily News*, 30 August 1924; "Girl Confesses Slaying Woman," *Chicago Herald and Examiner*, 31 August 1924; "Vote to Indict Two Girls as Slayers," *Chicago American*, 3 September 1924.

19. "Young Slayers, 2 Pretty Girls, Ask for Darrow," *Chicago Daily Tribune*, 2 September 1924.

20. "Comments on Decision in the Franks Case," *Boston Daily Globe*, 11 September 1924.

21. "Franks Decision Divides Public," *The Sun* (New York), 11 September 1924; "Poor Boy of 19 Seeks a Pardon in Illinois to Escape Hanging," *The Sun* (New York), 15 September 1924.

22. I. L. Bril, Editorial, "Our Civilization to Blame," *Jewish Daily News*, 11 September 1924.

23. "Comments," *Boston Daily Globe*, 11 September 1924.

24. Editorial, "We Must Make a Change," *San Francisco Chronicle*, 12 September 1924; Editorial, "Alienists in Criminal Trials," *Evening Star* (Washington, D.C.), 12 September 1924.

25. "Blanton Will Air New Charges Soon," *Evening Star* (Washington, D.C.), 1 April 1926.

26. [J. R. McCarl], *Investigation of St. Elizabeths Hospital* (Washington, D.C.: Government Printing Office, 1927), 126–127; "Condemns Hospital for Federal Insane," *New York Times*, 17 December 1926.

27. "Dr. William White, Psychiatrist, Dies," *New York Times*, 8 March 1937.

28. "Only Poor Hang, Darrow Says in Gotham Debate," *New York Times*, 27 October 1924; *Debate, Resolved: That Capital Punishment Is a Wise Public Policy. Clarence Darrow, Negative; Judge Alfred J. Talley, Affirmative* (New York: League for Public Discussion, 1924), 41.

29. "New Hospital Organized to Check Mental Diseases," *New York Times*, 11 May 1924; "Darrow Likes Plan for 'Crime Hospital,'" *New York Times*, 22 September 1924.

30. Edward Larson, *Summer for the Gods: The Scopes Trial and America's Continuing Debate over Science and Religion* (New York: Basic Books, 1997).

31. John Kobler, *Capone: The Life and World of Al Capone* (New York: Putnam, 1971), 176–179; Laurence Bergren, *Capone: The Man and the Era* (New York: Simon and Schuster, 1994), 162–165.

32. "Emmerson Wins by 400,000," *Chicago Daily Tribune*, 11 April 1928.

33. Nathan F. Leopold, *Life Plus 99 Years* (Garden City, NY: Doubleday, 1958), 87–88.

34. Ibid., 132.

35. Gladys Erickson, *Warden Ragen of Joliet* (New York: Dutton, 1957), 42–47; James B. Jacobs, *Stateville: The Penitentiary in Mass Society* (Chicago: University of Chicago Press, 1977), 20–25.

36. Jacobs, *Stateville*, 22; Leopold, *Life Plus 99 Years*, 173, 175, 177, 180–181, 193, 216, 223–235.

37. Nathan F. Leopold Jr. [William F. Lanne, pseud.], "Parole Prediction as Science," *Journal of Criminal Law and Criminology* 26 (1935–1936): 377–400; Leopold, *Life Plus 99 Years*, 251–264.

38. "New Evidence of Loeb Prison Rule Revealed," *Chicago Daily Tribune*, 1 February 1936; Erickson, *Warden Ragen*, 80.

39. "Horner Yields to Demand for Prison Inquiry," *Chicago Sunday Tribune*, 2 February 1936; "Prison a Homey Club with Dues, Felons Declare," *Chicago Daily Tribune*, 21 February 1936; "Two Convicts Tell Favors to Loeb in Prison," *Chicago Daily Tribune*, 3 June 1936.

40. "Kills Loeb; Prison Scandal," *Chicago Daily Tribune*, 29 January 1936; Seymour Korman, "Seek Death Jury to Try Convict Slayer of Loeb," *Chicago Daily Tribune*, 26 May 1936.

41. Leopold, *Life Plus 99 Years*, 266–270.

42. In 1929 Illinois changed its method of execution to the electric chair.

43. Leopold, *Life Plus 99 Years*, 284.

44. Ibid., 281–283.

45. "Prison Malaria," *Life* 15 (June 1945): 43–46, 48; Charles Remsberg, "The Convict & Medical Research," *Kiwanis Magazine* 46 (April 1961): 38–40, 49–50; Leopold, *Life Plus 99 Years*, 306.

46. George Wright, "Heirens Tells More Crime Details—Talks Five Hours,"

Chicago Daily Tribune, 24 July 1946; "Heirens Tells How He Strangled Suzanne Degnan, 6, and Carried Her Body from Home Down Ladder," *Chicago Daily Tribune*, 7 August 1946.

47. Genevieve Scott, "Heirens Just an 'Ordinary Guy' to Classmates," *Chicago Sunday Tribune*, 30 June 1946.

48. "Leopold Term Cut 14 Years; Parole Possible in 1953," *Chicago Daily Sun Times*, 23 September 1949.

49. Clayton Kirkpatrick, "Model Prisoner Leopold Numb at Idea of Freedom," *Chicago Daily Tribune*, 11 August 1952.

50. Marcia Winn, "Is 33 Years Enough to Pay? Asks Leopold," *Chicago Sunday Tribune*, 10 March 1957; Marcia Winn, "Should Leopold Be Paroled?" *Chicago Sunday Tribune*, 2 June 1957.

51. James Doherty, "How Leopold Asked Parole," *Chicago Daily Tribune*, 9 January 1953; John Bartlow Martin, "Murder on His Conscience," *Saturday Evening Post* 2 (23 April 1955): 135.

52. Martin, "Murder," 135.

53. Elmer Gertz, *A Handful of Clients* (Chicago: Follett, 1965), 97.

54. Doherty, "How Leopold."

55. "Leopold Parole Bid Denied," *Chicago Daily Tribune*, 15 May 1953; Martin, "Murder," 135.

56. "Florida Says No to a Job for Leopold," *Chicago Daily Tribune*, 12 March 1958; Gertz, *Handful of Clients*, 38–39; Roy Brown, "Leopold's Life Ahead," *Chicago Daily Tribune*, 13 March 1958.

57. Gertz, *Handful of Clients*, 54–55.

58. Ibid., 62–63.

59. Joseph Egelhof, "Misled by Loeb: Leopold," *Chicago Daily Tribune*, 6 February 1958; Gertz, *Handful of Clients*, 61.

60. Gertz, *Handful of Clients*, 100.

61. Ibid., 102.

62. "JACK EIGEN speaking," *Chicago Daily Tribune*, 8 March 1958; Gertz, *Handful of Clients*, 103.

63. Tom Littlewood, "Leopold Wins Freedom after 33 Years in Cell; Touhy Also Gets Parole," *Chicago Daily Sun-Times*, 21 February 1958; Gertz, *Handful of Clients*, 115–116.

64. Gertz, *Handful of Clients*, 116.

65. Joseph Egelhof, "Illness Mars Leopold's First Day on Parole," *Chicago Daily Tribune*, 14 March 1958; Gertz, *Handful of Clients*, 117.

66. "Leopold Due on Job Today in Puerto Rico," *Chicago Daily Tribune*, 15 March 1958; Leopold Lands in Puerto Rico; Happy, He Says," *Chicago Sunday Tribune*, 16 March 1958. Leopold's graduate thesis was published as Nathan Freudenthal Leopold, "Caracteristicas Sicosociales de un Grupo de Miembros Pertenecientes a la Socieda de Alcohólicos Anónimos en la Penitencieria Estatal" (MA thesis, University of Puerto Rico, 1961).

67. Brown, "Leopold's Life Ahead"; "Leopold Will Study Year at Puerto Rico U.," *Chicago Daily Tribune*, 1 August 1959.

68. "Leopold Sues Levin, Zanuck over Novel," *Chicago Daily Tribune*, 3 October 1959.

69. Meyer Levin, *The Obsession* (New York: Simon and Schuster, 1973), 225, 227.

70. "Leopold Loses His Privacy Suit," *Chicago Tribune*, 28 May 1970.

71. Ray Brennan, "Leopold's Fiancée Tells of Romance in Letter," *Chicago Sun-Times*, 12 January 1961; "Leopold and Widow Marry in Puerto Rico," *Chicago Daily Tribune*, 8 February 1961.

72. Elmer Gertz, *To Life* (New York: McGraw-Hill, 1974), 192–193.

73. "Nathan Leopold Dies at Age 66," *Chicago Tribune*, 30 August 1971; "Leopold 'Atonement' Over, Widow States," *Chicago Tribune*, 31 August 1971.

LEOPOLD AND LOEB IN FICTION

1. Harry Salpeter, "F. Scott Fitzgerald Becomes Oracle," *The World* (New York), 3 April 1927.

2. Nigel Jones, *Through a Glass Darkly: The Life of Patrick Hamilton* (London: Scribner, 1991), 153–159; Sean French, *Patrick Hamilton: A Life* (London: Faber and Faber, 1993), 101–104.

3. Donald Spoto, *The Art of Alfred Hitchcock: Fifty Years of His Motion Pictures*, 2nd ed. (New York: Doubleday, 1992), 166–172; Robin Wood, *Hitchcock's Films Revisited* (New York: Columbia University Press, 1989), 349–357; Patrick McGilligan, *Alfred Hitchcock: A Life in Darkness and Light* (New York: HarperCollins, 2003), 419–420.

4. James Yaffe, *Nothing but the Night* (Boston, MA: Little, Brown, 1957); Mary-Carter Roberts, *Little Brother Fate* (New York: Farrar, Straus, and Cudahy, 1957); Meyer Levin, *Compulsion* (New York: Simon and Schuster, 1956).

5. Barbara Leaming, *Orson Welles* (New York: Viking, 1985), 440–445.

6. John Logan, *Never the Sinner: The Leopold and Loeb Story* (New York: Overlook, 1999).

SOURCES

1. Hal Higdon, *The Crime of the Century: The Leopold and Loeb Case* (New York: Putnam, 1975); Paula S. Fass, "Making and Remaking an Event: The Leopold and Loeb Case in American Culture," *Journal of American History* 80 (1993): 919–951; Laurel Duchowny, "*Life Plus 99 Years*: Nathan Leopold and Chicago Criminology," *Journal of Contemporary Criminal Justice* 21 (2005): 336–349; Scott W. Howe, "Reassessing the Individualization Mandate in Capital Sentencing: Darrow's Defense of Leopold and Loeb," *Iowa Law Review* 79 (1993–1994): 989–1071.

2. Darrow published his version of the speech as *Clarence Darrow's Plea in Defense of Loeb and Leopold* (Girard, KS: Haldeman-Julius, 1926).

3. Lloyd Wendt, *Chicago Tribune: The Rise of a Great American Newspaper* (Chicago: Rand McNally, 1979), 480–486.

4. The history of the Hearst newspapers in Chicago is recounted in George Murray, *The Madhouse on Madison Street* (Chicago: Follett, 1965).

5. Frank Luther Mott, *American Journalism: A History, 1690–1960*, 3rd ed. (New York: Macmillan, 1972), 562–564, 662.

6. Joseph P. Savage, *A Man Named Savage* (New York: Vantage, 1975).

7. Clarence Darrow, *The Story of My Life* (New York: Scribner, 1932), 226–243.

8. Nathan F. Leopold Jr., *Life Plus 99 Years* (Garden City, NY: Doubleday, 1958).

INDEX

ILLUSTRATION CREDITS

1.   **The defendants with their lawyer.** Reproduction number DN-0078021, *Chicago Daily News* Negatives Collection, Chicago History Museum.

2.   **Robert (Bobby) Franks.** Frontispiece to Jack Franks, *My Blessed Little Pal* (n.p., 1926), in Box 1, Nathan F. Leopold Collection, Special Collections Research Center, University of Chicago Library.

3.   **The drainage culvert.** *New York Herald Tribune* Photograph Morgue, Long Island Division, Queens Borough Public Library.

4.   **The Harvard School.** Frontispiece to *The Harvard School for Boys* (n.p., 1923) in Box 80, Records of Hyde Park Historical Society, Special Collections Research Center, University of Chicago Library.

5.   **Richard (Dickie) Loeb.** *New York World-Telegram and Sun* Photograph Morgue, Prints and Photographs Division, Library of Congress.

6.   **Richard Loeb.** *New York World-Telegram and Sun* Photograph Morgue, Prints and Photographs Division, Library of Congress.

7.   **Il Circolo Italiano.** From *Cap and Gown*, 28 (1923): 186.

8.   **Nathan (Babe) Leopold.** *New York World-Telegram and Sun* Photograph Morgue, Prints and Photographs Division, Library of Congress.

9.   **Zeta Beta Tau fraternity house.** Zeta Beta Tau Fraternity, Inc., 3905 Vincennes Road, Suite 300, Indianapolis, IN 46268.

10.   **The ransom demand.** Chris Jouan, Jouan Illustration.

11.   **The ransom letter.** Harold Hulbert Collection, University Archives, Northwestern University Library.

12.   **The Law School, University of Chicago.** Picture of Stuart Hall, ID: apf2-07881, Series II (Buildings and Grounds), Special Collections Research Center, University of Chicago Library.

13.   **Willys-Knight automobile.** Collection of the author.

14.   **The kidnapping.** Chris Jouan, Jouan Illustration.

15.   **Disposal of the body.** Chris Jouan, Jouan Illustration.

16.   **Inside the state's attorney's office.** *New York World-Telegram and Sun* Photograph Morgue, Prints and Photographs Division, Library of Congress.

17.   **Clarence Darrow.** Box 22, Elmer Gertz Collection, McCormick Library of Special Collections, Northwestern University Library.

18.   **Robert Crowe.** *New York World-Telegram and Sun* Photograph Morgue, Prints and Photographs Division, Library of Congress.

19.   **The reform movement.** From *Chicago Daily Tribune,* 17 January 1923, American Newspaper Repository Collection, Special Collections Library, Duke University. Courtesy of Tribune Media Services.

20.   **Waiting for habeas corpus.** *New York Herald Tribune* Photograph Morgue, Long Island Division, Queens Borough Public Library.

21.   **Leopold and Loeb enter Cook County jail.** *New York Herald Tribune* Photograph Morgue, Long Island Division, Queens Borough Public Library.

22.   **John Caverly.** Photographic History Collection, Behring Center, National Museum of American History, Smithsonian Institution.

23.   **Psychiatrists for the defense.** *New York Herald Tribune* Photograph Morgue, Long Island Division, Queens Borough Public Library.

24.   **Cook County Criminal Court and jail.** From Paul Gilbert and Charles Lee Bryson, *Chicago and Its Makers* (Chicago: F. Mendelsohn, 1929), 487.

25.   **Radio transmission.** From *Chicago Daily Tribune,* 19 July 1924, American Newspaper Repository Collection, Special Collections Library, Duke University. Courtesy of Tribune Media Services.

26.   **Richard Loeb enters court.** *New York World-Telegram and Sun* Photograph Morgue, Prints and Photographs Division, Library of Congress.

27.   **The defense team.** *New York World-Telegram and Sun*

Photograph Morgue, Prints and Photographs Division, Library of Congress.

28. **Crowd outside the Criminal Court.** Reproduction number DN-0078043, *Chicago Daily News* Negatives Collection, Chicago History Museum.

29. **William Alanson White.** Reproduction number DN-0077454, *Chicago Daily News* Negatives Collection, Chicago History Museum.

30. **Clarence Darrow.** Folder 9, Box 39, Elmer Gertz Collection, McCormick Library of Special Collections, Northwestern University Library.

31. **A joke in court.** *New York Herald Tribune* Photograph Morgue, Long Island Division, Queens Borough Public Library.

32. **Suicide watch.** *New York World-Telegram and Sun* Photograph Morgue, Prints and Photographs Division, Library of Congress.

33. **The battle of the books.** From *Chicago Daily Tribune*, 14 August 1924, American Newspaper Repository Collection, Special Collections Library, Duke University. Courtesy of Tribune Media Services.

34. **Clarence Darrow in court.** Folder 1, Box 22, Elmer Gertz Collection, McCormick Library of Special Collections, Northwestern University Library.

35. **Leopold and Loeb enter Joliet Prison.** *New York Herald Tribune* Photograph Morgue, Long Island Division, Queens Borough Public Library.

36.   **Nathan Leopold.** Reproduction number DN-0078242, *Chicago Daily News* Negatives Collection, Chicago History Museum.

37.   **Richard Loeb.** Reproduction number DN-0078243, *Chicago Daily News* Negatives Collection, Chicago History Museum.

38.   **Joliet Prison.** Folder 16 (Prison Building), Box 6, Joliet Prison Collection, Chicago History Museum.

39.   **Stateville Prison.** *New York Herald Tribune* Photograph Morgue, Long Island Division, Queens Borough Public Library.

40.   **The happy couple.** *New York Herald Tribune* Photograph Morgue, Long Island Division, Queens Borough Public Library.